W9-AGM-533

LATVIA'S TRANSITION TO A MARKET ECONOMY

STUDIES IN RUSSIA AND EAST EUROPE

This series includes books on general, political, historical, economic and cultural themes relating to Russia and East Europe written or edited by members of the School of Slavonic and East European Studies in the University of London, or by authors working in association with the School.

Recent titles include:

Roger Bartlett and Karen Schönwälder (*editors*)
THE GERMAN LANDS AND EASTERN EUROPE
Essays on the History of their Social, Cultural and Political Relations

John Channon (*editor*)
POLITICS, SOCIETY AND STALINISM IN THE USSR

Geoffrey Hosking and Robert Service (*editors*)
RUSSIAN NATIONALISM, PAST AND PRESENT

Krystyna Iglicka and Keith Sword (*editors*)
THE CHALLENGE OF EAST–WEST MIGRATION FOR POLAND

Marja Nissinen
LATVIA'S TRANSITION TO A MARKET ECONOMY
Political Determinants of Economic Reform Policy

Jeremy Smith
THE BOLSHEVIKS AND THE NATIONAL QUESTION, 1917–23

Jeanne Sutherland
SCHOOLING IN THE NEW RUSSIA
Innovation and Change, 1984–95

Keith Sword
DEPORTATION AND EXILE
Poles in the Soviet Union, 1939–48

Studies in Russia and East Europe
Series Standing Order ISBN 0–333–71018–5
(*outside North America only*)

You can receive future titles in this series as they are published by placing a standing order. Please contact your bookseller or, in case of difficulty, write to us at the address below with your name and address, the title of the series and the ISBN quoted above.

Customer Services Department, Macmillan Distribution Ltd
Houndmills, Basingstoke, Hampshire RG21 6XS, England

Latvia's Transition to a Market Economy

Political Determinants of Economic Reform Policy

Marja Nissinen
Researcher
VTT/Technical Research Centre of Finland
Espoo
Finland

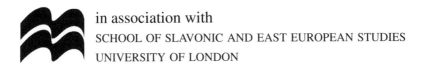

in association with
SCHOOL OF SLAVONIC AND EAST EUROPEAN STUDIES
UNIVERSITY OF LONDON

First published in Great Britain 1999 by
MACMILLAN PRESS LTD
Houndmills, Basingstoke, Hampshire RG21 6XS and London
Companies and representatives throughout the world

A catalogue record for this book is available from the British Library.

ISBN 0–333–73942–6

 First published in the United States of America 1999 by
ST. MARTIN'S PRESS, INC.,
Scholarly and Reference Division,
175 Fifth Avenue, New York, N.Y. 10010

ISBN 0–312–21989–X

Library of Congress Cataloging-in-Publication Data
Nissinen, Marja, 1967–
Latvia's transition to a market economy : political determinants
of economic reform policy / Marja Nissinen.
p.   cm. — (Studies in Russia and East Europe)
Includes bibliographical references (p.   ) and index.
ISBN 0–312–21989–X
1. Latvia—Economic policy—1991–   2. Latvia—Politics and
government—1991–   I. Title.   II. Series.
HC340.5.N57   1998
338.94796—dc21   98–40719
                                                              CIP

HC 340.5 .N57 1999

This book is printed on paper suitable for recycling and made from fully managed and
sustained forest sources.

10   9   8   7   6   5   4   3   2   1
08   07   06   05   04   03   02   01   00   99

Printed and bound in Great Britain by
Antony Rowe Ltd, Chippenham, Wiltshire

Contents

Tables and Figures

TABLES

FIGURE

Abbreviations

CDU/CSU	Christian Democratic Union/Christian Social Union (Germany)
CIS	Commonwealth of Independent States
CMEA	Council for Mutual Economic Assistance
CP	Communist Party
CPSU	Communist Party of the Soviet Union
CSCE/OSCE	Conference on/Organization for Security and Cooperation in Europe
DPS	Democratic Party Masters (Saimnieks)
EBRD	European Bank for Reconstruction and Development
EU	European Union
FDI	Foreign direct investment
FSU	Former Soviet Union
GATT	General Agreement on Tariffs and Trade
GDP	Gross domestic product
IMF	International Monetary Fund
IT	Information technology
KDS	[Latvian] Christian Democratic Union
KGB	Committee of State Security
L	People's Movement for Latvia (Siegerist Party)
LC	Union Latvia's Way
LDP	Latgale's Democratic Party
LNNK	Latvian National Conservative Party
LSDP	Social Democratic Party of Latvia
LSP	Latvian Socialist Party
LVL	Latvian lats
LVP	Latvian Unity Party
LZS	Latvian Farmers' Union
MFN	Most favoured nation
NATO	North Atlantic Treaty Organization
NCL	Non-Citizens' League
NGO	Non-governmental organization
OECD	Organization for Economic Cooperation and Development
PFL	Popular Front of Latvia
Phare	EU programme for assistance to countries of Central and Eastern Europe
R&D	Research and development

SDR	Special drawing rights, IMF-approved currency
SSR	Soviet Socialist Republic
TB	Union For Fatherland and Freedom
TPA	Political Union of Economists (Tautsaimnieks)
TSP	National Harmony Party
US	United States
USSR	Union of Soviet Socialist Republics
VAT	Value added tax

Part I

The Research Question and its Foundations

1 Introduction

The irony of the postcommunist transitions to capitalism is that while they are aimed at eventual reduction of political involvement in the economy, their success depends crucially on political developments. Politics is again in command. Liberal capitalism is being constructed by the force of the blueprints formulated by the new elites and their economic advisors. Market anxiety is not motivated solely for economic reasons, such as greater efficiency of resource allocation; the driving force behind the economic transformation is also political and ideological. A market economy based on private ownership is envisaged as the counterpart in the economic domain of democracy in the political arena. Likewise, the consequences of economic reform are not limited to the economic area. The early effects of market-oriented economic reforms increase insecurity, inequality and apparent foreign influence, just as major sectors of the population begin to find themselves empowered politically. Under such conditions, democracy in the political realm easily works against economic reform.

The tension between economic reform and democracy has generated an intense debate over the capacity of new democratic regimes to manage the daunting political challenges of economic reform. Adjustment is complex and controversial at a technical level but immensely conflictual at ideological and political levels. The situation is complicated by the exceptional dual character of the transition processes. Simultaneous economic and political liberalization distinguishes the postcommunist transitions from classical transitions from authoritarianism or from earlier economic adjustments. The problem in the new situation is that marketization and democratization interact in complex ways that are less complementary than conflicting. This factor further heightens the high politicization of the transition process.

Yet we need not seek out such an extreme case as systemic reform to realize that economic policy-making is an essentially political process. This requires, however, that we move beyond the view of policy-making implicit in most economics books. They tend to see policy primarily as a response to prevailing economic conditions and policy-making as a resolution of technical issues. To some degree, the idea is quite valid, but such a view is far too simple and incomplete. Economic policy is made by governments, which are political creatures. Unless economic policy-making is insulated from the influence of politics – which, indeed, is impossible in a democracy – we can expect political variables to have a decisive impact on the policy outcomes. Politics enters the policy process in multiple ways. Interested groups press for congenial policies; politicians and civil servants jockey for influence over the outcome; political problems occur in the implementation phase. On the other hand, the range of policy alternatives is limited by a matrix of international, social and institutional constraints and incentives. A better understanding of the political forces that govern economic policy-making is likely to contribute to more realistic and sustainable solutions to economic and social problems.[1]

The latter conviction is held at least by the proponents of political economy. *Political economy* – understood in a revised sense – is an interdisciplinary field which is concerned with the effects of politics on economic policy choice and performance. This concern with the political determinants of policy choice was brought into connection with the study of democratization in the 1980s, when the focus was directed toward the politics of economic reform in the Third World. Dissatisfied with the neglect of economic factors in the democratization process, a group of political scientists already engaged in research on the political dimensions of economic policy seized upon this shortcoming and the result was a rapid proliferation of studies focusing on the politics of economic adjustment. The initial impetus for such studies came from the differences in national strategies introduced to cope with the economic crisis. The diversity of responses raised critical questions for comparative political analysis. Why do nations choose different policy paths and divergent political strategies to deal with similar economic problems? To what do the economic policies of the state respond? Comparative political economy examines similarities and differences in economic policy as a basis for comparing political systems in order to test the relationship between economic policy and various independent variables.[2]

The present study addresses the factors that influence the determination of both the overall strategy and the specific policies of transition in one post-communist country, namely Latvia. The economic policy outcome of interest to us (the dependent variable) is Latvia's reform strategy and its practical applications. The purpose is to account for why exactly the Latvian governments have adopted the kind of policy courses they have. For instance, why has Latvia pursued orthodox policies, instead of experimenting with heterodox policies, as Lithuania has?

Continuing the above line of argumentation, the study takes the view that political variables have a definite impact on the character and direction of economic policy. Economic policy is supposed to be determined not simply by prevailing economic conditions, but also by political dynamics. The principal concern is with *the ways in which political factors shape government's adjustment choices* as well as the implementation of those decisions. The implicit concern underlying the problem formulation is whether politics constrains or jeopardizes economic reform. Political influence is assumed to be mediated principally through party politics. This formulation should not be taken as a restriction that leads to a total neglect of other essential factors, such as institutions, economic conditions or international pressures. Indeed, they are usually so entangled with politics that one cannot simply avoid taking them into account. Moreover, the emphasis placed on political explanations should not be misinterpreted as an attempt to resolve the controversy over the alleged primacy of political versus socioeconomic factors in the determination of policy. Rather, it reflects the author's bias.

The choice of an explanatory model is more complex than that between political and, say, economic variables. We face a perplexing set of issues: what kind of political variables are we talking about? How should we identify and conceptualize the most influential political factors? To take a position on the determinants of policy is implicitly to endorse a particular understanding of politics. Behind contemporary analyses of economic policy we find competing functional, cultural, public choice, group conflict and state-centric models of politics. They are by no means entirely consistent with one another, but each still claims to have the correct understanding of politics.[3] Therefore, the key theoretical issue is to outline a paradigmatic understanding of the policy process. In this study, the most central role is accorded to the pluralist group conflict but, in addition, the independent role of exogenous ideologies and the organizational features of the political system are recognized as factors to be taken into account in the explanation.

To put it succinctly, the idea is to view Latvia's economic reform strategy as a subject of political conflict. The task is twofold: first, the differences in proposed measures will be depicted in order to identify the points at issue; second, the different parties will be grouped according to their positions, applying a proper theoretical criteria. These steps will pave the way for an attempt to trace the various proposals to their motives: what makes political parties advocate different solutions to the same problem? The other objective is to assess the compatibility of political feedback with the requirements of the transition strategy. It is feared that the rise of populist or postsocialist movements will derail the reform process, but even without their existence democratic politics tends to necessitate compromise. How are the initial reform policies modified in response to societal pressures in the course of the transition process?

Far-reaching demands for modifying the reform strategy convert the question to the sustainability of that strategy. To discover whether the chosen path is worth preserving or not, it is necessary to examine the content and goals of the implemented reform policy. Latvia's approach has been praised at least by international financial organizations. The inherent tensions are revealed by contrasting the government's orthodox strategy with the competing schemes proposed by the political opposition. The motivation for the comparison is to introduce the perspective of political risk analysis. In this way the continuation of a business-friendly or in other respects economically favourable regime can be evaluated.

The risk analysis angle calls for the incorporation of contextual elements affecting the political risk. One aspect that does not derive from the formulation of the research task as directly as the others is the problem of Latvia's Russian-speaking minority. Still, the assessment of the probability of a national conflict is of utmost importance to almost any question related to Latvia, because national politics has a bearing upon all aspects of life, including many issues of policy and the party system. Owing to the unusually stark ethnic and linguistic divisions, the nationality issue is so fundamental – and the potential risk so enormous, if things should go wrong – that the cleavage structure of Latvian politics cannot be comprehended fully if it is neglected. Most foreigners who start to collect information about Latvia tackle the nationality problem spontaneously to begin with. A question to be investigated is, does the existence of a large Russian-speaking minority influence the design of economic policy? Do economic interests follow national lines? Have Russian-speakers some special interests according to which they would like to direct economic policies?

The ambitions of the study go beyond an inductive case study to provide a survey of the political forces shaping adjustment decisions. The objective is to forge connections to the actual theoretical debates in comparative politics and political economy. In view of the latter, the research task will be related to a wider-ranging question regarding the compatibility of a market reform with the logic of democratic politics: Will voters compromise the prospects of reform in order to alleviate the pain? Will the interest group conflict over the distributional consequences of reform bring the process to a stalemate? Latvia will be treated as a case to test the capacity of a young democratic regime to solve social conflicts related to the costs of economic transformation. The sustainability of economic reform under austerity entails a conflict between economic efficiency and social acceptability, the dilemma of which also lies at the heart of another major academic debate. Scholars who disagree on the optimal approach to economic reform are divided into shock therapists and gradualists. The 'shock versus gradualism' division is also reflected in political differences, which is the reason justifyng why the analytical frame for the examination of the government and parties' reform strategies will be anchored to it. In general, the description of a particular will be cast in terms of broadly applicable analytic constructs. The case study is to be framed in such theoretical terms that its findings could be integrated into cross-national comparative projects.

The leitmotif that runs throughout the whole study is the confrontation of politics and economics in all its ramifications. The collision of economic rationale and political need affects every level of decision-making. Consider, for instance, the problem of the gigantic all-union enterprises in the Baltic states, which went bankrupt after losing their markets and which were technologically outdated. Should the government immediately close down the unviable, loss-accumulating factories that cannot be integrated into the small national economies of the independent Baltic states, if their closure means laying off thousands of Russian workers? Unemployment is generally taken to be *the* economic variable that matters most for the dynamics of public opinion, but the situation is exacerbated by the sensitive nationality question. Mass unemployment among the Russian minority would furnish the aggressive Russian nationalists in Moscow with a powerful weapon in the propaganda war. Therefore, the segregation of society may force economic reforms to be more cautious than is otherwise desired.

The tension between the different logics of political and economic spheres is not exclusively characteristic of the transition stage but rather it is system-immanent. The uneasy relationship between democracy and capitalism stems from the root difference between a polity that distributes power and status relatively equally and an economy that distributes property and income relatively unequally. The compatibility problem also reflects the paradoxical relationship between liberalism and democracy. The use of markets as the basic regulator of economic transactions is more closely related to the creation of limited sovereignty than to the introduction of popular sovereignty. That is, the preconditions required for the creation of capitalist markets are not as much democratic as they are liberal.[4]

Transformation is not only a politico-economic process but it also involves a sociological and psychological change, a switch in values and public spirits. The idea of a collision between mutually contradictory values provides a helpful perspective with which to explain the compatibility dilemma. The inconsistency can be extrapolated from the fundamental contradiction between freedom and equality, the two values that Milton Rokeach (1973) singled out for special mention by all political ideologies. The conflict between freedom and equality is particularly sharp, conspicuous and actual in the specific historical context in Eastern Europe. The former communist ethos is diametrically opposed to the contemporary market ethos. The new political elites may have adapted themselves swiftly to such market-conforming values as competitiveness, self-initiative, innovativeness and risk willingness, but the masses still bear the burden of the communist socialization which rejected the enterpreneurial spirit. The legacy of communist egalitarianism is often seen as a threat to the creation of a market economy. Public opinion does not tolerate large income differentials; it clings to social welfarism; and it is suspicious of private property and profit. This sociopsychologic problem might be interpreted, among others, as a manifestation of the individualism–collectivism dimension. An economist reduces the clash between freedom and equality to the distinction between production and distribution.[5] One could introduce variations on the theme indefinitely. Some of these variations will constitute the intellectual backbone of the present study.

2 The Political Sources of Economic Policy Choices

For the very imperfect laboratory of the social sciences, the postcommunist transitions provide an unusual opportunity – a chance to measure national particularities through different responses to a common stimulus. While all countries responded to the economic crisis by changing their economic policies, the actual content of those changes differed. East European countries solved similar problems with different means at respective stages of their transformation processes. Not only did initial macroeconomic conditions and varying experiences of market socialist reforms in the past influence the design and time schedule in individual countries, but divergent intellectual arguments and inconsistent priority-settings also led to differing interpretations as to the appropriate methods. Although the ultimate goal appeared seemingly consensual, since both ordinary people and the ruling elite in Eastern Europe were convinced of the need for a far-reaching transformation that encompasses not only the economic but also the political system, the specifics of the resulting system again left room for wide variations. While it was self-evident that Western Europe offers attractive and appropriate models for transformation, disagreement prevailed over which West European models or which elements of the various models would be most suitable. Should one imitate the Thatcherite free market model, the Swedish welfare state model, or the German *soziale Marktwirtschaft* model?[6]

The choice between alternative paths to different capitalisms in a situation in which no clear, unambiguous conclusion can be drawn as to the superiority of one approach over the other raises the question of the determining criteria of such a choice. How is the choice between various possibilities made, if no 'laws of nature' define a fixed response? When the claim for a single best solution is abandoned, the understanding of the transition problem changes its character. Rather than an economic problem it appears more in terms of a political dilemma. Although there are contradictory conclusions concerning the alleged primacy of different types of explanatory factors – whether they be interests, institutions, ideologies or whatever – it is obvious that these explanations lie mainly within the realm of political science, when the problem is treated from the vantage point given above. The blanket category of 'political motives', neglected by many economists especially in the past decades, is likely to hold a clue as to the sources of economic policy choices.

The currently recognized fact is that economic policy does not simply respond to prevailing economic conditions but that political determinants have a crucial impact on its direction. Both the experience of developing countries during the 1980s and the ongoing transformations in former communist countries have made it clear that devising successful policies requires an understanding of the forces that govern policy-making. Many fundamental issues of economic adjustment transcend narrow economic analysis and have to do with maintaining political support for the transition policies. The growing awareness of the centrality of political factors in economic policy-making has increased the interest of economists in politico-economic modelling. As Rodrik puts it, 'an experience like this is simply too interesting to be left to political scientists'.[7] For the present, political science offers richer methodological premises for the study of the interaction between politics and economic change, as politico-economic modelling is only an emerging field in economics.

The significance of political factors is accentuated by the deficiencies in economic theorizing within the field of economics of transformation. First, while strong beliefs have developed around these issues, very few rigorous arguments have been presented as yet. Argument by metaphor – 'you don't cross a chasm in two leaps' or 'when driving at 100 miles per hour you don't come to a full stop immediately' – has too often been substituted for systematic thinking. The fact is that there is no generally accepted, comprehensive theoretical model for economic system transformation. It is also questionable to transfer theoretical elements from the analysis of market economy to the analysis of transitional economies. Second, while it is easy to identify the integral components of the market system from a theoretical construct, it is exceedingly difficult to specify what the crucial elements are that have to be present for a real market economy. As mentioned above, there are many 'alternative capitalisms' which differ markedly from each other with respect to their institutional configurations. Third, there are no historical models for dual transitions of such scale. Previous experience as to how the economic actors involved will behave is unavailable. Because of such high indeterminacy on the economic side, whatever adjustment strategy is chosen it is likely to be a product of internal and external political capacities.[8]

Even when recognized as a component of policy analysis, the role of political factors remains controversial as long as their contribution to economic policy-making is seen from different angles. The argumentation of many neoliberal economists brings politics into the picture as an obstacle course filled with impediments to the adoption of 'correct' economic policies. The view that for a given social problem there is one best solution easily leads to the assumption that disagreement is ipso facto irrational and Eastern

Europe is facing the choice 'us or populism'. At this point democratization tends to slip out of focus: in the present tense it is seen as a political minefield full of threats to economic rationality; in the future tense it is seen as a hoped-for consequence of the present prescribed economic policies. While the economist's view treats people as the main obstacle to reforms, the opposite thesis maintains that 'there can be no democracy without public opinion and no economy without people'. Political scientists of sincerely democratic views argue that after the launch phase there is no way of avoiding the justified demands for broader participation and that politics is not necessarily the enemy of reform. Once society becomes a genuine political actor in its own right, it will insist on economic reform, especially insofar as preserving its newfound democratic freedoms requires such self-restraint.[9]

Neoliberals who are concerned only with the efficient implementation of a sound economic plan insist on the insulation of policy-makers from politics so that they could apply their universalistic rationality without regard to the particularist claims of various obstacle groups. If this rhetoric sounds redolent of authoritarianism, it is no accident. Both old-fashioned authoritarians and new-fangled technocrats base themselves on the premise that those who occupy high office know better than the rest of society, and therefore have not only the right but also the duty to impose that superior knowledge.[10] Democratically minded theorists warn radical reformers about the dangers of an autocratic political style for democratic institutions. Cookbook capitalism that begins with blueprints ignores the ways in which actual policy-makers are shaped and constrained by citizens. A free press and political opposition serve as important early warning systems by means of which policy mistakes can be corrected. Moreover, there is no reliable expert knowledge, only competing expert claims, which means that there is the need to make a political decision in choosing between them.

The parallels in the argument for guardianship and the neoliberal conception of reform as well as respective equivalences in the defence of gradualism and a democratic transition period dispose the theoretical link between a regime type (authoritarian/democratic) and a transition strategy (radical/gradualist). Much of the academic discussion in the 1980s and the 1990s drew its dynamics from the assumption that certain economic strategies are more natural concomitants of certain regime types than others: particular kinds of economic solutions favour corresponding political arrangements and vice versa. To use an analogy, one could speak of strong and weak linkages in reference to the internal consistency of specific combinations. The term was first coined by Janos Kornai (1992a) who classified economic systems in terms of resource ownership and coordination mechanisms in the 1980s. The insulation of policy-makers from politics implies automatically an authoritarian transition period, because economic reforms cannot be insulated from politics in a democracy. The gradualist strategy emphasizes the social acceptability of reforms, seeking to ensure the popular support for their continuation by minimizing the social and economic costs of the transition. The way in which the arguments in one field reinforce the proposals in the other field points out the interception of the two major debates in transition studies – one in political science and the other in economics.

The paradox of the postcommunist transitions is that, despite the logical affinity between specific regime types and transition strategies, the emergent real-life combinations have not followed theoretical patterns (Table 2.1). The strong linkage between authoritarianism and radical reform strategy has not been realized anywhere in Eastern Europe. Instead, one of the weak forms has proved to be the most widespread and successful model in the region. The most rapidly and firmly democratized countries, like Poland, the Czech Republic, Estonia and Latvia, have adopted the radical economic programme with relatively small complications. In these countries, both political and economic reforms have advanced swiftly, bringing the most promising results in the area. On the contrary, haltingly democratized countries, such as Russia and Romania, where many old communists remain in high office, have followed a stop-go gradualism. Gradualism is not necessarily motivated by democratic concerns, while people in a democracy may support a radical programme with high transitional costs if they are confident in the future.[11] Internal variation within the regime category invalidates the traditional focus on the implications of a regime type on economic success, and diverts attention to intra-system features. In parallel, the differentiation between 'spontaneous' and 'artificial' combinations disappears.

Table 2.1   A Typology of Communist and Postcommunist Reform Models

Transition Strategy	Regime type	
	Authoritarian	*Democratic*
Radical	*Technocratic ideal*: insulation of policy-makers from politics * no country examples	*Gain maximization*: orthodox policies * Poland 1989–93 * Czechoslovakia * Estonia, Latvia
Gradualist	*Consumption communism* * China 1978– * Hungary 1968–89	*Pain minimization*: heterodox policies * Hungary, Lithuania * Russia, Romania

This last conclusion casts the generic problem of transformative politics in a new light, although the reformulation does not negate its existence. According to Bruszt (1992) and Stark (1992), the dilemma is not that of the compatibility of democracy and marketization in general but that of different types of democracies and different types of marketizations, that is, different paths, not to a general market economy, but to new types of economies with different mixes of market and non-market elements. Instead of studying that relationship at a general level, we should study the different capacities of the different mixtures of democratic institutions and policies, the different types of coalitions, the different types of market and non-market solutions in the economy and the theoretically seemingly impossible mixtures of different organizational principles. That is to say, it is the relationship between different types of democracy and different types of capitalism rather than the abstractions of democracy and capitalism that holds the key to explaining differences in contemporary Eastern Europe.[12]

The reformulation of the transitional dilemma brings the discussion back to the starting point of this chapter. In accordance with the earlier inference, the selection of a reform model can be hypothesized to be a deliberate political choice. The fate of democratic consolidation does not lie in any particular economic reform programme or vice versa, rather it lies in the hands of political elites. Whether political and economic reforms falter or are sustained depends primarily on the extent to which political leaders wish to maintain them and are willing to pay the costs of doing so instead of giving priority to other goals. The crucial factor influencing the future of systemic changes is the ability of political elites to form coalitions and come to a consensus.[13]

Even after the abandonment of causality in the relationship between regime type and transition strategy, both elements of the model continue to be relevant. They are subject to political choice independently of each other. Nor do pressures against political and economic reforms disappear. While political scientists are primarily concerned with the consolidation of democracy, economists are principally interested in the optimal approach to reform in order to secure the irreversibility of economic transformation.

Part II

Theoretical Underpinnings

3   Transitional Dilemma

Throughout history the interconnections between economy, society and polity have inspired scholars. The current processes of change in Eastern Europe have reopened and actualized the age-old theme. In recent literature the relationship between democracy and the market has been analysed in the context of the postcommunist transitions, but the problem is not specific to countries in transition. The relationship between democratization and marketization can be interpreted as a special case or subcategory of the generic problem involving the relationship between democracy and capitalism. Democratization and marketization appear then as weaker forms of democracy and capitalism.

Contemporary research has approached the relationship between democratization and marketization from three points of view. First, it has defined the dilemma specifically in the East European context, underscoring the unprecedented area-specific features that distinguish the postcommunist transitions from previous historical experience. Second, the present events have given an impetus for the reappraisals of classic masterpieces, intending to highlight the intellectual underpinnings of the contemporary discussion. They point out how the now fashionable topic has lain at the heart of political economy and philosophy since ancient times. Third, a more practical focus examines the linkages between economic crisis and political outcomes by comparing the implications of a regime type on economic success.

THE DEMOCRATIC SUSTAINABILITY OF MARKETIZATION

The nature of the failed communist systems calls for a transition which is as comprehensive in its objectives as were the systems themselves before they failed. The polymorphous nature of communist regimes characterized by the lack of a clear distinction between political and economic institutions requires the simultaneous reconstitution of both political and economic systems. The distinctive feature of the transition in Eastern Europe is its double character. Postcommunist societies are simultaneously undergoing two massive and closely related transformations: the political shift from authoritarianism to democracy and the economic shift from central planning to market economy. The interaction between the democratization of the polity and the marketization of the economy presents a specific problem that creates an additional dimension of conflicts and tensions which are absent in classical transitions from authoritarianism.[1]

The tension between the two dimensions of the transition process arises from the pressure for a revolutionary transformation that has put the developments in Eastern Europe out of sequence. On the economic side, there is a commitment to building capitalism in Eastern Europe, but in a most unusual economic context. The East European economies are already industrialized and feature both skilled labour and to some degree a welfare state, but at the same time they are capital short, primitive in their financial and legal infrastructure and without either private property or bourgeoisie. On the political side, there is a commitment to building a liberal democratic order, but again in a most unusual context. The publics are both mobilized and fully franchised and representative institutions are in place, but at the same time the infrastructure that supports democratic politics is missing. The socioeconomic base of political pluralism is not yet in place and social organizations, interest groups, unions and political parties are weak. To put it briefly, the cart – that is, some results of capitalism and democracy – has been placed before the horse – that is, social, political and economic developments that induced the transition from feudalism to capitalism and from authoritarianism to democracy in the West.[2]

Unlike in the Western capitalist countries in the nineteenth century or in the newly industrialized countries in the Far East, the creation of embryonic democratic institutions has preceded the development of capitalism in the postcommunist countries. Although the changes in the political and economic systems started at the same time, it takes more time to privatize the bulk of state-owned enterprises than to organize free elections. The asymmetry in speed produces a historically new sequence: mass democracy (or at least political pluralism) first and market capitalism later. The new sequence implies that market-oriented reforms have to be introduced under democratic arrangements. The crucial question confronting the postcommunist states is to what extent the introduction of democratic regimes prior to economic reform is an obstacle to the latter, when transition measures hurt a majority of the population in the short term. Will these societies accept the social costs of transition or will the support for reform erode during the course of action?[3]

It is the political accountability that generates the tension between democratization and marketization. Accountability makes politicians nervous about the social costs of economic transformation, whilst the reform requires decisions which will be extremely unpopular with the electorate. Under democratic conditions, where the discontent can find political expression at the polls, even the most promising reform strategies may be abandoned. Either politicians are concerned about electoral support and reverse policies that will cause them to lose elections, or they lose to competitors more attuned to the political consequences of structural transformation. Even if the measures might seem to be in society's broad interest, there is no guarantee that they are in the interests of the political coalitions that aggregate social interests.[4]

The question concerning the compatibility of the logic of democratic politics with an economic reform under austerity has been answered both negatively and affirmatively. Pessimists assume social solidarity breaking down because of the new opportunities to voice demands. The creation of wealth for a segment of the population will give rise to demands to redistribute it. The argument that the population would be willing to make sacrifices for a common cause appears valid to only a limited degree. Its validity rests on the degree to which sacrifices are shared equally and on the availability of opportunities to avoid making them altogether. Optimists believe there are ways to minimize the social costs of transition and to gain society's tolerance of these costs. Social support – or at least passive tolerance – can be generated through inclusive politics which increases the range of democratic institutions and political actors included in the decision-making. Optimists also stress the ability of governments legitimated by a popular consent to impose temporary sacrifices on the population. The collapse of communism lays the foundation for a social contract: leaders forgo the use of arbitrary power, while the population agrees to sacrifice its standard of living during the economic adjustment.[5]

THE FRICTION BETWEEN CAPITALISM AND DEMOCRACY

The immanent tension between capitalism and democracy reflects a structural problem. It stems from the root difference between a polity that distributes power and status relatively equally and an economy that distributes property and income relatively unequally. This poses a dilemma no matter how well the economic system is performing at a given moment. After the demise of communism, capitalism has been linked with the struggle for democracy. Yet the link between the two in contemporary Eastern Europe is more a product of peculiar historical conjuncture related to the character of the previous regime and the evolution of the international economy. Democracy is not a requirement of capitalism in any logical or institutional sense. The relationship does not exist of necessity. Non-democratic capitalism is as common as democratic capitalism.[6]

That economic freedom is not a sufficient condition for political freedom does not mean there would be no interaction between democracy and capitalism. The relationship between capitalism and democracy is indirect rather than reciprocal. Capitalism in itself does not generate direct pressures for democracy. It is perfectly compatible with many forms of authoritarianism (though obviously not with communist totalitarianism). But capitalism is a more efficient engine of economic growth than socialism, and thus it is more likely to generate the rapid socioeconomic change that favours the emergence of stable democracy. It is this observation that offers a clue as to why all the established democracies are located in countries in which economic production and accumulation are largely in the hands of privately owned firms and in which distribution is mainly effected through market mechanisms. In all of these polities, however, the outcome of the market processes is affected by public intervention that has been decided by democratic governments. Controlling capitalism rather than abolishing it has become the normal practice. The paradoxical conclusion is inescapable that (1) capitalism must be a necessary (though not sufficient) condition for democracy, but (2) capitalism must be modified to make it compatible with democracy.[7]

The condition that capitalism must be tamed by government intervention before it can be made compatible with democracy gives rise to another controversy: to what degree and in what ways should it be modified? A fundamental disagreement as to whether one can rely on the omnipotence of the market allocation or whether the market outcomes should be corrected divides the economic science into two camps. One strand of economics suggests that where market failure occurs, the state must actively intervene; another strand shows how state action may fail to coordinate the economy even more significantly than the market. The economics of transformation, 'transfonomics', is heavily influenced by the latter school of thought, which is an heir of the liberal tradition. Neoliberalism triumphed in Eastern Europe where disillusionment with state socialism was thorough.

Liberals from Locke to Hayek have always been attuned to the dangers of too much democracy, and especially its threats to liberal freedoms and the capitalist market. The principle of popular control has often been restrained by the fear of democracy at odds with the requisites of efficient governance. For liberal theorists, there has been an aspiration to hold the economic and the political apart or to insulate the economic sphere from the democratic control. It is true that neoliberal commentators have always made much of the (exclusive) historical affinity between democracy and capitalism. However, just as frequently, they have insisted that this happy coincidence is dependent upon the ways in which the jurisdiction of democracy is strictly delimited. Their model for democracy is an appropriately and necessarily limited democracy.[8]

The relationship between liberalism and democracy is notoriously paradoxical. On the one hand, the justification for democratic procedures most commonly rests on liberal assumptions. On the other hand, liberal institutional arrangements, such as the separation of powers or the rule of law, have frequently been interpreted as constraints upon democracy, albeit necessary ones if democracy is not to undermine itself. This paradox is resolved at a formal level by the presence of two notions of democracy at work within liberal thought. The first conception views democracy as a deliberative process between independent, reasonable agents concerned with the elaboration of general norms designed to regulate their mutual interaction. The second conception sees democracy in more instrumental terms as a process for arriving at decisions between self-interested agents. It is this second form of democracy that liberal constitutional arrangements seek to exclude or limit by bringing it under the control of the first form.[9]

Friedrich A. Hayek is one of the most consistent advocates of the liberal constitutional ideal. His theory is organized around a set of antinomies reflecting two different conceptions of social order. These contrasting views of society give rise to the two different conceptions of the democratic process. One of these notions of democracy is compatible with liberalism, whereas the other one is not.[10]

Hayek's conception of the rule of law and its relationship to individual liberty plays a pivotal role in his constitutional theory. That 'equality before the law leads to the demand that all men should also have the same share in making the law' is, for Hayek, 'the point where traditional liberalism and the democratic movement meet'. However, liberals and democrats have different views of the function and character of democracy. The liberal regards democracy as a protective device for guaranteeing the rule of law. It offers a procedure for the peaceful change of government and a check on arbitrary rule. The democrat sees democracy as a form of popular rule. It offers a mechanism for the aggregation of interests and the imposition of the majority will. Although in both instances Hayek equates democracy with a majoritarian decision process, the appeal to the majority is very different in each model. In the liberal conception of democracy, democracy is a means of consulting majority opinion. The majority do not make law, they 'discover' it in the internalized general rules that underpin the spontaneous order. This innovation does not involve remodelling the law according to some preformed rational schema. In contrast, those whom Hayek calls dogmatic or doctrinaire democrats see democracy as a system of majority rule in which the will of the people determines the law. He associates this notion with constructivist rationalism. Whilst positive liberty and social justice are compatible with a constructed order, only negative rights and commutative justice are consistent with the universal, equal, abstract, goal-independent character of law.[11]

Whereas the liberal version of democracy is compatible with the desire to limit the coercive power of government by subjecting it to the rule of law, the democratic version of democracy is not since there can be no law other than that made by the demos. When unrestrained, the second version leads to the undermining of the spontaneous order in the attempt to implement a created order by a tyrannous majority. In order to gain majority support for its programmes, governments will engage in bargains with interest groups. Horse trading rather than substantive agreement on the merits of particular policies decides what measures get adopted. Democracy slowly degenerates into vote-buying. The only way to prevent government becoming a prey to special interests and adopting totalitarian policies is to limit the powers of government by restricting the scope for which it can use its coercive powers. The government needs to be deprived of the ability to grant discriminatory benefits to specific groups. In essence, this means bringing the government within the boundaries of the rule of law.[12]

Hayek believes that a free and just society can only be secured on the basis of 'catallaxy', the neologism he uses to describe the special kind of spontaneous order produced by the market. He ascribes a correspondingly limited role to the state. The duty of the public authority is not to pursue its own ends but rather to provide the framework for the rule of law within which 'catallaxy' may develop. Hayek is a fierce opponent of sovereign and unlimited government often associated with the rise of democracy. He claims that where Parliament is sovereign, governments become the plaything of organized sectional interests. The vices of unlimited government are particularly damaging in the hands of socialists or social democrats because interventions in the market will always produce suboptimal outcomes. 'The mirage of social justice which the socialists pursue is, at best, a nonsense, and, at worst, pernicious and itself unjust. It means undermining the justice of the market, confiscating the wealth of the more successful, prolonging the dependency of the needy, entrenching the special powers of organized interests and overriding individual freedom. Indeed, it is irreconcilable with the rule of law.'[13] The last sentence in the quotation demonstrates Hayek's insistence on the universal application of law without regard to its particular results. Although Hayek would doubtless have considered himself a democrat (of a very particular kind), he is still more an advocate of individual freedom.[14]

The same antagonism toward the political version of democracy is expressed in public choice theory. Public choice theory sets out to show that individually rational decision-making under established democratic procedures will tend to generate collectively suboptimal outcomes. The differential costs and benefits of organized action create a systemic bias in which the unorganized majority ends up carrying the burdens of self-serving pressure group activity by well-placed minorities. Public choice theorists posit that policy-makers behave as standard economic theory assumes *Homo economicus* to behave: they maximize their personal well-being. Their policy prescriptions are aimed at minimizing the role of government so as to curtail the damage done by policy-makers seeking to maximize what has sometimes been termed a 'social illfare function'.[15]

The modern neoliberal market theorizing has germinated various theorems about the relationship between the market and democracy. What they share is a common assumption that too much politics is bad and too many people demanding things is bad for politics. The old liberal refrain is repeated in a new guise: defining democracy as a version of the market enables a new set of arguments to be deployed. One is that since self-interest prevails there, the chief question is how it is to be contained. A second is that since democracy is an inferior form of the market, its agenda should be restricted as much as possible in favour of the arena of real choice. The general message is to keep politics limited in terms of both agenda and access.[16]

The *necessity theorem* defines the market as an essential locus of individual freedom. The proposition that the market constitutes a necessary condition for democracy is based on the argument according to which there exists an intrinsic connection between economic freedom and political freedoms that are integral to democracy. The need for a plurality of power centres to balance and check one another, and hence to protect political freedom, is most surely guaranteed by the separation of economic and political powers.[17]

The *analogy theorem* argues that democracy works by analogy with the market so that the market provides the paradigm for understanding the democratic process. Electoral competition between political parties corresponds to the competition between firms in the consumer market, except that the reward for success is not enhanced profit but political power and the penalty for failure is not bankruptcy but exclusion from office. The analogy theorem elaborated by Downs (1957) and Buchanan and Tullock (1962), among others, offers a logical extension of the utilitarian theory of representative government advanced by Bentham and Mill.[18]

The *superiority theorem* claims that democracy is an inferior form of the market. The market is more democratic because it allows far more people's choices to be realized and a much greater variety of choices to be expressed. Compared with the choices made in the consumer market, choices in the public policy market suffer from a number of disadvantages. They are aggregated, indirect, uncertain and ineffectual; that is, a minority choice may be overridden by the majority.[19]

The *disability theorem* seeks to expose the consequence of empowering too many people in the democratic market place: the integrity of the economic market and thus ultimately that of democracy itself will be undermined. It reverses the causal relationship proposed by the first necessity theorem by underlining the negative effects of democracy on the market.[20]

In past decades, market-oriented liberals have turned their attention to societies escaping from authoritarian political economies – whether in Latin America or, now especially, Eastern Europe. Neoliberal reformers argue that effective economic reform is endangered by democracy under the conditions facing postcommunist and developing nations. They maintain that democracy must be postponed until marketization has produced growth, prosperity and a pluralist society. Their claim is, as Sachs once put it: 'Let's do it before these new democracies wake up.' The problem of democracy is that the considered opinion of wise economists as to what is better will not be decisive. What will be decisive is the natural way of making political decisions, and that means putting difficult or painful decisions off for a while. The political factors result in permanent postponements and partial solutions which prevent the implementation of a comprehensive reform 'surgery'.[21]

The neoliberal notion appeals to the rationality of guardianship, the idea, first proposed by Plato, that some elite should govern because of its monopoly on expertise. In this case, the relevant expertise is possessed by the neoliberal economists. Marketization involves the imposition of a technical economic blueprint which ordinary people, especially those with no experience with a market system, cannot be expected to understand. The sheer complexity of many public policy issues means that neither ordinary people nor democratic politicians can be entrusted with them. Therefore, the precondition for a good economic policy is that technocrats are in charge of making it. While public choice theorists rejected the Platonic ideal of the elite's selfless dedication to the public good, current neoliberal economists are building a myth of socially regarding, public-spirited economists-cum-politicians. Williamson defines such a technocrat as an economist who uses his professional and technical skills in government with a view to creating an economic system that will further the general good. Common to neoliberal and public choice theories is that democratically elected politicians who are subject to political competition are distrusted.[22]

While the introduction of democracy to Eastern Europe is highly desirable for many reasons, it is unfortunately unclear if enacting a major economic transformation is one of them. The basic preconditions required for the creation of self-regulating markets in the economy are not so much democratic as liberal. The political requirements for economic reform lie less in the introduction of institutions for popular control of the state than in the establishment of mechanisms that limit the use of political authority in the economy. As such, the use of markets as the basic regulator of economic transactions appears much more closely related to the creation of limited sovereignty than to the introduction of popular sovereignty. It is quite possible to envision a polity that conforms to the canons of liberalism but is fundamentally undemocratic, as well as a polity that embraces democracy but, given rising social tensions, finds itself unable to maintain the guarantees of liberalism. And it is exactly the second possibility that worries neoliberal reformers in Eastern Europe.[23]

One classic masterpiece which has attracted renewed attention in the light of the present events is Joseph A. Schumpeter's famous text *Capitalism, Socialism and Democracy*, published in 1942. The excitement of reading *Capitalism, Socialism and Democracy* arises from the clash between the prevailing spirit of the late 1930s and that manifest in the early 1990s. Schumpeter was writing his work during the heyday of fascism and concluded that the facts seemed to suggest 'a pessimistic prognosis' for bourgeois democracy. Today democracy is ascendant as never before and for the first time in history almost everyone claims to be a democrat – at least when it comes to the public justification of one's programmes, if not the reality of one's actions. The same conditions that compelled Schumpeter to fear for the prospects for democracy led him to reject capitalism, as well. Unlike some other famous prophets of capitalism's doom, however, he was not a socialist but a pessimist. As he put it: 'Prognosis does not imply anything about the desirability of the course of events one predicts ... One may hate socialism ... and yet foresee its advent.' Such a conclusion could not be further removed from the intellectual climate of the present day. Now it is socialists who find themselves proclaiming the indispensability of the market and the inevitability of capitalism.[24]

History proved Schumpeter wrong about the political failure of capitalism, but the record shows that he was right about the difficulties of making socialism work as an economic system. Whatever its substantive weaknesses, Schumpeter's alternative theory of democracy captured the nature of existing democratic arrangements far better than the classical model he rejected. Such concepts as 'Schumpeterian democracy' and 'creative destruction' have left an indelible imprint on economic and social sciences. Numerous reappraisals attest to his work's continuing importance. The fundamental issue raised by Schumpeter remains very much alive.[25]

ECONOMIC OR POLITICAL LIBERALIZATION FIRST?

In recent years, no issue in comparative politics has received more attention than the appropriate sequence of political and economic transition. The investigations have most commonly addressed the question as to how the type of political regime affects the likelihood that economic reform policies will be launched and sustained. Early 'conventional wisdom' maintained that authoritarian regimes are distinctly advantaged in undertaking macroeconomic stabilization and liberalization, because they are able to ignore or repress opposition from groups that suffer from reform measures in the short term. Recently, this thesis of 'economic reform first' has been challenged by a number of scholars who point to the intrinsic difficulties of initiating reform under authoritarian conditions as well as to the substantial progress of economic reform in many new democracies.[26]

The Case for Authoritarianism

Until recently, it was widely accepted that democracies – especially fragile, uninstitutionalized new democracies – have difficulty initiating and sustaining major economic reforms because the unpopular consequences of economic stabilization and liberalization make reform politically suicidal to elected officials. As the third wave of democratization crested in the 1980s, sceptics questioned the capacity of new democratic governments to manage the political challenge of economic reform. They doubted the compatibility of simultaneous democratization and economic reform. There were two versions of this 'transitional incompatibility' thesis. The first version focused on democratization's potential to undermine the coherence of reform policy, generating a downward economic spiral. The second version contended that the heavy costs of economic reform can turn crucial social actors against democratization.[27]

Concerns about policy stalemate or democratic breakdown led to efforts to resolve the transitional incompatibility dilemma. The simplest way to overcome the problem is, of course, to avoid simultaneous reforms, either by consolidating economic reform before embarking upon democratization or by consolidating democracy before initiating economic reform. The 'democracy first' option is rarely discussed openly in international development policy circles. One reason may be that most policy consultants conceive of their primary task as furthering economic reform. Another reason is perhaps that a stubborn scepticism prevails about the economic efficiency of democracy, although no strong empirical evidence supports this doubtful belief. In practice, however, the 'economic reform first' option seems to remain as the only viable alternative, meaning that policy recommendations generally give primacy to economic reform.[28]

The 'economic reform first' option reflects three related theses: (1) economic liberalization must precede political liberalization; (2) market reforms can be successfully introduced only under authoritarian regime; (3) only when successful economic development has occurred can conditions favourable to democracy emerge. The pro-authoritarian theses rest on the argument that dictatorships enjoy a greater political capacity and a higher level of insulation from particularistic demands than do democratic regimes. Only when a state is insulated from particularistic pressures can it behave as the universalistic agent it needs to be. Authoritarian regimes meet this requirement because they are less dependent on political support and do not have to concern themselves with electoral cycles. Therefore they find it easier to ignore the complaints of groups hurt by reforms.[29]

By contrast, democratic leaders, constrained by the local version of the political business cycle, find it difficult to stand firm. Democratization means giving a political voice to groups that previously had not been able to make their demands heard. Most demands relevant to public policy require additional expenditures. Thus governments that recently have become more politically inclusive often turn to economic populism – that is, politically motivated economic policies that expand total government expenditure for current consumption and investment. From the viewpoint of democratizing politicians, the implications of economic transition are particularly distressing owing to four structural characteristics of reform process. First, although adjustment's costs pinch immediately, its benefits lag. Second, the costs of adjustment tend to be unevenly distributed. Third, beneficiaries of reform are unlikely to realize it. Fourth, winners are often not organized to protect their emerging stakes. They are less motivated than losers to try to influence the government. For these reasons beneficiaries may not provide much of a counterweight to groups with vested interests in the old arrangements. In virtually all cases, market-oriented reform generates temporary income losses to society overall and steeper losses to groups engaged in types of production that are no longer profitable after reform. In other words, economic restructuring is inevitably painful. When the reform necessitates short-term pain (inflation, unemployment, inequality), voters cannot be trusted to stay the course. In demanding the pain to be alleviated, they are likely to compromise the prospects of economic reform.[30]

Just as democratization can undermine economic reform, reform can undermine democracy by placing undue strains on fragile politics. If the government sticks with its programme despite its painful consequences, rising popular frustration may derail democratization in three different ways.

First, the unavoidable costs of reform are likely to lead to increasing political opposition from those who feel them most. The lower classes particularly feel the economic costs through higher unemployment and higher prices for basic wage goods. Consequently, the public may become seriously disillusioned with democracy, thus becoming available for recruitment into leftist or rightist anti-system movements. Alternatively, propertied or middle-income groups may become so frightened by lower-class protest that they use their influence either to increase state repression or to change the rules of the political game in ways that render them less democratic. Finally, failed economic reforms can undermine the credibility of new democratic governments, which can be blamed both for the costs of whatever partial reforms were imposed and for the costs of a return to an interventionist regime. In sum, as long as weak leadership remains the norm, economic conditions will continue to deteriorate, eventually undermining democratic rule.[31] To put it more systematically, the case for authoritarianism can be reduced to five main arguments.

(1) *The need for a strong government.* If one wishes that the reforms are carried out in as rapid, comprehensive and simultaneous a fashion as possible, it is self-evident that such a monumental task can be accomplished only by a strong government. Democratic governments are almost by definition weak governments in the sense that their capacity to design and implement comprehensive reform packages is extremely low.[32] Kornai complains: 'The sluggishness and constant delay with which the government drafts legislation and the rate at which Parliament can cope with its legislative load form one of the most distressing bottlenecks in the advance toward modern market economy.'[33] Sachs warns that the greatest political risk facing Eastern Europe is not a resurgence of communism, but the Argentine trap of political and social paralysis, in which coalitions of workers, managers and bureaucrats in the declining sectors succeed in frustrating the needed adjustments. The decades-long agony of Argentina is for Sachs proof enough that a country can become trapped in a seemingly endless political stalemate that blocks effective restructuring of the economy.[34]

Kaltefleiter defines the necessity of compromise seeking as the fundamental problem of democracy in situations where a comprehensive systemic reform would require strict consistency in policy. The majority rule enforces concessions which water down the sound economic blueprints. The system theoretical conceptions do not endure half-heartedness because they lose their effectiveness if they are realized incompletely. This is exactly the reason why democracy is dysfunctional in the realization of economic reforms.[35]

Democratically minded theorists are forced to formulate highly restrictive conditions under which a democratic government could act as a strong government. In order to be strong, a democratically elected government should enjoy high legitimacy based on popular consent to enforce economic change. Its authority should rest on a real popular mandate to set the economy right with a firm hand. In the case of Eastern Europe, where the political base is extremely fragmented and labile, the requirement for solid social support seems unrealistic. The institutional minimum prerequisite for building strong governments is the introduction of electoral rules based on majority principle. Voting based on proportional representation tends to produce weak multiparty coalition governments.[36]

(2) *The dangers of populism.* The immense social costs imposed on the majority of the population make it unlikely for a democratic government to meet the restrictive conditions described above. Populist parties will attempt to profit from public disillusionment and force the reformist government to dilute its policies.[37] By referring to the Latin American lesson of the 1980s, Lipton and Sachs point out how a fragile democratic opening combined with a deep economic crisis is a fertile brew for populist policies. Cutbacks in subsidies, rise in unemployment and reductions in consumption will produce ample opportunities for politicians who promise illusory low-cost paths to reform.

> In the short term, populist pressures will lead to opposition to cuts in subsidies and calls for 'reactivation' of the economy through wage increases and demand expansion. In the longer term, populist politicians will find support among workers in declining industries, who will press for protection, subsidies, and other steps to halt the necessary industrial restructuring ... There is little doubt that one dubious scheme after another will be proposed to try to circumvent the difficult processes of structural change.[38]

In these conditions, egalitarian ideologies with strong populist and nationalistic overtones can be mobilized against both democracy and reforms. Growing social inequality is an inevitable consequence of marketization, yet a population whose values have been shaped by communist egalitarianism will have a low tolerance of rising inequality. The values, beliefs and attitudes to sustain a market economy – individualism, personal initiative, risk-taking, competitiveness, acceptance of significant social and economic inequalities – are diametrically opposed to the values, beliefs and attitudes dominant under communism. A democratically elected government will be incapable of ideologically justifying the reordering of individual rights and responsibilities if in the eyes of a majority of the population its initial results are perceived as unjust. Especially those adversely affected will refuse to adopt market ethics, and quite reasonably so. They will see that primarily members of the old *nomenklatura* and criminal elements benefit from the newly created economic freedoms, while many hard-working, decent people lose their jobs. The adaptation to market ethics must be guided by a regime that has power to resist the temptations of responding favourably to demands rooted in collectivist ethics. The government must be capable of continuing with the construction of a legal framework which will compel people to adapt their values to the market environment.[39]

(3) *The erosion of confidence in democratic institutions and the sustainability of economic reform.* If the government cannot ignore, silence or push aside the groups with vested interests that are opposed to the reform programme, it is forced to slow down the pace of reform. Over time it becomes more and more improbable that it is capable of maintaining its commitment to a long-term strategy.[40]

As pressures mount, democratic governments begin to vacillate between mutually inconsistent political styles, namely between the technocratic political style inherent in market-oriented reforms and the participatory style required to maintain consensus. Since the idea of resolving conflicts by agreement is alluring, governments turn to making bargains when opposition against reforms heightens; they turn back to the technocratic style when the compromises imperil reforms. They promise consultation but shock the eventual partners with decrees. In electoral campaigns candidates promise painless adjustment, only to launch austerity programmes upon taking office. As a result, governments appear to lack a clear conception of reforms. The state begins to be perceived as the principal source of economic instability. The contradictions between popular demands for consultation and government's tendency toward technocratic decision-making cause distrust which erodes fragile confidence in democratic institutions.[41]

Once confidence is eroded, each new government tries to make a clean break with the past by doing something that people have not yet learned to distrust. Reforms are addictive: a stronger dosage is needed each time to soothe the accumulated desperation. Elites may learn from the past mistakes to design better programmes, but citizens learn from past failures to expect that new reforms will also fail.[42]

(4) *Weak civil society.* An underdeveloped civil society in postcommunist countries means that organizations have not yet emerged that could represent their membership in a bargain with the government. The intermediary level of institutions is too weak to act in a cooperative manner albeit not too weak to be an obstructing factor. According to Przeworski, reforms are least likely

to advance when political forces – in particular, opposition parties and unions – are strong enough to sabotage them but not large enough to internalize the entire cost of arresting them.[43]

(5)(a) *Historical lessons* ... The most recent success stories of Singapore, South Korea, Taiwan and Chile or the more distant cases of Germany or even England offer little comfort for those believing in the compatibility of marketization and democratization. Moreover, history shows that a democratic regime at the wrong time may plunge a country into the worst forms of oppression and disaster (the Weimar Republic), while an authoritarian regime at the right time can create most favourable conditions for a successful democratization (the French Second Empire).[44]

(5)(b) ... *and legacies*. The East European countries are not only carrying the heavy burden of Leninist legacy but also that of their authoritarian past stemming from the precommunist era. The communist system did not represent a complete departure from the prewar period; rather, it carried along some elements of the precommunist order. The dictatorship of the proletariat was not built on the ruins of working democracies but rather on the remnants of various forms of right-wing authoritarianism. The point is that democratic polity was never really in place in Eastern Europe, with the exception of Czechoslovakia.[45]

A Critique of the Case for Authoritarianism

The critique of the case for authoritarianism does not confine itself to undermining individual arguments made in support of the 'economic reform first' option. Rather, it attacks the fundamental assumptions which form the grounds for the pro-authoritarian argumentation. Critics seek to show, for instance, that many neoliberal claims indeed rest on shaky theoretical and empirical ground.[46] The most effective critique will therefore start by examining the tacit conception implied in the defence of an authoritarian transition regime.

The force of the case for authoritarianism derives in large measure from a particular formulation of the problem of economic transition. This particular understanding of the reform task entails a set of political requirements that democratic regimes are unlikely to meet. Interpreting the transitional problem as a purely technical problem to be solved by purely technocratic means clearly favours authoritarian solutions. If it can be shown that this implicit formulation of the transitional problem is faulty or inadequate in important respects, the pro-authoritarian thesis needs to be reassessed from a new vantage point.[47]

The orthodox formulation rests on three, often unstated, assumptions. First, the goal of economic reform in postcommunist countries is to make the transition from one economic system to another. Second, the basic knowledge concerning the integral components of the market system is available. Third, corresponding general strategies as well as specific policies of economic reform can be derived from assumptions 1 (the goal) and 2 (the available knowledge). Each of these assumptions is highly problematic.[48]

First of all, the conception of a market economy as a system is misleading as a description of the context of economic reform. The system analogy is useful in the confines of the neoclassical model in order to demonstrate, for example, the allocative efficiency of free markets or the benefits of private property. It quickly reaches its limits when the problem situation at hand deviates from the conditions postulated in the model's premises.[49]

The second point of criticism denies the availability of the knowledge concerning the integral components of a market economy. While it is easy to identify the integral components of the market system from a theoretical construct, it is exceedingly difficult to specify the crucial elements necessary for a real market economy. The conclusions derived from textbook definitions of a market system are not empirically valid. Actually existing market economies differ markedly from each other with respect to their institutional configurations: the extent and type of state intervention, the role of non-governmental organizations (NGOs) in regulating the economy as well as the provision of social security vary significantly from country to country. Clearly, the Anglo-Saxon model is not the only viable model of the market economy; many 'alternative capitalisms', such as the German, French, Swedish or East Asian models, have proved to be successful. Yet debates over neoliberalism have frequently become polarized in ways that have obscured and mischaracterized the political options available to new democracies.[50]

Finally, the critics accuse neoliberal blueprints of 'neo-Bolshevism' by comparing the current debate with the Marxist debate on the transition to socialism. In their view, the same sense of confidence of possessing the correct scientific knowledge, the same sense of disdain for the ideologically blinded and for political reactionaries, shines through the case for authoritarianism. The orthodox formulation is utopian in precisely the sense that the communist project of engineering radical social change was utopian. The danger of utopian formulations is that they will produce unintended consequences. The more utopian the approach to economic reform, the more authoritarian its implications.[51]

When the basic conception of authoritarian transition is seriously questioned, the individual arguments in support of such a solution change their character as well, for they derive much of their force from the orthodox formulation of the problem. In the changed context they make their appearance, not as arguments backing an ill-defined problem, but as arguments suggesting the impossibility of a democratic solution to the redefined problem. This reformulation of the transitional problem suggests that a political regime should be capable of maintaining political order, stability and the conditions for the implementation of reform policies. Let us consider each argument to see if they add up to a convincing case against democracy's capacity to maintain political order and stability.[52]

(1) *Need for a strong government?* Political order and stability are not equivalent to a strong government. Rather, they refer to regime stability. A succession of weak governments as such is not a threat to the stability of a democratic regime.[53] As Samuel Huntington has pointed out:

> The legitimacy of particular rulers or governments may depend on what they can deliver; the legitimacy of the regime derives from the electoral processes by which governments are constituted. Performance legitimacy plays a role in democratic regimes, but it is nowhere near as important as the role it plays in authoritarian regimes and it is secondary to procedural legitimacy. What determines whether or not new democracies survive is not primarily the severity of the problems they face or their ability to solve these problems. It is the way in which political leaders respond to their inability to solve the problems confronting their country.[54]

The pro-authoritarian thesis was initially presented in the context of analyses of development that focused on the problem of how to promote high rates of investment. New democracies were seen as vulnerable to demands for immediate consumption because of a collective-action problem: the short-term interest of social groups in turning economic policies into a distributive game would prevail at the expense of the long-term benefits that would eventually have accrued from cooperative sacrifices. The political result of such vulnerability would be instability of the regime. Successful economic reform was thus assumed to require an authoritarian regime that is internally insulated but externally malleable.[55]

Yet it is the latter double requirement that creates the paradox pointing to the basic problem with the pro-authoritarian thesis. In general, authoritarian regimes have more limited incentives and more limited access to information than democratic regimes. When the focus of development strategies moved from the accumulation of investment to the productivity of investment, the problem of incentives became salient. As for the supposedly greater resilience of dictatorships, Samuel Huntington has convincingly argued that the overlapping of procedural and performance legitimacy can make them more vulnerable than democracies to economic crises, particularly when their claim to legitimacy is based on economic performance.[56]

(2) *Dangers of Populism?* From the perspective of architects of radical reform programmes, any political opposition to reforms appears to be irresponsible populism. Yet two questions merit more serious reflection. First, is it reasonable to expect politicians competing under democratic conditions not to exploit dissatisfaction with reforms for partisan advantage? While populist leaders may be able to take advantage of public disillusionment, it does not pose any serious threat to political stability. On the contrary, democratic governments have an incentive to respond to the concerns expressed by populist leaders in order to reduce their electoral appeal. The second important question to be considered is, should we not expect that unless opposition to reforms finds an expression through the democratic process, it will erupt in some other ways? If economic reforms are not to undermine political stability, distributional conflicts must be institutionalized: all groups must channel their demands through the democratic institutions and abjure other tactics. It is the strength of democratic insitutions, not the exhortations by technocrats, that reduces the political space for the pursuit of immediate particularistic interests; that is, for populism. Populism is an endogenous product of technocratic policy styles.[57]

Contrary to Sachs's expectations, labour has not been able to translate its opposition to adjustment policies into credible threats to punish the initiators of reform. The opposition has not routinely led to threats of regime breakdown or the wholesale abandonment of market-oriented policies. Labour by itself is not powerful enough to hinder reform; it needs the support of the rest of the urban sector but it can be isolated from the rest of the urban sector in numerous ways, depending on local circumstances and the political skills of leaders. There are also two other complementary explanations for the political ineffectiveness of working-class opposition. First, unemployment and economic crisis decrease the bargaining power and political influence of labour. Second, democratic politicians have more autonomy from societal interests than old theories gave them credit for.[58]

The broad climate of both popular and elite opinion favours participation and consultation. East European experience already demonstrates that economic reform cannot long be insulated from politics and that politics is not always the enemy of reforms. There is no avoiding the challenge of balancing access to decision-makers with adequate autonomy for economic policy-making.[59]

(3) *The erosion of confidence in democratic institutions and the sustainability of economic reform.* Since the neoliberal strategy entails significant social costs and hence political opposition, reforms tend to be initiated from above and launched by surprise, independent of public opinion and without the participation of organized political forces. The political style of implementation is autocratic; a government seeks to demobilize its supporters rather than compromise its programme by public consultation. In reality, however, reforms can never be quick enough to prevent the emergence of divergent opinions and political conflict. It is impossible to build democracy by trying to beat the democratic process to the punch.[60]

The autocratic policy style of market-oriented reforms debilitates representative institutions, personalizes politics and generates a climate in which politics becomes reduced to fixes. Society is taught that it can vote but not choose; legislatures are trained to think that they have no role to play in policy elaboration; political organizations are taught that their voices do not count. Economic blueprints that treat politics as nothing but an extraneous nuisance may result in long-term damage both to reform and to democracy. If democratic institutions are neglected or bypassed, their prestige is harmed and their future effectiveness jeopardized. If a government has made many enemies, the negotiations that become essential later on, when mandates have been eroded, will be more difficult. The price of the insufficient attention to political factors is the erosion of support for reforms as well as the fragility of nascent democratic institutions.[61]

It should be reminded that authoritarian political systems also suffer from problems that derive from their particular nature, such as overly concentrated decision-making, deficient feedback, dependence on performance legitimacy. Empirical evidence based on a comparison of 44 authoritarian and 39 democratic regimes suggests that authoritarian rulers are no more successful than democratic governments in accomplishing fundamental economic reforms.[62]

(4) *Weak civil society?* The widely held view that communist rule effectively destroyed autonomous forms of social life is increasingly being called into question. Di Palma points out that the breakthrough in pursuing a new civic culture was made by dissident movements. Uncharacteristic of intellectual mobilization in backward countries, East European movements made an anti-Leninist – hence, anti-Jacobin – choice, one that entrusts progress to the proper constitution of citizens' relations to one another rather than to a guiding state.[63]

A further source of confidence in the ability to set up a working democracy is the perception that the forces responsible for the removal of the communist parties demonstrated great restraint in dealing with their opponents. The self-restraint suggests that people in postcommunist countries are already prepared for democracy built on respect for an opponent, preference for negotiations and time for differences of opinion to subside. This pattern of democratic proceeding is reinforced by the fact that communism was replaced not by individual efforts but rather through organized ones. Popular activism was by and large of a grassroot nature, a feature usually equated with democratic politics.[64]

(5) *What lessons from history?* Conventional wisdom claimed that authoritarian governments are more capable of initiating and sustaining major economic reforms. Evidence that appeared to support a relationship between regime type and likelihood of economic liberalization came from the earliest liberalizers, especially Chile, South Korea, Taiwan, Mexico and Ghana. Many of the studies of these cases are classic examples of what social scientists call 'selection on the dependent variable': cases were chosen for examination because they had experienced the outcome the analyst sought to explain – in this instance, economic liberalization. The flaw in this research design is that the failure to examine cases that do not exhibit the 'right' outcome lures the analyst into identifying any plausible characteristics shared by the selected cases as causes of the outcome. Conclusions reached in this way are wrong because unexamined cases may also have the traits the analyst has identified as causes. When an unbiased sample is used, the data supporting a causal link between regime type and likelihood of economic liberalization is weak. Internal variations within the regime categories are more important for successful economic reform than whether the regime is democratic or authoritarian. Only in Asia does authoritarianism appear conducive to economic liberalization, but even there the evidence is not entirely one-sided. The success of the East Asian reform projects seems to be attributable more to these countries' turn to an export-oriented strategy as well as their high rates of literacy than to the authoritarian nature of their regimes.[65]

To a very great extent, pro-authoritarian conclusions are rooted in a particular time period. A regression of the average rates of economic growth in 82 countries between 1980 and 1987 on an index of democracy for the same countries for 1980 shows that democracy did have a positive effect on growth. As Adam Przeworski and Fernando Limongi have noted, from 1987 onward a majority of comparative quantitative studies reported better economic performance by democratic regimes than by authoritarian ones. Under the harsh economic circumstances of the 1980s, democracies proved to be more economically efficient and less vulnerable to economic crises than expected, while dictatorships fell short of expectations regarding resilience, insulation from interest group pressures and economic performance as a whole.

Dramatic fiscal crises, overwhelming external debts, and soaring inflation rates were more frequently traceable to the developmental efforts of dictatorships than to the populism of new democracies.[66]

In Eastern Europe, prolonged and painful economic mismanagement could have persisted only under conditions of authoritarianism: the social costs would not have been tolerated under democratic conditions. Authoritarian politics also made the implementation of necessary economic reforms impossible. Little economic pluralism was allowed to develop under communism, for the interests of the *nomenklatura* dictated otherwise. Modest changes were thwarted by party and state bureaucrats and more ambitious transformations were prevented by the regimes of individual countries or by the USSR. Such reform-inhibiting phenomena as the overlapping of the economic and political realms, widespread opportunistic, rent-seeking behaviour and the absence of good economic information could be traced not only to the economic institutions of the communist countries but also to the institutions of authoritarian politics. The failure of communist countries to stabilize their economies provided strong evidence that effective economic reform could not be accomplished without democratization.[67]

Eventually, democratic elections provided a window of opportunity: elected governments turned out to have the legitimacy necessary for the launching of reforms. In developed postcommunist countries, there is a striking empirical correlation between democratization and the transition to a market economy. Economic liberalization has gone furthest in two of the most democratic countries of the area, Poland and the Czech Republic. The transition to capitalism has faced the stiffest resistance in precisely those parts of Eastern Europe and the former Soviet Union where the political system has changed the least. Haltingly democratized countries where many old communists remain in high office have been susceptible to populist politics.[68]

The bottom line is that no strong evidence supports the conventional wisdom. The relationship between regime type and economic efficiency is inconclusive. Although some authoritarian governments have carried out successful transitions to more market-oriented economies, there is little support for the thesis that authoritarianism as such increases the likelihood of such transitions. The strategy prescribing economic reform prior to political reform is risky for two reasons. First, most authoritarian governments, including the former communist governments in Eastern Europe, fail to liberalize their economies. Those governments which indeed do carry out a successful economic reform find that success reduces the short-term demand for democracy.[69] Second, generalizations about the greater political capacity of authoritarian regimes are based on sloppy methodological practices and the natural lag between events and scholarship. More importantly, the studies of economic transitions illustrate Albert Hirschman's remark about 'paradigms as a hindrance to understanding'. In this instance, three paradigms converge to hinder the understanding: pluralist theory, traditional Marxism and the standard economist's view of politics. The unspoken assumptions underlying expectations about the course of reform process can be traced to these three paradigms. What they have in common is (1) a focus on interest groups or classes, without consideration of the ways in which political arrangements (except for authoritarianism) affect the political influence of interests; (2) a focus on material interests to the exclusion of other kinds of interests; (3) a black-box view of the state. The focus on societal interests leads analysts to expect that the main impediment to economic reform is the opposition of groups hurt by it. Politicians' careers depend on pleasing constituents; if large and well-organized groups of constituents are hurt by policies, they will respond with demonstrations and votes against the politicians who initiate adjustment policies. Consequently, elected politicians do not take the risk of initiating unpopular policies or, if they do, they will lose the next election. In the end, economic crisis, caused either by reform or by its postponement, will lead to political crisis.[70]

The story sounds plausible. However, something went wrong because scholars failed to predict democratic stability in the face of severe economic crisis. It is increasingly evident that earlier theoretical explanations are inadequate. There is a reason to believe that the political process is more complicated than that posited by the simplest versions of democratic theory which extrapolate from societal interests to policy outcomes. To understand why a certain outcome occurs in one place but not in another, one should examine who the people are who make policies, what the interests located within the state are and what shapes those interests. In this way the state ceases to be an unexamined black box. All generalizations about the political feasibility of economic reform should be treated tentatively at this time.[71]

The Case for Democracy

The construction of the case for democracy continues from the point at which the critique of the case for authoritarianism ends. Faced with the evidence that the general authoritarian prescription cannot be defended on either theoretical or empirical grounds, democratically minded scholars have been asked to explore the opportunities for dual transitions. In order to overcome the democratic disadvantage, they seek an answer to the question: 'What are the conditions that facilitate the success of economic reform and the persistence of democracy?' Adopting democratization as the primary goal of transition implies a tacit valuation of democracy per se, but it also hinges on the conviction of the better economic performance of democratic regimes. A strong case can be made that economic reforms are more likely to succeed in a democratic political context. Political pluralism generates more and better information to use in economic decision-making. A free press and a political opposition serve as important early warning systems by means of which policy mistakes can be corrected. In the absence of institutionalized consultation with legislators and interest groups, decision-makers are deprived of feedback that may be essential for correcting mistakes, and their reforms are more exposed to the possibility of popular backlash. The case for effective non-expert participation is based on two considerations. First, there is no reliable expert knowledge but only competing expert claims, which means that there is the need to make a political decision between them. Second, many questions of economic reform are not reducible to technical problems but represent normative questions about fundamental values and the future state of society.[72]

Democratic institutions may reduce the transaction costs of economic performance as well as restrict predation of public resources. The competition entailed by democratic political markets provides a valuable mechanism of punishment and reward. Politicians suffer the consequences of their own policy mistakes in the form of reduced popularity and are therefore more interested in avoiding such mistakes. The same dependence on electoral support and the establishment of a good reputation among voters inhibits opportunistic and self-serving behaviour. It is no wonder then that democratic regimes have proved themselves capable of learning more from the past unsuccessful reform experiences than authoritarian ones. In an effort to stabilize their economies and ensure the survival of democracy, governments of both the left and right have abandoned populism, economic voluntarism and experimentation.[73]

When economic hardships are required by the reform process, the greater legitimacy enjoyed by democratic leaders allows them to obtain more easily the cooperation of citizens, who feel a greater sense of responsibility for their society. Majority rule limits the influence of particularistic interests on politicians, meaning that political parties and trade unions can better be persuaded to accept trade-offs or to moderate their demands. Because their legitimacy is not so dependent on their economic performance and because they foster greater diffusion of power and responsibility, democratic regimes are more resilient during economic crises.[74]

Decretismo in economic decision-making reinforces tendencies toward what Guillermo O'Donnell has called 'delegative democracy', in which elected executives attempt to rule through broad media appeals and personalist movements, bypassing intermediate institutions. Even where the reform initiatives of plebiscitarian presidents yield positive economic results, there is a substantial risk of a slide into a kind of soft authoritarianism in which economic success is used by the ruler to chip away at constitutional limits on his power. If both economic reforms and democracy are to be consolidated, executive authority must be depersonalized and integrated into a broader framework of accountability.[75]

The analytical argument for the capacity of democracy hinges on the belief that the general population as well as politically powerful groups can have both instrumental and intrinsic attachments to democracy. In the transitional stage, compliance with democratic rules depends on the probability of winning with democratic institutions, while established democratic regimes develop symbolic, emotive significance for their populations. Democratic procedures are valued not primarily for the benefits they bring to citizens, but for their own sake. Once democracy becomes the only legitimate political system, the tolerance on the part of both the mass public and powerful interest groups for the costs associated with economic reforms rises significantly, as long as the decision to reform is perceived as having been made via democratic procedures. Legitimacy and pluralism promote the development of a strong civil society which will be crucial in building a meaningful social and political consensus on reform measures. Consensus on economic policy can even substitute for a strong electoral mandate. To achieve such a consensus, democratic governments need to listen, to negotiate and to persuade. Democratic institutions must offer the politically relevant groups incentives to process their demands within the institutional framework.[76]

Democracy should not be expected to emerge as a byproduct of some structural logic of marketization. A great deal depends on the commitment of political and economic elites to strengthening democratic institutions. Rather than being an unaffordable luxury, democracy is perhaps the single most important precondition for successful economic reform in Eastern Europe.[77]

Beyond Dichotomies and Toward Consensus

From a wide range of perspectives, there emerges a surprisingly strong consensus on the need to move beyond the debate over 'economic reform first' or 'democracy first' to finer-grained questions regarding the specific institutional arrangements that enable governments to undertake reform, the imperatives and constraints at different stages of the reform process and the degree to which democratic procedures must be modified in order to facilitate reform. The demands for a more differentiated and elaborated approach reflect the perception that the economic reform agenda changes significantly between the launch phase and later phases. Respectively, the character of politics also changes as the early transition period yields to more structured patterns. As both economic and political reforms evolve over the course of the transition period, the interactions between them change, too.[78] A theme that resonates through many of the latest writings is the sharp difference between the first stage of reform, in which stabilization and liberalization are implemented by a small technocratic team, and the second stage of reform which involves far-reaching institutional changes and requires the mobilization of political support. The need for an analytical distinction between the successive stages of transition derives from the simple fact that different processes of economic reform have different maximum possible speeds. Decision-makers should remain mindful that complex institutional changes like the reform of the tax system or the privatization of the public sector run on a slower clock than stabilization and liberalization policies.[79]

Academic research has traditionally focused on the initial stages of economic reform: the factors behind a government's decisions and the immediate political reactions to these choices. The political dynamics of consolidating reforms has received much less attention, even though it is equally important. Experience in many countries suggests that sustaining reforms differs from initiating them but is by no means easier. Some tactics that are useful in the initiation phase may be dysfunctional during the period of consolidation. In the long run, democracies cannot sustain reform without the use of democratic methods.[80]

The initiation of reform usually requires a substantial concentration of discretionary political authority to surmount resistance from status quo interests as well as collective-action problems facing potential beneficiaries. Early stages of adjustment are carried out almost everywhere in an autocratic and technocratic manner, even in countries with firmly democratic systems. Reflecting the crisis context, reform packages are introduced with little or no public preparation and are pushed through legislatures rapidly or launched by decree. Governments launching market-oriented reforms normally enjoy unusual degrees of central executive autonomy.[81]

In many cases, political leaders concentrate authority for economic management in change teams, recruited from the ranks of non-officials. This small circle of senior economists is then made responsible for the formulation and implementation of reform policy. Given the stong backing by the top political leaders, the change team is protected and insulated from political pressures originating both from outside and from within the government. The group around Leszek Balcerowicz in Poland is a typical example of such a change team. The explanation why the first steps of reform can be formulated and implemented by a small circle of senior economic officials lies in the nature of initial reform packages. Measures taken to stabilize and liberalize the economy are administratively uncomplicated.[82]

The first round of reform is driven by the urgent desire to get a crisis under control. It is characterized by concerns about economic collapse and democratic reversal. Yet the flux and confusion of the political arena actually provide insulation for the reform effort. In such a context, scattered protest against economic austerity measures is likely but large-scale coordinated opposition in the legislature or from well-organized groups is not. Groups opposed to reforms are mostly discredited or in disarray. Moreover, the launch phase is often accompanied by a negative consensus that old economic strategies and institutions have failed. This was the case in Eastern Europe, too. At the outset of transition, there was a widespread agreement that communism had performed poorly as an economic system and that it should be replaced by a market model.[83]

Leszek Balcerowicz calls the first stage following the breakthrough a period of extraordinary politics. During the period of extraordinary politics, the readiness to accept radical economic measures is exceptionally high. New political structures are still fluid, the old elite is discredited and political liberalization has produced a special state of mass psychology. Unfortunately, extraordinary politics quickly gives way to the mundane politics of contending parties and interest groups. Where the initiation of reforms was delayed, the governments lost the opportunity of taking advantage of the period of extraordinary politics and are likely to meet more resistance and delays than instant reform launchers. The brevity of the extraordinary period means that a radical economic programme, launched as quickly as possible after the breakthrough, has a greater chance of being accepted than either a delayed radical programme or a non-radical one that introduces difficult measures in piecemeal fashion. For the same reason, time-consuming institutional and structural reforms are likely to meet more resistance than swiftly implemented stabilizing and liberalizing measures.[84]

The main political challenge in initiating a reform is coping with inevitable opposition, whereas the main challenge of consolidating a reform is generating positive support. Crucial to the success of the reform effort in democratic systems is a change in the nature of consensus. While a negative consensus may suffice for launching a reform, later stages depend on the building of a positive consensus on the ultimate goals of transition. The success of economic reform depends not just on the commitment of the government initiating it, but on whether there is a consensus in the broader political arena regarding the basic direction in which society should be moving. Yet the initiation of far-reaching adjustments has often reflected a political logic that is not easily reconciled with the formation of broad-based coalitions and effective representative institutions. Democratic governments cannot sustain the reform process in the second stage by using the same methods of secrecy, surprise and delegation that brought the initial success in stabilization. To carry restructuring forward, they must build political coalitions for reform. That requires not only showing some positive results but also educating people as well as strengthening the associational infrastructure of civil society. Furthermore, the new challenges include the construction of a capable state bureaucracy and the mobilization of the newly emergent beneficiaries of reform. It should be noted, however, that as winners emerge, they do not automatically provide the government with useful political support.[85]

The transformations taking place during the second round are likely to be more incremental, but no less crucial for the consolidation of capitalist democracy. Compared with the first round, measures that come later – such as financial sector reforms, privatization of state enterprises, liberalization of labour markets, restructuring of social security systems – are much more complex, requiring sweeping institutional and legal changes. While they involve the legislature, the courts as well as a wide range of central and local government agencies, the later-stage reforms are more vulnerable to dilution, delay and derailment. In addition, while the initial costs of stabilization are temporary and distributed evenly over the whole population, sectoral and institutional reforms result in permanent losses to specific groups, thus prompting vigorous resistance. Moreover, tensions between different elements of the reform programme increase over time, contributing to heightened disagreement in later stages. Tough trade-offs within the reform programme itself fuel protracted struggles among conflicting interest groups.[86]

In later phases of reform there is a shift not only in the character of the economic reforms but also in the political context in which they are carried out. Honeymoons end, diffuse support fades, disabled opposition groups reorganize, elections approach, the opportunity to blame the old system draws to a close. If the signs indicate that the acute economic crisis has been contained, the public's willingness to make sacrifices will decrease. On the other hand, if initial results are disappointing, confidence in the government will erode. Either outcome serves to heighten political difficulties. Under these conditions, people need a vision of what kind of society is being sought. The market-oriented agenda by itself does not provide an adequate vision.[87]

4 Radical and Gradualist Strategies for Reform

The wave of systemic changes has triggered a lively theoretical discussion on the course of the overall reform programme. The major dividing line in the theoretical debate is between the radical 'big bang' school, also called the shock therapy approach, and the gradualist, evolutionary school. Shock therapists advocate the application of sweeping, state-led reforms attacking all aspects of the economy at once. Gradualists prefer a self-grown order and a carefully prepared sequence of steps, each preparing the ground for a smooth introduction of the next one. The controversy generated by the debate on shock therapy versus gradualism reflects in large measure differences over speed. At issue is the desirability of effecting a quick break with the old system by adopting a rapid transition strategy. This contrasts with a slower approach to transition, in which the institutions inherited from the old system are gradually modified ostensibly in line with the social, political and cultural specifics of a given country.[88]

Speed can be broken down into three separate aspects: timing of launching, sequencing and pace. The timing of launching refers to the interval between the political breakthrough and the start of the economic reform. Sequencing describes the relative phasing and the order of implementation of different measures. Pace describes the implementation rate for each main component of the reform.[89]

The attitude of shock therapists reflects the feeling that the economic situation under communism deteriorated to such a desperate level that no time should be wasted on gradual measures. Pressing ahead as fast as possible is the best way to establish the institutional, behavioural and policy changes necessary to create well-functioning market mechanisms. The motivation is to cut the uncertainties facing the public with regard to the new rules of the game in the economy. Rather than creating protracted turmoil, uncertainty and political resistance through a gradual introduction of new measures, the goal is to set in place incentives for the new economic system immediately. Only a consistent set of steps across the entire economic panorama can produce positive results, while any gradual reform is self-contradictory due to incompatibilities between the new and old elements of the system during the transition. A command economy and a market economy are completely alien to each other and no convergence has proved possible.[90]

The logical core of the argument for shock therapy comes in two varieties, which are politically complementary but analytically distinct: (1) shock treatment as 'bridge burning', and (2) shock treatment as 'sneak attack'. The case for shock treatment as 'bridge burning' rests on the claim that incremental reform lacks credibility. Households and firms must have confidence that the new system has come to stay and it is worthwhile to adjust to a market economy. The greater and more persuasive the steps are, the more people will believe that the market economy is actually coming about. If actors conclude that reforms will be halted or reversed, they will hesitate to respond to any positive incentives. Because it is very difficult for a government to commit itself to reforms that are intended to be implemented only in the distant future, a gradual reform is likely to foster doubts about future government policies. It was the partiality and the indecisiveness that were responsible for the failure of the earlier communist reform efforts. Communist reforms are often characterized as a windmill of inconclusive attempts, where too few steps were taken to prevent the system from returning to its starting point. The critics have always seen that *style* as one of their sins.[91]

The second group of reasons pertains to the nature of democratic politics. Economists frustrated with the apparent lack of political determination claim that democratic politics will not willingly carry economic reforms to their necessary conclusion. The reason is that individuals discount future benefits relative to present benefits. Radical reformers hope to have passed the point of no return before the political opposition coalesces. People will accept a fair amount of hardship for a while, but their patience is limited. It is important to do as much as possible before the sense of crisis and willingness to sacrifice give way to discontent and impatience. Moreover, it is politically easier to have severe measures adopted as a big package. If many changes are introduced at the same time, it is difficult for anyone to assess who will win or lose.[92]

Attributing widespread dissatisfaction to shock therapy is erroneous, because under conditions grave enough to elicit such radical measures, any economic policy package will generate discontent. There is no a priori reason to expect that the dissatisfaction attendant upon radical measures will be greater than that attendant upon non-radical ones. Even cursory examination of the East Central European experience shows no clear link between the intensity of displays of social discontent and the type of economic programme pursued. Declines in economic activity have been dismissed by shock therapists as phenomena artificially exaggerated by official statistics that have inflated these declines.[93]

Gradualists claim that there is a trade-off between cutting inflation and maintaining national income. They focus on the excessive social costs of a rapid transition, suggesting that there is an alternative approach causing less suffering. The gradual evolution into a market system has the advantage of being more easily accepted by the population. Carrying out economic reforms by means of stealth and deception undermines democracy.[94]

Another set of criticisms pertains to the impossibility of undertaking massive changes very fast. Restructuring is a process that necessarily takes time. Moreover, human learning is a long and complicated process, which is not favoured by sudden abruptions. Gradualists rely on organic economic processes. The phasing out of old institutions must be smooth and incremental, in companion with the rise of the new institutions of the private sector. If the private sector assumes a self-grown, slow path, so too must the public sector be permitted to withdraw in a spontaneous way. A lengthy phase of dual economy implies that the state has to operate parallel economic arrangements for state-owned and private enterprises. Gradualists cling to the severe implementation problems faced by the radical reformers. These problems damage the coherence of the programme that is the most important property of the big bang model.[95]

Proponents of gradual change emphasize the absence of the private and public sector institutions that a well-functioning capitalist economy requires. Relying on nascent market forces that cannot function effectively is a recipe for disaster. Some gradualists accuse shock therapists of trying to recreate a form of capitalism that is obsolete in the West. They point out that the 'free market' is an intellectual construct not evident in real-world capitalist economies since the 1930s. Adopting a rapid programme is tantamount to choosing a *laissez-faire* version of capitalism as an end goal. Shock therapists are less likely to make this connection between ends and means. They in turn answer that the state simply cannot afford large welfare expenses during the depths of the postcommunist budget crisis.[96]

The decision to employ the shock treatment strategy requires a high degree of confidence in the economic design of the proposed reforms. If the technical design is anything less than perfect, a gradual strategy would allow for crucial modifications at a lower economic cost. It also allows for a more elaborate preparation of particular reform components, thus diminishing the risks of making policy mistakes. Instead, if the wrong bridge is burned, the cost of rebuilding it – in terms of both time and resources, not to mention government credibility – may be extremely high. Gradualist critics often complain that radical measures smack of neo-Bolshevism. In their view, the truly important lesson from the communist past is not that gradualism does not work. Really relevant is the experience of the formative years of state socialism rather than that of the mature age. The notion that the more rational institutions can be implemented by a conscious design thus duplicates the rationalist fallacy evidenced during the introduction of communism. The origins of capitalism in the West were not created by a blueprint but by routine.[97]

Although the 'fast versus slow' debate has generated much heat, it has shed little light on the appropriate transition strategy, leaving the problem largely unresolved. Each side is only able to prove the other side wrong. The widely recognized failures of market socialist reform in the 1980s make arguments against gradual transition plausible, especially when the dismal economic conditions the democratic governments inherited are taken into account. A 'third road' hybrid is inconsistent with the realities of the modern world, where no viable alternatives to capitalism exist. The weaknesses of the state in the 1990s argue in favour of reducing the role of state administration in the transition in order to avoid overloading the state with tasks it cannot accomplish. The argument that no capitalist country leaves matters of critical importance solely up to the invisible hand of the market is equally correct. Confusion in the debate is deepened by the passions it arouses and by the protagonists' propensity to caricature their opponents. Proponents of rapid transition brand their opponents closet communists whose opposition to a quick break is really a cloak for their aversion toward the creation of capitalism. Gradualists charge that shock therapists, in their ideological zeal to destroy the old system, are willing to ruin the national economy.[98]

Each side can draw upon respectable intellectual arguments in support of their position but they draw upon different scholarly traditions (Table 4.1). Neoliberal economic theory – including the Austrian school with Hayek – provides radical reformers with arguments on what represents the effective economic regime, specifically, allocation through competitive markets. The emphasis placed on property rights reflects the influence of property rights theories, which are in great esteem among postcommunist reformers. The intellectual underpinnings for gradualism are provided by two distinct sets of theories: evolutionary economics and conservative political philosophy. The modern presentation of evolutionary economics begins with Schumpeter (1942); the most detailed current exposition is that of Nelson and Winter (1982). The leading works in conservative political philosophy are Burke (1790), Popper (1971) and Oakeshott (1962).[99]

Some practical men find the distinction between gradualism and shock therapy simplistic, journalistic and unnecessarily divisive. They regard it as misleading, since an effective transition programme requires both immediate and piecemeal measures.[100] The previous discussion has shown however that different approaches to reform rest on distinctive paradigms with different philosophical worldviews. The impact of the underlying reform philosophy penetrates the entire reform strategy right down to individual measures. The choice of certain priorities tends to preclude the use of certain mechanisms

Table 4.1   Radical and Gradualist Approaches to Economic Reform

Radical	*Gradualist*
1. *End point driven.* Choice of initial policy determined by the goal for the final outcome of the process. All actions directly related to the attainment of the envisioned endpoint. Immediate implementation of the features of a mature market economy. Doing as much as possible as soon as possible.	1. *Focus on immediate problems.* Concentration on the most urgent problems, trying to solve them by largely ignoring the effects of today's decisions on the long-run equilibrium. Acceptance of compromises and temporary solutions that might be inconsistent with the end-state. Pragmatic assessment of present requirements.
2. *Destruction of old institutions.* Cleans the slate. Emphasizes the interrelatedness of society's problems and therefore the need to make a decisive break with the past, with the necessity of institutional destruction in the first stages.	2. *Gradual replacement of old institutions.* Uses existing institutions. Recognizes that new structures can be created only slowly. Accepts that old institutions are usually better than none or hastily constructed alternatives. Respects the information contained in the continuing operations of existing organizations.
3. *Large leaps.* To make a decisive break with the past, advocates bold policy steps that involve packages of many new institutions. Fast pace and large-scale experiments.	3. *Small steps.* Restricts the scope of experiments. Emphasizes the risks of going too fast and the impossibility of creating a network of interrelated institutions anew.
4. *Irreversibility.* Commitment and credibility. Willingness to accept large irreversible changes.	4. *Reversibility.* Advocates policies that facilitate feedback on their effects and that can be stopped. Reason: incompleteness of knowledge.
5. *Faith in the new.* Willingness to trust in theoretical reasoning as the primary input for the design of society's new arrangements.	5. *Scepticism.* Views with scepticism reforms that use wholly new schemes derived purely from theory. Search for existing models to help in the formulation of changes.
6. *Reliance on theoretical design.* Faith in reason over experience. The most important intellectual resource for policy-makers is the knowledge held by theoreticians and technocrats.	6. *Judgement and practice.* Extrapolation of present experience. Valuation of accumulated experimental wisdom of society.
7. *Unified, liberalized market place.* Market product. Economy-wide liberalization as an absolute priority for a first step.	7. *Dual economy.* Market process. Encouragement of an organic growth of a new private sector.
8. Society as a *resource allocation* device.	8. Society as an *information processing* device.

Sources: Murrell 1992a, 13; Murrell 1992b, 87–92.

to achieve them and vice versa. The dependence of lower-level policy choices on the basic approach can best be demonstrated by those dimensions of economic reform which contain a rich set of optional modalities and sequences. Privatization is such an element: there is a wide array of alternative privatization methods to be sought out at each level. The implications of the overall strategy for privatization methods are assessed in the light of six considerations: (1) speed; (2) mass versus piecemeal privatization; (3) top-down versus bottom-up privatization; (4) mechanisms of privatization; (5) actors targeted for the acquisition of assets; and (6) private versus public property.

(1) *Speed.* The key issue in privatization is how quickly and in what form assets can be taken out of the immediate control of the state. Advocates of rapid privatization believe that the efficiency gains from private ownership and private capital markets are so overwhelming that the process must be speeded up as much as possible. The potential costs of overly rapid privatization must be traded off with the high cost of maintaining the present system in which state-owned enterprises lack clear incentives in the face of market forces. For other analysts, privatization should take place at a more measured pace in order to ensure the development of effective ownership. The privatization strategy should focus on establishing effective ownership and corporate governance, rather than simply transferring nominal ownership to the private sector. The secondary market for corporate control, which might operate, for example, through take-over bids on a stock market, will not be reliable enough to ensure efficient matches between enterprises and owners.[101]

(2) *Mass versus piecemeal privatization.* Those who advocate once-and-for-all privatization are sometimes called wholesalers in contrast to retailers who recommend a careful case-by-case approach. Since the primary objective of wholesalers is to put a quick and final end to the government's control over the enterprise activities, a large number of privatizations must be carried out simultaneously on a mass scale. Mass privatization requires the creation of wholly new procedures (e.g. voucher schemes) and institutions (e.g. mutual funds) not found elsewhere. In the opinion of retailers, privatization ought to be carried out in a process of acquisition and merger that is normal to capitalist economies. The search for natural owners of firms is based on employing traditional market mechanisms to identify buyers.[102]

(3) *Top-down versus bottom-up privatization.* Top-down privatization concentrates on the denationalization of the existing state sector from above, while bottom-up privatization stresses the development of the nascent private sector from below. In the first case, reforms are state-led, whereas in the latter

case, the majority of changes in property structure takes place independently of the state. Denationalization forms the core of radical transition programmes. Evolutionarists, by contrast, lay primary emphasis on the gradual expansion of a new private sector through the formation of new firms made possible through economic liberalization[103]

(4) *Mechanisms of privatization.* Four basic mechanisms can be followed for privatization: (a) sale of assets; (b) free distribution of assets; (c) spontaneous privatization; and (d) usufruct divestment. Each mechanism can be implemented through a variety of techniques which are not perfect substitutes for each other. The issue of which mechanism and technique to select is not merely a technical question since each method responds to different objectives in privatization.[104]

When governments decide to proceed with sales, rapid privatization can be achieved only if the state is ready to sell at very low prices, given the shortage of domestic capital and the difficulty in attracting foreign capital. This in itself is not a bad thing: on the one hand, the revenues are lower than those the state could achieve with a more long-term privatization programme; on the other hand, the outlays on debts, subsidies and restructuring decrease. The real danger of selling at low prices lies in the probable speculation and corruption. Moreover, fire-sale prices obstruct the competition between prospective buyers and sellers in a transparent environment.[105]

To cope with the problem of pace, many new governments have developed an ingenious idea of distributing shares of state enterprises transformed into joint-stock companies to citizens through so-called vouchers. Conflicts between the various objectives of privatization are noticeable in voucher privatization particularly. Divestiture of state property by free transfers is advocated in view of equity, valuation problems, the inadequacies of capital markets and the population's lack of funds to buy state assets. It also promotes popular capitalism and recognizes that the citizens are already supposed to own all state property collectively. However the grand voucher schemes are viewed by evolutionarists as a way of exposing a large segment of society to what is essentially the implementation of a theoretical idea. Voucher privatization is opposed on practical economic grounds, too: (1) Budget revenue will be reduced. (2) Unlike the sale of shares, free transfers do not absorb any of the monetary overhang. Inflationary pressures may even increase. (3) Free distribution runs the risk of putting assets at the disposal of people who neither value them properly nor are able to enhance their value by exerting a meaningful influence on the management of the firm. People who get shares free may have less interest than those who buy them in the operation of the respective enterprises. (4) The dispersion of share ownership impedes effective corporate governance. (5) There exists the problem of fairness in the face of differences of value between firms. 6) Unlike foreign investments, free transfers do not infuse new capital, technology nor management skills.[106]

(5) *Actors targeted for the acquisition of assets.* In internal privatization, the shares are given or sold exclusively to workers and/or managers employed in a firm. In external privatization, the shares are given or sold to individuals or groups whose composition extends beyond the firm's boundaries. Bidders for an enterprise can be private persons, institutions or foreign investors, the last mentioned including both legal and natural persons. Institutional endowments can be made to mutual funds, holding companies, pension funds or banks.[107]

Spontaneous privatizations, where managers or workers take over the ownership of firms, constitute a form of internal privatization. Public outcry against spontaneous privatizations has been sharp, not least because these take-overs have often been engineered through networks of privileged *nomenklatura*. *Nomenklatura* enterprises are generally viewed not only as economic anomalies but also as unjustified compensation for socially ill-deserving persons. Not all the former critics of communist rule, however, oppose *nomenklatura* enterprises. Interestingly, some of the most vocal support for political capitalism has come from the ultraliberals. The ultra-liberals are not concerned with how an effective capital market is created but rather with how quickly it is done. Who gets the capital first, is irrelevant, since once real market competition emerges, only those individuals who possess 'animal spirit' will survive.[108]

(6) *Private versus public property.* Whilst the radical strategy attempts to erase all non-capitalist ownership forms, the gradualist strategy claims that unclear property rights can be resolved without immediate privatization. The strengthening of certain types of property rights might be an appropriate response to organizational inefficiency, even if these property rights might not be deemed suitable in the long run. One method is to strengthen workers' management rights.[109]

Part III

Setting the Research Task

The transitional dilemma will be investigated in the light of the experience drawn from Latvia. Examination of the Latvian case should highlight the way in which a political system mediates the relationship between democracy and economic reform. The political preconditions for a successful economic transition are characterized in terms of political feasibility, which is introduced as an auxiliary concept to operationalize the problem.

According to Majone's definition, a feasible policy is one which satisfies all the constraints of the problems which it tries to solve where a 'constraint' means any feature of the environment that (a) can affect policy results and (b) is not under control of the policy-maker. Conversely, to say that a policy is infeasible means that various obstructive factors prevent the realization of the proposed course of action. As the definition of political feasibility suggests, the actual focus on feasibility analyses is directed toward *political constraints*. Constraints related to gaining or preserving political power can be defined as short-term constraints and institutional, structural or system immanent constraints as long-term ones.[1] Majone's classification of political constraints is organized around David Easton's system metaphor. The distinction between inputs and outputs corresponds to that between reform's initiation and consolidation stages.

1. *The availability of political support.* The first constraint is related to the input side of the political system. The problem is how to mobilize voters behind the idea of transition to a market economy. During the take-off phase of a reform, consensus among political elites is decisive. In the short term support among aware citizens may be enough, but in the long run reforms must win a mass acceptance.

2. *Distributional constraints.* These constraints have to do with the outcome of the political process. They consider the extent to which the social and distributional consequences of the economic transition are acceptable to major groups in society. The outcomes of the policy are reflected in support for the reform through a feedback mechanism.

3. *Institutional constraints.* The freedom of choice of a policy-maker is always restricted by a set of political institutions which must be taken as given. Institutions entail the historically shaped patterns of the mediation

between state and society. They are manifested in the distinct capacities of the regimes to channel the conflict into the framework of democratic politics and to generate support for economic changes.[2]

Political constraints are expressed through detrimental intrusions into economic policy-making of aspirations which contradict the objectives of reform. Such demands are motivated by values or priorities that differ from those of economics and they include, among others, particularistic, egalitarian or nationalist (pre-industrial) concerns. The 'Washington consensus'-type standard package based on a neoliberal strategy is used as a yardstick in all evaluations and comparisons, because this version of reform has proved successful both in Latvia and fast-moving East Central European countries, such as Estonia and the Czech Republic. The experience of the past seven years begins to show that countries that have attempted rapid transitions from communism have generally fared better than those that have adopted gradual transition strategies. The neoliberal strategy was adopted by Latvia's first postcommunist government at the outset of transition, it laid the foundations of the market economy in Latvia and it has been pursued by the later elected governments, including the current one. Competing propositions, influenced by gradualism, emerged only later when new opposition parties challenged the established parties in power.

The economic programmes of the Latvian parties constitute the primary data on which the examination of proposed economic solutions will be based. The party programmes are first presented one by one without comments. Drawing on this body of raw data, the issue dimensions of Latvian politics are derived from the principal themes included in the programmes. The points at issue are also instrumental in mapping the content of the socio-economic cleavage. The socio-economic cleavage defines the space of party competition in terms of left–right issues. The unit of analysis is the content of a carefully extracted policy area, and the study aims to test the relationship between economic reform policy and various political variables. Policy analysis is understood here as a field concerned with the initiation and development of specific policies, the modification of policies in the political process and the effects of those policies under implementation.

Insulating the analysis of economic policies from the overall political context would easily lead to distortions or misinterpretations. The role of country-specific factors in explaining policy outcomes must be taken into account. Each political system has distinctive organizational features: a particular set of political parties, operating within the context of electoral laws and customary practices. The expressive capacities of the electorate will be limited by the nature of the party organizations already established for this purpose. The inertia qualities within the existing party system can limit the possibilities for new electoral coalitions to form.[3] Thus, integrity of observation requires that the political system is depicted in its essential parts. Since the ethnic division is conspicuously stark in Latvia, special attention is devoted to ethnic politics and especially the intertwinement of economic and national interests. Indeed, the collision of economic and national objectives manifests a special case of political constraints.

Although the whole study as such addresses the interaction of politics and economics, privatization is distinguished as an especially illuminating example of this relationship. Therefore, privatization and its political attributes are analyzed as an analogous miniature case within the frame of the major case study. The study, which is carried out in a cross-sectional manner, mainly focuses on a two-year period from 1995 to spring 1997. By the mid-1990s, Latvia had achieved the parallel shift from a launch phase to a consolidation phase on the economic front and from extraordinary politics to mundane politics on the political front. In contrast to earlier research, attention is directed to the political dynamics of consolidating reforms and the challenge of coping with the reorganized opposition. The second postcommunist national election in the autumn of 1995 is treated as a test case for a democracy's ability to stay on the reform course. The two government crises and the second local elections in March 1997 are examined from the same vantage point. The background of events is highlighted only to the extent necessary for understanding the present, as the approach is not historical.

Specialization in a well-defined geographical area with a limited focus on one country – Latvia – invites almost automatically the case study method. The combinaton of several explanatory models further supports the decision to select the case study method (see below, 'Paradigm'). Case study is the method of choice when the phenomenon under study is not readily distinguishable from its context and when the investigator deliberately wants to cover contextual conditions, believing that they might contain important explanatory variables. The desire to treat the topic broadly, rather than narrowly, is inherent in the strategy. The inclusion of the context as a major part of the study creates distinctive technical challenges. Among others, the study cannot rely on a single data collection method but will likely need to use multiple sources of evidence.[4] In the study under consideration, the data base consists of three different types of source: expert interviews, survey data and documents, including party platforms, memoranda and other administrative documents, progress reports, laws, formal studies, newspaper articles. The majority of the interviews, with a few exceptions, were conducted in Riga in September 1995 and from January to May 1997. The interviews took an open-ended but focused format and they were complemented by a short structured questionnaire.

Documented materials cover satisfactorily the official declarations and the goal-setting of the government as well as other state institutions. Respectively, a wealth of reliable information about the economic development and legislation is available. However, exclusive reliance on documents would allow merely a formal description of official Latvia. The availability of documents is sharply reduced when one wants to investigate party politics or the politicial dimension – that is, the unofficial side – of decision-making. Only a few parties have comprehensive programmes in writing, and even those are often so vague or muddled that they do not alone give a clear picture of the party's profile. In Latvia, where deficiencies in documentation and knowledge of the national language are problems for a foreign researcher, interviews are an especially important data collection method. The inside stories and the hidden interests of conflicting parties, which shed light on the true nature of many public events, can be comprehended only through confidential interviews with informants who have access to information beyond that found in newspapers. Interviews can provide deep, focused and unique information in a time-efficient manner, but their danger is partiality and subjectivity. The validity problem can be counterpoised by increasing the bulk of interviews so that it is possible to discuss the same theme with several people representing different views. Moreover, if one researches the subject extensively and lives in the country for a longer time, one will achieve a general overview which helps to judge individual comments critically, particularly when one knows the interviewee's reference group or political opinions. In some uses of interviews, subjectivity is an advantage, when it is exactly the 'self-portrait' that is looked for. An effective way of increasing objectivity is to combine in-depth interviews (or documents) with unbiased survey data which presents the general trends and average responses reliably. Survey results can be generalized but their interpretation may remain thin and schematic without a profound familiarity of the phenomenon under consideration. This may result in the assumptions of a researcher distorting the reporting. Giving a voice to some living persons makes flesh and blood of dead statistics.

Paradigm

Economic policy has important consequences for the material interests of social groups. In the case of a major reform, interest conflicts are particularly drastic. As an economic transformation leads to a broad reallocation of wealth and power, there are many interest groups which are clashing over the final type of change to be implemented. First, the costs of economic adjustment do not spread evenly over the population. Second, various sectors of the population are hit differently, depending on what specific measures are taken. Therefore the preferences of major political groups for particular reform policies differ in terms of the opportunities different policies offer them in meeting their economic needs and in enhancing their relative political power. The political resources that interest groups utilize to influence the economic reform policy have a decisive impact on the course of policy. As a result, the economic strategies of the government will reflect the coalition of the political forces in power.[5]

The pluralist model implies that politics is ultimately about the conflict among groups with divergent interests for claims on scarce resources. This contest for control over scarce resources pits one social group against another and defines the content of politics. The great virtue of the pluralist paradigm is the insistence that coalitional support must be found for any policy and that the range of policy alternatives will then be constrained by the relative balance of group power. Stress on the economic aspects of group support stems from the assumption that policy preferences are mainly shaped by an economic location. Adhering to behaviourist principles, pluralists believe that individuals' behaviour reveals their policy preferences: their interests can be discerned by seeing which policy options they choose.[6]

In the pluralist model, the political process rests on the interaction between two principal sets of actors. The first set of key actors in the making of economic policy are societal actors, those individuals and organizations of individuals which confer electoral power in the political system and/or have leverage over policy because of their control over vital economic activities. Societal actors begin with an economic situation, to which they link an economic policy preference and then seek out a political strategy to make that preference prevail. While societal actors seek politics that suit their policies, politicians, in contrast, seek policies that suit their politics. Politicians begin with a political situation, for which they need support, and then seek economic policies which provide that support to win office and govern. Consequently, politicians judge economic policy alternatives – at least in part – by the effects those policies have on the holding of office, because they must be concerned with the mobilization of consent and the maintenance of social peace.[7]

It is essential to notice that neither politicians nor societal actors can act alone and in isolation. The intermediary which brings politicians and social actors together is the party organization. A political party can be understood as referring to an association of individuals who have certain ends in common and cooperate with each other to achieve them.[8] Voting is the main experience of political participation in a democracy for most citizens, who authorize the candidates put up by parties to represent their interests.

The outlined model provides the tools for an empirical analysis to trace the political dynamics of economic policy-making. Its building blocks include political parties, elections, interests and the societal sources of policy. Political parties are the principal avenue through which the electorate can influence the direction of economic policy. Parties articulate the available political alternatives, which they formulate and 'serve' to the electorate in the form of political platforms. The societal response to these policies is measured at elections and polls as well as in strikes and demonstrations. The divisions that lay the foundation for political conflicts are conceptualized with a cleavage metaphor.

Although the unspoken assumptions that underlie the empirical analysis are traced to pluralist theories in the first place, it is acknowledged that one set of variables is not usually capable of explaining the policy outcome alone but it rather results from a complex interaction of several causal factors. One cannot simply extrapolate from societal interests to policy outcomes, while ignoring the actors and interests located within the state. Politicians, officials and their allies also have much at stake in the economic liberalization. Moreover, policy is not made from a *tabula rasa*: policy-makers are profoundly influenced by the labyrinth of institutionalized relations. Pluralist accounts also leave open the question of how different actor groups come to perceive and define their interests in a particular way, as they neglect the role of ideologies in political economy. They are incapable of dealing with exogenous ideas and values whose presence cannot be associated with any given social location. The appearance of unexplained 'grey areas' that are not fully comprehensible within the terms of the main paradigm can be resolved by incorporating complementary accounts, which are understood as correctives to each other's biases and limitations. A proper selection of complementary paradigms will help to outline a more complete picture of the subject, because it makes it possible to infuse a greater number of partial aspects of reality into the study.

Part IV

Empirical Case Study

5 Latvia's Transformation Strategy

'WASHINGTON CONSENSUS'-TYPE STANDARD PACKAGE

Within a general framework of systemic economic changes, three types of changes can be discerned:

1. *Sectoral economic reforms.* Sectoral economic reforms affect specific branches of economic activity or particular domains of economic policy. These reforms are usually named after the sector to which they are related (e.g. monetary, financial, fiscal). Sectoral reforms ensure a gradual, smooth adjustment to technological and other environmental changes as well as the assimilation of experience from foreign countries.
2. *Comprehensive economic reforms.* When a country fails to undertake timely necessary sectoral reforms, when it neglects its external or internal imbalances or when non-economic considerations extend so far that the economy cannot be put in order by usual means, a comprehensive economic reform must be undertaken. Although it contains changes in a number of domains, it alters neither the foundations nor the general logic of the given economic system. By redistributing the economic power, it usually reduces the impact of non-economic forces and opens greater room for the operation of market forces.
3. *Alterations of economic systems.* Both of the above-mentioned changes in economic systems are evolutionary changes, whereas a replacement of an economic system is a revolutionary process. When a number of changes as well as their character are so drastic that the very foundations and the general logic of an economic system are reversed, an alternation of that system is taking place. In this last case, one can speak of a transition from one system to another. A replacement can bear different meanings in disparate historical situations. As in the case of postcommunist transitions, an economic system may become outdated in the face of technological and social developments and appear inefficient in terms of performance criteria. As a consequence, it is superseded by another system which is assumed to be superior to it.[1]

Since the early 1990s, the thrust of economic policy in the ex-communist states of Eastern Europe has shifted from reforming the existing system of central planning to fundamentally transforming these economies toward market regulation and private ownership. One after another, the ex-communist

61

countries have adopted comprehensive programmes of reforms aimed at a single strategic objective: the establishment of a modern market economy of a Western type. In fact, the very term 'reform' has in the last few years become synonymous with a transition from an administered to a market economy. Thirty-five years ago the same term conjured up distribution of land to peasants in Latin America or tinkering the planning system in Eastern Europe. Today it is tantamount to the reign of markets. The shift in the content of the terminological usage reflects the different ideological credos that guide the present and past reforms.[2]

Most of the reform packages applied in Eastern Europe and sponsored by the IMF are based on the liberal-monetarist philosophy which dominated mainstream economic thinking in the 1980s. In the monetarist tradition, a sound currency, competitive markets and private property form the pillars of prosperity. The standard approach to economic adjustment is to limit drastically government involvement in the economy through cutting subsidies, liberalizing prices, deregulating economic activity and then letting the market do the job. The programmes typically include strong deflationary measures in the form of monetary and fiscal restrictions, aimed at reducing domestic demand. Institutional and structural changes focus on foreign trade liberalization, the introduction of currency convertibility, privatization of state-owned enterprises and reform of the financial sector. To put it another way, the standard reform package incorporated in the neoliberal 'Washington consensus' consists of four principal elements: macroeconomic stabilization, microeconomic liberalization, restructuring and privatization, and creation of a market-conforming institutional and legal framework.[3]

Latvia has pursued consequent reform policies since regaining independence in order to accelerate its transition to a fully fledged market economy. Latvia's reform strategy has been conformed to fulfill the strictest requirements of a monetarist policy. Adherence to a liberal economic regime implies almost exclusive reliance on the market mechanism and principled rejection of economic regulation and state interventionism. Latvia belongs to the most exemplary pupils of the class of transitional economies whose achievements are frequently praised by international financial organizations. One of the concrete acknowledgements is a substantial standby credit approved by the IMF to support the government's economic programme. The IMF is extremely circumspect in granting standby credits.

Prime Minister Skele assures lenders that 'the government will realize its course toward the development of a free market economy in Latvia'. The government will work to ensure a stable national currency, independence of the central bank, a balanced state budget, an open land market and a favourable climate for foreign investment, an intensified privatization process and development of the transport and transit systems. Implementing these principles will allow Latvia to integrate into the European Union.[4] The government's firm resolve to stick to sound economic policies is finally starting to bear fruit. The postcommunist recession hit Latvia hard so that the economic recovery started as late as 1994. The positive development was interrupted by the outbreak of the banking crisis in 1995 but already in the next year the economy returned to the growth track. The Ministry of Economy forecast a growth rate of 3.5 per cent in gross domestic product (GDP) for 1997.[5]

LIBERALIZATION

Liberalization of the economy from the old administrative methods is the first prerequisite for a transition to a market economy. Internal liberalization means free domestic prices as well as open domestic markets both for residents and foreigners. Price reform – including wages and interest rates – ends price control and rationing so that the price mechanism can be made responsible for the decentral coordination of the economy. Technically, it is quite simple to lift price restrictions, but the problem concerns the political and social acceptability of the measure. To create a competitive economy, government must abolish all barriers impeding the entry of new firms into the market. Deregulation will ensure that regulations are justified only by such criteria as safety, environmental protection or prudential supervision of financial institutions. External liberalization includes decentralizing foreign trade, reducing trade protection and establishing currency convertibility. The resulting integration with the world economy transmits corrective price signals about the comparative abilities of the domestic market, which, in turn, induces the restructuring needed to exploit these abilities. A liberal foreign exchange regime and unrestricted repatriation possibilities are instrumental to enhancing foreign trade and attracting foreign direct investment (FDI).[6]

Price Liberalization

Latvia started to dismantle its administrative price-setting mechanism as early as January 1991. The initial reason for price reform was the effort to reduce spillovers of excess demand in other areas of the ruble zone and to prevent internal shortages. In addition, the liberalization of prices and reduction of subsidies were correctly seen as fundamental components of a broader economic reform. The liberalization process was implemented in several stages so that prices were freed gradually. Yet sequencing did not mean sluggishness. On the contrary, liberalization of prices advanced with vigour, with the biggest changes concentrated in winter 1991–92. At the end of 1992, less than 8 per cent of goods and services, as measured by their weight in the consumer price index, remained subject to control.[7]

Even though no formal price controls have remained, the prices of some services are still administratively determined, mainly by local governments. Among commodities remaining subject to ceiling prices are housing rents, energy, transportation, telecommunication, public utilities and medical services. Household energy prices are the most important items still under regulation, which has kept them significantly below full cost levels.[8]

Interest rates were deregulated in Latvia in mid-1992. Since then all banks have been free to set their interest rates. One of the side-effects of financial liberalization has been the persistence of very high nominal deposit and lending rates, despite significant decline in the inflation rate and nominal appreciation of the domestic currency against convertible currencies. The spread between lending and deposit rates has also remained very high at 25–35 per cent. The level and structure of interest rates reflect both the structural weaknesses of the financial and enterprise sectors – resulting in high credit risk – and exceptional opportunities to finance highly profitable short-term transactions created by the existence of controlled prices on certain commodities in other former Soviet Union (FSU) countries.[9]

Foreign Trade Liberalization

The trade regime adopted in Latvia resembles those common in Western countries and can be characterized as a relatively liberal one. Although Latvia exercises some protection with tariffs against agricultural imports, it 'remains committed to open economy and liberal trade in a multilateral framework'. The tariff framework is designed according to the General Agreement on Tariffs and Trade (GATT), since Latvia had submitted its request to join the World Trade Organization during the preparation of the tariff framework. Tariff rates vary according to the particular agreement concluded with each individual country (free trade, most favoured nation, no agreement). There are virtually no licensing requirements for either imports or exports. The few quantitative restrictions (quotas) in exports are made for health or national security reasons. There are neither export nor import subsidies. The milestones of Latvia's foreign trade policy include an associational agreement with the European Union, a treaty to create a Baltic Free Trade Zone and an agreement with Russia on the most favoured nation (MFN) status.[10]

Currency Convertibility

Since leaving the rouble zone in the summer of 1992, Latvia has made advances in convertibility that can be described as the greatest success to date in its transition. This achievement stands out, even if it is compared with any of the former communist countries. Latvia has established one of the most liberal foreign exchange regimes in the world. A special feature of Latvia is the existence of private foreign exchange offices, which have been set up in large numbers over a short period time.[11]

The lats, Latvia's national currency, is freely convertible both for current account purposes and for capital account purposes. Foreign exchanges and lati may freely enter and leave the country. Both resident and non-resident individuals and enterprises are allowed to hold cash and bank accounts either in domestic or foreign currency and to use these funds for domestic payments. That is to say, even the use of foreign currencies as a domestic means of payment is allowed. There are no restrictions on the repatriation of either capital or dividends by non-residents. Latvian enterprises are not obliged to repatriate their foreign currencies earned abroad, but the state taxes these foreign exchange earnings. The Bank of Latvia has officially promised to buy and sell any amount of hard currency to commercial banks at their request and without any restrictions.[12]

In February 1994, the lats was informally pegged to the special drawing rights (SDR) at the rate of 1 SDR = 0.8 LVL (Latvia lats). Through pegging the Latvian currency regime converged with a fixed exchange rate system. Although Latvia in principle follows a traditional central bank-led currency regime, it has informally applied a currency board system since spring 1994.[13]

Foreign Direct Investment

Latvia is faced with the problem of building capitalism without capital. Investment needs in the Latvian economy are huge, as investments in the productive sector have collapsed since 1990 and production facilities are generally outdated. The authorities in Latvia are anxious to generate a strong flow of FDI to provide capital, technology and management skills required for the country's economic development. FDI is expected to contribute to the restructuring of the economic structure as well as to the expansion of the private sector. A further objective is to develop export potential. On the other hand, the Latvian authorities are aware of the vigorous international competition that exists for such investment. Therefore, the need for a strong promotion programme to attract FDI is seen as a high priority of policy.[14]

The Latvian government is dedicated to continuously improving the business climate for foreign investors. The latest improvements concern a move toward a free land market, capitalization of the debts of state enterprises, introduction of a tougher bankruptcy law and relaxing of visa regulations for long-term residents. All elements of the economic legislation have been built with a view to making the country attractive to foreign investors. Enterpreneurial activity by foreign investors is regulated by the Law on Foreign Investment and the Law on Enterpreneurial Activity. Within the framework of these laws, a foreign investor is entitled to the same rights and duties as natural and legal persons of the Republic of Latvia. No special permissions or licences are needed to set up a business, with the exception of certain extra-ordinarily sensitive areas, such as state defence and security, weapons and explosives, securities, banknotes, coins and stamps, mass media, education, natural resources, fishing, hunting or port management. Property rights are embodied in the Constitution.[15]

The basis for corporate legislation is set out in the Law on Enterpreneurial Activity which states the general regulations that apply to foreign-owned companies, as well. The law stipulates the company forms allowed in Latvia as well as the main principles of their formation, registration, operation and liquidation. Foreigners may establish only limited liability companies or joint-stock companies.[16]

Foreign direct investment can take three major forms: green field investment into a new company, joint venture investment into an existing company or investment through privatization. There are no quantitative requirements concerning the amount of share in an enterprise. A foreigner may be the sole founder of an enterprise. Foreign investors may freely repatriate both their capital and profits after the payment of taxes. Latvian law ensures the protection of foreign investment against illegal confiscation. If a foreign investment is forcedly alienated in the interests of the Republic of Latvia, its owner will be compensated for the full extent of his losses in convertible currency within three months. Latvia has concluded agreements on mutual promotion and protection of investments with most West European countries. A foreign company registered in Latvia is entitled to purchase land in cities and rural areas if investments come from a country with which Latvia has entered into the agreement on mutual promotion and protection of investments or more than a half of the authorized share capital belongs to citizens of Latvia.[17]

The latest incentive schemes focus on the establishment of free ports and special economic zones. The Riga Commercial Port has been transformed into a free port which offers exemption from customs duties, value added and excise tax (though under certain restrictive conditions). Similar laws on Ventspils and Liepaja have been passed. In Liepaja, the benefits of a free port will combine with those of an enterprise zone. The generous benefits of the enterprise zone will include:

- a 100 per cent exemption from local property tax and land tax;
- 80 per cent allowances for corporate income tax;
- favourable calculation of the base of corporate income tax;
- possibility to double the speed of the depreciation rate.

To be entitled to tax benefits not more than 20 per cent of the production should be sold to the territory of Latvia.[18]

One of the policy instruments created to promote FDI in Latvia is the Latvian Development Agency. The Latvian Development Agency is an independent, quasi-governmental institution that enjoys a certain degree of autonomy from the ministries. Its area of responsibility concentrates on external economic activities. It supports the implementation of the national economic development programme by (1) marketing Latvia as a business site; (2) providing information to potential investors; (3) analysing investment projects; (4) promoting Latvian exports; and (5) encouraging the development of capital markets. The Latvian Development Agency offers potential investors a 'one-stop-shop' for easy access to reliable, up-to-date information and advice concerning the local business environment, investment opportunities, taxation, duties, market structures, business practices, laws, policies and national programmes affecting FDI. It assists the investor in setting up a new business by providing liaison services between governmental institutions and the investor and by seeking contacts with potential partners. In addition to these facilitation services, the Agency participates in image-building activities. It produces information materials, organizes media campaigns, arranges meetings and seminars.[19]

Latvia takes a middle position among the transitional economies in terms of the value of FDI. The stock of FDI amounted to around US$ 700 million at the end of 1996. The biggest investments into the share capital were made by the traditional trading partners from the Baltic Sea region: Denmark, Finland, Sweden, Germany and Russia. There is also a substantial amount of investment from Britain and the United States. The largest foreign investors per company are Cable & Wireless (UK) together with Finnish Telecom, Statoil (N), Kellogg (USA), Radisson-SAS (USA), Vika Wood (S), Shell (UK), Karl Danzer Furnierwerke (D), House of Prince (DK), Enso (FIN) and Cultor (FIN). The sectoral breakdown shows that transport and communications have drawn most foreign capital, finances occupying the second place. Food, beverages and tobacco, textiles and clothing, wood-processing and chemicals have been the most popular industrial sectors. Over 90 per cent of foreign investors have their activities in Riga or in Riga's vicinity.[20]

STABILIZATION

Concurrently with price liberalization, macroeconomic discipline is needed in order to prevent the inevitable initial price surge from setting off a vicious cycle of price–wage spirals leading to hyperinflation. Macroeconomic austerity, i.e. tight monetary and fiscal policies, should avoid inflationary spiral, balance domestic demand with domestic production and realize price stability in which prices reflect relative scarcities. The negative consequence of austerity programmes is that output falls sharply as a consequence of reduction in demand. Stabilization measures aim at controlling inflation, restoring fiscal stability and balancing external payments. The standard approach assigns a central role for nominal anchors. The money supply has emerged to be the dominant nominal anchor together with the uniform exchange rate and the incomes policy playing a supportive role. Such a strategy is attained by keeping the growth of money supply below that of nominal GDP, by setting the exchange rate at a market-clearing level and by controlling wages. Control of money supply can be achieved by raising interest rates to levels that exceed inflation, instituting strict policies on central bank credit to commercial banks and reducing bank financing of government budget. Although fiscal consolidation may be achieved by either cutting spending or increasing revenues, the elimination of subsidies and hardening of budget constraints should have a priority. Fiscal reform involves balancing the budget, limiting the role of the state, making explicit the hidden transfers that permeated the old system and raising revenue through more efficient collection of taxes.[21]

Reformers in Latvia have recognized that the elimination of macroeconomic imbalances, particularly the reduction of inflation rates, is key to the success of the long-term transformation of the economy. They have also realized that the restraint must not be relaxed, when the first signs of success emerge, but that establishing of tenable development requires long-term commitment to stabilization policies. A comprehensive reform package centring on macrostabilization was adopted at the beginning of 1992. The stabilization programme was prepared in close cooperation with the International Monetary Fund (IMF), and it is similar to those pursued by the leading reformers in East Central Europe. The importance of an IMF programme is that it signals to the world that the country has embarked upon policies that are deemed rational and worthy of support. Therefore these programmes have an important catalytic role in the channelling of private and public funding and expertise assistance.[22]

The success in macroeconomic stabilization is one of the chief achievements of Latvia's economic policies. Today Latvia has the lowest inflation in the Baltics. The inflation rate was 16 per cent in 1996 and the target for 1997 has been set below 10 per cent. A monthly inflation rate is stipulated to be lowered to 0.5 per cent by the year 2000. In terms of assessing Latvia's ability to satisfy some of the key Maastricht criteria, Latvia is in particularly good shape in relation to foreign debt and budget deficit. In 1996 the foreign debt amounted to 8 per cent of GDP and the budget deficit was only 1.6 per cent of GDP. The year 1997 began with a balanced budget without any deficit. The government is committed to the principle according to which the internal and external debt of the state must not exceed 20 per cent of GDP. Latvia's trade balance is negative but it is compensated for by the surplus in the service balance.[23]

Monetary and Exchange Rate Policies

As long as Latvia remained in the rouble area, the possibilities for control of the money supply were limited. Only the early departure from the rouble zone made the imposition of tough monetary controls possible. The successful introduction of a national currency became the cornerstone of monetary stabilization.[24] The role of the exchange-rate-based stabilization was accentuated with the pegging of the lats to the SDR.

Latvia did not leave the rouble zone immediately, but it decided to issue an interim currency, the Latvian rouble or 'rublis' in May 1992. From the outset, it was clear that the Latvian rouble would be merely a temporary measure, remaining in circulation until Latvia's regular currency, the lats, could be restored. The last Latvian rouble notes were withdrawn from circulation in October 1993. Since October 18, 1993, the lats has been the sole legal tender, although free circulation of foreign currencies is permitted.[25]

Today the lats is one of the strongest and most stable currencies in the transitional economies. After 1994, the lats has faced hardly any fluctuations. It is backed 100 per cent by gold and convertible foreign currency reserves. The price of the strong currency is that Latvia has been faced with the trade-off between stabilization and recession. From abroad Latvia has generally received little but praise for its commitment to tight monetary and exchange rate policies, but Latvian enterprises particularly have been critical of the central bank's policy. Nevertheless, the Bank of Latvia remains strongly committed to exchange rate stability in the future, too.[26]

Stringent control of the money supply, emission and credit restrictions, along with high interest rates, have remained the main monetary policy instruments. The sharp slow-down in the level of economic activity has made the reduction of the rate of growth of money supply easier, but temporary credit creation ceilings have additionally helped to make anti-inflation policies work.[27]

The institutional preconditions for a disciplined monetary policy are secured in the Law on the Bank of Latvia. The central bank law resembles the German 'Gesetz über die Deutsche Bundesbank' conspicuously. Its essential content is that it ensures a high degree of independence for the central bank. In fulfilling its tasks, the Bank of Latvia is not subject to Parliament nor to the government. The alternative that the central bank would finance state budget deficits through inflationary printing of money is legally restricted to highly exceptional cases.[28]

Fiscal Policy

Monetary stability cannot be maintained against fiscal expansion. Latvia has pursued a policy of balanced budgets since the very beginning as far as it has been realizable under the prevailing fiscal situation. The sudden explosion of the budget deficit in 1995, leading to a severe crisis of the public economy, took the Latvian authorities by surprise. The budget crisis was caused by the banking crisis which coincided with some other unfortunate incidents. The budget was again balanced within two years.

Budgetary reform is an essential part of the overall task of trimming the public sector. The budget has to be freed from functions that in a market economy are taken care of by private actors. On the negative side, the insufficiency of budget revenues forces a dramatic cut in social welfare expenses and public investments. Pensioners especially find it very hard to meet their daily expenses. Curtailing subsidies is not enough but the state must simultaneously seek ways to raise revenue by reforming the tax system, as well. The aim of tax reform should be in broadening the tax base and cutting the marginal tax rates. Tax reforms are induced by the serious problems that collection of tax revenues poses in all transitional economies. First, tax administration and control mechanisms are only in the formation stage. Tax avoidance is therefore quite common, especially in the enterprise sector. Second, due to economic difficulties, the capacity of state enterprises to pay taxes is limited. The tax arrears of state enterprises constituted 2–3 per cent of GDP in 1993. Latvia's tax system is being harmonized with the tax legislation in the EU.[29]

The Latvian tax system is conducive to business and investment, and the corporate tax system provides a maximum of simplicity. Latvia has a unified tax rate of 25 per cent which applies to all types of businesses. The law allows substantial depreciation rates on fixed assets. Foreign-owned companies are eligible for a wide range of discounts and allowances. Foreign investors are liberated from payment of value added tax and customs duties for fixed assets as imports of a long-term investment, investment into the capital or securities, and export of goods outside Latvia. In addition, they are exempt from the same taxes and duties for commodities which have been brought to Latvia to be processed on a temporary basis. The standard rate of value added tax is 18 per cent, but there are plans that under favourable budget conditions it might be lowered to 16 per cent.[30]

Social tax is applied to salaries, fees, royalties and other compensations. 28 per cent of the taxed income is paid by the employer and 9 per cent by the employee. The tax rate will be reduced gradually by 1 per cent each year until by July 2001 the current 37 per cent rate will have reached 33 per cent. The employer proportion will then be 18 per cent and the employee proportion 15 per cent. The other taxes effective in Latvia are excise tax, personal income tax, property tax, land tax, tax on natural resources and customs tax. Latvia has concluded tax conventions on the prevention of double taxation with nearly 20 countries.[31]

THE INSTITUTIONAL FRAME FOR A MARKET ECONOMY

A market economy presupposes the existence of certain economic freedoms. These economic freedoms need to be underpinned and protected by a legal framework that is consistent with the principles of a market economy. Institutional and legal reforms have an important function in creating a market-conforming institutional environment and policy regime which will enable the enterprise sector to play an effective role in the economy. The government must take positive steps to develop a formal set of rules of the game to provide an appropriate context for commercial activity. A legal system should entail a guarantee of the market order itself, protection against political arbitrariness and the enforceability of claims resulting from private contracts. An essential part of such a context is a modern system of commercial law to provide property rights, regulate contracts, enforce competition, guarantee free entry to and exit from the market and recognize different company forms.

Not only must the whole economic legislation be constructed from scratch in all transitional economies but also an infrastructure for transacting real and financial claims is needed to organize streams of capital assets. The latter goal requires the establishment of capital markets and intermediate financial institutions. Financial sector reform should establish a two-tier banking system by separating the monobanking system into an autonomous central bank and commercial banks. The role of the financial sector in a market economy is to collect and channel financial savings to those uses which contribute most to welfare and to provide an efficient clearing and settlement system. An effective financial sector is a precondition for the development of private enterprises in the transitional economies. Last but not least, administrative reform should enhance the capacity of state bureaucracy and the creation of a social safety net should soften the hardships of the adjustment process.[32]

Legal Reform

Latvia has enacted a fair amount of legislation in a relatively short time. The creation of a new legal framework has suffered from many handicaps, particularly at the beginning of the process. Rules and regulations changed too frequently, even for the state of transition Latvia found itself in. This was due to a non-systemized, piecemeal approach to legislative development. The legislation was not based on a systematic concept but was enacted on a case-by-case basis with an emphasis on the short-term perspective. In the selection of a legal system, a country ought to take into consideration the countries with which it intends to establish close political and economic relations, while legal harmonization with these countries is advisable. Latvia has on a number of occasions expressed its desire to forge close political and economic ties with the EU, and it is harmonizing its legislation accordingly. Latvia's prewar legal system was heavily influenced by German laws.[33]

The system of commercial law is in place, comprising property, contract, bankruptcy, competition and company laws. Although Latvia's economic legislation is presently comparable with that of the advanced capitalist countries, implementation and enforcement does not reach the same level.[34]

Banking Reform

During 1992, the commercial and central banking activities of the Bank of Latvia were gradually separated. The active formation of commercial banks started after the passage of the Law on Banks in May 1992. As witnessed by the large number of registrations, entry into the banking market was hardly restrained. The number of banks peaked to over 60 in the wildest days. The mushrooming of banks was a byproduct of the money flows set in motion by the realization of Soviet property in the West, in which Latvia was used as one of the corridors. As the Latvian banking legislation was more liberal than the Russian one, part of the money stayed in Latvia.[35]

Unprofessionalism and mismanagement together with inadequate regulation contributed to financial scandals. The Latvian banking sector drifted into a serious crisis in spring 1995, when banks were 'dropping like flies', as one newspaper put it. The crisis started with smaller banks but led to a chain reaction due to the network of interbank credits. As the jitters spread, the oil capital from the FSU countries was withdrawn from Latvian banks with the result that many banks faced a liquidity crisis. The series of suspensions culminated in the dramatic collapse of Banka Baltija, Latvia's largest bank. Banka Baltija was considered to be the cornerstone of the Latvian banking sector. It had one-fifth of the Latvians' deposits. Its shutdown was estimated to cause a drop of 10 per cent in the GDP. The government sought a criminal conviction against the former leadership of Banka Baltija for deliberate sabotage, because the bank's liquidity crisis resulted from the secret transactions with a shady Moscow bank.[36]

Already in the midst of the banking crisis, the Bank of Latvia together with the government commenced an extensive action programme to improve the banking legislation, tighten the supervision and restrict the activities of unsound banks. Banks themselves moved to tighten their internal controls and to develop their risk management. Thanks to these rationalization measures, banking is now concentrated in about 20 banks. The 15 largest banks account for over 80 per cent of the total assets of all commercial banks. According to an opinion poll among bankers and financiers, the five safest banks are Unibanka, Parex Bank, Rigas Komercbanka, Rietumu Banka and Hansabank-Latvia. Western observers consider the banking crisis in Latvia a natural part of changes toward a market economy. They believe that it overhauled and strengthened the country's financial system, instead of harming it, because inexperienced banks had adopted inappropriate practices. Estonia and Lithuania went through similar banking crises at about the same time: Estonia a year before and Lithuania a year afterwards.[37]

RESTRUCTURING

Restructuring is necessary to increase the efficiency of resource allocation in the economy. Industrial restructuring results in a decline of the share of the industrial sector to the advantage of the emerging service sector (deindustrialization), shifts in the relative importance of industrial subsectors and decentralization of the extremely concentrated economy, as large units give way to small-scale private business. Firms undergo internal changes in management and organization. The demise of the Council for Mutual Economic Assistance (CMEA), in which national specialization and bilateral exchange with the Soviet Union played a major role, forces East European countries to reorientate their foreign trade in terms of both export goods and trade partners. The active reorientation of foreign trade toward Western hard-currency markets has both economic and political reasons. The foreign trade sector exerts dominant influence on the economic development of the small postcommunist countries.[38]

Industrial Restructuring

Latvia's production sector was seriously distorted under the Soviet indus- trialization. The central authorities in Moscow emphasized industrial development in machine building, metallurgy, electronics, chemicals and electric power industries. In 1990, the non-traditional industries of engineering and chemicals contributed more than 33 per cent to industrial output and more than 44 per cent to industrial employment. The production of consumer goods as well as the provision of services were neglected, as the emphasis was put on heavy industry and military production. Although data on the military share is not published, according to an authoritative estimate, more than 15 per cent of the Latvian labour force was employed in military production in 1985.[39]

The first changes in the economic structure have been in bringing Latvia's production structure closer to the structure typical to Western industrial countries. The share of industry and agriculture is declining, while services are increasing their volume. Latvia's industrial strategy aims at moving production away from energy-intensive goods toward higher value added goods for exports. Production based on imported raw materials should be replaced by skills-based production, which encourages the use of domestic materials. The government foresees support particularly for technology and research intensive products. The diversification of the production structure is aimed at helping to overcome Latvia's one-sided dependence on Russia and to prepare for the country's integration into the European Union. The goal of the structural adjustment is to promote those industrial sectors in which Latvia can claim to have a comparative advantage.[40]

The Latvian government has conducted a series of sectoral studies with the assistance of foreign consultants in order to identify the industrial sectors with the best developmental potential vis-à-vis export markets. FDI is encouraged especially in these earmarked priority sectors. The following industries are treated as priority sectors: (1) wood-processing, furniture, paper and pulp; (2) information technology, radio electronics and electrical engineering; (3) chemicals and pharmaceuticals; (4) mechanical engineering and metal processing; (5) clothing and textiles; (6) food-manufacturing; (7) construction and building materials.

Wood-processing
The timber and furniture industries are prognosticated to be at the forefront of Latvia's economic revival. The forecast is well-founded since these branches are the biggest contributors to Latvia's exports. The wood-processing branch has the advantage of drawing on rich natural resources. Latvia possesses the largest unused forest resources in East Central Europe. Approximately 2.9 million hectares – that is, nearly 45 per cent of the total land area – is classified as forest land. Currently wood resources are under-utilized. The wood-working industry is supported by long-standing traditions in the mechanical and chemical processing of wood. However, in the last years of the Soviet rule, no capital investments were made to maintain the inherent capacity of the industry. The production of pulp and paper has almost stopped due to obsolete technology and environmental problems, although there are bottlenecks in the supply of neither raw materials nor technical skills. The Latvian government has undertaken a project for a greenfield pulp mill with an annual capacity up to 600,000 tons.

Information Technology
Globalization of information technology (IT) offers lucrative opportuni- tites for contract manufacturing and software outsourcing in a country like Latvia which combines a highly qualified work force with low manpower costs. The average monthly salary of a software engineer is US$ 400, making one-tenth of the rate for a comparable post in the United States. Many Latvian software professionals have profound experience of genuinely large- scale projects, a skill which is scarce but in high demand. Until 1991 Latvia had a system of scientific institutes, involved in 'industrial science' – they were part of the Soviet military industrial complex, employing a staff of 10,000 persons. The new industrial strategy intends to transform all surviving credible R&D (research and development) institutions into Western-type units. There are at least ten software companies which are developing impressively, showing great potential for growth. These companies have a particularly high sophistication in financial system software, localized financial packages, LAN integration and small and medium-size custom system software. The founding

company of the Latvian IT sector is Dati (formerly Software House Riga), which pioneered a large-scale third party contracting in Latvia. Today Dati is an international class company in the design of CASE tools.

Chemicals and Pharmaceuticals

Latvia developed a strong base in the manufacture of fine chemicals and pharmaceuticals during the postwar period. Latvia was a leader in organic chemistry and pharmaceutical research in the Soviet Union. A high level of scientific expertise was secured by a range of academic institutions, the most famous of which was the Institute of Organic Synthesis. The Institute of Organic Synthesis has developed an anti-cancer drug, ftorafur, which sells particularly well to Japan. The disintegration of the Soviet Union drove the branch into a crisis in the early 1990s, but the surviving companies are now showing a stable upsurge. Some laboratories do research by order of foreign firms. The production profile of the Latvian chemical and pharmaceutical industry carries a great variety of articles, ranging from petrochemicals and man-made fibres to paints and bioenzymes.

Public investment programmes have been used in the rehabilitation of the infrastructure in transportation, telecommunication and energy. Latvia aspires to win a position as an important trade link – as a gateway – between the West and the Commonwealth of Independent Stakes (CIS) on account of its advantageous geographical location. Transit cargo accounts for more than 90 per cent of the cargo handled in the Latvian ports and 70 per cent of the cargo transported by railways. Ventspils, the world's twelfth largest port, continues to be the overwhelmingly busiest port in the Baltics. During the Soviet time Ventspils was the main port serving oil and oil products transport in the European part of the Soviet Union. It was also an internationally known shipping centre for metals, salt, ammonia and chemicals. Joint-stock company Ventspils Nafta is the largest crude oil and oil products transshipment terminal on the Baltic seashore. Latvians believe that even a small country can be a great power in transit.

Latvia does not exercise direct industrial policy influencing individual sectors but rather it relies on indirect measures aimed at developing conditions for industrial performance and competitiveness. The state sees its role as one of assistance, and it tries to avoid violating the rules of the emerging market economy. The goal of its policy is to create a favourable institutional framework in which market forces are capable of allocating resources so as to accelerate structural adaptation. Nor does the financial situation of the state leave much room for active structural policy.[41]

A real positive increase in manufacturing was registered in 1996 for the first time after the start of reforms. The highest growth rates in manufacturing are projected for those industries that are oriented toward exports: timber and wood products, textiles and foodstuffs. Those industries that were deeply integrated into the national economy of the USSR are unable to free themselves from stagnation. Electronics, telecommunication equipment, motor vehicles and agriculture are in continuous decline. Over 50 per cent of the industrial output was produced in the private sector in 1996. During that year 62 per cent of the work force was employed in the private sector. The official unemployment rate was around 7 per cent in 1996 but the real level of unemployment is believed to be higher, and regional variation is also substantial.[42]

Restructuring of Trade

In the first years of independence, Latvia sought new trade partners exclusively from Western Europe. The radical reorientation of trade was motivated by political reasons and the instability of the CIS countries. Not only were the relations with Russia and the other CIS states ranked low by Latvian politicians, but also the free trade agreement between the Baltic states came into force only after a long delay. Pressure for the formation of the Baltic Free Trade Zone came from outside rather than from inside the region. It was the EU that stressed the need for cooperation among the Baltic states as a prerequisite for wider cooperation with the Union. The Baltic countries regarded themselves more as competitors than as partners in the world markets. Currently the government of Latvia realizes that economic policies must utilize the existing relationships with the Baltic neighbours as well as with the CIS countries: 'Foreign economic policy ... will be conducted in line with multilateral principles *on a non-discriminatory basis*. Because of geographical proximity and historical ties there is a necessity to continue close economic relations with the FSU countries.' The special status granted to the Baltic Sea countries reflects the revival of the Hanseatic idea which is popular in Latvia.[43]

Latvia's ability to shift foreign trade toward countries outside the CIS is an important indicator of progress in economic transition. The EU's share in Latvia's foreign trade is becoming more and more predominant, while the significance of the CIS is simultaneously declining. The EU accounted for 45 per cent of Latvian exports and 49 per cent of imports in 1996. The CIS took 36 per cent of exports and provided 26 per cent of imports in the same year. The fact that Latvia serves as a major transshipment and re-export centre for Russian metals and petroleum keeps Russia's share in its trade high. Russia is the single largest trade partner to Latvia with its 23 per cent share of exports and 20 per cent share of imports. The second and third largest export countries are Germany and the United Kingdom.[44] Latvia's most important foreign trade partners are presented in Table 5.1.

Table 5.1   Latvia's Main Trade Partners, 1996 (%)

Country	Share of exports	Share of imports
1. Russia	23	20
2. Germany	14	14
3. Sweden	7	8
4. Great Britain	11	3
5. Lithuania	7	6
6. Finland	2	9

Source: LDA 1997.

Table 5.2   Structure of Foreign Trade Turnover:
Main Export and Import Goods, 1996 (%)

Exports	%	Imports	%
1. Wood, articles of wood	24	1. Minerals	20
2. Textiles	16	2. Machinery and equipment	19
3. Machinery and equipment	12	3. Chemical	8
4. Foodstuffs	9	4. Base metals	5

Source: LDA 1997.

The commodity composition of Latvia's foreign trade has changed along with the industrial restructuring and the reorientation of trade (Table 5.2). Latvia's main export articles are timber and wood products, followed by textiles, machinery and electrical equipment. The main import goods are minerals, machinery and electrical equipment, and chemicals.[45]

6 Privatization

PRIVATIZATION AS AN ECONOMIC PHENOMENON

The cornerstone of a capitalist market economy is the private enterprise operating in a competitive environment. Private sector development can be divided into two components. First, the state must be taken out of the decision-making on the allocation of assets it nominally owns by transferring the ownership of state property to other agents. The second part of private sector development concerns the emergence of entirely new private companies. In Latvia the bottom-up expansion of a private sector has been encouraging, while the privatization of a state sector has been troubled with many difficulties. The government sees its main task as the stimulation of new private activity rather than as the divestiture of state enterprises, because state companies are usually in such a bad shape that their privatization will not improve the economic situation. Privatization is only a step toward their liquidation. Hence, Latvia's slow progress in the privatization of state enterprises has not had a dramatic impact on the marketization of the economy.[46]

Privatization is usually lumped together with a property rights' reform, although the two as a norm are distinct concepts. Property rights' reform contains several dimensions, one of which revolves around the assignment of property rights associated with existing assets. This aspect exhibits an obvious link to privatization. Privatization as an operational category is often ill-defined. Confusion arises because in the context of mature market economies the notion has been used to describe a whole range of activities to improve the functioning of a market economy, including deregulation. Here privatization is defined to mean the transfer to other agents of the right of the state to influence directly the allocation of existing capital resources. When it refers to enterprise reforms that alter the firm's legal position from being a state agent into some joint-stock company, whose property rights are initially entrusted to but not necessarily all exercised by some state agency, the term 'corporatization' is used. When corporatized firms are furthermore subjected to a hard budget constraint, that is, they have to be profitable or otherwise be sold or dissolved, the term 'commercialization' is invoked. Commercialization involves notably the fine-tuning of managerial incentive schemes so that management seeks to maximize the net value of existing assets. Finally, the notion 'divestment' includes sale as well as free distribution of assets.[47]

Privatization can serve various economic, social and political objectives which are not necessarily consistent with each other. The relative weight of divergent goals varies from programme to programme. That variation gives the special flavour to different country strategies. Economic motives include, among others, the following objectives: the introduction of a market economy (competition, profit maximization), economic efficiency (productive, allocative and X-efficiency), finance growth, government revenue and shareholding culture. Privatization is intimately linked to other fields of economic reform. In the sphere of macroeconomic stabilization, it affects budget revenue and expenditure. Privatization can absorb monetary overhang and help to achieve restraint on the growth of wages in connection with an incomes policy. Through sale of state assets to foreign investors, privatization can improve a country's balance of payments. Privatization is affected by competition policy, tax reform, banking reform and deregulation of the labour market.[48]

Privatization is normally divided into programmes dealing with small and large enterprises because the size and complexity of a unit affects the ease with which its privatization can take place. The dividing line cannot be drawn precisely but, generally speaking, a small enterprise refers to an enterprise where the operator can afford to be the owner, in contrast with an enterprise that is too large for owner operation. Often the size of the enterprise, as measured in employees or in terms of book value of assets, is used as a yardstick. Small or petty privatization is concerned with shops, retail outlets, restaurants, hotels, workshops, housing and agricultural land. Big or mass privatization refers to the divestment through share sales or free distribution of shares in the vast bulk of core industries which tend to be large, highly monopolistic and organized in conglomerates. The objectives of such divestment as well as the ways in which it could be achieved are considerably more complicated than in the case of small privatization.[49]

Since small privatization has proceeded fairly smoothly overall, it has not been a source of great concern or controversy. The serious disagreements concentrate on the specific methods of implementing big privatization. The situation reflects the unprecedented scope of the required privatization effort, which reduces the value of lessons from other countries. Therefore, the debate over the problems and methods of privatization in the transition economies concentrates on mass privatization, which will be the case here, too.

The privatization of small businesses was launched in Latvia in November 1991. Privatization commissions for each municipality were established to undertake the privatization of qualified objects under their jurisdiction. Although small privatization began slowly during the first quarter of 1992, it accelerated during 1993 and it was by and large completed by 1995.[50]

Characterization of the Privatization Strategy

Private ownership did not exist in Latvia between 1940 and 1990. After the Soviet annexation in 1940, all enterprises were taken out of private hands, because under the Soviet system the state was the sole owner of means of production. As new industries were established in Latvia, the largest and the most profitable of these enterprises were placed under the control of the All-Union ministries in Moscow, rather than the republican authorities in Riga. This was one of the principal methods by which Latvia's independent national economy was integrated into the Soviet economy. The Latvian government claimed legal ownership over All-Union enterprises on declaration of economic independence from Moscow in early 1990. When non-state-sponsored cooperatives began appearing in the countryside in the late 1980s, legal ownership still belonged to the cooperatives and not to individual members.[51]

These initial conditions suggest the enormous magnitude of the transformation. Many West European countries, such as the UK, France, Germany and Portugal, carried out privatization programmes during the 1980s, but their programmes involved dozens or hundreds of firms. By contrast, in Latvia as well as other postcommunist countries the number of firms to be privatized is in the thousands. Prior to privatization in the UK the ratio of the state sector to the private sector was approximately 1:9 whereas in Latvia the state sector constituted the entire economy, including small businesses, retail outlets and services. In addition, newly privatized firms in the East must operate in an infant market economy without working examples of private firms.[52]

The privatization programme commenced cumbersomely in Latvia. The pace of privatization dragged far behind its Baltic neighbours until the mid-1990s, when the EU Phare (the programme for assistance to countries of Central and Eastern Europe) advisors described Latvia's privatization programme as a disaster. Confusing regulations and a complicated procedure were important reasons for the implementation difficulties. The concept on mass privatization was worked out three times between 1990 and 1994. The last reorganization finally brought results. Together with the decisive measures introduced by Skele's government, the process was speeded up so remarkably that Latvians had reason to be proud of their privatization programme for a change. The procedure was rationalized, among others, by adopting the same decisions in the case of similar enterprises. The year 1996 became a turning point in mass privatization. The main bulk of enterprises were privatized in 1996–97, while the target was set to complete the privatization by mid-1998.[53]

Once the Privatization Agency completes privatization, Latvia will have completed its transition to a market economy. All real business units should have been privatized by the deadline. What cannot be privatized will be liquidated, assures the General Director of the Privatization Agency: 'We could not permit hopeless, failing enterprises to continue operating, thereby increasing losses which eventually would have to be covered by the people of Latvia.' Also the giants of the Latvian economy, monopolies and strategic enterprises are assigned for privatization, although the state will keep a minority share in some cases. The most massive privatization projects include such nationally significant objects as Lattelekom (telecommunications), Latvia's Gas (gasworks), Latvenergo (electric power utility), Ventspils Nafta (oil transshipment terminal), Latvian Shipping Company, Latavio (national airline), VEF (State Electronics Factory), Unibank (Latvia's largest commercial bank) and the Latvian Savings Bank. The only exclusions, which are not assigned for privatization, are objects deemed to be of national strategic interest or of cultural value. This remainder includes very few, if any, truly business-like organizations. Those nearly 200 organizations consist of regional road maintenance units, agricultural units (such as research stations and laboratories), cultural entities (such as sports clubs) as well as ports, airports, the railway company and the postal system.[54]

Independent[55] Latvia's first step towards privatization and denationalization was taken in November 1990, when the Council of Ministers submitted a resolution on the Conversion of State Property. The basic principles enunciated in this resolution had important implications for the further development of Latvian privatization policy. They included, first, individual treatment of sectors, which was later reflected in the power given to branch ministries in the privatization process. Second, eligibility for denationalization was made independent of citizenship. Third, the means of payment in privatization was declared to be 'the currency currently in use in Latvia', which led to fears that many Latvian assets would be acquired by foreigners with Russian roubles. Finally, the use of vouchers was proposed, although the Law on Certificates was passed only two years later. The goal of the first concept, worked out in November 1990, was to find owners for large enterprises as soon as possible, mainly by administrative methods. The enterprises were expected to be transferred to (a) municipalities, (b) the employees or (c) private enterpreneurs by leasing or selling. The process was soon interrupted because a substantial segment of society believed that the enterprises were appraised at prices below their actual value. Consequently, the government prepared a new set of regulations with the technical assistance from the EU Phare Programme.[56]

The second scheme for privatization procedure operated in a *decentralized* way, with separate laws for each sector. Responsibility for each industrial sector rested with the relevant branch ministry rather than with a specialized agency, as in Estonia or East Germany, while small businesses such as shops and restaurants came under the aegis of the appropriate municipality. The Ministry of Economic Reforms performed only the role of monitor, reviewing and approving the privatization projects carried out by the branch ministries. In other words, there was no single institution for overall control and implementation of the privatization process. Decentralized administration was designed to take into consideration the specifics of different sectors. Its disadvantage was that it was slow and bureaucratic, requiring a lot of paperwork. Each ministry prepared a list of enterprises to be privatized within its area of responsibility. The Ministry of Economic Reforms compiled a comprehensive list of enterprises to be privatized on the basis of the lists supplied by the responsible ministries. This list of privatization objects was submitted to the Council of Ministers for approval. After that the list was published but both the responsible branch ministry and the Ministry of Economic Reforms had to approve the projects once again. A proposal to initiate a privatization project could be submitted by any physical or legal person. The privatization project was first reviewed by the ministry or committee responsible for the object of state property or the municipality responsible for the object of municipal property. Then the bid was sent to the Ministry of Economic Reforms for approval. Individual privatization projects were approved by the Council of Ministers in cases where convertible currency or objects of cultural importance were involved. Finally, the Ministry of Economic Reforms nominated a privatization commission (one per enterprise) on the recommendation of the branch ministry. The privatization commission evaluated the value of the enterprises, negotiated with the bidder and implemented the privatization. Many of these commissions were characterized by a lack of adequate technical knowledge and a low level of commitment. It took a year on average to go through all these complicated phases.[57]

The decentralized case-by-case approach to privatization proved a failure. To speed up and simplify the privatization process, Latvia changed over to a *centralized* system in March 1994. Under the centralized system, the Latvian Privatization Agency and the State Property Fund became the key institutions involved in the privatization process. Both were independent agencies supervised by the Ministry of Economy and Finance, respectively. The State Property Fund was responsible for the management of ongoing state enterprises under commercial criteria. The State Property Fund was amalgamated with the Privatization Agency in 1996. Consequently, all remaining state-owned enterprises, previously held by the State Property Fund, were assigned to the Privatization Agency for privatization. After the streamlining, the Privatization Agency remained as the sole professional institution responsible for the management and sale (or liquidation) of state assets on behalf of the Cabinet of Ministers. The Privatization Agency is a non-profit state-owned joint-stock company which manages the practical privatization process. It evaluates the assets, works out the principles of eventual restructuring, selects the privatization method, negotiates the sale agreement and supervises the sale contract.[58]

The privatization procedure commences with a submission of the privatization proposal to the Privatization Agency. Any natural or legal person, including the ministry or other institution in charge of the respective state enterprise, may submit the application, stating the preferred method of privatization and the planned commercial activities. The Executive Board of the Privatization Agency investigates whether the enterprise is ready for privatization and whether it can be included in the list of the enterprises to be privatized. Such a list has to be submitted to the Cabinet of Ministers for approval. The government announces the enterprises open to privatization by publishing its decisions in the newspaper *Latvijas Vestnesis*. Only after that does the Privatization Agency take the asset unit into its jurisdiction. The Privatization Agency specialists organize the enterprise's valuation and develop privatization regulations. The purpose of these regulations is to offer the enterprise to a potential buyer with all the conditions denoted by the state, such as job preservation or maintenance of manufacturing expertise. The regulations are forwarded to all interested bidders and subjects entitled to pre-emption rights. *Latvijas Vestnesis* also publishes the terms of privatization as well as the deadline for submitting the definite proposals. The last stage comprises negotiations with potential buyers and, finally, signing of a contract.[59]

The decision concerning the method of privatization is made by the Privatization Agency. The law provides the following means of privatization: (1) sale by auction, (2) sale by public tender, (3) cash sale without selection of bidders, (4) credit sale to a particular bidder, (5) transformation into a joint-stock company and sale of shares (three variants), (6) liquidation and separate sale of fixed and liquid assets. Normally various methods are combined in one privatization. If several prospective bidders have submitted a bid for the same asset unit, the Privatization Agency organizes an auction. When foreign investors are targeted, international tenders and public offerings of shares are the principal methods.[60]

Public offerings are carried out through the banks, the Riga Stock Exchange and the Latvian Central Depository. Subscription takes place at the banks, where bidders fill in a special form which at the same time serves as a contract with the Privatization Agency. The contract provides for receipt of shares in the case of successful bidding. After the deadline for application submissions, the banks submit them in the form of an electronic file to the Riga Stock Exchange, which handles the bidder selection. Criteria for the bidder selection is the bid price for one share. Given the bids and the amount of vouchers offered, the auction price of the shares is computed. Those bidders whose bid price exceeds or is equal to the auction price obtain the shares. All successful bidders obtain the shares for the same price.[61]

The Privatization Agency has organized international tenders with the help of German financial aid and advice. Information on the enterprises admitted to tenders was published in the most prominent newspapers of the world, including the *Financial Times, The Economist, Handelsblatt* and *Dagens Industri*. An opportunity was arranged for the prospective buyers to visit the enterprises and meet with their managements. Based on the information obtained, the bidders prepared and submitted their proposals to the Tender Bureau in the Privatization Agency. The bids contained the purchase price, terms of investment and a business plan. After the tender's closing date, the envelopes were opened and the bids were registered. To clarify the contents of the bids, negotiations were conducted with each bidder.[62]

The Privatization Agency evaluates applications according to specific criteria: (1) the conditions of work, employee training and the number of vacancies; (2) the amount and purpose of the proposed investment; (3) an outline of the activities for environmental protection. The buyer will assume the liabilities of the enterprise, unless the buyer and the Privatization Agency have concluded a different agreement. Two legislative changes have improved the position of the buyer in the latter respect: capitalization of the tax payment principal debts to be transferred into the state budget and protection for privatizers against undeclared liabilities appearing after the privatization. Liberalization of land ownership has had the positive effect that foreigners may purchase the land associated with an enterprise being privatized, instead of relying on 99-year leases.[63]

Transparency is the cornerstone of Latvia's privatization strategy. The Privatization Agency is committed to create a trustful atmosphere where the buyer can feel confident that the sale of enterprises is carried out openly, all prospective bidders have equal chances and the same requirements are applied. The Privatization Agency has developed a special information system to ensure regular, direct information flow. Announcements on enterprises at different privatization stages are published in *Latvijas Vestnesis*, local newspapers and the most popular daily and weekly periodicals. The mass media are regularly informed of the decisions adopted by the responsible minister as well as the Executive and Supervisory Boards of the Privatization Agency. Press conferences, where the directors of the Privatization Agency together with the management of the privatized enterprises present an analysis of the current situation, are held once a fortnight. The weekly TV and radio programmes *Mine Will Be Mine* and *Privatization News* provide detailed information about the privatization process, specific projects and the adopted decisions.[64]

Privatization certificates (vouchers) were invented to speed up the economic transformation in the postcommunist countries. In Czechoslovakia the voucher privatization programme turned out to be an enormous success. In Latvia the effect was just the opposite: vouchers slowed down the implementation of privatization. The intricacy of the Latvian voucher scheme may have been the reason for its failure. Latvia has the most complex voucher scheme in Eastern Europe. Introduction of the voucher scheme has been judged as a political solution which is economically inviable. Political motives constitute the main arguments for a free distribution method everywhere. The ideal is to involve as many inhabitants as possible in privatization. First, widespread ownership of shares in firms or investment trusts promotes popular capitalism. It creates the political stake in the system which makes the whole reform programme less likely to be derailed. Moreover, giving assets to the inhabitants is a swift way of establishing the private property basis of a market economy. Second, equal transfers to all residents will reduce inequality in the distribution of wealth. Third, free transfer recognizes that the residents are already supposed to own all state property collectively and seeks to split part of this property into divisible shares.[65]

Vouchers not only proved an inefficient way of transferring state property into private hands but they also retarded the start of the whole mass privatization programme. Although the use of vouchers was enunciated as one of the basic principles of the Latvian privatization strategy as early as March 1991, both the overall concept and its detailed elaboration remained controversial for a long time. It took three years to set up the voucher scheme with all necessary laws due to the lengthy, painful discussions in Parliament about the principles of the programme (allocation criteria, field of application, etc.) The Law on Privatization Certificates was finally passed in November 1992 and amended in May 1994. Distribution of vouchers began in September 1993 and their allotment was terminated by the end of 1995. Numerous technical difficulties troubled the distribution of vouchers to the residents. It came out that the total value of the certificates issued exceeded the value of the targeted state property, until the privatization of flats was included in the voucher scheme. With necessary legislation not enacted and scepticism high, vouchers lost their value in trading. Handed out with a face value of 28 lati (US$ 52) each, they bottomed out at 50 santims (US$ 1) each. In 1997 their market value amounted to 1 lats. Some political parties made an electoral issue of this loss of value, arguing that the state must engage itself to redeem the vouchers at their face value for the sake of social justice.[66] Residents of Latvia, defined as citizens or permanent residents, received an assigned number of vouchers in accordance with their length of residence. Citizens received one voucher each per year of living plus 15 extra vouchers. Non-citizens received one voucher for each year of residence in Latvia without the extra 'bonus' of 15 vouchers. Time worked for KGB (the Committee of State Security) institutions or in high Communist Party posts was subtracted from years of residence. Special regulations concerned specific categories of people. The previous owners of nationalized or otherwise illegally confiscated property or their heirs were entitled to compensation for such property which could not be returned in nature. Politically repressed individuals received vouchers proportionate to time spent in prison or labour camps.[67]

Vouchers can be used as means of payment to varying extents in the privatization of land, housing and medium- and large-scale enterprises. In the public offering privatization they can be used at their face value of 28 lats. Vouchers can also be invested in mutual funds or pension funds. The scope of the voucher programme is more modest than in Czechoslovakia. Free distribution is envisaged as a secondary method so that vouchers can be used for the privatization of a limited fraction of state property only. The Privatization Agency urged Parliament to amend the laws to lower the per centage of vouchers required to buy into companies in order to attract more foreign capital. Not more than 20 per cent of the shares can be purchased through vouchers. Earlier their tradability was limited to transactions through the accounts at the State Savings Bank and they could not be traded to foreigners. These restrictions have been removed so that foreigners may buy vouchers on the secondary market. Vouchers are actually not material but they exist only in a registered form as accounts at the State Savings Bank.[68]

Comparative Typologization

The privatization strategy Latvia has chosen to follow is only one available option among a multiplicity of possible strategies. The fact alone that Latvia has varied its strategy a couple of times suggests that different combinations of privatization techniques can be viable. Both theoretical literature and comparative studies identify alternative strategies typifying distinctive privatization programmes. Stark (1992) and Pedersen (1993), among others, have developed typologies to portray differences in the privatization programmes adopted by various East Central European countries (East Germany, Poland, Czechoslovakia/the Czech and Slovak Republics, Hungary).

Stark and Pedersen each propose three dimensions conceptualizing three central questions that must be addressed by any privatization programme. To capture the essential features of Latvia's privatization strategy, we shall apply Stark and Pedersen's typologies to the Latvian case. Drawing on their analytic categories, we shall explicate the following four aspects from the Latvian variant: (1) Which methods of divestiture are being used in transferring state assets to private hands? (2) Which instances conduct the selection, valuation and restructuring of state assets? (3) Who can acquire state assets? (4) What kind of resources are converted to acquire ownership rights? A longitudinal analysis will compare within the Latvian case the successive modifications made in the concept on enterprise privatization during the first six years of independence. The results presented are based on the currently prevailing state.

1. Method of Divestiture

Options: A. Sale: public offering through capital market operations (o – openness), public auction (o), auction to selected bidders (c – closedness), public tender (o), closed tender (c), employee or management buy-out (c), B. Free transfer = vouchers to citizens (o) or employees (c).

Latvia's choice:

First stage: Open subscription for shares, open and closed auction, tender, direct sale to physical and legal persons (small) or sale of shares (big), employee/management buy-out, leasing with an option to buy.

Second stage: A. Different methods of divestiture are utilized simultaneously: sale of shares by public offering, international tender, direct sale or auction of an enterprise, sale of shares to employees. B. Vouchers can be used as means of payment to obtain a limited amount of specifically defined enterprise shares. Vouchers were distributed to all residents without employee preferences.[69]

Pedersen defines privatization strategies in terms of their openness (o) or closedness (c). More specifically, he makes a distinction between open and closed methods of divestiture according to the possibility of unrestrained participation in the privatization process. The Latvian privatization strategy sets transparency as its prime value. All methods used entail the principle that everybody must have an equal opportunity to participate in privatization. Closed tenders are not stipulated by the law. By law, employees have no pre-emption purchase rights. A company established by employees or managers takes part in the auction on equal condition with other bidders. All kind of enterprises are subject to the same fixed procedure. To ensure the transparency of privatization, efforts are made to inform inhabitants of how, to whom and on what conditions state property can be sold.[70] To conclude, Latvia's method of divestiture can be classified as an open one.

2. *Executor*

Options: Bureaucratic agency and administrative measures > < companies themselves and market mechanism.

Latvia's choice:

First stage: Branch ministries → privatization commissions appointed by branch ministries.

Second stage: Privatization Agency (Latvian Treuhand).

Irrespective of whether the administration has been organized in a decentralized or centralized way, Latvia has relied on administrative methods in the selection and valuation of enterprises to be privatized. Most sale techniques still leave room for bargaining or competitive bidding so that the price setting is influenced by a market mechanism. Restructuring is usually left to the purchaser owing to the scarcity of public funds. Despite these deviations from purely bureaucratic measures, the implementation is decidedly statist in its orientation. Privatization is centralized in one single bureaucratic agency with a strong legislative mandate to supervise all aspects of the privatization process.

3. *Actors Targeted to Acquire Assets*

Options: Corporations, managers, workers, citizens, multiplicity of agents (mixture).

Latvia's choice: Latvian and foreign physical and legal persons.

Latvian legislation is vague on the question of who can participate in the privatization. The law does not designate any specific target group. The programme combines civic principles with economic principles. The voucher scheme, which targets civic persons, seeks to involve wide layers of society in the privatization, while the sale methods are directed toward enterpreneurs in the first place. Western investors are especially welcomed for participation in the privatization. Formally there are no employee preferences but in small privatization they have nonetheless been granted in practice.[71] Nevertheless, the emphasis is on corporations; the other methods are only complementary and often subject to restrictive conditions. To sum up, a multiplicity of agents is targeted simultaneously, but on the other hand the bias toward corporations justifies the characterization of the approach as semi-corporate.

4. Resources Utilized to Acquire Ownership Rights
Options: Monetary > < positional.
Latvia's choice: Monetary.

In the precursory stage of privatization, when spontaneous privatizations were more frequent, positional resources were essential to acquire property rights. Managers, for instance, were able to utilize their occupancy for advantage in gaining effective ownership rights. Early programmes also mentioned that a certain part of state property must be transferred to the employees of the enterprise to be privatized, but later privatization through occupancy was rejected as a method. Today privatization rests on the utilization of monetary resources exclusively. There is nothing for free. If a part of shares is to be distributed to employees, employees will receive their share in exchange for vouchers. Transparency and equal opportunity for all are the slogans of the Privatization Agency which underscores the rejection of insider privatization.

The four dimensions derived from Stark and Pedersen's articles are cross-classified in Tables 6.1 and 6.2 to yield two complementary typologies of privatization strategies. The purpose of the typologies is to point out typical traits by means of simplification rather than produce an exhaustive description of the full range of privatization programmes in each country. Thus, location of a particular country in a given cell is not meant to capture all aspects about its course of privatization. Country cases are found to exemplify specific intersections of the dimensions.[72] Comparison of the Latvian case with the more commonly known Central European cases makes it easier to identify the distinctive features of the Latvian privatization strategy. Comparison provides a basis for evaluating the Latvian programme relative to conceptual criteria.

The typologization reveals that the Latvian privatization programme is composed of mixed elements and the legislation rests on no unified concept. For instance, free competition on state assets is invited within a centralized, bureaucratic framework. Latvia is the opposite of Czechoslovakia, which adheres to market mechanisms in a consistent fashion. Each aspect in Czechoslovakia's privatization programme follows logically from the same underlying concept, whereas Latvia's programme lacks such a distinctive guiding principle. The Latvian model is based on discretion, a case-by-case approach and reliance on experience. The Law on Privatization requires that separate privatization regulations are developed for each enterprise being privatized. These regulations are usually based on proposals and discussions carried out with potential buyers.[73] With regard to the implementation mechanism, Latvia's current strategy resembles East Germany's Treuhand model. The difference is that Latvia is not targeting corporations as exclusively as East Germany. Latvia has also introduced a voucher scheme similar to that used in Czechoslovakia, although it is of secondary importance in Latvia. Latvia does not favour insider privatization like Poland and Hungary; on the contrary, the exploitation of positional resources contradicts Latvia's privatization legislation.

Table 6.1   A Typology of Privatization Strategies in East Central Europe: How?

Method of divestiture	*Executor*		
	Market/ atomized	*Hybrid/ state-market mix*	*Administrative/ centralized*
Open	Czechoslovakia spontaneous market mechanism	Poland state-market mix	*Latvia Privatization Agency*
Semi-open			East Germany Treuhand
Closed		Hungary positional bargaining	

Table 6.2   A Typology of Privatization Strategies in East Central Europe: To Whom?

Resources utilized to acquire ownership rights	*Actors targeted to acquire assets*		
	Civic persons	*Multiplicity of agents*	*Corporations*
Financial/ outsiders	Czechoslovakia citizens	*Latvia: companies & citizens/ semi-corporate*	East Germany companies
Positional/ insiders	Poland workers		Hungary managers

PRIVATIZATION AS A POLITICAL PROCESS

Privatization is undoubtedly the most politicized area of postcommunist economic reforms. Economic reasons constitute only one component of the grounds on which privatization measures are justified. Indeed, the driving force behind privatization both in the West and the East is explicitly political. The political motives include such goals as de-etatization, removal of *nomenklatura*, strengthening of democracy and securing of social stability through the formation of a middle class. Likewise, the consequences of privatization are not limited to economic effects. Privatization leads to a broad reallocation of wealth and power. There are many interest groups which are clashing over the final type of privatization to be implemented. The mobilization of conflicting political forces is due to many variants of property rights which differ in terms of the opportunities they offer various social groups. As a consequence, the group preferences for particular privatization models vary. Understandably, the primary obstacles to progress in privatization are political ones.[74]

The conspicuous entanglement of political motives and aspirations in an apparently economic process makes privatization a most interesting phenomenon in regard to the research problem of this study. Privatization is an ideal example of the impact of politics on economic decision-making. Therefore, we shall examine more closely how political factors have influenced the design and the implementation of privatization both in the immediate past and in the present.

The Political Modification of the Strategy

The very first version of the Law on Privatization favoured employee and management participation. The early programme granted preferential rights to those who had spent a long time in a certain working place. Privatization through occupancy was promoted by both the Popular Front and the Equal Rights faction but for markedly different reasons. As the immigrants tended to work in industry, transfer of assets to employees was advantageous to Russian-speakers. Thus, the Equal Rights movement had a vested interest in advocating insider privatization. The Popular Front, instead, was calculating how to win the sympathies of the Russian-speaking labour force in a turbulent political situation. A lot of workers were oriented to Russia at that time, and there were political strikes and demonstrations. As long as Latvia's independence was at stake, the government tried to persuade the Slavic workers to side with them by supporting privatization through occupancy, although this method contradicted its basically liberal stance.[75]

The Latvian privatization programme started relatively late (early 1992), moved ahead slowly and cumbersomely with a narrow focus on municipally owned small objects. Delay was partly intentional because certain problems of vital importance to the economy and the state were still unresolved. First, privatization was held back until the introduction of the national currency. The reason for waiting was not solely the galloping inflation in the rouble zone, which raised a fear that sale of assets would attract a flood of currency from the Soviet Union, leading to a loss of control over real assets in exchange for a piece of paper of uncertain value. The political leadership was worried about prospective buyers, as most Latvians did not possess sufficient financial means to participate in the privatization. In 1990–91, only a few business groups had enough money to purchase privatization objects – and this money was mostly of Russian origin. The government was concerned about the danger that Latvian property would fall into the hands of Russian businessmen, whose loyalty to the independent Latvian state was distrusted. In fact, the fear that Russian money is entering the country in large quantities – most often through third-country intermediaries – and is gaining a grip on the Latvian economy has not disappeared even today.[76]

Second, tense relations with a powerful hostile neighbour, the indefinite presence of the Russian military in Latvia and inconclusive talks on regulating the Russo-Latvian relations on account of Russia's delaying tactics had a direct bearing on privatization. The Russian Parliament deferred ratifying the interstate accord which contained provisions relevant to privatization. Without the ratification these provisions had no legal force. Similarly, the situation was unclear with respect to the take-over by the Latvian authorities of property or enterprises used by the Soviet military. Two ship repair plants, formerly under the jurisdiction of the USSR, refused to accept the authority of the Latvian Ministry of Maritime Affairs. Instead, the enterprises claimed they were under the oversight of the Russian Federation. When informed of the declaration, the Russian authorities were reluctant to accept the fact that Moscow no longer had legal authority over the plants.[77]

The decentralization of the privatization administration was a reflection of internal political tensions. The original draft programme worked out by the Popular Front of Latvia (PFL) liberals recommended the establishment of one central agency responsible for the management and divestment of all state property after the German Treuhand model. In 1991, privatization was indeed subject to a single institution, which was a department in the Council of Ministers. During the government crisis in November 1991, Prime Minister Godmanis decided to split these functions between branch ministries because there were worries about an excessive concentration of power. It was feared that a small circle of people would take over all decision-making power. A centralized privatization agency was conceived of corresponding to a huge ministry. The respective bill was rejected by Parliament where the majority of the deputies supported a decentralized organization.[78]

As long as Latvia lacked a citizenship law the government was unable to design a comprehensive approach to privatization methods. Particularly the debate over the guidelines of the voucher programme was influenced by a distorted nationality structure. The voucher controversy centred on the question of which population groups should be addressed – all residents or merely citizens – and whether employees should take precedence over the population at large. According to the 1989 census data, 63 per cent of Latvia's industrial labour force was Slavic, with Russians making up 41 per cent of the workers. Most of the top management, appointed during the Soviet era, were Russian. The Slavic workers and especially the Slavic enterprise managers tended to support the preservation of the USSR, the Communist Party and the Interfront. By the same token, they opposed Latvia's efforts to regain economic autonomy and political independence. Therefore, many Latvians were afraid that if these people were issued privatization certificates, they would use them to preserve the Soviet system, albeit under a different label, in order to safeguard their own positions. Latvians were also worried that issuing vouchers without adequate safeguards could lead to foreign ownership of Latvia's economic assets. The Slavic workers considered vouchers to be their due by virtue of having worked in Latvia and to be an affirmation of their rights to residence, citizenship and property ownership. In accordance with the Law on Certificates, vouchers were issued to all residents without employee preferences. The allocation was based on the number of years a resident had lived in the country, with additional certificates available for citizens. The rejected proposition, advocated by the trade unions, was based on labour years. Labour certificates were to be issued relative to one's investment in the accumulation of national welfare; that is, relative to the years worked in Latvia.[79]

In a similar way as in the debate over the criteria for the allocation of vouchers, the nationality conflict was intermingled with the preparation of the law on residential privatization, passed in June 1995. While Latvian citizens already had buying rights for flats and land, non-citizens' rights in this sphere were unclear, thus making it difficult for them to lease or sell flats. The long-anticipated law addressed the so-called 'residents problem'. It laid out the general guidelines governing the privatization of flats, which had proven slower than privatization in the corporate sector. The new law guaranteed citizens and non-citizens equal rights in purchasing flats. The only remaining difference was that non-citizens could not buy land, they could only rent it.[80]

Apartment privatization continued causing discrepancies in party politics when it came to implementation. Latvia's Way wanted to ensure privatization on a fast track, stressing the security of property ownership and increasing freedom to change flats, whereas the Democratic Party Masters (Saimnieks) advocated a slower approach to protect tenants: 'Our constitution guarantees a roof over everyone's head. If apartments are privatized quickly and for wrong reasons, residents may not be able to afford housing.' The Social Democratic Party was similarly defending the rights of tenants. Fatherland and Freedom wanted to include a provision that an apartment can be privatized by other persons if its tenant fails to do so within six months of the house being put up for privatization. All other parties rejected compulsory privatization of state-owned apartments by their tenants. As of 15 May 1997 approximately 40,000 state and municipal apartments were privatized, about 10 per cent of the total.[81]

Politics need not always be an obstructing factor, as it is usually described, including the examples discussed above. A strong positive political will can also give a push to the privatization process. Skele's radical economic programme accelerated privatization drastically. Over 250 enterprises of all sizes were assigned for privatization in 1996. The secret of the sudden success has a great deal to do with the Prime Minister's personality. Skele possesses profound first-hand knowledge of privatization, since he knows its pitfalls from a personal experience. Skele was responsible for the privatization of agriculture and food-processing industry in the Godmanis government. Then he was deeply involved in the creation of the privatization legislation. Finally, he was the first unofficial General Director of the Privatization Agency. The Privatization Agency commends Skele's support for privatization.[82]

Skele's government had set itself the political goal of finishing mass privatization by mid-1998, which seemed a realistic target in the light of the current progress of the process. One reason why the plans for the completion of privatization were prepared in quick succession was the approaching of national elections in the autumn of 1998; Skele's government wants to ensure the irreversibility of privatization so that any government reshuffle cannot endanger the development.[83]

Controversial Privatizations

Eternal questions of privatization include, among others, the scope of state involvement, the degree of openness in the procedure, valuation of the speed, a desirable ownership structure, social guarantees and the interpretation of the essence of privatization (see pp. 178–81). Privatization of natural monopolies, strategic enterprises and infrastructure objects has stirred intense debates in public, which have followed the political left–right divide in the first place but also the traditionalism–modernism divide to some extent. The issue is not whether to privatize or not but whether the proposed strategy is cautious or unconditional, whether it stresses social or economic aspects. Hence, it is easy to perceive in the tangible context of Latvia how the controversy over privatization is a derivative of the 'shock versus gradualism' controversy. The principal differences were embodied in the privatizations of Latavio, Lattelekom and Latvia's Gas, which all came into the firing line.

1. Latvia's Gas is a monopoly supplying natural and liquefied gas to Latvia and it is the sole owner of an underground gas storage facility in the Baltic states. Latvia's Gas imports, stores, transports and distributes gas to consumers. Approximately 3,500 employees work at the state-owned joint-stock company. The privatization of Latvia's Gas was initiated in 1995, when the government was ruled by Latvia's Way and the Political Union of Economists (Tautsaimnieks). Latvia's Way placed no preconditions on the privatization, but Tautsaimnieks wanted to proceed cautiously. Tautsaimnieks called for a thorough investigation into the different alternatives, the results of which should be submitted to a broad-based political discussion. The party succeeded in pushing through its demand not to privatize more than 49 per cent of the shares. When the Privatization Agency started the privatization, it soon turned out to be impossible to privatize only 49 per cent. The Privatization Agency appealed to politicians to grant permission to sell as much as was necessary. The request was discussed in the government and in the parliamentary commissions. Under changed circumstances in the political arena the exemption was cancelled. Skele's government gave the green light to a comprehensive offering.[84]

Over ten foreign gas companies submitted proposals for the privatization of Latvia's Gas to the Privatization Agency. Four of them remained at the end of the competition. Saimnieks insisted that at least one strategic partner must always come from the East in the privatization of large companies. (The Eastern orientation of Saimnieks implies, among others, that it wants to attract Eastern capital to Latvia.) Saimnieks's demand was accepted by Parliament with the result that Russian Gazprom was invited to participate in the privatization of Latvia's Gas. When the privatization of Ventspils Nafta reaches the proper stage, one strategic supplier will probably be selected from the Eastern side and one buyer from the Western side.[85]

2. The modernization of the Latvian telecommunication system induced enormous public polemics. The Latvian State Telecom (Lattelekom) signed an agreement in January 1994 with the Tilts Communications consortium of British Cable & Wireless and Telecom Finland on updating Latvian telecommunications. The government had announced an international tender to find a strategic partner for the modernization programme, and this tender produced two serious bids: one from the British-Finnish and another from the German-Swedish consortium. The former won the project. Tilts Communications pledged to invest US$ 160.3 million to acquire a 49 per

cent stake in the restructured Lattelekom. The remaining 51 per cent was to belong to the Latvian state.[86]

Neatkariga Cina, the second largest Latvian daily, launched a lengthy campaign against a privatized Lattelekom in its pages. Being influenced by Bojars at that time, the newspaper published a series of articles denouncing the deal with Tilts Communications as disadvantageous to Latvia. *Neatkariga Cina*'s fight culminated in an address signed by around 16,000 people in protest against an alleged 'shady transaction' regarding Lattelekom. The signatures were submitted to Parliament together with a demand to create an independent committee to study the issue.[87]

The main objection presented in the political debate focused on the heavy foreign involvement in such a strategic sphere as telecommunications. Reservations about the participation of Western investors in Lattelekom were voiced by the parties leaning to the left in their political thinking. It was suggested that while Lattelekom is a joint-venture involving the British-Finnish consortium Tilts Communications, there is a danger of the Latvian state becoming marginalized by the Western partners, with the final result of Lattelekom being entirely under Western control. It may turn out in the end that the actual owner of Lattelekom's 20-year monopoly will be Tilts Communications. The law grants Lattelekom exclusive rights to telecommunication services until 2010.[88]

While others were enthusiastic about the huge foreign investment, critics maintained monopoly profits are taken from the pockets of Latvians so that everybody is paying back the investment with interest to the investors. The criticism was directed against the pricing policy of the private foreign monopolist which is in a position to set the tariffs. There were complaints that the prices were too high while the quality of services was too low. The tariff rates of foreign calls were cited as an example of the overpricing. It costs five times more to call from Latvia to the United States than from the United States to Latvia. More importantly, high prices were related to a social aspect, for a great part of the population cannot afford to pay the new tariffs. Opponents believed that if the monopoly were in the hands of the government there would be various ways to exert pressure on price-setting. According to the counter-argument, the aversion to tele tariffs is derived from the old system in which the use of the telephone was free of charge.[89]

The critics were dissatisfied with the implementation of the modernization activities as regards subcontracting. Latvia is supposed to get one of the world's best digital telephone networks by the year 2001, but Latvian producers will not have much of a role in setting it up. Janis Smilga, Chairman of Latvia's Radio Technical Centre, summarized the complaints as follows: 'I do not agree that all Latvian telecommunication developments should take place without any Latvian industry being involved. The fact that the monopoly for choosing which companies supply the equipment lies with British specialists from Tilts Communications has led to foreign companies being favoured over Latvian companies.' Those who claimed there is too little Latvian involvement in Lattelekom asked why Lattelekom relied exclusively on foreign deliveries when Latvian factories could have composed the same units. They could not understand why VEF did not receive any orders. VEF was the largest manufacturer of telephones in the Soviet Union. One instance in which Latvian companies were shunned in favour of foreign firms was the relatively low-tech area of cable splicing. A Latvian company won a US company's licence to produce cable splicing parts, but Lattelekom did not use them. The reason why Lattelekom favoured foreign companies was believed to be that Tilts Communications received a 5 per cent commission on equipment and supplies purchased for the modernization project. This contractual arrangement did not provide an incentive for Tilts to seek the best prices. According to the critics, there were no grounds for such extensive capital investment to carry out the project. They argued that too much of the equipment was being replaced and the equipment itself was too expensive.[90]

The advocates of the agreement with Tilts admitted that there may have been some legal mistakes in its formulation but on the other hand the updating of telecommunications is of utmost importance to Latvia. It would be a remarkable competitive advantage to the country if Latvia were able to switch over to an ultramodern digital network as the first Baltic state. This aim was acknowledged by foreign experts to contain real economic insight. Furthermore, the advocates stressed that the quality of the technology must be the prime concern. They pointed out that the technological level of telecommunications was low in the former Soviet Union. Even if Latvia had a qualified labour force to realize the project, it would have to buy the technology from abroad, which would be very costly and problematic, if not impossible, without foreign partners. Latvians also lack the managerial skills necessary to organize the process. The liberal right parties argued strongly for the joint venture with Tilts Communications.[91]

3. Latavio was the Latvian state airline. Latavio was constantly troubled with financial problems, and in the autumn of 1994 the airline sank so far into debt that it became obvious it would never be able to pay back its creditors. Latavio's biggest creditor Banka Baltija submitted a privatization proposal to the Privatization Agency. The Privatization Agency accepted the proposal and forwarded it for Cabinet consideration. The government approved the plan to establish a new national airline company in Latvia. According to the Privatization Agency's plan, Latavio would be turned into a cargo and charter carrier and it would lose its passenger flights to the new

national airline, Air Baltic Corporation (ABC). Air Baltic Corporation would be the only Latvian air company to carry passengers, which would bring about a general restructuring of civil aviation. Namely, there was also another smaller but more successful carrier in Latvia, Baltic International Airlines. Baltic International Airlines was a joint venture between the Latvian state (holding 51 per cent of the shares) and a private American partner, Baltic International USA Inc. (BIUSA). The restructuring decision entailed the government passing the state capital shares of Baltic International Airlines to the Privatization Agency for privatization. The new airline was going to merge Latavio's passenger services with the services of Baltic International Airlines. Once formed, the new airline's finances were expected to consist of 51 per cent state capital, while 49 per cent of the starting capital would be derived from BIUSA, SAS and two Scandinavian investment funds.[92]

Latavio was angry over the way the Privatization Agency handled the project. From top management to labour union members, Latavio employees stepped up protests against the privatization of Latvia's national flag carrier. They accused the Privatization Agency of selling the company much too cheaply and of reorganizing it on terms that would bring about its eventual liquidation. The best part, capable of generating profit, was given to foreigners, while the unprofitable part was kept under Latvian ownership. A further complaint concerned the transformation of Latavio's original function. The former leadership claimed that this concept violated the law: privatization rules require that a company to be privatized maintains its profile of activities. Latavio officials insisted on keeping the passenger services and demanded potential investors to cover the 6 million lats (US\$ 12 million) debt owed to Banka Baltija. Referring to the latter point of view, Latavio regarded it as a mistake to choose only one strategic partner. Latavio's former Vice President attacked the heavy involvement of SAS, saying that 'SAS is not interested in Riga to become a competitor to Stockholm or Copenhagen'. The trade union also opposed the heavy foreign involvement in ABC. The striking employees were afraid for their jobs, as they believed that 50 per cent of the new company's employees would be foreigners. In an open letter to Parliament, Latavio demanded an official investigation into its privatization. The Privatization Agency denied causing Latavio's liquidation and pointed to the company's mismanagement and inefficiency as a source of its financial difficulties.[93]

One interpretation saw the troubled privatization of Latavio as a struggle between two capitals interested in breaking into the Latvian market. This struggle was reduced to a competition between Western (American-Scandinavian) and Russian capital. In principle, there were two bids: Baltic International Airlines and SAS, and Latavio and Banka Baltija. A major part of Banka Baltija's capital was of Russian origin, but also the management of Latavio had connections with Russian capital as well as with Latvian Social Democrats. As the stakes were high, competing lobbies tried to influence the decision to be made by all possible means: money, press campaigns, rumour-mongering. The opposition was not directed against privatization per se but against the specific way the project was realized. As the losers refused to give up, they tried to prevent the new company from commencing to work. It is telling that the outcries occurred only when the new activities were scheduled to begin, not when the discussions about the form of privatization took place. The late timing seems to confirm the suspicions of the questionable motives on the part of Latavio's managers. Employees, who were concerned about safeguards for their jobs, were manipulated by the old leadership of Latavio.[94]

4. Insolvent state enterprises, facing no choice other than liquidation, constitute the most difficult cases for privatization, especially when they employ thousands of workers. Politicians may not have enough courage to liquidate the failing giants due to the employment effects. Politicians press the Privatization Agency to find an investor who would take over the liabilities of an indebted enterprise, even when common sense notes that the task is hopeless. The light industry factory Vokce is an illustrative example of the political inability to shut down a bankrupt enterprise. Vokce employed over 3,000 workers in a small provincial town where no other potential employer was available. The factory was in such bad shape that nobody was interested in buying it but nevertheless it was hard for the Privatization Agency to liquidate Vokce.[95]

To preserve or to liquidate is not a dichotomic question but rather a continuum with many intermediate degrees, ranging from the liberal to the socialist position. Political conflict over the treatment of bankrupt state enterprises reveals the differences within the party system.

- Latvia's Way wants to close down bankrupt state enterprises if they are not privatized in the first few rounds. The state must not run unprofitable factories under any circumstances. Latvia's Way is not concerned about the effects of liquidation on employment. It believes that economic growth and expansion of the private sector will compensate the loss of working places. It further argues that places where the big factories are located do not suffer from alarming unemployment rates. Their rates lag far behind the European levels of unemployment. Areas where unemployment is very high do not have threatened factories. Latvia's Way leaves the responsibility for restructuring to the purchaser of an enterprise.

- Saimnieks is not as consequent and uncompromising as Latvia's Way, allowing exceptions to salvage troubled industries. Saimnieks is ready to accept a somewhat slower speed of privatization in exchange of rescued working places. Those enterprises which cannot find a buyer should be restructured by the state. Both the technology and the finances of such companies could be improved within the context of a special programme.
- The Socialist Party and the Social Democratic Party put their stance unambiguously: the maintenance of working places always has an overriding priority. Therefore, each case must be carefully investigated to find out if there is any possibility of keeping the factory running. Large state enterprises, such as VEF, must not be allowed to go bankrupt on any account. If the Privatization Agency cannot find an investor who would take over all employees and guarantee their jobs, the state must continue funding those factories. The government must restart production in many state-owned enterprises that have come to a standstill due to the lack of markets.[96]

Political Control over Privatization by Law

Before going more deeply into the political dimensions of privatization, it is useful to determine the scale of the phenomenon by comparing the degree of politicization in Latvia with the other Baltic countries. A comparison shows that political influence is smaller in Latvia than in Estonia or Lithuania. Latvia's emphasis on transparency, competitiveness, professionalism and uniform rules limits the scope of political interference. Decisions concerning privatization of a given company fall within the jurisdiction of the Executive Board of the Privatization Agency, which is composed of civil servants, i.e. professionals. In Estonia, on the other hand, respective decisions on large enterprises are made by politicians. The Board of the Estonian Privatization Agency consists of the representatives of the government. In Latvia, all privatization objects from pharmacies to banks go through the same standard procedure. No specific regulations or restrictions are adopted by Parliament under any circumstances. In Lithuania, Parliament has assembled a list of objects (mostly strategic enterprises) not to be privatized. The Lithuanian Parliament may also pass a separate law on the privatization of, say, a specific bank.[97]

Latvia's liberal approach to privatization aims at the minimization of political regulation, although political influence can never be fully avoided. The choice of a technocratic strategy is, however, a political choice. It reflects Latvia's Way and Skele's liberal economic policies in the same way as Lithuania's approach reflects the ideology of the Social Democratic government. An apparently non-political result can come from a conscious political decision.

Privatization is subject to parliamentary supervision in Latvia, too, although the level of control is relatively relaxed. Political control is realized on two levels: first, legislation envisages a domain for political representation by institutional arrangements; second, significant privatization decisions cannot be kept beyond the reach of parties by isolating them from the political process.

According to the law, political influence is channelled through the Supervisory Board of the Privatization Agency. The Supervisory Board is composed of one representative from each parliamentary party as well as five additional members from the Ministry of Economy appointed by the Chairman of the Supervisory Board. The Chairman of the Supervisory Board is the Minister of Economy (in 1996–97 Guntars Krasts), who is a political figure. He represents not only the government but also his own party (in Krasts case the Union for Fatherland and Freedom (TB)), whose interests must be kept in mind, too. The Executive Board of the Privatization Agency reports monthly to the Supervisory Board about large and medium-sized privatizations. All significant projects need the 'blessings' of the Supervisory Board in practice. It also monitors the procedure and defines the guidelines of privatization.[98]

The purpose of a parliamentary controlled supervisory board is to guarantee a permanent collaboration with all political forces – not just with the government parties – so as to avert accusations of wasting state property. Despite this good intention, there is a danger that interest groups will exploit the lobbying opportunity with the consequence that privatizations may be postponed or cancelled. Slight violations of social or regional policy objectives can lead to demands to submit the project for fresh consideration. Correspondingly, if the project under consideration appears inconsistent with 'Latvian national interest', the parliamentarians may feel an incentive to start a long-lasting discussion round. The worst scenario envisages the Supervisory Board of the Privatization Agency turning into a battlefield of political power struggles. Such horror visions have not so far materialized, although the Privatization Agency admits that its problems are primarily political.[99]

Although the Executive Board of the Privatization Agency officially consists of non-political professionals, their appointment is still a political decision, reflecting the central importance of privatization to national economy. The General Director of the Privatization Agency is maybe the third most important person in the economic field after the Prime Minister and the Minister of Finance, because almost all state monopolies and the largest state enterprises are under the governance of the Privatization Agency. How this bulk of enterprises is managed affects the revenue of both the state budget and the social budget as well as several economic indicators. How and whom to privatize has immense distributional effects on the allocation of wealth. The General Director, who also acts as a Chairman of the Executive Board, is appointed by the Cabinet of Ministers for a three-year period. When the Privatization Agency was established in 1994, Latvia's Way was the governing party in Latvia. Hence, it naturally won the eligible post of the General Director. The first three-year period expired in April 1997. Although Latvia's Way had lost its dominant position in party politics, Janis Naglis was allowed to continue as General Director thanks to his personal merits, since he was acknowledged to have worked flawlessly and successfully. The political dispute arose over the nomination of the four department directors – that is, the other board members – who are appointed by the Minister of Economy at the General Director's suggestion.[100]

Naglis wanted to continue with his old team, but Minister Krasts refused to reappoint the same directors for another three-year period. Krasts argued that the appointment of directors should occur through a competition in order to introduce more openness to privatization. It was obvious that Fatherland and Freedom and possibly some other parties wanted to have their representatives in the Executive Board, instead of leaving it under the sole control of Latvia's Way's. Finally a compromise was reached in which two directors were selected through a competition and two on the General Director's suggestion. The freedom the General Director has in the selection of the board members depends on the circumstances under which he has been appointed. If the prevailing balance of power is not advantageous enough to his party, he must adjust his team to the requests of the other political parties.[101]

Although the Executive Board of the Privatization Agency is authorized to decide on the execution of privatization, important privatization projects are always discussed at the weekly meetings of the ruling coalition beforehand. Only after the principles of privatization have been agreed among the political parties, can the Executive Board of the Privatization Agency afford to make its decision, which will be adjusted to the requirements put forth by the parties. Bargaining focuses on such questions as whether a state share should be left after privatization, who will be targeted by the privatization (local or foreign investors), which goals should be achieved through privatization, etc. Political parties have their representatives on the boards of the large state enterprises that are managed by the Privatization Agency.[102]

Stakeholders and *Nomenklatura* Privatization

There are always stakeholders with a vested interest who want to participate in the determination of conditions for privatization. Trade unions or employee

groups, management of state enterprises as well as parties' sponsors and
backers from business[103]all try to influence the procedure to their advantage.
Trade unions are generally weak in Latvia, especially in small and medium-
sized enterprises, but there are still a few branches which are exceptions to
the rule. Energy, shipping and pharmacy belong to the sectors with strong
union power. It has become a customary practice to involve the trade unions
in the privatization of energy enterprises. A share of the stock to be transferred
to employees, restructuring of the enterprise, guarantees for the job maintenance
and the social effects of privatization are crucial points in the negotiations
with the trade unions. The law allows the unions the right to express their
opinion on the regulations at the board meetings of the Privatization Agency.
The forthcoming negotiations with Latvenergo's trade union are expected
to be difficult, because the privatization of an inefficiently working state
monopoly will inevitably lead to dismissals of workers.[104]

Privatization of pharmacies was preceded by a prolonged battle with the
trade union. At first the union resisted privatization altogether, since state
employment had been lucrative for employees. They had had relatively high
salaries, because pharmacies had typically avoided the profit tax by hiding
the profit through the payment of higher salaries. A peculiar feature of the
pharmacy branch is the small size of the units which has the effect that almost
all employees are engaged in the management of a pharmacy. At the next
stage the trade union demanded pre-emptive purchase rights for employees
or for companies which are majority owned by employees. They secured the
latter demand through Parliament.[105]

Managers tend to oppose the initiation of privatization at the launch stage.
The systematics holds for both individual cases and longitudinal treatment
of privatization's history. Resistance was more vigorous in the early years
of the privatization process. State enterprise managers were also more
powerful at that time owing to the embryonic state of the private sector: the
state had to rely exclusively on state enterprises as suppliers. To keep the
power in their hands managers opposed privatization. Today managers are
no longer in such a strong position to resist privatization, and in many cases
they are not against privatization as such. Rather, they try to manipulate specific
privatization projects in such a way that the realization would serve their
interests. They want to ensure a large management share of the privatized
assets or to involve their own company or a clientele company in the privatization. As long as a 'friendly' company is guaranteed precedence, managers
are supportive of the privatization of a state enterprise. If a rival company
appears too competitive, managers try to obstruct the privatization by all
possible means. Managers prefer to carry out the privatization on their own
without the interference of the Privatization Agency and without a public

auction or a tender. When facing the prospect of losing control, they lack the motivation to prepare the company for external investors.[106]

Today privatization is relatively open and controlled, but at the very beginning of the process, when the legislation and the institutions were not yet in place, spontaneous privatizations were a problem. The disorderly dissolution of collective farms benefited the leaders and the specialists of the collective farms. The leaders seized the machines and other valuable assets, whereas the ordinary labourers got nothing. The leaders also arranged themselves extensive domains.[107]

The mechanism of *nomeklatura* privatization in industry was to set up a private enterprise which parasitized a state enterprise. Already in Gorbachev's time private enterprises were permitted under certain restrictive conditions. A director of the state enterprise established a company of his own which used the equipment of the state factory or entered into a favourable contract with it. The director sold raw materials or products from the state enterprise to his private company at a very low (administrative) rouble price. The private company sold them further, for instance, to the West at a world market price, receiving the payment in hard currencies. All profits accrued to the director's private company, while the losses were carried by the state enterprise. When the state enterprise was assigned for privatization, the director involved his company in the privatization, manipulating the conditions to its advantage. He was a quasi-seller and buyer simultaneously. He might have used some off-shore company as an intermediary, but nevertheless the end result was that he privatized the failing state enterprise cheaply for himself.[108]

RESTITUTION – A DOUBLE-EDGED SWORD

One of the social and political aims of property reform is the redress of past injustice when private property was expropriated by the state without proper compensation. Denationalization and reprivatization – in brief, restitution – of the illegally confiscated property is the other aspect of the restoration of private ownership rights. While less of an issue in Russia, where the confiscations occurred over 70 years ago, restitution is an acute question in the Baltic republics, where nationalizations were overtly imposed by a foreign occupying power and where elder citizens and their children well recall what they once owned. Symbolically, the process of restoring former owners is seen as the economic counterpart of restoring political independence. Hence, restitution enjoys widespread political support among the population.[109]

Restitution refers to the return of property nationalized after 1940 to previous owners or their heirs, irrespective of their present citizenship. The principle holds not only for physical persons but also for legal entities who present a valid ownership claim. Three separate restitution programmes are going on for land, buildings and enterprises. The property is primarily returned in nature, if the property still exists and if its return does not conflict with national interests. However, the return of property can be bound with restrictions on property rights, if there are binding lease or tenancy contracts which must be respected by the legal owner. If the property cannot be returned as such, compensation is to be achieved by issuing special compensation certificates for use in privatization sales. These compensation certificates may be used to obtain property of equal value to that lost; in the case of a previous (part) owner of a factory, to obtain shares in the new statute company established on the basis of his former business or shares in another statute company; to purchase apartments and land owned by the state or municipalities; and to pay for newly built housing or to establish individual farms. Industrial property belongs to the bottlenecks of restitution, since industrial plants have changed drastically since 1940. The problem is how to separate the expropriated property from the units added during the 50-year occupation. For this reason, the government relies mainly on monetary compensation in the case of industrial property.[110]

The distribution of rural land targeted for the restoration of the prewar situation, restitution being the principal method of divestiture. The former owners and their heirs automatically had the right to claim restitution of their property without anyone asking whether they can till the soil and whether they have resources or capabilities for cultivation. Many acres of arable land have been lost from cultivation owing to the indequate compensation mechanisms since the owners, who may be urban dwellers, treat their land simply as security against evil days. It is easy to see how the prevailing restitution provisions may collide with the economic interest of society by hindering the efficient use of the denationalized object, when agricultural land or business assets are involved. Legal owners are often elderly people or they have no money to invest in the rehabilitation of their property, whereas the present user is more likely to be able to continue the activities he or she has thus far carried out. Simultaneously restitution may contradict the rights of those who actually hold the confiscated property so that old injustices will be replaced with new ones. Sometimes several heirs of the former owner have a claim for the same asset, which again leads to a conflict situation. Restitution of land, characterized as a political solution, is contrasted with the Gorbachev-era experiment in the countryside. The then Minister of Agriculture Edvins Bresis created a small class of private farmers in accordance with an economic criterion. Able agricultural labourers who wanted to leave a collective farm were offered the opportunity to become land owners.[111]

The source of the problem is that restitution has priority over privatization in the legislation. All relevant laws are written in favour of former owners. To cite an example, the former owner has the absolute right to have his land returned, irrespective of what has been built on that land after the confiscation. Consequently, the owner of the ground and the owner of the factory can be two different persons. This odd state of affairs is exacerbated by a deficient legislation which leaves open many questions concerning the relationship between the owners of the land or buildings and those of business assets. Furthermore, former owners and their heirs, who have claimed restitution of their property rights, possess pre-emptive purchase rights for privatization objects.[112]

Lawsuits between the proprietors of denationalized land and of the property built on that land afterwards have flooded the courts. Lindeks, one of the leading wood-processing companies in Latvia, had a large sawmill on land returned to the previous owner. The sawmill had been built there in the 1980s. Lindeks had detailed plans to expand the capacity of the sawmill three-fold; however, not only the extension plan but also the whole operation of the sawmill came to a standstill lasting for months due to a conflict with the land owner. The land owner refused to sell or lease the land at a reasonable price despite repeated offers and compromise proposals. Each day the sawmill was lying idle caused considerable losses to Lindeks, not to mention workers who were presumably laid off. As the unsuccessful negotiations came to a deadlock, Lindeks had no choice but to bring the matter before the court, although it had hoped to the last to avoid a lawsuit. The court proceedings took still more time.[113] The land on which the Riga Airport is sited is the most famous case of the attempt by the former owners to milk it for money. Saeima was forced to adopt a special law on the airport land.[114]

The Latvian experience shows that it is necessary to balance the renewal of property rights with the interests of the present users and, even more importantly, to direct the process in such a manner that it does not impede privatization. Restitution has severely hampered privatization because new owners cannot be certain about the true ownership of the property when they buy it. Provisions which prevent land and buildings from being privatized together with other business assets retard the development of small business. The restitution law forbids the renting of vacated space to new tenants as well as the renovation of buildings until they are returned to their former owners. At the time of passing the restitution decree, 90 per cent of space suited for business in Riga was located in buildings waiting for denationalization. Initially, the period for filing restitution claims for land in towns and cities was ten years and for buildings three years. Although these deadlines were predated, the period for filing restitution claims still remained excessively long, partly due to repeated extensions of the deadline. Previous owners were in no haste to submit their claims with the result that property rights remained unclear in the meantime. In cases where former owners renewed their ownership rights, the small supply of commercial space led to extremely high rents.[115]

Restitution is a shining example of a situation in which economic rationale conflicts with political need and social fairness. The political sensitivity of restitution is heightened by its intertwinement with the nationality question. Extensive restitution favours prewar residents and their descendants, i.e. ethnic Latvians. The pronounced role given to restitution in the property reform reflects the wish to create a Latvian class of property owners. The National Bloc parties and part of Latvia's Way have pushed hardest for the restitution laws, whereas the left-leaning parties have been more critical about the precedence of restitution. However, the means used do not always lead to the intended end, if the configuration of causal relations is more complex than might be expected from superficial observation.[116]

The Law on the Denationalization of Buildings was designed to serve the interests of the ethnic Latvians but, to everyone's surprise, the effect turned out to be quite the opposite. Originally, people who campaigned for this law kept on talking about the 'national interest'. In actuality, the return of buildings to their prewar owners is mainly directed against ethnic Latvians, not Russian-speakers. The unintended result is to be explained by the demographic composition of Riga's different districts. The highest percentage of ethnic Latvians is concentrated in the central districts where the older buildings are located, whereas the new districts around Riga are populated by Russian-speakers. More specifically, while the proportion of ethnic Latvians amongst Riga's inhabitants was a third in the early 1990s, their proportion in the central districts was a half. During the Soviet time, migrants were granted a privilege to new flats, because it was argued that they had no place to live when they came to Latvia from other parts of the USSR. Native inhabitants had difficulties in getting flats in the new suburbs with the consequence that they had to stay in the old districts. Hence, the restitution of buildings affects especially Latvian nationals, since buildings built during the occupation have no previous owners.[117]

7 Economic Programmes of the Political Parties

Modern democracy is a party democracy. The realization of a representative democracy is based on the existence of a competitive party system. Modern government is a party government. Parties formulate and design policies when they exercise legislative and executive power. Parties, as bearers of competing policy alternatives, define the relevant policy options. Responding to this supply of policies, people decide in the elections which option should be forwarded during the next electoral period. In the long run, parties respond to the demands extracted from society and formulate their programmes in accordance with these demands but in the short term, as during a pre-electoral campaign, parties are suppliers and voters consumers. The rivalry between alternative policy options pursued by various parties gives expression to interest conflicts inherent in civil society. The structure of the party system constitutes one of the most crucial elements of the institutional framework affecting policy-making.

The banal presentation of the self-evident truths above addresses the point that political parties are in charge of policy-making. On account of their key role in the policy-making process, a policy analysis cannot ignore them. On the contrary, political parties seem to provide exactly the right point of departure for such an analysis. Even if the idealized, theoretically constructed textbook model justifies the selection of political parties as a subject of analysis, a critical reader might ask whether they are the real actors on the political scene in Latvia. Maybe the Latvian party system is a mere façade, while the true locus of power lies elsewhere. In some East European countries the development of the party system is still at such an embryonic level that the true forces must be sought elsewhere. Also in the case of Latvia, one sometimes hears claims that 'Latvia has no real party system' or 'Latvian parties are cadre-type groupings around power-hungry leaders without any real political platforms'. Such drastic generalizations are going too far, although the existence of shortcomings conforming to these allegations cannot be denied. The essential point is that the formulation of national policies is unambiguously in the hands of political parties. There is no competing locus of power that could replace the government or the parliament in general policy-making. For instance, corporatist structures are virtually non-existent in Latvia and the pressure group activity is principally limited to ad hoc lobbyism in cases where the interest of a given business is directly concerned.

The most natural way to study political parties is to take a look at their programmes, an approach which allows one to chart the alternative policy options provided by them. Programmes alone do not cover all relevant aspects in the behaviour of parties, and sometimes their content may not correspond to actual practices but, in spite of these reservations, they undoubtedly reveal something essential about the political alternatives at hand. When the content of the party programmes is related to the requirements for a successful continuation of reform, the analysis of the programmes will give hints regarding the prospects of the transition process in Latvia. Moreover, the presentation of Latvian parties serves the purpose of producing new authentic information, because the Latvian party system is unknown outside Latvia. Familiarity with Latvian parties is relevant to those people, among others, who wish to weigh and foresee the influence of government reshuffles on the business climate. If one knows something of the new decision-makers beforehand, one will be able to anticipate what kind of stands they will take. The international press has all too often circulated a false image of certain parties as the result of insufficient knowledge. Parties should be given the opportunity to 'speak out' before any outsider makes conclusions on their behalf. On these grounds it is considered sound to highlight their programmes extensively in a descriptive fashion.

Each programme review will follow approximately the same formula in order to make comparison between parties easier; that is, the programme summaries will deal with the same themes, though in a slightly divergent order depending on the significance of a given topic for each party. Those topics that have a high priority in the goal-setting of the party under consideration are emphasized in the programme review correspondingly, and they are normally presented at the beginning of the review. The economic issues addressed in the reviews have been selected in view of their theoretical and practical relevance. Luckily, both criteria have pointed to similar themes. The topics debated among scholars have been disputed among politicians in everyday politics and pre-electoral campaigns. The review of economic policies will be preceded by a brief introduction to the background and the overall profile of each party in order to anchor the economic platform within a wider frame. The standard structure of the programme reviews is outlined below.

A. General characterization of the party's political profile and social base.
   1. Origin.
   2. Ideology and location on the left–right spectrum.
   3. Reference group: related/sister parties abroad.

4. Preferred coalition partners among Latvian parties > < main opponents, unacceptable parties.
5. Constituency.

B. Economic policy advocated by the party.
  6. Economic system aspired to, the particular model for market economy among 'alternative capitalisms'.
  7. Role of the state in the economy, the extent and type of state intervention.
  8. Privatization.
  9. FDI and foreign ownership of land.
  10. Stabilization, fiscal policy, monetary policy, exchange rate policy, independence of the central bank.
  11. Agricultural policy.
  12. Principles of foreign trade: customs policy, trade partners, attitude toward the EU.

C. Citizenship policy.
(D. Eventual special emphasis.)

The twelve political parties whose programmes will be analysed comprise all the Latvian parties that have gained seats either in the 5th or 6th Saeima elections (or both), meaning that their electoral support has exceeded at least 4 per cent in 1993 or 5 per cent in 1995. Politically insignificant petty parties that have never been able to exceed the 4 or 5 per cent barrier are left outside the analysis, with one exception. The big winner of the last local elections will be included in the presentation, because it is forecast to emerge as a winner in the next Saeima elections. Thus, the twelve parties presented here play more or less central roles in Latvian politics, and are commonly known among the electorate. The reason why the parties are presented from right to left (and not from left to right) is that the rightist position represents a status quo orientation whereas the leftist alternatives can be treated as challengers to the status quo. In some cases, it is very difficult to place parties on a traditional unidimensional left–right dimension because it does not fully capture the multidimensional political reality in Latvia. Therefore, the order in which parties are arranged may be somewhat dubious but it offers a rough classification of the party system, distinguishing at least between the main blocs. The so-called National Bloc parties – Fatherland and Freedom, the National Conservative Party, the Christian Democratic Union and the Farmers' Union – are grouped together, discussed in succession and contrasted with the opposite pole, the Russian parties – Harmony and the Socialist Party.

THE UNION FOR FATHERLAND AND FREEDOM

The national conservative Union For Fatherland and Freedom (*Tevzemei un Brivibai* – TB) was founded in January 1995, when a political party called the November 18th Alliance and a national movement called Fatherland joined together. As an electoral coalition, the November 18th Alliance and Fatherland had already run together for the 5th Saeima elections in 1993, but the alliance was sealed officially in a joint congress held on 21 January 1995, at the outset of the pre-electoral campaign for the 6th Saeima elections.

The origins of the party date back to the Citizens' Congress and the radical wing of the Popular Front. Initially, the Citizens' Congress was supported by moderate political parties and organizations as well, but its militancy soon alienated many supporters. It was understandably one of the Latvian organizations most frequently criticized by the Russian-language press in Latvia. The Citizens' Congress played a pivotal role in focusing public attention on the need for Latvian citizens to have their rights restored and to exercise those rights fully in determining the future of Latvia. The Congress was seen as the legal representation of the state authority of the Republic of Latvia founded on 18 November 1918. It was elected exclusively by the citizens of Latvia, unlike the Supreme Soviet which was elected by all residents almost simultaneously. Distrusting the Supreme Soviet and the government endorsed by it, the Citizens' Congress tried to act as an alternative legislature for the citizens of Latvia. As the Citizens' Congress was a quasi-parliament, it could not enter political life as a political party. The first political party to rise out of the Citizens' Congress was the November 18th Alliance, which was later to become one of the founding organizations of Fatherland and Freedom. The legacy of the political platform of the Citizens' Congress is clearly recognizable in the programme of Fatherland and Freedom. The present party platform is rooted in the legal approach advocated by the Citizens' Congress.[118]

When outlining its policy, Fatherland and Freedom keeps to national conservative principles:

> ... respect for the nation, property, family, religion or any other form of world outlook as a moral and legal basis for the state recognition of the leading role of private property and competition for forming a balanced economic and social policy, at the same time rejecting both ultimate liberalism and state capitalism ... strengthening the institutions that bridge an individual and the state – family, school, NGOs – in order to exclude exaggeration of the role of both the state and the individual.

The TB wants to 'develop a strong state based on the inherited values, traditions and experience of the Latvian nation'.[119] The TB treats all conservative parties in Europe as its reference group. It has contacts especially with Estonian Pro Patria, the Lithuanian RSP and the Swedish Moderates. Within the Latvian party system, it prefers to cooperate with the Latvian National Conservative Party, the Farmers' Union and the Christian Democratic Union. The uniting feature between these parties is the wish to see Latvia as a national state and to work concretely for this goal. The TB considers the Socialist Party, Harmony, Tautsaimnieks and Saimnieks to be its main opponents. Its relationship with Latvia's Way is reserved, even though it sees possibilities for cooperation with some individual members of Latvia's Way. In the case of Latvia's Way, the main difference lies in the citizenship policy. The other four above-mentioned parties differ from the TB not only in terms of a more cosmopolitan approach to the citizenship question, but also in terms of their economic policy and international orientation.[120]

In their own words, the electoral basis of the TB 'comprises the conservative part of all layers of society, but never a separate social group. They are people who manage to combine respect for the long-lived traditions with accepting certain fundamentally considered novelties.' That is, the party denies representing any special social strata. Although the social basis is not to be defined sociologically, the party has a relatively stable constituency. It draws support from people who suffered considerably under the Soviet occupation, who themselves were repressed or whose relatives were harassed. As for demographic distribution, these people mostly belong to an elderly generation but there are also young supporters. The dramatic personal history of Fatherland and Freedom leader Maris Grinblats is illustrative of the background of the party's typical electorate. It also makes the party's uncompromising stand on many issues understandable, most prominently on citizenship. The Grinblats clan, like so many other Latvian families, was severely cut down in number by the Soviet deportations of 25 March 1949. This dark chapter in the family history left its mark on Maris Grinblats. Upon graduating from the School of Philosophy at the University of Latvia, Grinblats fell foul of the Soviet authorities. His refusal first to join the Communist Party and later to work as a KGB informant was punished with banishment to menial work as a concierge and night watchman.[121]

The prime concern of the TB focuses on the citizenship issue, even after the adoption of the citizenship law. In accordance with this programmatic emphasis, the party defines the unsatisfactorily resolved citizenship question as the most burning issue of Latvian politics. This conflict dimension is seen as dominant over other political cleavages. 'Citizenship is a basis for every national state. Unless the citizenship question is resolved as we wish, it is impossible to implement any economic programme in the interests of the Latvian people.' Political opponents label the TB as a radical nationalistic party pursuing a discriminatory policy toward non-Latvians. The TB stresses that it does not focus on the nationality issue but on the citizenship issue, which is quite a different matter, even though the latter is sometimes misinterpreted as a national question. The approach of the TB does not differentiate between Latvians and non-Latvians; instead, it differentiates between citizens and non-citizens. Among the legal citizens of Latvia, the proportion of non-Latvians is about 25 per cent.[122]

The approach of the TB to the citizenship law stems from the recognition of the legal continuity of the Republic of Latvia, proclaimed in 1918. According to international law, the legal continuity of the Latvian state could be restored in 1991 because Latvia had been an occupied state. The implication of recognizing the occupation was that it was not necessary to create Latvia anew as an independent state. The logical consequence following from this situation is that citizenship should also be based on continuity; that is, on descendancy. Therefore, the TB recognizes as citizens only persons who were citizens of Latvia in 1940 as well as their descendants. Furthermore, the TB refers to the Geneva Convention of 1949 which declares that the occupying state has no right to move its population to the occupied state. If that has nevertheless happened, the occupying state must remove all its civil population in the case that the occupation ceases.[123]

The TB has set forth the elimination of the occupation and colonialization as well as their consequences. In other words, it wants to promote the repatriation of the colonialists. As a first step, the TB demands the immediate departure of the demobilized militarists of the occupation army and their families. In this connection, it criticizes sharply the prevailing Law on Aliens for legalizing the status of the retired Soviet army officers. From the perspective of the TB, civil occupants are economic victims who were artificially converted into a cosmopolitan mass without any ethnic consciousness. Civil occupants may be issued wih an interim residence permit of up to five years. However, the state must stop granting naturalization to people who arrived in Latvia during its occupation. Using political and economic means, it should organize a process for repatriation of those civilians who were transported illegally to the territory of Latvia during the occupation. The aim of a strict citizenship policy is 'to ensure the survival and flourishing of the Latvian nation in a national, judicial and economically developed state'.[124]

The conspicuous emphasis on the citizenship question is reflected in the economic and social policies advocated by the TB. One could say that the citizenship policy conditions all other spheres of the party's policy which are subordinated to the issue with the highest priority, the protection of the Latvian nation. Many concrete proposals in economic and social fields are linked with citizenship in the way that serves the interests of the Latvian citizens. The following points from the pre-electoral programme of the TB are illustrative in this regard. The pro-Russian Equal Rights Party objects fiercely to the idea of providing social benefits only to one part of the population: 'If one speaks about social guarantees without mentioning equal rights, one is in the realm of national socialism.'[125]

1. The pension system should be differentiated. Citizens of Latvia should be entitled to full service pensions for the entire period of employment; non-citizens should be paid only for the period worked in Latvia.
2. The state should ensure a free health service for needy Latvian citizens.
3. A national fund should be set up for the support of young and large Latvian families.
4. Latvian citizens should take precedence over non-citizens in recruitment. If two applicants (a citizen and a non-citizen) have the same qualifications, the citizen must be employed. Social tax paid by employers for employees must be indexed so that the employer pays less tax for a citizen employed than for a non-citizen. The purpose of these measures is to provide jobs for citizens.
5. Entrepreneurship must be organized so that citizens of Latvia will be protected. Non-citizens may continue participating in business but they should not be allowed to own big business companies as major shareholders. The majority of shares should always remain in the hands of citizens. Presently all economic values are in the hands of illegal immigrants whose stay has been legalized under the pressure of Russia.
6. Citizens as well as juridical persons of the former occupant states should be denied the right to own land in Latvia.[126]

The TB is in favour of market-oriented economic reforms and a market economy based on competition and private property. Its general position on economic policy does not differ so drastically from that of Latvia's Way, the Latvian National Conservative Party or the Farmers' Union that it would impede cooperation within the same government coalition, although the economic policy advocated by the TB is more cautious than that of the most rigorous liberal reformers, such as Latvia's Way. The TB may be radical and strongly rightist on the citizenship question, but it is not particularly radical or rightist on economic policy. The liberals classify it as slightly leftist in this area. The TB rejects both ultimate market liberalism and state capitalism and, instead, seeks a proper balance between these two extremes. In other words, it stands for a 'balanced economic system'.[127] Moreover, economic principles alone do not guide the decision-making of the TB in many questions related to economic reform, but rather the political aspects referred to earlier often play a predominant role.

The TB stands for reducing state involvement in the economy. The responsibilities of the state must be limited to strategic planning and to the creation of a functioning economic space. The task of the state is not to regulate the everyday activities of enterprises: state orders must be placed with private producers. Neither should the state rely on direct sectoral interventions in any branches of industry. Except in the area of agriculture, subsidies are not generally acceptable. In spite of these basic principles of liberal economy, the role of the state in the economy remains more pronounced in the programme of the TB than in the respective versions of the distinctly liberal parties. The TB wants to preserve a state monopoly in some areas where it exists only on paper today. Fast privatization of state enterprises is not necessary in such sectors as energy, water supply and ports. Moreover, the TB wants to bring the privatization process under a stricter state control, instead of freeing all operations and leaving them to market forces. The state must take the lead in privatization and exercise utmost care in precluding the waste of state assets.[128]

The TB stresses the necessity of accelerating privatization in the interests of Latvian citizens. The defence of the interests of Latvian citizens is related to the desire to introduce more state control in the implementation of privatization. The authorities should check the background of bidders in order to prevent property from falling into the wrong hands. The TB rejects the idea that the state should concentrate on privatizing unprofitable enterprises in the first place, while postponing the privatization of profitable companies in order to get revenue from their profits. Privatization is not the instance where the state should try to fill its empty pockets. Part of the funds acquired through privatization can be used for paying compensation to the private owners for any losses incurred. The TB is one of the most vocal parties championing restitution. It demands that unfair restrictions on the rights of former owners must be lifted.[129]

Foreign investments should be directed toward the establishment of infrastructure in such areas as energy, oil refining and aviation. In addition, priority should be given to such foreign investments which help in eliminating the consequences of the occupation. For instance, investors who build accommodation for those immigrants who would like to leave Latvia are welcomed by the TB. Foreign ownership of land is rejected. The TB was the main force in Parliament opposing the establishment of a free land market.[130]

The TB supports a strong lats policy. It is against a devaluation of the national currency. According to the party leader, a comparison of pros and cons reveals that a devaluation of the lats would foster Latvian exports but the export promotion would be the sole positive effect. It should also be noted that state enterprises in their present shape are not capable of exporting. The situation will be different after the privatization process is completed. Now devaluation would only raise the prices of imports, including the price of energy, raw materials and foreign technology. This would lead to negative consequences: the funds would be deposited in foreign currency accounts, which would further depreciate the value of the lats and raise interest rates. These funds would not benefit production. The currency policy advocated by the TB can be understood in the light of its general goal-setting. The party emphasizes the necessity of reducing inflation, of encouraging decline in interest rates and of facilitating long-term credit.[131]

The principles of taxation outlined in the electoral platform of the TB contain many elements common to all political parties. Even the central idea is universal: in order to be able to reduce tax rates, it is necessary to put in place an effective tax collection system which is difficult to evade but which is convenient for a tax-payer. To restrict the possibilities for avoiding taxes, deals with cash money must be limited and the circulation of cash money must be brought under control. For the most part, the TB agrees with the present taxation system. It sees the problems as being in the implementation of the tax laws rather than in the laws per se. An exception is the social tax law. According to the TB, the proportions paid by the employer and employee should be changed to the advantage of the employer.[132]

The approach to agricultural policy rests on the view that agriculture does not mean merely food production. It is the only source of livelihood for rural people. Therefore, agricultural policy includes functions of social, regional and environmental policy, as well. It is necessary to support rural areas and farming population with subsidies, cheap loans and protective tariffs. The intention of protecting agriculture is to keep people in rural areas and to encourage the supply of Latvia's own products to the domestic market. However, supportive measures have to take into account both the interests of the national economy and those of consumers. Latvia is also compelled to adjust to the agricultural policy of the EU in order to be in a good position for joining it. The state should set annual quotas for the state purchases of farm products (e.g. for the army, schools, hospitals) and fix the prices of these purchases over a period of three years. The form of production in agriculture must rely on family farming, even when the price of splitting up of collective farms is making them too small to be productive. When realizing a land reform, it is not possible to preserve large units without abandoning restitution and privatization. The creation of a land market will lead to a competitive size of farms in the future.[133]

In foreign trade policy, the TB wants to make Latvia economically independent of Russia, to promote cooperation between the Baltic states and to facilitate Latvia's return to Europe. In the first place, Latvia should orientate itself toward the Nordic, Baltic and West European countries in seeking trade as well as other partnerships. The integration of Latvia into the European Union must occur in a step-by-step fashion – not abruptly – to avoid disturbances to Latvia. Full membership should be preceded by a four- to five-year-long transition period during which Latvia's legislation will have been harmonized with EU legislation and society should be prepared for the keen standards of competition in the common market. [134]

THE LATVIAN NATIONAL CONSERVATIVE PARTY (LNNK)

The Latvian National Independence Movement is one of the oldest political organizations in Latvia. As its name suggests, the Latvian National Independence Movement was established to restore the independence of the Republic of Latvia, proclaimed on 18 November 1918, as well as the rights of the Latvian citizens. It was largely responsible for persuading the Popular Front to come out in favour of a pro-independence course in June 1989. Although the Latvian National Independence Movement started to operate as early as July 1988, it was converted into a political party only in June 1994. On that occasion, it also changed its name to the Latvian National Conservative Party (*Latvijas Nacionali Konservativa partija*), while still keeping to the old well-known abbreviation LNNK. Before the 6th Saeima elections, the LNNK joined in an electoral coalition with the Latvian Green Party (*Latvijas Zala partija*) but the coalition did not turn out to be successful. For the small Green Party, it was of vital importance to find a bigger coalition partner as it was predictable from the very beginning of the pre-electoral campaign that it would not surpass the 5 per cent threshold on its own. The Green Party was not represented in the 5th Saeima due to a barrier preventing the participation of small splinter groups in Parliament, because it had received only 1.2 per cent of votes in the previous elections.[135]

A coalition between the Greens and the National Conservatives may strike Western observers as odd at first sight but a closer look at the history of the Green Party makes the alliance understandable. In the 1980s, the nascent national consciousness found its first expression under the guise of an environmental movement. Toward the end of the Soviet reign, environmental clubs rose in importance, attracting widespread support among the Latvian population. Simultaneously, the character of the clubs changed from a non-political ecological movement to a disguised opposition movement against the Soviet Union. The environmental movement offered a legal possibility to be in opposition to the Soviet empire, as the Soviet policy paid hardly any attention to the protection of environment. The approach of the Latvian environmentalists rested on a wider concept of environment than a strictly ecological definition; the clubs were set up to defend the environment of the Latvian nation. Ultimately, the environmental movement gave rise to the Popular Front and the Latvian National Independence Movement. The Green Party itself, registered in January 1990, took an active part in the struggle for independence. Because of this extraordinary background, the Latvian Green Party differs from the West European Green Parties in many respects. The Latvian Greens are conservative rather than leftist. In the citizenship question, they stand very close to the LNNK.[136]

In addition to the electoral coalition with the Green Party, the LNNK signed a resolution together with the Farmers' Union, the Christian Democratic Union and Latgale's Democratic Party in which these five parties announced to jointly form a coalition government after the 6th Saeima elections, if the electorate gave them the necessary mandate. Fatherland and Freedom was encouraged to participate in the eventual government coalition, even though it did not belong to the signatories of the agreement. If that were not enough to get a majority, the reasoning went on, cooperation with Latvia's Way should be considered seriously but only as the last choice. The order of preference for partners was clear in the LNNK: the other National Bloc parties were preferred to Latvia's Way. The National Bloc parties share for the most part similar views both on the citizenship issue and on the guidelines of economic policy. There are some minor differences, for example between the LNNK and the Farmers' Union in farm policy, but they are conceived as being surmountable in view of the national need to form a strong nationally oriented government. In contrast, cooperation with the Socialist Party, Saimnieks, the Unity Party and the Siegerist Party is rejected on account of their leftist orientation.[137]

The LNNK defines itself as a national conservative party, referring to two aspects in its ideology: 'We are conservative in our thinking and we are for the Latvian national.' Among the foreign sister parties, the LNNK has the strongest allies among the British and Norwegian Conservatives. Compared with Fatherland and Freedom (the other national conservative party in Latvia), the LNNK is less radical, less principled, more pragmatic and more flexible, although the premises of policy are essentially the same in both parties, especially on the citizenship question. The constituencies of the LNNK and the TB are very similar, which has caused shifts in electoral support resulting from voters' mobility between the parties. Many rank-and-file members of the LNNK participated in the campaign organized by the TB for collecting signatures for the citizenship referendum. The forces behind the LNNK are, however, more heterogenous than those behind the TB. Indeed, the LNNK has two wings: the conservative wing is inclined to cooperation with the TB, whereas the liberal wing has sympathies toward Latvia's Way.[138] When the LNNK decided to merge with the TB, some of the liberal LNNK politicians joined the new Reform Union, because they could not accept the idea of belonging to the TB.

The LNNK does not approve the present citizenship law but it did not raise this issue in its pre-electoral campaign as emphatically as the TB. In general, the political profile of the LNNK is more diversified than that of the TB. The citizenship question no longer plays a dominant role in the political platform of the LNNK. Despite the diminished attention, the LNNK has not totally given up its demand that the citizenship law should be tightened. According to the citizenship policy advocated by the LNNK, the extent to which citizenship rights are admitted to non-Latvians should be related to the number of Latvian nationals at any given time. The proportion of ethnic Latvians should never fall below 73 per cent of the citizens. Hence, the size of the naturalization quotas should be made dependent on the per centage share of Latvian nationals. If the number of ethnic Latvians increased, the number of citizenships granted to non-Latvians could go up as well. The LNNK rejects the idea that everyone who has lived in Latvia for a certain period is eligible to obtain the citizenship. If every resident is granted the citizenship, Latvia will become a very troubled country. History has proven in most cases that a country cannot escape civil unrest – which may lead to a civil war in the worst case – if almost one half of the citizens belong to a separate ethnic group. To protect the position of the Latvian language, the LNNK suggests that education in the instruction of the state language alone should be financed from the budget.[139]

The economic policy of the LNNK remains very close to that of Latvia's Way. In theory at least, it tries to keep some distance from Latvia's Way but practice reveals that its approach to economic problems is almost identical to Latvia's Way's policy. The LNNK used to be a supportive rather than fighting opposition in the 5th Saeima so that the party was classified as standing close to the ruling coalition.[140]

The LNNK claims to pursue conservative economic policy based on three main principles: (1) the private initiative of the individual, (2) lessened state interference in people's personal affairs, and (3) the responsibility of the individual for his own welfare. This highly individualistic approach confronts forcibly the socialist system by rejecting the state as a social safeguard, empowered with manifold welfare functions. It relieves the state of most social responsibilities, except for a limited responsibility for the poor, the old and the unemployed. Accordingly, the LNNK rejects state involvement in the economy. The party stands for a free market economy without hesitation. The government should simply put into place the rules of the game – that is, provide the proper legislation for a market economy – while leaving the rest to freely functioning market forces. There is no need for any state regulation in national economy. The only exceptions to this rule are certain specifically defined sectors which cannot survive without the government's support. One such sector is Latvia's underdeveloped agriculture. In these exceptional cases, the state should set the objectives of a development plan and arrange financial assistance to entrepreneurs working in these sectors.[141]

State ownership in industry must be reduced to a minimum. The policy implemented in the UK serves as a good model in this respect. The state could maintain a strong position in some key industries but that would not necessarily mean a majority holding. A minority position in a joint venture with private investors would suffice. As the value of the company later rises, the state could sell off its share and, thus, create a larger increase of funds. Privatization is a corollary to the aim for minimal state ownership in the economy. The LNNK is in favour of speeding up the privatization process but at the same time it envisages restructuring prior to privatization, if it appears to be beneficial in a given situation. Both speed and maximization of the state revenue should be taken into consideration with privatization.[142]

The LNNK supports consistent economic reforms, stringent macroeconomic stabilization and a non-deficit national budget. It stands for stable monetary and currency policies as well as for the independence of the Bank of Latvia in determining these policies. It is unconditionally committed to maintaining the present value of the currency and does not accept a devaluation of the lats under any circumstances. A devaluation would increase inflation with the result that everybody, exporters included, would be worse off afterwards. Another counter-argument against devaluation is that there are funds available in the economy but these funds are not invested in production.[143]

Tax reductions could be financed by two means: by improving the system of tax collection and by hardening penalties for those who do not pay taxes. The LNNK would computerize all departments and border transit points to make the supervision easier. The lowering of the social security tax would be accompanied by a redistribution of the tax burden between the employer and the employee according to a 50:50 principle so that each would pay half of the imposed tax. Reductions in export-import tariffs would cover agricultural tariffs, too.[144]

The LNNK regards foreign investments as an essential factor in the recovery of the Latvian economy. Although foreign investments are of vital importance to Latvia, Latvians must not be subordinated into the position of slaves in their own country. Therefore, the limits on foreign ownership in enterprises must be defined very carefully. G24 credits should be used for the improvement of the infrastructure especially in those areas which serve the transit trade, because Latvia should become a transit country. Export promotion should not concentrate one-sidedly on extending the bulk of exports but the degree of working up should also be raised to increase the value of export articles. Rather than ship raw timber at a low price Latvia should develop its plywood industry and furniture manufacturing. Prospective sectors should be promoted by tax incentives and by the offer of low-cost credit from the government. In view of the balanced regional development, the state should take care that industries do not concentrate solely in Riga.[145]

In the field of agricultural policy, the LNNK wants to hasten the completion of land reform. It criticizes Latvia's Way for cutting the resources that were devoted to the development of the land registration facilities. The land registration system is a necessary prerequisite for the establishment of a real estate market. In supporting agriculture, the government should rely on subsidies rather than on customs tariffs. However, there are also forces in the LNNK who suggest introducing import quotas for agricultural products in order to protect the domestic market. In addition to financial support, the government should provide advisory services offering information as to how farmers can increase their productivity. Farmers should specialize in their production and seek subsidiary sources of income in forestry, farm tourism or food processing plants. Special attention should be devoted to the development of food processing industries with the help of low-cost credits.[146]

The LNNK hopes that Latvia will be a member of the European Union in the year 2000. It stresses the necessity to harmonize Latvian legislative acts and quality standards with those of the EU. At the same time, it emphasizes the importance of regional cooperation among the Baltic states and the Nordic countries.[147]

THE CHRISTIAN DEMOCRATIC UNION

The Latvian Christian Democratic Union (*Latvijas Kristigo Demokratu savieniba* – (KDS) was founded in 1990. It entered the 6th Saeima elections in a coalition with the Farmers' Union and Latgale's Democratic Party. The aim is to form a permanent coalition with the Farmers' Union after the fashion of the Christian Democratic Union/Christian Social Union (CDU/CSU) in Germany, provided that the cooperation in the 6th Saeima develops propitiously. The motivation behind the eventual coalescence is to bring the Christian Democratic ideas into the context of a big people's party. What unites the KDS and the Farmers' Union is the common emphasis on lawfulness and responsibility for the social sphere.[148]

Despite a basic agreement on the general guidelines of policy, the programmes of the other National Bloc parties contain some elements which contradict the principles of the KDS. In the case of the TB, the difference lies in the approach to the citizenship law. The KDS considers the TB too extreme in this regard. The LNNK, on the other hand, is seen as too liberal in its free market ideology which does not sufficiently take social responsibilities into consideration. Saimnieks is an outcast in the eyes of the KDS. The KDS regards Saimnieks as a democratically unacceptable force because the leadership in this party is alleged to be in the hands of the former KGB and CP people. The KDS has severe doubts about their trustworthiness: 'It is entirely uncertain for whom they will work, what their fundamental values are and whether they will keep their promises.'[149]

As its name already suggests, the KDS identifies with the West European Christian Democratic parties.[150] It also has contacts with the Conservative parties in Norway and Denmark. Within this reference group, it is the German CDU that has served most clearly as a model for the Latvian Christian Democrats in inspiring their ideological platform. Following the pattern of the German CDU, the KDS tries to make a synthesis of free market liberalism, Christian social ethics and respect for traditional values, i.e. conservatism. The KDS believes that a socially responsible market economy combined with Christian values provides the best premises for the restoration of a democratic state. Conservativism does not mean to the KDS that the party would stubbornly stick to some outdated principles without facing the actual problems of the modern world which simply did not exist 50 years ago. Instead, one has to be open to the realization of new ideas while at the same time being able to retain the useful things from the past.[151]

What differentiates the KDS most distinctly from other Latvian parties is a manifest formulation of the fundamental moral values underpinning the party programme. The chairman of the party, Paulis Klavins, puts it as follows: 'Other parties give simply action programmes of how to solve practical problems but they do not say who they are. We find it very important to explain in the first place who we are and what our fundamental values are so that everybody can decide whether we are acceptable or not.' The fundamental platform of the KDS is rooted in the 'Christian understanding of man's responsibility before God ... The political programme is not directly made from Christian doctrines of different denominations but the Christian belief gives the specific foundation of ethical responsibility for the fulfillment of common tasks.' The KDS aspires to restore the traditional European moral values in people's everyday life and to replace the spiritual degradation left by atheistic indoctrination with a new spirituality.[152] The religious emphasis is clearly recognizable in the discourse of the party programme.

The secular cornerstones of the KDS's programme can be grouped into three clusters: (1) law and order, (2) the dignity of human life, and (3) free enterprise and market-conforming legal framework. The first point refers to the need to create the conditions for a *Rechtsstaat* and to bring order into the legislative work in Parliament. Two aspects should be considered in this connection. On the one hand, lawful order is the prerequisite for a functioning economy and, thus, for prosperity. On the other hand, unless lawful order is established in the economic sphere, the state will not be able to meet its social responsibilities. The state authority is responsible for providing social security for those who are not able to take care of themselves, like the old, the invalids or the orphans. The dignity of human life means that everybody has the equal right to live up to a standard which allows an individual dignity. The Christian love for one's neighbour calls for solidarity, that is, for assisting the weak who lack the sufficient mental or physical resources to be able to survive under the conditions of free competition.[153]

The strong pro-life position of the KDS is manifested in the party's concrete priority setting. For instance, the KDS holds that the state should not assume massive cultural projects to be forwarded as long as it is incapable of taking care of life. It reminds voters that 80 per cent of the Latvian population lives at the minimum level of subsistence. Another proposition recommends the dissolution of the army in its present form. Military forces should not be developed after the pattern of large Western countries because such a strategy cannot work in Latvia's geopolitical conditions. Instead of spending money on expensive weapon systems, Latvia should adopt a defence strategy based on guerrilla tactics and modern communication techniques. In this way the state could save money for channelling into social welfare. Furthermore, the KDS draws attention to the 'robbery' committed by the state. When the USSR ceased to exist, the pension funds disappeared with the result that retiring workers lost their savings. Latvia should make an issue of this injustice at an international level. A certain proportion of the international aid to Russia and Eastern Europe could be allotted to the restoration of pension funds.[154]

The KDS understands that economic growth is the only way to assure the well-being of society as a whole. The economic system must be organized according to market principles so that free enterprise constitutes the basic unit in the economy. The enterprise structure should consist of small and medium-sized enterprises whose emergence could be promoted by enabling them access to low-cost credit. It is not the task of the state to engage in ordinary everyday business. The state should only prepare a favourable framework for private economic activity through legislation and tax policy. Wise tax laws are not greedy: they do not suppress embryonic business but give young enterprises time to prosper from two to three years. That is to say, jobs should take precedence over the immediate tax revenue. In general, job creation holds one of the highest priorities in the economic platform of the KDS.[155]

The KDS accepts no state ownership in the economy. In its view, the waste of government funds on the subsidization of state enterprises is inexcusable. There is no sense in keeping unprofitable enterprises under state control, when they keep on accumulating debts for the state. The KDS complains that Latvians do not understand the true meaning of privatization. The common attitude holds that, 'If something belongs to the state, we as a people are its owners. As soon as we give it away we give away something that is ours.' According to the KDS, the state should get rid of its property as quickly as possible. A private owner working with the property contributes to economic recovery more than anything else. The state should try to maximize its income through the results of private activity rather than through profit from the sale of state enterprises.[156]

Special attention in the programme of the KDS is devoted to restitution in the rural areas. 'Taking into consideration man's natural rights to property, it is possible that Latvian citizens' rights to property, which were destroyed by the Soviet power, are to be justly renewed.' At the same time, the KDS underscores that the interests of the previous owners have to be harmonized with those of the current users in order to ensure the efficient use of the cultivated land without any interruptions. 'A pattern of agreement with the user of the area upon how to continue this use for a certain period of time is to be provided in such cases in which the land is used for agricultural production or other kinds of business undertaking and in which the rightful owner does not want to continue that production or business.' The KDS is ready to allow the foreign ownership of land on condition that the land is not used for speculative purposes. To prevent the speculation with land, Latvia should follow the German pattern. Land could be sold only to investors who commit themselves to definite projects which are bound with a certain number of employees. The responsibility for the sale of land should be delegated to local communities which would get an opportunity to improve their employment situation through these agreements.[157]

The dissolution of collective farms was an inevitable step in the process of breaking away from the Soviet system but it was a very harmful development because it meant a return to the agricultural structure of the 1920s. The KDS recommends that many small farmers could specialize in gardening or biological cultivation with an eye to Central European markets. The KDS wishes to preserve the traditional Latvian landscape and to prevent the depopulation of the countryside. The KDS demands the protection of the agricultural sector until Latvian agriculture reaches a normal level of development, since agriculture is subsidized in Western countries, too.[158]

The KDS disputes the negative side-effects of the strong lats. In its view, other factors contribute more to the living standard than the value of the national currency. However, the party does not belong to the sworn protectors of the strong currency. It does not exclude the alternative of a slight devaluation: a small devaluation might not do much damage as long as it does not endanger anti-inflationary policies. The KDS supports the tight monetary policy of the previous governments. In other respects, the KDS is not so satisfied with their economic policy. It accuses the Gailis government of dealing irresponsibly with money and of being unable to establish a transparent system of laws. One consequence of this almost criminal negligence was the banking crisis. Another manifestation was the uncontrolled use of foreign loans. Foreign loans were wasted by using them for eating and heating or by distributing them to insolvent, unserious companies which disappeared after having received the money. The state should borrow money from abroad only to the extent it is able to ensure the proper use of these credits.[159]

The KDS agrees with the criticism according to which Latvia's Way neglected the development of industry while putting too much emphasis on trade and finance. As a consequence, the population got poorer and poorer. The utilization of the transit routes to Russia is, of course, very important but transit trade cannot provide the main source of income.[160]

The KDS stands for Latvia's membership in the EU. Before joining the EU, however, the Baltic states should agree on a common economic border. The KDS prefers the intensification of economic relations with Latvia's immediate neighbours, the Nordic countries and Germany.[161]

The KDS regards the citizenship law as a reasonable compromise. The crucial point is the manner in which the law is put into practice: how strictly or leniently local authorities apply it. The KDS criticizes the implementation of the citizenship law for unjustified severity, which has unnecessarily obstructed the naturalization process. Latvians must learn to live with large minorities. The KDS acts to avoid any national animosity or ethnic discrimination and to integrate loyal non-Latvians into Latvian society. Ethnic minorities are entitled to cultural autonomy. To secure the survival of the Latvian identity and culture, the Latvian language must be the official language of the state.[162]

THE FARMERS' UNION

The Latvian Farmers' Union (*Latvijas Zemnieku savieniba* – LZS) originates from the first republic. The party was established in 1917 for the first time, and it used to be the most influential right-wing party in the interwar period. It was led by Karlis Ulmanis, the many times nominated prime minister and from 1934 the dictator of Latvia. Today the presidential power is again in the hands of the Farmers' Union but by virtue of the result of a democratic election. President Guntis Ulmanis is not only a member of the Farmers' Union, he is also Karlis Ulmanis's great nephew. The Farmers' Union revived its activities in 1991, first as an agrarian faction within the Popular Front and later as a separate political party. It participated as a junior partner in the government formed by Latvia's Way after the 5th Saeima elections. After eleven months – that is, in July 1994 – the LZS suddenly withdrew its three ministers from the coalition which led to the resignation of the Birkavs government. In leaving the government, the LZS was protesting against the liberal tariff policy advocated by Latvia's Way. It could not accept that Latvia's Way had rejected its demand for the imposition of higher tariffs on imported farm products. Farmers' Union representatives accused that this rejection of the tariff hike was merely the latest violation by Latvia's Way of the coalition agreement to support Latvian agriculture.[163]

The Farmers' Union entered the 6th Saeima elections in coalition with the Christian Democratic Union and Latgale's Democratic Party. The coalition agreed officially on cooperation with the LNNK by signing a document on the formation of a joint government after the elections. The coalition also expressed its willingness to cooperate with the TB. The LZP distances itself from parties that it considers extremist, such as the Socialist Party and the Siegerist Party. Competition over the same votes evokes the rejection of the Unity Party, as well. In seeking contacts with other agrarian parties abroad, the LZS has established the most active relations with the Swedish Centre Party.[164]

The LZS defines itself as a centrist party whose ideological position is located between liberals and social democrats. In economic policy the LZS advocates liberal ideas, whereas in social affairs its approach is similar to social democratic welfare policies. It stands for a state welfare system and tripartite collective bargaining in the labour market after the pattern of the Nordic countries. There is only one exception to its generally liberal stance on economic questions, namely the demand for support for the rural community. The LZS insists on taking responsibility for the country people. In its terminology, the party avoids consciously using the more restrictive expression 'agriculture' since agriculture constitutes only a part of the wider concept embracing the whole rural community. Furthermore, the LZS denies being an exclusively agrarian party which would be dedicated to defend only the interests of farmers. On the contrary, it tries to build an image as a people's party or as a catch-all party after the pattern of its Nordic counterparts. 'Rural issues do not have a priority in our party programme. They only constitute an important part of it. Many other issues rank at the same high level in our goal-setting.' Yet the fact remains that the LZS draws its support mainly from farmers as well as from the rural population at large.[165]

The LZS considers agriculture an integral component of Latvia's economy and a small farm a basic unit of Latvia's agriculture. The party gave its unconditional support to the breakdown of the collective farms of the Soviet era and the return of farmland confiscated by the Soviet authorities to its rightful owners. Now it argues that the country's economic self-sufficiency is tied to its ability to produce agricultural products and to offer them at fair prices to the population. Latvia does not need agricultural imports, which means that the domestic market must be protected from foreign dumping prices. Imported farm products are not cheap because of low production costs but rather because of the export subsidies paid by the neighbouring countries. Therefore, it is justified that Latvia subsidizes its agriculture likewise. The subsidies should be directed to the improvement of the quality of agricultural production, for instance, to the breeding of high-quality cattle. The subsidies also have a wider function in the maintenance of the rural community, not just agriculture. The Nordic countries offer useful examples for Latvia as to how a reasonable rural policy can be realized. Each country has its special strength within this field from which Latvia could learn: Sweden's agricultural policy and environmental protection, Denmark's intensive cultivation, Finland's regional planning and Norway's rural development.[166]

Interest in regional policy is a natural concomitant of the party's rural orientation. The LZS considers it important to foster sustainable development of all regions by means of decentralization. Decentralization should include the tax system so that taxation could be used efficiently as an instrument in the development of local communities. In the view of the LZS, centralization is too strong in the prevailing system where most taxes are state taxes that are collected in a centralized way. It proposes that all major taxes should be divided between the state and the municipality. The LZS is dissatisfied with the principles of taxation in other respects, too. Tax policy should be based on patriotic considerations. Moreover, the LZS wants to introduce a progression in the taxation so as to meet the objectives of social policy better. In any case, it is necessary to increase the efficiency of the tax collection.[167]

The LZS does not accept direct state interventionism in the economy, but it insists on more regulation and statutory control over the markets. Wild, unrestrained markets, i.e. *laissez-faire* capitalism, will lead to unpredictable consequences. For instance, the government should tighten its hand on the supervision of banks and the management of state enterprises. Correspondingly, privatization should be realized under strict state control. The authorities should make sure that the buyer will pay a price corresponding to the real value of the property. In addition, the LZS proposes some legislative changes to accelerate privatization. The state should allocate money for the purpose of speeding up the privatization process, especially the privatization of land. It is often the bureaucratic barriers that constrain the proceeding of privatization, as the case of the deficient land registers indicates. The distinctive feature in the approach of the LZS is that it divides property into two categories which it treats differently, namely into rural and urban property. Its attitude toward foreign ownership varies according to the type of property. As far as business undertakings are concerned, it does not make any difference who the owner of the company is if the jobs can be secured. In contrast, the party does not permit the sale of rural land to foreign physical and legal persons; the ownership of land should be confined solely to the citizens of Latvia. Although the LZS gives priority to private ownership, it does not fear the existence of state-owned companies along with the private sector, if monopoly control is functioning adequately. Moreover, the party reminds liberals that 40 per cent of the forests belonged to the state in the prewar era. Comparable state ownership might be acceptable today, as well.[168]

The main task of economic policy-making is to end the acute crisis in the economy. The government must continue stringent stabilization as well as follow a stable currency policy because Latvia needs neither an inflationary spiral nor a vicious circle of repetitious devaluations. However, the currency rate should be set at a realistic level so that the value of the lats would reflect fluctuations in the values of the big currencies, such as the dollar. Instead of being 'super-fixed', the Bank of Latvia should let the lats float. The present overvalued rate distorts the balance of payments.[169]

The LZS points out two priority sectors in the economy which it suggests may have good prospects in the future: transit trade and high tech industries. The special emphasis on education in the party programme is related to the latter vision. The educational system should be state financed. The creation of a wide middle class is crucial for social stability. Similarly, the objective of the citizenship law is to advance stability in the country. The LZS agrees with the current citizenship law.[170]

The LZS sets as a key goal the integration of Latvia into the European economic structures, while simultaneously preserving the country's national identity. It stresses the necessity of achieving a closer integration amongst the Baltic states before they enter the European Union. It also stands for more intensive cooperation with the Baltic Sea countries. The final decision to join the EU must be confirmed by a referendum. The LZS invites foreign investors from both the West and the East, and particularly from the Far East. Yet the state must not lose control over investment activities.[171]

LATVIA'S WAY

Latvia's Way (*Latvijas Cels* – LC) emerged as a pre-electoral association for the 5th Saeima elections in 1993. Well-known, popular politicians who had been active members of the Popular Front, the *Satversme* faction or the World Federation of Free Latvians united in this electoral association. The *Satversme* faction was a breakaway group of the Popular Front formed in the autumn of 1991 by the right-wing deputies who had supported the restoration of the Republic of Latvia, proclaimed in 1918. They called themselves the *Satversme* faction to underscore their desire to uphold the authority of the *Satversme* (the constitution of the interwar Republic of Latvia). In spite of some differences in political views, the *Satversme* faction emphasized its loyalty to the Popular Front and regarded itself as a political ally rather than a competitor of the Popular Front. The World Federation of Free Latvians was an umbrella organization for the Latvian communities living in exile who wanted to restore the independent Latvian state. After Latvia regained its independence, the World Federation of Free Latvians committed itself to helping to shape Latvia into a democratic and economically prosperous state. It organized various aid and expertise-sharing programmes. It encouraged Latvians abroad not only to vote in the elections but also to run for seats in Parliament. A further force behind Latvia's Way was Club 21. Club 21 was founded in late 1991 by 21 people with political clout, wealth and business acumen. The club is considered to be highly elitist and it is compared to the Masonic Lodge. New members can join the club only on invitation and their candidacy must be approved by the members. What is said at the meetings of the club is not publicized. A notable feature of the first Latvia's Way government was that about half of the cabinet ministers, Prime Minister Birkavs included, were members of Club 21.[172]

The great diversity of LC's membership – some members had made their careers in the Soviet Latvian government and the Communist Party (Anatolijs Gorbunovs), while others were leaders of the anti-communist Latvian organizations in the West (Gunars Meierovics) – was probably a boon at the 5th Saeima elections since it broadened the appeal of the group. Although LC did not win an absolute majority, 36 seats enabled the formation of the overwhelmingly largest and most influential faction in the Saeima. As this was not enough to ensure the smooth passage of laws, LC decided to join forces with the somewhat more right-of-centre Farmers' Union (which consisted of twelve deputies). The ruling coalition was the strongest, though not always controlling, force in the Saeima. LC's chairman Valdis Birkavs became prime minister and Anatolijs Gorbunovs was elected as chairman of the Saeima.

The Birkavs government was forced to step down, as the Farmers' Union abruptly suspended all its activities in the government and withdrew its ministers from the coalition in July 1994. The principal reasons why the uneasy coalition collapsed were fundamental differences over Latvia's economic development and particularly over agricultural policy, as well as personality conflicts between the leading spokesmen from each side. Frequent controversies over agriculture caused displays of personal animosity between Minister of Agriculture Janis Kinna (LZS), on one side, and Minister of Economy Ojars Kehris (LC) and Minister of Finance Uldis Osis (LC), on the other. The straw that broke the camel's back was the passage of the bill on tariffs.[173]

As Andrejs Krastins's (LNNK) attempt to form a new government failed, the President nominated LC's Maris Gailis, Minister of State Reforms in the departing Birkavs government, as a candidate for prime minister. The Cabinet proposed by Gailis managed to pass a vote of confidence in Parliament with the result that LC returned to power in September 1994. The minister posts were occupied predominantly by the members of LC but the government included representatives from the left-of-centre Tautsaimnieks as well as from the Farmers' Union, LC's former coalition partner. The participation of the Tautsaimnieks meant a slight transition to the left compared with the former government. Gailis himself was also classified as more socially oriented than Birkavs who had profiled as a liberal reformer. The Gailis government ruled uninterrupted until the normal formation of a post-electoral government after the 6th Saeima elections.[174]

During the months following the electoral victory in June 1993, it turned out to be necessary to broaden the party organization over the whole country in order to implement the electoral platform and to meet the standards adherent to European parties. These requirements were the reason why Latvia's Way was registered as a political party in September 1993. At its first congress in October 1994, LC decided to join the International Liberals. This fixing affirmed its self-definition as a liberal party: 'The Union Latvia's Way is a liberal party whose aim is to transform Latvia into a modern European country with free market economy, parliamentary democracy and liberalism in all spheres of life.'

However, the party programme refers to the fact that the world has become so complicated today that it can no longer be understood in the classic sense of conservative, liberal or social democratic categories. The confusion of ideas is manifested in the ideology of LC, too. Fully aware of the ideological mix, LC has included in its programme some values typical of conservative ideology. Liberal ideas are evident in the emphasis on both individual and economic freedom as well as on the individual's responsibility for himself and his family. LC defends openness, tolerance, pluralism and competitiveness. The influence of conservative ideology appears in the stress laid on the preservation of national traditions and the strengthening of family, which is defined as the foundation of a nation. LC declares that Latvia is a national state where the Latvian nation may live in harmony with its own philosophy of life, its cultural and spiritual (Christian) values. Special attention must be paid to the protection of the Latvian language, folklore and do-it-yourself projects. In parallel, cultural autonomy of the national minorities must be continuously guaranteed.[175]

LC is a moderate right-of-centre party which is located at the centre of the political spectrum. Its centrist position contributes positively to its ability to enter into political alliances with various partners. When this factor is combined with relatively large electoral support, it is no wonder that LC possesses a key role in Latvian politics. It is difficult, if not impossible, to form a government without LC. LC is prepared to cooperate with all political forces that are loyal to Latvia and support Latvia's integration into the EU. First and foremost, LC prefers a coalition with the LNNK because the programmes of the two parties are very similar. The old coalition partner Farmers' Union is another preferred partner. Cooperation with the Democratic Party Saimnieks is found acceptable, too. By contrast, LC is firmly opposed to any relations with the Siegerist Party. The LC chairman describes the Siegerist Party as 'unpredictable' and composed of 'odd leaders'. Furthermore, it is pretty obvious that there is not much ground for cooperation with the Socialist Party and the Social Democratic Party. The electoral base of LC is very diversified. The party appeals, among others, to businessmen and the middle class.[176]

LC has one of the most thoroughgoing and best-documented party programmes in Latvia. The economic strategy of LC is formulated in Latvia 2000 and Latvia 2010 reform programmes, drafted by the leading Latvian economists. LC's principles in economic policy are commonly known owing to the party's activity in the government. As a leading party in the government, it had naturally the last word to say about the design and implementation of economic reforms so that Latvia 2000 and Latvia 2010 programmes laid the foundation for the respective government programmes. LC is firmly committed to the continuation of market-oriented economic reforms. Indeed, the party is identified with the reform course and liberal economic policy. It is known as the *primus motor* of the transition and the most dedicated reformer among the Latvian parties. The reform strategy of the Latvia's Way governments is characterized as a soft shock therapy. All tools are used to create a private sector as fast as possible, but certain caution is still followed in order to avoid political shocks, strikes and demonstrations.[177]

LC stands for a socially responsible free market economy based on private ownership. The economic system aspired to resembles the German *soziale Marktwirtschaft* model. LC sees no need to increase economic regulation by the government but it considers it necessary to fortify the legislative framework controlling the markets. According to Birkavs, liberal policy means the curtailment of state regulation but simultaneously it presupposes effective control by the state. LC underscores the assertion that the state must not support any industrial sectors by direct means, such as by subsidies, but only by fostering a favourable atmosphere through legislative acts. Neither is it permissible to practise protectionism. In this connection Latvia has to take into account the EU directives. LC considers that the promotion of competition is one of the most urgent tasks. Legal provisions for effective competition should be put in place and the emergence of small and medium business should be promoted.[178]

Diversification of the economic structure is tied to substantial investments. LC wants to create a favourable business climate in order to attract foreign investors to Latvia. To maximize the inflow of foreign investments, equal business conditions must be offered to both local and foreign business. For instance, foreign investors must be allowed to purchase land both in towns and in the countryside. Foreign investments are not only of economic importance but there is also an aspect related to security policy involved. Birkavs cites Aleksanders Kirsteins (LNNK) who has said that Grozhny would not have been bombed if the Coca-Cola Company were there. While LC is unreservedly in favour of FDI, it has a cautious attitude toward foreign credits. LC believes that the policy of increasing the national debt must be contemplated very carefully. State-guaranteed credits must be directed to objects of infrastructure included in the state investment programme. State investment must be increased to 3 per cent of the gross domestic product annually.[179]

LC puts heavy emphasis on the development of banking and transit trade. The prominent role given to these sectors is derived from the geographical location of Latvia. As State Minister Olgerts Pavlovskis puts it, it would be foolish not to use this geographical advantage. Both trade and finances are very profitable, they are much easier to build than, say, heavy industry and they can absorb the surplus population which will be released from agriculture in the future. Modernization of Latvia's industrial base should concentrate on sectors that are neither energy nor material intensive but where Latvia has experience as well as a qualified labour force. LC is certain that Latvia has the potential to compete successfully in the Western market with the medium developed countries.[180]

Tax policy plays a crucial role in promoting investment in business, particularly in export branches. In order to reduce the negative effects of taxes on business, the LC government introduced a unified corporate income tax rate of 25 per cent, which is one of the lowest in Europe. New regulations for ammortization of assets are intended to stimulate the acquisition of modern technology in manufacture. It is also necessary to achieve a procedure for collecting taxes which will make it difficult to evade taxes.[181]

LC opposes a devaluation of the lats. It argues one has to keep an eye on all macroeconomic indicators simultaneously. A devaluation would just lower the standard of living without ameliorating the operational facilities of the industry. LC supports the role of the Bank of Latvia in the economy as well as the monetary policy pursued by it. It is important that the Bank of Latvia remains independent from the fluctuations of political power.[182]

LC is of the opinion that state enterprises should be privatized as fast as possible, including the large ones. LC believes that the privatization of small and medium-sized enterprises could be accelerated, if auctions were used as the chief method of privatization. The privatization of large companies is a complicated process, subject to a development concept of the enterprise, i.e. a business plan. The fate of large enterprises must be evaluated from the long-term perspective of Latvian industry. If the enterprise turns out to be in a desperate state and there is no hope of finding serious buyers, it will be closed down. The government does not plan to run bankrupt businesses just to save the jobs.[183]

LC stresses the importance of establishing market principles in all spheres of economy, including agriculture. Consequently, it has tried to do without subsidies and tariffs favouring Latvian producers. For instance, it accepted only reluctantly the idea of higher tariffs on agricultural imports. Although its long-term objectives involve a gradual marketization of agriculture, LC admits that one has to be much more careful in applying market principles to agriculture than to industry. There are two factors affecting the need to proceed at a slower pace. First, giving up farming is tied with more severe hardships than changing jobs from one factory to another. It attacks the whole family and forces relocation. Second, the percentage share of rural dwellers is so high that abrupt changes would cause insurmountable difficulties in absorbing the unemployed farmers into other branches. Despite some concessions, LC insists on the principle that agriculture must be subordinated to the development of the economy as an integrated whole and it cannot be developed at the cost of other economic sectors. It is unthinkable that agriculture would be subsidized from the state budget to achieve narrow political goals. To cite an example, when the consumption of butter is decreasing all over the world, Latvia should not pour in money to support uncompetitive butter production artificially.[184]

LC stands for the continuation of agrarian reforms related both to the privatization of farm land and the restructuring of agricultural enterprises. Strong private farms of various sizes and types must form the backbone of the production structure in the countryside. Employment in agriculture is impossible for the present number of rural dwellers. Accordingly, a significant factor in the development of the rural environment is the expansion of employment opportunities for the rural and small town population. Infrastructure projects and regional tax policies can be used to attract investment to rural regions. Special attention should be paid to forestry, fishing and tourism as well as to exportable agricultural products. The government should fix guaranteed purchasing quotas for agricultural products for the state food reserve.[185]

LC maintains that integration into the EU must guide priority setting both in foreign and domestic policies. LC is convinced that the EU membership will help to guarantee Latvia's international security. Reaching toward Europe also signifies a return to Latvia's cultural roots. However, LC accepts only the kind of integration into Europe which permits Latvia to preserve its national identity. The goal of foreign trade policy is broader than just the entering into the West European market. The CIS market should be maximally expanded as far as the level of risk remains low enough. Latvia should try to find opportunities for export to the Near East and the American continent. The main partners are still in the Baltic Sea region. LC ranks the preferable partners in the following order:

1. Baltic countries
2. Nordic countries
3. West European EU countries
4. East Central European countries (i.e. postcommunist countries)
5. Russia and other CIS countries.[186]

LC holds the middle position in the controversy over the citizenship law. The citizenship law proposed by LC was a compromise between two parts of society. All residents were not automatically granted a Latvian citizenship but they all were shown the way how to eventually obtain it. The law informs each resident about the conditions for gaining a citizenship. Citizenship will be granted individually and gradually, taking into consideration the knowledge of the Latvian language, the number of years the person has lived in Latvia, conditions in the family and merits for the benefit of Latvia. LC believes that the citizenship law ensures the development of Latvia as a national single-community state.[187]

THE PEOPLE'S MOVEMENT FOR LATVIA (SIEGERIST PARTY)

The People's Movement for Latvia, known as the Siegerist Party after its leader Joachim Siegerist, (*Tautas Kustiba Latvijai/Zigerista partija* – L) is one of the newest parties in Latvia, founded in November 1994. Joachim Siegerist was a well-known politician even before the formation of the People's Movement for Latvia. He ran for the 5th Saeima elections in the list of the LNNK. Although a LNNK candidate, he had a somewhat separate pre-electoral campaign already then because he possessed the sufficient financial means to campaign on his own. Siegerist was elected to the Saeima but there he soon came into conflict with the leadership of the LNNK. His rough-hewn style, knack of drawing controversy as well as extraordinary strokes discordant with the national conservative image made him a burden to the LNNK. Dismissed from the LNNK, Siegerist found himself as an independent deputy in Parliament. He united with a splinter group of two deputies and formed his own party in support of these deputies.[188]

The distinctive feature of the Siegerist Party is that it is identified exceptionally strongly with its leader Joachim Siegerist. One could claim it is a typical one man's party, a product of extremely personalized politics. A textual analyst would certainly pay attention to the high frequency with which Siegerist's name repeats in the pre-electoral pamphlet: 'Joachim Siegerist did ...' and 'Joachim Siegerist said ...'. The party organization seems to follow an authoritarian pattern in which all decision-making power is concentrated in the hands of the party leader. The followers' respect for the party leader verges on a personality cult. They persist in praising Siegerist's peerless achievements for the benefit of Latvia but independently they are reluctant to give any comments or interviews concerning the party platform. One deputy of the Siegerist Party characterizes 'the personal significance' of Mr Siegerist as follows:

A lot of people in Latvia are thankful to God that we have the Roman Catholic pope who is a big mental investment for Latvia's development. We [the Siegerists] suggest that Mr Joachim Siegerist is a big political investment for Latvia. Siegerist's personal role is important because he knows the market philosophy, while he represents the Western market. Many politicians in power do not profoundly understand the market philosophy.[189]

On the above-mentioned grounds, the study of the Siegerist Party cannot be separated from the vicissitudes of Siegerist's political career. Siegerist is undoubtedly the most colourful politician in Latvia who has attracted attention even in the international press. Siegerist is a German citizen who has spent most of his life in Germany. In 1992 he suddenly discovered his Latvian ancestry and made his way to Latvia to conquer the country's political scene. Siegerist claimed Latvian citizenship through his father, a German Baltic soldier who had served in the German army and had perished in Siberia under Stalin. What irritates Latvians enormously is the fact that Siegerist speaks only halting Latvian. Instead of bothering to learn the state language, he tried to handle the matters in German. His speeches in the electoral meetings were interpreted from German to Latvian. After having been elected to the Saeima in 1993, he promised to pick up the Latvian language within two months, but in the next elections his ignorance of Latvian prevented him from running for a seat. Actually, his career as a deputy had already finished earlier. He was expelled from Parliament in August 1995 for non-attendance. Parliamentary regulations allow for the annulment of mandates of deputies who miss more than half of the plenary sessions throughout the year. Siegerist was the only politician to be excluded from Parliament for failing to attend more than half of the meetings.[190]

Siegerist's track record is marred by scandals. He had made a notorious political career already in Germany where he belonged to the extreme-right German Conservative Community. In his native country, he was known for unsuccessfully trying to slander the former Chancellor Willy Brandt. In 1994, he was charged by the court of Hamburg for inciting public hatred against gypsies ('*Volksverhetzung*') and was sentenced to 18 months in prison. Yet that was not the first time that he was prosecuted for racist activity. Siegerist himself denies being an ultrarightist extremist. He responds to such accusations in a newspaper interview in which he offers a different interpretation of the events.

The roots of my image as a radical lie in my break with the German Christian Democratic Union. I left the party ranks some years ago over money being sent to the Honecker regime in East Germany. We are certainly not the party in Latvia with anti-semitic or racist tendencies. For that one should look to Le Pen's sister party Fatherland and Freedom.

Siegerist admits that he has legal problems with gypsies but for different reasons than claimed.

I am a chair of an international child fund. I saw with my own eyes Romanian gypsy women selling their babies or injuring them so that they could beg for money in the streets of German cities. I wrote articles criticizing these gypsy mothers, saying that they should be expelled from the cities and their children should be taken into state custody.

Siegerist accuses Latvia's Way of defamation: 'This [his dismissal] is the product of a campaign orchestrated by Latvia's Way.'[191]

The electoral poster of the Siegerist Party caused a stir in the autumn of 1995, because it was embellished with an enormous portrait of Stalin, and the message of the poster was misunderstood. Not only was the electoral poster sensational but also Siegerist's vote-winning strategies both in the 5th and 6th Saeima elections were unconventional. In 1993, Siegerist distributed several wagonloads of bananas to his would-be voters and organized bus transport from the countryside to the nearest polling station. In 1995, he sold sugar at an extremely low price and served free soup to the poor. He ran a permanent charitable centre in Riga which distributed free medicines and shoes to needy pensioners. Anyone receiving an aid package automatically became an affiliate of his party. The financing of these charitable activities led to official investigations in Germany. It was suspected that Siegerist had misused humanitarian aid from Germany for financing his political activities. Yet nothing could spoil Siegerist's good mood immediately after the elections. During a press conference he gave the representatives of Latvia's Way (the loser of the 6th Saeima elections) bananas for allegedly helping him in his campaign. At the time when he believed he would get nominated for Minister of Economy, he declared that he would sell off all cars belonging to the state and replace them with lorries by which he would transport humanitarian aid to the countryside (the Latvian state has put very expensive luxurious cars at the disposal of the top politicians).[192]

What makes Siegerist such an unpredictable actor on the political scene is that one never knows what rabbit he will pull out of the hat next. He does not hesitate to make a complete volte-face on his propaganda. Before the 5th Saeima elections, Siegerist played on the anti-Russian and anti-communist themes with a nationalistic flavour, but in the next electoral round he appealed to the Russian-speaking population and demanded closer ties with Russia. For instance, he boasted of having good friends among Russian politicians, mentioning particularly Grigori Yavlinski. Siegerist is a maverick, enigmatic politician and a temperamental, sharp-tongued personality who confuses his opponents with his unscrupulousness. He does not tolerate any criticism directed against him but treats his opponents as personal enemies whom he automatically labels as communists. Politicians from the mainstream parties warned that Siegerist's strong showing would introduce a wild card into Latvian politics. Siegerist's nomination in the government was feared to undermine Latvia's relations with Germany as well as to retard integration into European organizations. This problem disappeared by itself as Siegerist met with a serious accident in Italy, resulting in a neck vertebrae injury which prevented him from moving. His political opponents questioned the information saying that it may have been a mere political trick. LNNK faction head Aleksandrs Kirsteins claimed he had heard lobby talks before 'the accident statement' that 'Siegerist will blame health problems for withdrawal from the cabinet list.'[193]

The key question is whether the Siegerist Party can be classified as an anti-democratic brown-shirt party, as it is often suggested. Siegerist's radical background in German politics easily tempts one to jump to such a conclusion. Moreover, the glaring fashion in which he propagates his ideas – his style of speech-making has been compared to Goebbels's public appearances – is reminiscent of the national socialist rhetoric. Siegerist offers simple solutions and strong leadership, if people decide to follow him. He intentionally provokes controversies, ferments discontent with the government, singles out scapegoats and quarrels with the press. He fights a fierce battle against ex-communists and Bolsheviks whom he lambasts as the root cause of Latvia's ills. According to him, a change for the better has not occurred after independence because the same old communists occupy the posts in the government as in the Soviet period. All Latvian parties have communists among their ranks, which makes it impossible to cooperate with them. The main enemy to Siegerist is Anatolijs Gorbunovs, one of the leaders of Latvia's Way. In a pre-electoral edition of his party newspaper, he compared Gorbunovs to a devil responsible for deportations of Latvians. 'Communists, who served as high up as he did, served the devil.' In the same issue, Siegerist declared that 80 per cent of Latvian politicians are bandits. His party, by contrast, fights crime and corruption. The party programme proposes the establishment of a special anti-corruption unit within the police.[194]

Despite many suspicious traits, it is difficult to point out unambiguous evidence that would confirm the accusations of right-wing extremism. For example, the party programme does not contain any racist or discriminatory elements. Siegerist asserts the same point: 'I would love to see any written documents from our party or hear any speeches that lend credence to such a claim.'[195] Although the party's vote-winning methods are eccentric and its political rhetoric is brash, the actual goals in economic and social spheres hardly differ from those of any other party. Siegerist is undoubtedly an unprincipled opportunist and there is no question that his party is strongly populistic, but that still does not justify calling it a neofascist brown-shirt party. A Finnish journalist aptly likens the Siegerist Party to the Finnish protest party from the 1970s which defended the victims of the structural transformation in the countryside, pursued corrupt politicians and bureaucrats in the capital and vigorously opposed President Kekkonen[196]. To summarize, the conclusion here is that the Siegerist Party clearly represents populism but not necessarily right-wing extremism.

The Siegerist Party defines itself as a right-of-centre party. It adheres to a Christian social conservative ideology and equates itself with the Christian Social Union in Bavaria. The Christian social ethic lays the foundation for the pronounced social programme of the party. The Christian orientation was tangibly expressed in the list of the deputy candidates. Siegerist tries to paint an image of a politician who is concerned with the socially weak. 'Mr Siegerist has come here with a sense of what Latvia needs and is willing to institute policies that other politicians have shown little interest in pursuing', commends Odisejs Kostanda, a leading candidate on the For Latvia list in the last elections. The party programme is clearly geared to voters reeling from the economic dislocation brought on by market reforms. The Siegerist Party collects protest votes from the losers who have lost their trust in the established parties. The economically hard-hit areas in the countryside together with the pensioners form the core of the party's supporters. These constituencies are typically poor, less-educated people who are characterized by Siegerist's political opponents as *Lumpenproletariat*. What struck even Siegerist himself by surprise was that such a large proportion of Latvia's Russians voted for his party. The trend was particularly evident in the Catholic Latgale region.[197]

The Siegerist Party underscores the urgency of the social question, for 80 per cent of the population lives in absolutely poverty. The first duty of the government is to foster economic development and, at the given stage of development, to provide social guarantees to whatever extent it is possible. The Siegerist Party understands that the level of social security cannot be high in the present economic situation but efforts should be made to channel the few available resources to social purposes. People should be guaranteed the satisfaction of the basic needs: food, shelter, clothes, medicine and medical care. The Siegerist Party does not regard economic development and social defence as contradictory but rather as complementary tasks. Both have to do with solving everyday problems. Not only do altruistic motivations urge the establishment of a social network but also political stability as well as the continuation of reforms necessitate it. The transition to a market economy leads unavoidably to downward mobility. The hazard is then that widespread poverty induces a sharp shift to the left and the communists are returned to power. People will say that life was better under the communists. The irony is that one cannot dispute the argument because it holds true! Large, prosperous firms should be forced to participate in the costs of the transition. Social payments are more advantageous for businessmen than the alternative that the communists return to power with the consequence that they will lose everything. Siegerist's aide Egils Ziedins summarizes the approach of the party: 'Reforms must be carried out as fast as possible but people must not be forgotten during the transition phase.'[198]

In spite of its special attention to social problems, the Siegerist Party assigns the economy a key role: 'If the economy does not function properly, doctors and teachers cannot get higher salaries.' As Latvia cannot make it alone, it is essential to attract investments from abroad. Western investors bring not only capital but also experience and know-how. Therefore, the promotion of FDI is included in the main priorities of the Siegerist Party. To put this objective into practice, Siegerist inserted a large paid advertisement in *Frankfurter Allgemeine Zeitung* inviting German investors to Latvia. The Siegerist Party prefers joint ventures with Western companies or private persons to cooperation with the state structures. The profit principle must guide all activities so that they offer mutual benefit to both sides. The Siegerist Party also refers to the security policy aspect, arguing that foreign investments furnish security against Russia in the same way as bank deposits protected Switzerland during the Second World War. If Latvia has no foreign investments, Russia can do there whatever it wants. The Siegerist Party blames Latvians for underestimating the significance of foreign investments. The false attitude becomes apparent each time a foreign company enters Latvia. Immediately certain groups raise a great hullabaloo if they consider some national values or particularistic interests to be offended. Ziedins cites two illustrative examples: Lattelekom and McDonald's. In the latter case, some people complained that the hamburger restaurant is located too close to the Freedom Monument.[199]

A controversial point related to foreign investments is whether foreigners should be permitted to own land in Latvia. The Siegerist Party strongly supports the sale of land to foreigners. Hastening the establishment of a free land market is one of the priority issues of its programme. The party argues with an analogy: would you build a house on land that does not belong to you? That is to say, a prohibition against the sale of land to foreigners would seriously curb foreign investments in Latvia. Moreover, there is no shortage of land in Latvia; rather, the problem is that there is a lot of land that is utilized by nobody. The Siegerist Party advocates the model known from East Germany where the buyer is obliged to invest a certain amount of money and to provide a certain amount of jobs.[200]

The Siegerist Party is unsatisfied both with the pace and the manner in which privatization is being carried out. First, privatization proceeds too sluggishly. Second, privatization is incorrectly equated with redistribution. Instead of redistributing possibilities to make profit from the existing property, one should focus on the developmental potential inherent in the companies to be privatized. The right way is to tie privatization to investments. It is not so important how many lati the state will earn from selling a bad enterprise; it is much more essential to set the wheels turning, provide jobs and involve investments. The Siegerist Party stands for the complete privatization of industry. The only sector in which it accepts some sort of state involvement is the infrastructure serving transit trade. The state must keep control over the ports but that does not necessarily mean exclusive state ownership. Belgium provides a good example of transit policy which combines private and public capital. The party leader would like to see state television privatized in order to bring the state extra revenue and to raise the quality of programmes. Siegerist is particularly irked by the fact that state media is under the thumb of 'certain political interests', calling this 'impermissible' in a democratic state.[201]

The Siegerist Party stresses property rights and private entrepreneurship. In its view, it is not the task of the state to be involved in entrepreneurial activity. The state must only guarantee stability, provide a convenient legislative framework and create a business-friendly climate. The Siegerist Party defines its approach to economic policy as a conservative one. It adheres to the model of market economy represented by Ludwig Erhard and Margaret Thatcher because these models, according to the Siegerist Party, minimize state influence and emphasize the role of the individual. Mart Laar's Thatcherite reform strategy in Estonia is seen as a noteworthy example for Latvia. The party does not acknowledge any contradiction between its libertarian free market model, on the one hand, and its strong emphasis on social defence, on the other hand. Furthermore, the Siegerist Party supports currency policy aimed at preserving the value of the lats as stable and strong. The most urgent task in the field of economic policy is to lower tax rates dramatically. The Siegerist Party believes that the higher the taxes are the emptier the pockets of the state are. If the tax rates were put on a tolerable level, many decent Latvians would prefer to pay them to be able to sleep their nights peacefully. In the current situation they are compelled to practise tax evasion if they want to survive.[202]

Agriculture is taken as an exception to the application of market principles in the economy. If agriculture were marketized in a rush manner, there would be 100,000 unemployed in Latvia, which would threaten the country's political stability. State regulation is needed to work out the heritage of the past 50 years. Limited forms of subsidies as well as public investments in specific fields, such as linen production, may be permitted. The present tariffs on agricultural imports are also acceptable. The Siegerist Party proposes the creation of model farms up to Western standards to accelerate the reform in agriculture.[203]

The Siegerist Party envisages the prospect of Latvia becoming a bridge between the East and the West. Latvia could gain a position as an experimental laboratory or a launching point for Western firms interested in the Russian markets. First they would gather preliminary experiences in Latvia, after which they could continue to Russia. As the competition among transit countries is fierce, Latvia should quickly invest in the relevant infrastructure so as not to lose the game to its neighbours. As a defender of the country people, the Siegerist Party points out that Latvia is not just Riga.[204]

The Siegerist Party supports Latvia's integration into the EU because EU membership is a means of promoting national welfare. Simultaneously, it stresses the necessity of creating healthier links with Russia, reasoning that Latvia cannot choose its neighbours. In its view, six countries (or country groups) should be given priority when developing foreign relations:

1. the Vatican
2. Israel
3. Germany
4. the USA
5. Russia
6. the Nordic countries (less important).

The precedence of relations with Israel and the Vatican is stressed on moral grounds. Though desirable, the Siegerist Party does not believe in real chances of stimulating intense cooperation among the Baltic states due to the diversification of their national economies. Laar and Meri's press statements as well as the fish war with Estonia further deepen this pessimism.[205]

The Siegerist Party describes the current citizenship law as a reasonable compromise of all opinions. In affirming its satisfaction with the law the party speaks in conciliatory tones. All nationalities must learn to live in peace with each other. Latvia must try not to provoke Russia. The danger does not come from outside but rather from inside: the alarmingly low birth rates threaten the survival of the nation. Moreover, the Siegerist Party stresses that the nationality question belongs to the past whereas the economic question is the most burning issue at present.[206]

THE UNITY PARTY

The Latvian Unity Party (*Latvijas Vienibas partija* – LVP) was founded in 1993, but it had no visibility in Latvian politics until Alberts Kauls joined the party. In the 5th Saeima elections the Unity Party belonged to the faceless mass of insignificant petty parties that did not manage to overcome the 4 per cent barrier, but the victory in the 6th Saeima elections was rewarded with a ministerial post in the government. The success story turned out to be short-lived, as the party was dissolved in the same legislative period. Its deputies went over to Saimnieks or the Farmers' Union. The LVP's problem was that it was a single-issue party focusing almost exclusively on agriculture, while its programme in other respects was vague.[207]

The success of the LVP rested on the personal charisma of its leader Alberts Kauls. Kauls gained immense popularity in the 1980s when he was a director of Adazi, one of the largest and most prosperous collective farms in Latvia. Adazi used to be a well-led model farm which was proudly presented to foreign visitors. Kauls also served as an agricultural advisor to Mikhail Gorbachev. Despite these indisputable merits, Kauls was discredited during the struggle for Latvia's independence. He earned his notoriety when he aligned himself with the so-called Latvia's Salvation Committee, an organization hastily established by Latvia's Communist Party bosses to counter the nation's struggle for independence. The alleged Soviet organizational activity after 13 January 1991 prevented Kauls from running for Parliament. In accordance with the electoral law, persons who have been active members in the CPSU, All-Latvia Salvation Committee or in a few other Soviet organizations after 13 January 1991 are not eligible for the Saeima. A lack of tangible evidence linking Kauls to the outlawed activities led to a month-long scandalous tug-of-war over whether or not Kauls should be struck from his party's candidate list. Mutually contradictory court decisions alternated one after another. Once one court had deleted Kauls from the candidate list, another court declared null and void the earlier ruling. Observers said it was the negative coverage surrounding the deletion of Kauls from the candidate list that made him a martyr for some voters. In any event he received enormous publicity in the mass media. Kauls's formidable campaign machine completed the media circus. Kauls's frequent radio advertisements interrupted the regular radio programme every 15 minutes in the first election day.[208]

The LVP became known colloquially as the Kauls Party, reflecting the same kind of personification of politics as is evident in the Siegerist Party. Kauls was compared to Siegerist in many respects: he was labelled as a strong populistic leader who plays on the misery of the rural population, promising them abundant social benefits. Saimnieks leader Cevers said after the

6th Saeima elections that many Latvians had voted for two Santa Clauses – Kauls and Siegerist. In a Kauls-led Latvia pensions and public sector wages would increase by leaps and bounds, health care and education would be free of charge, unemployment would be drastically reduced and organized crime would be totally eliminated. The actual political objectives, going beyond plain electoral slogans, remained obscure during the pre-electoral campaign since the LVP leadership was disinclined to enter into substantial discussions.[209]

The LVP portrays itself as a rebellious protest movement against entrenched leadership which is beggaring the population. It compares itself to the Perot movement in the US and the Reform Party in Canada. The party ideology rests on the principle of social justice and on conservative moral values. In terms of the left–right continuum, the LVP considers itself a moderately left-leaning party. The confusing mix of leftist and conservative elements can be perceived in its selection of congenial parties. The LVP prefers to collaborate with Saimnieks, the Siegerist Party, Fatherland and Freedom and Harmony. The Socialist Party, Latvia's Way and the LNNK are considered parties with which the LVP wants to have nothing to do.[210] The former government party Farmers' Union is seen as a rival and is deemed accountable for the current situation in the countryside.

The leading candidate on the Unity list defines Kauls's party as a party of the 'Red Baron' composed of individuals who made their reputation in rural areas. In other words, the membership of the LVP is composed of former collective farm directors. One could claim that the LVP serves as an interest group for the high-rank leaders of Soviet agriculture who are trying to restore their position to whatever extent it is possible. The target group of the LVP is 'the thoroughly disillusioned and increasingly impoverished' part of the electorate, who are disappointed with the performance of the Farmers' Union in the previous government.

Alberts Kauls symbolized good life in the countryside. His pre-electoral campaign was designed to create an impression that he knows the real problems of the countryside and he is capable of taking the responsibility for the country people. The LVP favours concentration of agricultural production in bigger units than small family farms. It does not demand a return to the full collectivization of agriculture but it advocates a hybrid between the old and new systems. In its view, there must be different kinds of farms depending on the needs of farmers so as to achieve optimal results. The LVP campaigns for increasing state support for agriculture as well as for protecting the domestic market from agricultural imports. The state must guarantee fixed quotas for the purchase of farm products. The LVP strictly opposes the sale of rural land to foreigners.[211]

The LVP pursues a mixed but market-based economy, combining a diversity of property forms. Privatization of strategic objects should be suspended, and in general, too, the transition should proceed gradually in a step-by-step manner. The LVP stresses the necessity of enhancing domestic production while restricting liberalism in economy. Currency policy should be coordinated with the needs of the industry. Taxes should be used to stimulate production and capital formation. Elements of a welfare state should be introduced to correct income distribution. The LVP stands for a traditional nation state but simultaneously it wants to guarantee the rights of the immigrants.[212]

THE DEMOCRATIC PARTY MASTERS (SAIMNIEKS)

The Democratic Party Masters (*Demokratiska partija Saimnieks* – DPS) was founded in April 1994 when the Democratic Party merged with the Party Saimnieks. The Democratic Party (originally called Democratic Centre Party) came into being as a parliamentary faction within the Popular Front in February 1992. It was founded by former liberal communists who tried to fill the vacuum in the political centre, though without much success. (It was Latvia's Way that seized the role of the leading centrist force in the Latvian party system.) Saimnieks was registered in the party register as late as September 1994 but the party turned out to be an immediate success. Saimnieks was established by Ziedonis Cevers, a then 36-year-old millionaire who had made his fortune through a private security firm called Droshiba Fonds. Before independence, Cevers was a Komsomol leader in Riga. During the failed hard-line communist coup in August 1991, he helped to organize the defence of Parliament against anti-independence OMON militia unit attacks.[213]

Political opponents were anxious to remind voters of Cevers's Komsomol background as well as the communist past of many other Saimnieks leaders. During the pre-electoral campaign, Saimnieks came under public fire due to the fact that a number of its top candidates had been high-rank Soviet officials or KGB collaborators. Saimnieks responded calmly to the accusations of its being a party of old communists and KGB agents. It admitted openly that it had representatives of the old *nomenklatura* in its ranks but considered such a membership composition natural in a postcommunist country. 'We have a part of our society [in our party]. We are people who have lived in Latvia all the time.' Cevers likened activity in Soviet organizations to a professional athlete being traded to a new team. Furthermore, Saimnieks pointed out that Anatolijs Gorbunovs (LC) was the ideological secretary of the Latvian

Communist Party for three years while Ivars Kezbers (DPS) held that post only for eleven months.[214]

An apter characterization which better captures the essence of the party's nature defines Saimnieks as an interest group on behalf of one part of the business community that is actively involved in transactions with Eastern countries. The influence of certain business groups can be perceived in its privatization and foreign trade policies, among others. Saimnieks itself says it represents the interests of domestic producers, as it regards local producers to be the backbone of a national economy. The link between these two definitions is that the traditional production sectors used to be heavily dependent on exports to the East. The core of the party members consists of state enterprise managers and new rich businessmen but the party draws support from small business and factory workers, too. It attracts electoral support even across ethnic lines, although it is mainly a Latvian party. Russian-speaking business has given Saimnieks its backing.

Saimnieks denounces being a left-of-centre party whose position in the middle of the party spectrum encourages wide cooperation with both sides. It would like to see itself as a mediator between the left- and right-wing parties that might not be able to make contact without external arbitration. Before the 6th Saeima elections, there were only two political parties on which Saimnieks cast doubts: the Siegerist Party and the Socialist Party. Even on this question, the party leader stayed true to his pragmatism and did not exclude compromises in the government formation: 'Politicians are like diplomats. We must always be open to opportunities when they arise.' When the Social Democratic Party gained popularity, Saimnieks dissociated itself from what it described as an unrealistic, leftist programme. Before the elections, Saimnieks felt kinship especially with the Political Union of Economists and the Farmers' Union. Both the programme and the membership structure of the Political Union of Economists are almost identical to those of Saimnieks, which makes it easy to find a common cause with Tautsaimnieks. The Farmers' Union shares a similar view to Saimnieks on the development of agriculture. Unity and Latvia's Way were also mentioned as potential coalition partners.[215]

Saimnieks bases its approach on pragmatism and professionalism. It bills itself as a movement of specialists, taking an anti-ideological stance and promising a government of professionals. Saimnieks rejects the possibility of realizing any 'isms' or abstract theories in a modern society, attacking liberalism and monetarism implemented by Latvia's Way. Although Saimnieks does not identify with any 'isms', some voices among its ranks have likened it to Western social democratic parties. Saimnieks stresses concrete thinking that seeks practical solutions to immediate problems by relying on experience, careful analysis and a case-by-case approach. It advocates piecemeal social engineering, warning about a policy of great leaps that may lead to insurmountable costs, if incorrect steps are taken. Somewhat surprisingly, Saimnieks has recently started to praise Skele's course and criticize social populism: 'We have to solve first certain fundamental questions, before we can start thinking about "normal" problems. We are still struggling for our survival. This is also the way Skele thinks. Now we have to work, work, work ...'.[216] The sharpened position may be interpreted as a reaction to the competition from the left; that is, the strong showing of the Bojars party.

Saimnieks assures concerned rightist parties that its orientation toward Eastern markets stems from pragmatic business thinking rather than from political sympathies. There are no bad markets for producers and Russia offers an enormous potential for Latvia. Latvia is not so rich that it can afford to lose the Eastern market because of vain pride when at the same time the West European countries are on the look-out for the same markets. Aivars Kreituss mentions Finland as a good example for Latvia of how to develop flourishing trade relations with Russia. He is simultaneously pessimistic about Latvia's chances of conquering the highly competitive Western markets with the current level of technology and he blames Latvians for wishful thinking. Saimnieks's platform recommends cooperation with all countries, asserting that hostilities between countries are outdated. Saimnieks stands for a balanced distribution of trade by country groups. The emphasis on the economic contacts with the CIS does not mean the party is turning its back on the European integration. On the contrary, Saimnieks gives a priority to reform measures preparing Latvia for the EU membership at the turn of the millennium.[217]

Saimnieks sets clear goals for both the long- and short-term development of the Latvian economy. In the long-run, the aim is to convert the Latvian economy into a modern free market economy where competitiveness holds the highest esteem. In the short-term, it is necessary to deliver Latvia from the economic crisis. Saimnieks makes a distinction between economic management during the transition stage, on the one hand, and the advantaged capitalistic stage, on the other hand, asserting that different rules of the game apply to different stages. The economy should gradually move toward deregulation and liberalization so that in the end the state would withdraw from the economy. Meanwhile, when the old system has just broken down but the new system is still evolving, economic liberalism is disastrous. Saimnieks complains that the prevailing state of anarchism does not even meet the criteria of true liberalism since there is no unified system of rules applying to all economic actors. In addition, the transition phase necessitates regulation and strategic planning by the government (not administrative planning). Saimnieks declares that economic reforms must serve the interests of the people. The reform policy must focus on the creation of jobs, the struggle against inflation and the elimination of poverty.[218]

Saimnieks emphasizes the importance of implementing an active industrial policy, demanding the re-establishment of a separate ministry of industry. It believes that the destruction of Latvian industry must be stopped and, instead, the government must seek out some priority sectors to be promoted by economic means. Until Latvia has achieved a competitive level in these selected sectors, they must be protected from foreign competition. Resources must be channelled into such branches that benefit from Latvia's natural resources or geographical location.[219]

Saimnieks promises state support not only to industry but also to agriculture. It wants to establish a system of long-term credit to farmers financed by the national budget. To avoid overproduction, agriculture should be subordinated to a regulation tied with fixed quotas. Saimnieks stands for the dissolution of the Soviet-type collective farms and the restoration of land as private property but it regrets that cooperative companies were also destroyed in the wake of the land reform. Individual farmers should be encouraged to form voluntary producers' cooperatives to give a stimulus to the modernization of technical equipment and the formation of processing plants for agricultural products. Protective customs tariffs are instrumental to act as a counterweight to cheap agricultural imports the price of which is based on export subsidies paid by the neighbouring countries. Saimnieks underscores the idea that Latvian agriculture cannot jump into a West European model in one night because the majority of Latvians live in the countryside.[220]

Tax and credit policies should be used to foster the expansion of private business. Cuts in tax rates should be accompanied by the enforcement of an effective tax collection system. Low-cost credits should be provided to small and medium-sized business but the distribution of loans should be monitored much more carefully than before in order to prevent the abuse of public funds. Financial discipline should be tightened up in the public sector, too. Saimnieks reproaches the LC governments with wasteful use of public funds for unproductive purposes. Despite a large budget deficit, the government has initiated grandiose construction projects in a great rush and has kept on sending deputies and civil servants on unnecessary excursions to foreign countries all over the world. To encourage foreign investments in Latvia, the government should create free trade areas and allow foreign investors to own the land needed for building the investment object. Saimnieks urges the setting up of a real estate market. A proposition concerning the establishment of free trade zones in the hard-hit Eastern region of Latvia reflects the wish to intensify cooperation with Russia and Belarus.[221]

Saimnieks criticizes the Bank of Latvia and the Ministry of Finance for not having participated sufficiently in the efforts to overcome the economic crisis. They ought not to realize such monetary and fiscal policies that do not deal with the problems of the national economy. Although the independence of the central bank must be preserved, the Bank of Latvia should work closely with the government in fighting for the country's economic interests. Saimnieks opposes the present currency policy because it contributes to a continuous appreciation of the lats. Such a currency policy weakens the competitiveness of Latvian exports, affects negatively the inflow of foreign investments and, thus, aggravates the economic crisis. Saimnieks does not demand a devaluation of the lats but it wants to rely on economic mechanisms in the determination of the value of the lats.[222]

Although Saimnieks supports privatization in principle, its approach is not quite consistent when certain business interests get involved, and it is not ready to go as far as the liberals. Certain strategic sectors, especially those including natural monopolies, that are vital to the maintenance of life should remain under state control, instead of being completely privatized, so that their tariff setting could be regulated. Energy, telecommunications, alcohol and part of the financial sector are examples of the fields to be kept in the hands of the government. Replacement of state monopolies by private monopolies cannot be permitted. Referring to this point, Saimnieks criticizes the privatization of Lattelekom by a private monopolist. Existing monopolies must be subjected to a strict control to avoid overcharging and to ensure the efficiency of their performance. Those enterprises that cannot be privatized due to the lack of buyers or that are purposefully kept under state ownership should be restructured. Both the technology and finances of the state companies should be improved within the context of a special programme. Saimnieks emphasizes the equal status of all property forms whether private or public. Privatization should be carried out in a controlled manner which prevents the waste of public property and maximizes the budget revenue from selling off state enterprises. Divestment of state property at a nominal price is not acceptable, even though it might speed up the privatization process. The funds gained through privatization can be used for the promotion of small and medium-sized enterprises in the private sector.[223]

THE POLITICAL UNION OF ECONOMISTS

The Political Union of Economists (*Tautsaimnieku politiska apvieniba* – TPA) was established as an independent political party in March 1994 when the electoral association 'Harmony for Latvia – Rebirth of National Economy' split up. The Economists who left the association were dissatisfied with the direction in which the policy of the Jurkans-led coalition was developing. In their view, 'Harmony for Latvia – Rebirth of National Economy' was becoming an ethnic single-issue party leaning almost exclusively on the electoral support of Russian-speakers. Hence, the industrial wing of the association, focusing on the economic problems rather than on the nationality question, founded the Political Union of Economists – Tautsaimnieks. Its core was made up of directors and middle management of large state enterprises and agricultural collective combines as well as high trade union officials. Unlike Harmony, Tautsaimnieks is primarily a Latvian party. Before the 6th Saeima elections, Tautsaimnieks negotiated with Saimnieks on an eventual coalescence but the planned merger failed due to a disagreement on practical arrangements rather than ideological differences. Tautsaimnieks participated in the Gailis government as a junior partner, being represented through two ministers and two state ministers.[224]

The merger plan reveals the similarity of the political programmes of Tautsaimnieks and Saimnieks. Tautsaimnieks is a left-of-centre party which traces its ideological roots to social liberalism. The centrist orientation makes it open to cooperation with nearly all political parties. In addition to Saimnieks, Harmony, Latvia's Way and the Farmers' Union are regarded as proper partners, whereas cooperation with Fatherland and Freedom as well as 'populistic socialist forces' is objected to. Divergent opinions about the citizenship law and relations to Russia might cause troubles with the LNNK, but the differences are not conceived of as being insuperable.[225]

Tautsaimnieks stands for a socially responsible market economy. It rejects ultraliberalism and shock therapy because they lead to a polarized society in which a tiny layer of the wealthy is counterpoised by crowds of the poor. The social question should be resolved through the strengthening of a middle class. The expansion of the middle class, in turn, depends on the existence of economic sectors capable of absorbing the skilled labour. Tautsaimnieks does not want to reintroduce a command economy but it holds it necessary to increase economic regulation during the transition phase. It cites the bankruptcy of Banka Baltija as an indication of the need for some degree of state control. It is also tempted to slow down the pace of reforms in order to ensure their continuation in future: that is, to avoid a political backlash. It urges reformers to pay attention to the social and economic consequences of transition. The focus on these consequences should guide all legislative work related to the reform process.[226]

In the view of Tautsaimnieks, the state must retain the ownership and management of strategic objects of national importance so that they can buttress capital accrual as well as the economic independence of the state. Moreover, the state must monopolize the alcohol production and combat the smuggling of alcohol and tobacco. In general, state-owned enterprises may exist alongside private enterprises, if they work efficiently under competitive conditions. To induce R&D activities in a capital poor country, it might even be desirable to have some large state enterprises that have sufficient means to put into practice new scientific ideas. Tautsaimnieks wants to proceed cautiously with the divestment of state property so that the state will not lose sight of the economic consequences of enterprise privatization. The party tries to influence the conditions of individual privatization projects to prevent hasty actions.[227]

Tautsaimnieks complains that there is no national view on the direction of the national economy at the moment. The main strategy for economic development should be outlined by the government and it should contain, among others, a conception of industrial policy: which branches should be prioritized and how the state could promote them. According to Tautsaimnieks, the state should actively support such branches of industry that have a base in Latvia and that are neither energy nor raw material intensive. Export industries particularly should be promoted by means of tax, credit and customs policies. Efforts should be made to raise the degree of the working up given to Latvian exports. It is senseless to export raw timber with a low price when this timber could be worked up already in Latvia. In the same way as Saimnieks, Tautsaimnieks underscores the primacy of a productive sector, arguing that Latvia has always had an 'excellent manufacturing culture' with a qualified work force. Tautsaimnieks criticizes the utopian idea of Latvia as a country of transit and bankers. It recognizes the significance of transit trade to Latvia, supporting the investments in ports and other related services, but simultaneously it points out that transit to Russia is extremely sensitive to political fluctuations and that the competition among the Baltic states and Finland is fierce within this field. A further disadvantage is that transit cannot employ great masses, whereas Tautsaimnieks puts a heavy emphasis on the creation of jobs. For these reasons, one-sided orientation toward transit is not the right solution. Finally, Tautsaimnieks demands that more resources should be allocated to science and education because industry depends on inputs from science and education.[228]

Tautsaimnieks is committed to the promotion of the Latvian enterprise sector. It promises assistance to every private, cooperative, municipal and state enterprise willing to become competitive. The customs tariffs must serve to protect the domestic market so that the principle of MFN will be applied to the import of energy and raw materials, on the one hand, and to the export of Latvian manufactures, on the other. Taxes must be reduced for small business, cooperatives and enterprises with a long production cycle.

Tautsaimnieks is prepared to freeze the tax debts of industrial enterprises incurred after the introduction of the Latvian rouble. Monetary policy must be subjected to the interests of the people and business. A devaluation of the lats is not recommendable since it would further shaken the fragile economic situation. Instead, the currency rate should be bound with the dollar. Foreign investors should have the right to buy land in Latvia but the state and the municipalities should control these purchases of land.[229]

Tautsaimnieks pushes hard for farmers' subsidies and higher tariffs on imported farm goods. It demands a loan system that would make long-term investments possible. Tautsaimnieks believes that small family farms are not capable of producing sufficiently nor can they bring their products to the market on their own. The solution proposed by Tautsaimnieks is the creation of a cooperative system. Producers' cooperatives could be helpful in the marketing and processing of farm products. That does not mean going back to collective farms because the basis would be private property. Tautsaimnieks sticks to the principle set by Karlis Ulmanis: 'Land belongs to those who till it.' Tautsaimnieks warns that if farmers are left totally at the mercy of the market forces, the social situation may become explosive in the countryside. However, the direction of supply and demand conditions must be determined by the market.[230]

Tautsaimnieks wants to make sure that Latvians will support Latvia's joining the EU in a referendum, asserting that the policy formulation will have to be designed to pave way for the full membership. The party considers the Nordic countries as natural partners to Latvia, whereas it is sceptical about the possibilities of the intra-Baltic cooperation.[231] One notable difference compared to the Saimnieks programme is that Tautsaimnieks puts less emphasis on the intensification of the economic relations with Russia; it is more Western-oriented.

THE NATIONAL HARMONY PARTY

The other half of the electoral coalition 'Harmony for Latvia – Rebirth of National Economy' took the name National Harmony Party (*Tautas Saskana partija* – TSP) when it established itself after the split in February 1994. As its name suggests, the National Harmony Party focuses on the nationality issue, representing the interests of the Russian-speaking minority. The electoral base of the TSP consists of non-Latvians mainly. In citizenship policy, the position of the TSP resembles that of the Socialist party – both parties advocate the so-called zero pattern – although the TSP is not as radical as the Socialist party in its demands. In other spheres of policy, the TSP has little in common with the goals of the Socialist Party. In fact, it places the Socialist Party into the group of political parties with which it is not particularly enthusiastic to cooperate. The main opponents of the TSP are the national conservative parties Fatherland and Freedom and LNNK which want to restrict the naturalization of non-citizens. The most preferred coalition partner for the TSP is Saimnieks, followed by Unity, Latvia's Way the Farmers' Union and the Christian Democratic Union. The TSP defines itself as a left liberal party, comparing itself to the Dutch Democrats. Its location on the left–right spectrum corresponds to that of Saimnieks and Tautsaimnieks; that is, the TSP is a left-of-centre party.[232]

The TSP summarizes its political aspirations as three concerns: (1) stability and compromise in society, (2) human rights and (3) integration of non-citizens. When the TSP speaks about harmony it does not refer solely to the ethnic relations or the relations between citizens and non-citizens, though they are important manifestations of the concord idea. Nor is the TSP so naïve as to build illusions of a conflict-free society. To be accurate, the Latvian word *saskana* does not mean precisely the same as the English translation 'harmony', as harmony is a state without contradictions. *Saskana*, instead, is a situation in which two or more groups coexist, they have normal relations with each other but these relations need not be warm or friendly. The state of *saskana* is similar to a choir with divergent voices. When the choir is singing, the different voices pull together. Following the example of Spain after the Franco era, the different political forces should put aside their political differences to agree on those issues most crucial to the majority of Latvians. Similarly, one should take a clear-cut attitude toward the Soviet past: 'OK, we had a very bad past but now we have to start a new life.' The TSP objects to any general restrictions related to an individual's former activity in the KGB, because the alleged KGB connections are very hard to prove. As the KGB used to be an integral part of the state structure, all people working in arts or science, for instance, had a connection to the KGB. Those who are found guilty of crimes can be prosecuted in accordance with the criminal law. Therefore, separate acts are unnecessary.[233]

Saskana's point of departure on the citizenship issue rests on the existing real situation rather than on the desirable or rightful situation (cf. the legal approach of the TB). The TSP admits that the current proportions between Latvians and non-Latvians have been created artificially by the Soviet policy, but that is quite another separate question which does not change the fact that nearly half of the residents are non-Latvians and almost one-third of the population has no citizenship. The TSP does not claim that non-citizens are without any rights but it complains that there are differences in the rights of citizens and non-citizens. In an ideal case, the difference ought to manifest only at a political level: who has the right to vote in national elections and who has not. The TSP fights for the elimination of any connection between citizenship and economic, social, labour and ownership rights. When non-citizens pay taxes as all others, they have a right to the same pensions and social security as citizens. If foreign investors are granted the right to buy land, which the TSP considers necessary, it is absurd if non-citizens cannot own land in Latvia. Integration of the ethnic minorities into Latvian society could be fostered by granting the right to vote at the local elections to all Latvian residents who have resided in their correspondent communities at least five years.[234]

The TSP is proud that the closest variant of the citizenship law adopted is the variant proposed by it from the very beginning. It takes the credit for the following two amendements: (1) the citizenship law was adopted without any naturalization quotas, (2) the citizenship law was amended in favour of the Eastern Latvians who are now obtaining the Latvian citizenship through registration. Despite its basic contentment with the existing legislation, the TSP pleads for some individual concessions in the liberalization of the law. The main changes that need to be implemented according to the TSP are easing requirements for elderly non-citizens who might have trouble with language tests, the granting of automatic citizenship to the children of non-citizens born in Latvia and the accelaration of the naturalization process. Moreover, it is one thing to have a law; it is quite another thing to have a mechanism for the implementation of that law. It is essential to observe the application of the citizenship law to eliminate arbitrariness of the executors.[235]

The basis of the TSP's economic approach can be reduced to the following simple principle: 'Freedom to those who are able to make it and support for those who cannot manage their life.' The TSP requires the elimination of all bureaucratic and political barriers to entrepreneurship. The TSP gives its unconditional support to a fast privatization procedure. It argues that privatization is needed in Latvia – not to obtain money for the budget but to make property work efficiently.[236]

The TSP blames the LC governments for destroying Latvian industry, sometimes merely on political grounds, like by neglecting Eastern markets. According to the TSP, Latvia needs at the state level a clear programme as to how to develop industry. The TSP is not homogeneous as to the form of the state support to industry. The party programme advocates preferential treatment of the Latvian producers in the allocation of state orders. The liberal businessman wing adheres to the neoclassical model, in which the state fosters only general tendencies in the economy. The TSP liberals reject state support to particular products as well as direct state investments in the priority sectors.[237]

In the opinion of the TSP, the responsibility for the economic development and the growth of exports is to be envisaged within the legislation not merely for the government but also for the Bank of Latvia. The TSP is not satisfied with the implemented monetary and currency policy. It regards the current state of affairs as tragicomical: Latvia has an utterly devastated economy but a very stable currency. The currency is like a stone: when everything else is dead, the lats persists. The reserves the Bank of Latvia keeps abroad could be used to credit the national economy to the extent that these reserves are exceeding the limits necessary to uphold the lats.[238]

The TSP regards decollectivization as a mistake because it destroyed the infrastructure but brought nothing new in its place. Latvian agriculture stagnated to the level of the 1920s with the consequence that it will have to go through the same process of unification of small farms into bigger, more viable units as it did in the 1930s. Another critical note concerns the prevalent restitution practice: land is returned to the previous owners irrespective of their intention to till it or not. A compensation mechanism should be set up to compensate those owners who are not interested in cultivating their land. The government's task is to restructure infrastructure in the rural regions to make the development of a provincial enterprise sector possible. Tax policy, regional policy as well as public investments should contribute to the structural change. The liberal wing of the TSP is sceptical about agricultural subsidies and higher import tariffs, whereas the other wing sticks to the protection of the domestic market.[239]

In the field of foreign policy, the TSP puts forward three interrelated priorities: (1) strengthening of the cooperation among the Baltic states, (2) concluding a partnership with Russia and (3) joining the European economic and security structures. The TSP urges the establishment of the Baltic Association of the Free Market and the assignment of a border agreement between Russia and the Baltic states. In regard to Russia, it demands the predominance of economic pragmatism over political passion. There would be enormous opportunities to do business with Russia, especially in Latvia's Eastern region Latgale where the unemployment rate is very high. The wish to intensify economic relations with Russia is related to the treatment of the Russian minority in Latvia. If the Russians are oppressed in Latvia, Latvia cannot hope for normalization of relations.[240]

THE SOCIALIST PARTY

The Latvian Socialist Party (*Latvijas Socialistiska partija* – LSP) was founded in January 1994 to continue the political activities of the Equal Rights (*Lidztiesiba*) movement. The leadership of the Socialist Party was made up of different persons from that of the Equal Rights movement, the condition of which caused intra-party tensions between the two wings in the long run. The Socialist Party split into two parts in the legislative period following the 6th Saeima elections, although the parties continued working within a common parliamentary faction. Those debuties who stressed human rights aspects first and foremost took the old name 'Equal Rights'. The Socialists are more leftest in economic policies than Equal Rights. In the second local elections, Equal Rights collected more votes than the Socialist Party, while the Socialists had one deputy more in Parliament.[241] From this point onwards the name 'Socialist Party' will be used to refer to Equal Rights as well.

The Socialist Party is a successor party to the Latvian Communist Party (LCP). Its roots can be traced back to the last Supreme Soviet elected in spring 1990. The voters as well as the candidates were divided into two camps: pro- and anti-independence forces. Those who wanted to maintain the status quo – an intact USSR dominated by the Communist Party, with the Latvian SSR as one of its republics – voted for the candidates fielded by the Latvian Communist Party. The communist group which called itself the Equal Rights faction included about one-third of the deputies in the Supreme Soviet. Most of them were ethnic Russians. After August 1991, the political composition of the Supreme Soviet gradually changed. The anti-independence forces declined numerically in the legislature. They also had to alter their policies since they were now deputies in the Parliament of an independent state.[242]

The Supreme Soviet's decision on 24 August 1991 to outlaw organizations (including the Communist Party) that had acted to overthrow the Latvian government led to a considerable thinning in the ranks of the Equal Rights faction. More than half of its adherents had actively supported the policies of LCP leader Alfreds Rubiks who had not only endorsed the attemped coup in Moscow but had also tried to seize control over both the Latvian government and the legislature. For this reason, these deputies lost their seats in the Supreme Council. Alfreds Rubiks is the only top Soviet era official to be convicted for supporting the failed coup. The former First Secretary of the Latvian Communist Party tried to rush Latvia's newly declared independence during the August coup against Mikhail Gorbachev. Six people were killed in Riga in clashes with police. The headline-making trial against Rubiks lasted for two years. In his final statement to the court in 1995, Rubiks remained unrepentant, denouncing Latvia's declaration of sovereignty as unconstitutional. Neither did he acknowledge Latvian statehood. He maintained that Latvia is a non-independent country which has 'crept under the wing of NATO [North Atlantic Treaty Organization]' after breaking away from the Soviet Union. Rubiks was found guilty of conspiracy and he was sentenced to prison for eight years. He also had all personal property confiscated. At the same time as the trial, Rubiks was fighting for his mandate in Parliament, which was suspended during the trial. In the 6th Saeima elections, he wanted to run for a seat again as a top candidate on the LSP list. The Central Electoral Committee barred him from the election list on similar grounds to Alberts Kauls. The co-chairpersons of the Socialist Party, Larisa Lavina and Filip Stroganov, were deleted by the Central Electoral Committee accordingly.[243]

The LSP appeals to Russian-speaking workers and pensioners. It has a lot of supporters among the non-citizens who cannot vote. Nationality policy unites the LSP and the Harmony Party, while in the field of economic policy the LSP feels itself totally isolated. Because it has not enough political weight to be able to determine the direction of policy, it has to consider its stance on each case separately. Consequently, it allies itself with very different partners from vote to vote, even with the National Bloc parties. In principle, the LSP treats the National Bloc parties as unacceptable coalition partners. On the international level, the LSP holds contacts, among others, with the dwarfed Finnish Communist Party.[244]

Citizenship and human rights issues have an overwhelming priority in the platform of the LSP. The LSP treats all other questions from the viewpoint of the citizenship issue, always stressing the rights of the non-citizens. Tatjana Zdanok, a member of the board and professor of mathematics, illustrates the fundamentality of citizenship with a term borrowed from the probability theory: conditional expectations. All other questions are conditioned by the requirement of equal rights. Latvia cannot proceed further with social and economic reforms until the citizenship question is resolved in a satisfactory way. The only satisfactory solution is to grant citizenship to all Latvian residents without any restrictions. The LSP demands that the citizenship law must be changed in accordance with the so-called 'zero pattern'. The LSP mentions Finland as a good model of how to arrange the relations between different nationalities.[245]

The problem of the LSP is that it constantly finds itself in the opposition since the economic model it advocates deviates considerably from the aspirations of all other political parties. As it is not likely to be able to realize its programme as such, it faces the choice between an orthodox or a realizable programme. It is confronted by the question of whether it should voluntarily take the attitude of a party which can only improve other programmes. When this standpoint is combined with the absolute priority given to the equal rights condition, the economic policy of the LSP may bring surprises in actual practice. It may appear inconsequent in the sense it does not necessarily correspond to the theses of the party platform. Many observers note that the voting behaviour of the LSP has often been more rightist than the policy pursued by more moderate left-wing parties. Although the party is supposed to be theoretically left, it may sometimes decide on rightist solutions. The decision is always made from the standpoint of the equal rights. If something works for this highest priority, the LSP will vote for it, even when it contradicts other principles of the party. In principle, the LSP opposes liberalism but it has noticed that liberalism is a circumstance which offers more opportunities to people[246] and, therefore, it is often convenient to support liberal policy. The case of land ownership is an illustrative example in this respect.[247]

In principle, the LSP is against private ownership of land. Were it the leading government party, it would not permit denationalization. It would distribute usufruct rights but it would prohibit buying and selling of land. However, under the prevailing conditions the LSP voted for the extension of property rights. As it was written in the Constitution that only citizens could be owners of land, the LSP supported an amendment allowing also juridical persons to purchase land. Juridical persons may also include non-citizens.[248] Accordingly, it later supported the establishment of a free land market to permit foreigners and non-citizens to buy land.

The LSP rejects the Western models for an economic system. Instead, it advocates the model known from China. The Swedish social democratic model in its traditional form is also considered worth examining. Sergei Dimanish, one of the party leaders, has developed in his dissertation a theoretically founded plan for how to pass from an administrative system to a market economy. Dimanish's approach is evolutionary, corresponding to the Chinese model. The reason why the LSP objects to a Polish-type revolutionary approach is its destructiveness. The rush modernization of the telephone network is cited as an illustrative example of the negative side-effects of the revolutionary transition strategy. Lattelekom's new tariffs are so high that most pensioners are forced to give up their telephones because keeping a telephone would cost half of their monthly pension. The LSP proposes that Latvia would preserve the old telephone system parallel to the new one. Those who can pay, like businessmen, could join the modern digital network while those who are in a very bad economic situation could continue using the old, less efficient system.[249]

According to the LSP, the government should regulate economy to ensure the coherency of goal-setting in different fields of the economy: for instance, to avoid inconsistencies between trade policy, industrial policy and private business activities. Reasonable supervision of industry is necessary to revitalize the productive potential of the country. The economic policy is to be targeted to stimulate the accumulation of national capital, to attract foreign investment both from the East and the West, to create new employment opportunities and to promote private business. People's savings should be channelled into investment projects, instead of letting them lie in doubtful financial institutes. The government must name two or three priority sectors in industry to be fostered and protected by the state. In addition, Latvia must utilize its geographical position between the East and the West to become a transit country.[250]

The LSP opposes the kind of privatization policy the current government is realizing. The intentional repudiation of public property reflects a worldwide trend. It ignores the possibilities of public property and monopoly profits in achieving various economic and social goals. The key industries and transports must not be privatized at all. State ownership must be extended to embrace large factories such as VEF, RAF and the Daugavpils chemical plants. Communications, the Latvian airlines as well as the sale, import and production of spirits must be subordinated to a state monopoly. Moreover, the government must restart production in many state-owned enterprises which have come to a standstill due to the lack of markets. The production of the restructured companies can be used as a payment for the energy imported from Russia, following a barter principle. The maintenance of working places has always been an overriding priority. Therefore, each case must be carefully investigated to find out if there is any possibility of keeping the factory running. The privatization procedure must be brought under social control. Vouchers should be used as a means of payment to a much greater extent than before. The government should redeem the unused vouchers at their nominal price. All types of property forms must be guaranteed an equal status. Private entrepreneurship is to be favoured, especially in services and small business.[251]

The LSP is a bitter opponent of the stabilization policy which is being practised. In its view, controlled inflation is a prerequisite for economic growth. The LSP also wants to restrict the independence of the central bank, proposing changes in the Law on the Bank of Latvia. As long as the Bank of Latvia has the status of 'a state within a state' the development of the country is impossible. The central bank should take responsibility for the national economy. The artificially upheld exchange rate hampers the growth of exports, ruins the industry and contributes to the decrease in budget revenue. Repse's stable lats does not suit the prevailing economic situation. The LSP requires a devaluation of the lats. The current fiscal policy leads to the impoverishment of teachers, doctors and other budget-paid employees. To cover the social expenses, the government should allow the existence of a budget deficit. Taxes should be set at such a level that businessmen are interested in investing their money in production and not just in speculative transactions on the black market.[252]

The LSP promises its support to farmers, insisting on subsidies, credits, higher tariffs and all measures necessary to protect the domestic market. The party was against the decollectivization of agriculture but it acknowledges it is impossible to reverse the process. The few existing collective agricultural enterprises should be preserved, despite the counter-pressure on the part of the government.[253]

The recovery of the Latvian industry depends on its ability to find export markets. The Eastern markets in particular hold the key to the expansion of Latvian exports. Tax and customs policies should work for this goal. The LSP accepts an economic association with the EU to the extent it deals with taxes, customs or other corresponding treaties. However, it rejects the Maastricht Treaty due to its political and military aspects. Thus, the LSP opposed Latvia's integration into the EU until an unexpected about-turn in October 1995 (see p. 175). The LSP puts the most important foreign partners to Latvia in the following order:

1. the Baltic states
2. the CIS countries, especially Russia and Belarus
3. the Nordic countries as well as the East Central European transitional economies, especially Poland
4. the West European EU countries.[254]

The LSP's attitude to the political system in Latvia diverges considerably from the views held by other major political parties. The radicalism of the LSP reflects this strong negative attitude. The extracts below illustrate the party's deep distrust in Latvia's democracy.

- Many people are afraid of admitting publicly that they are actually supporting the LSP, the opposition party, because Latvia has a totalitarian regime. Poll results are distorted.
- There are frequent human rights violations in Latvia. Therefore, the LSP has established a human rights commission to monitor the Citizenship and Immigration Department.
- There is a conspiratory plan to liquidate the Russian capital in Latvia. If radicals come to power, they will realize this plan. The collapse of Banka Baltija is a proof of the pressure directed against non-Latvian business.
- Nationalists are working for a two-community society.[255]

THE SOCIAL DEMOCRATIC PARTY

The Social Democratic Party of Latvia (*Latvijas socialdemokratiska partija* – LSDP) emerged as a result of the split in the Latvian Communist Party at its 25th congress in 1990. The Independent Communist Party was founded on 14 April 1990. The party was renamed the following September as the Democratic Labour Party. The party leadership decided to rename themselves once more in 1996, after hearing a rumour that Saimnieks was considering a name change that would include the word 'labour'. Professor Juris Bojars, Director of the Institute of Foreign Affairs at the University of Latvia, took over the party leadership in 1992, following Ivars Kezbers who is now a Saimnieks deputy. When the party came into being as the Independent Communist Party, it had 25,000 formal members. By the time of the leadership shuffle in 1992, the number of members had sunk to 5,000. Only the truly leftist forces had stayed in the Democratic Labour Party. Bojars reformed the party and wrote an extensive, diversified programme for it.[256] The LSDP is identified very much with its leader in the same way as the Siegerist or Kauls Party, being also known colloquially as the Bojars Party. Bojars himself cannot run for elections because he is a former major in the KGB.

Although Bojars was a well-known politician throughout the 1990s, the Democratic Labour Party fared miserably in all elections before the second local elections in 1997. The electoral coalition 'Labour and Justice' (*Darbs un Taisnigums*), in which Bojars's Democratic Labour Party took part, ran almost neck and neck with the threshold in the 6th Saeima elections, but a 4.6 per cent share of the national vote did not entitle the party to seats. Persistent political work finally bore fruit in 1997, when the LSDP came out a big winner in the local elections. It collected 23.5 per cent of the votes given to party lists across the whole country. In Riga it claimed 11 of Riga City Council's 60 seats. (17 of the 19 party lists found representation on the council.) In Daugavpils the LSDP gained 13 of the council's 15 seats. The LSDP is forecasted to win the next Saeima elections too, because it can benefit from a favourable position in opposition. Bojars is convinced of the victory: 'It is inevitable. Historical and political trends dictate we will rise to power.'[257]

Bojars was not surprised by his party's success in the local elections in the light of the catastrophic economic situation. 'This is inevitable, because people have had their taste of liberal parties', Bojars said to the journalists. 'The laws of political science are those of the stomach. When living standards go down, people look for alternatives.' He maintained that the electoral victory was 'the result of misguided social policies by four successive governments since liberation'. Critics describe the LSDP as another For Latvia, which owes its popularity in large part to demagogic appeal.[258] Bojars has indeed received much of Kauls's and Siegerist's votes as well as those of Saimnieks. Wage earners and especially the poorest strata form the LSDP's constituency. Bojars is regarded as a more dangerous populist than Siegerist, because he has expressed radically leftist demands that contradict the reform course. Newspapers stated that he would like to halt or even reverse the privatization process by renationalizing denationalized industries. Bojars denies such a statement.[259]

The LSDP ran both for the 6th Saeima elections and the second local elections in coalition with the Social Democratic Workers Party. The Social Democratic Workers Party is the original leftist party from the prewar period, but it has remained small and insignificant after the restoration of independence. The coalition 'Labour and Justice' was complemented by trade unions and some minor non-party organizations. Today Bojars blames the trade unions for betrayal and asserts that they still continue to be manned by the old *nomenklatura*. In the local elections the LSDP tried to cooperate with Fatherland and Freedom for tactical reasons, although the parties' political orientations have little in common. The LSDP aspired to obtain a governing majority in the Riga City Council, but Fatherland and Freedom allied itself with Latvia's Way and Saimnieks in the end. Bojars considers Fatherland and Freedom more acceptable than the other governing parties, because in his view Fatherland and Freedom is less responsible for the current economic crisis than the others. Latvia's Way and Saimnieks are the evils of Latvian politics in Bojars's eyes. According to him, both parties are greedy, and they aim at the privatization and monopolization of the whole economy for their benefit. Bojars outlines his reasons for putting a clear distance between the LSDP and Saimnieks: 'Saimnieks is a collection of economic interests, not a true leftist party.' He classifies Saimnieks as a centrist party. The LSDP has been equally unamicable with its neighbouring parties on the left. It completely dissociates itself from Equal Rights, the Socialists and other groups that emerged from pro-Russian or unreformed communist groupings. National policies make the difference in the latter case.[260]

The LSDP emphasizes that it belongs to the same category as the West European social democratic parties. The European Democratic Left is also seen as a reference group to some extent. The LSDP's programme is 'a synthesis of the best social democratic teachings in Europe and Australia'. Selected ideas have been picked up from the European Democratic Left, but they have been integrated into a general social democratic framework. The concept 'casino economy', which is borrowed from the Finnish Left Alliance (*Vasemmistoliitto*), is an example of the combination of ideas. Bojars equates the location of the LSDP on a left–right spectrum with that of the West European social democratic parties, but then again complains that they are centrist rather than leftist. Widespread opinion maintains that the LSDP is more leftist than the West European social democratic parties.

Prime Minister Andris Skele contrasted Latvia's '*sociki*' to Scandinavian social democrats in the sensational television speech on the eve of the 9 March 1997 local elections. Skele warned voters to beware of the rising tide of socialism and not to be deceived by the left-wing parties' promises of miracles. Skele went on to denounce the '*sociki*' as a collection of KGB agents and likened them to those who welcomed Soviet tanks in 1940. Bojars thought Skele had overstepped the mark by using national TV and taxpayers' money to defame his party. 'He [Skele] is the prime minister, and he should not be using his position to influence voters' decisions at election time', announced Bojars. Bojars endeavoured to sue Skele for moral damages. However, the court dismissed the anti-Skele lawsuit.[261]

The LSDP markets itself under the slogan 'patriotic left'. The Social Democratic Party of Latvia is a patriotic political organization which is committed to political and economic reforms to transform Latvia into a lawful, democratic, socially just, economically prosperous state. The LSDP does not support the dogmas of communism and Soviet 'socialism'. Bojars explains: 'We are pro-independence, pro-nation and won't stand for Soviet nostalgia.' Bojars, a former KGB officer, attacks heavily the continuing political power of the Soviet *nomenklatura* in Latvia, analysing, among others, the composition of Club 21 and Latvia's Way. 'The most active communists have turned into the most active capitalists and the most extreme liberals.' The LSDP rejects liberalism and shock therapy; it stands for a strong state and a gradual transition.[262]

Bojars is engaged in revealing corruption and misuse of state funds, not forgetting Prime Minister Skele's misdealings as a Deputy Minister of Agriculture. 'The governing elite is enjoying themselves at splendid press parties and receptions ... Organized crime together with corruption have resulted in a mass robbery of state assets. According to former Minister of Finance Uldis Osis (LC), some 10 billion US-dollars' worth of Latvian capital has been hidden abroad already under the Supreme Council.' Bojars further refers to the disappearance of the G24 credits. He is worried about the amalgamation of the government, political parties and law enforcement institutions. 'It is not acceptable that the State Control becomes an instrument of the leading party or coalition, thus undermining its usefulness, because its task is to monitor those same institutions.'[263]

Bojars stresses the importance of efficient law enforcement as a prerequisite for foreign investments. A strong system of safeguards is needed to make the investment environment predictable. 'Latvia should be made into a civilized state.' Bojars mentions constantly changing taxation, high crime rates and inefficient courts as the main impediments to the inflow of foreign investments. He welcomes foreign investors to Latvia. The only restrictions should be placed on foreign ownership of rural land. As long as poor Latvians are uncompetitive in the land market, foreign companies can buy the most fertile land for a song. The sale of land in connection with productive investments is acceptable.[264]

The LSDP's goal is to create a Nordic-type welfare state where social welfare is merged with an efficient economy. A social democratic state should act as a guarantee of social justice and an instrument to involve citizens in public control. The LSDP advocates a mixed economy, combining multiple forms of ownership: private small and medium-sized enterprises, cooperatives and large state-owned enterprises, including monopolies. 'The main condition for a free market economy is not the form of ownership but a sound competition in markets and efficient management of enterprises.' A strong, dynamic state sector should compete with the private sector. Economic inequality could be reduced by creating broad sectors of national economy based on public capital, where speculative private capital would be excluded. Exclusion would not include capital originating from personal initiative. Part of the public enterprises should be owned by municipal investment banks, pension funds or mutual insurance funds. The LSDP champions economic democracy and employee ownership. Workers' collectives should guarantee the right to work, employees' participation in the management of enterprises and profit-sharing schemes. Agricultural production, likewise its processing, should be organized on the basis of farmers' cooperatives. A non-profit system of consumers and tenants' cooperatives would realize the idea of public democratic control.[265]

The LSDP resents employees' interests being sacrificed in the name of privatization. Bojars describes the existing privatization model as follows: a factory is closed down, workers are thrown onto the street with no rights and enormous social tax debts are left unpaid. As a consequence, the dismissed workers are entitled to neither social benefits nor pensions. The other main grievance over privatization concerns the practical monopolization of privatized property. State and cooperative property have been robbed by the communist *nomenklatura*, which has stayed in power. They are turning their political power into economic power by privatizing the whole economy for themselves. According to Bojars, a great many of the privatizations which have taken place are criminal.[266]

An equally grave mistake in privatization is to invite foreign monopolies to Latvia. Lattelekom is a warning example of the consequences of monopoly power: prices rise rapidly, while the population is left unprotected. Now the same mistake is being repeated in the energy sector. Latvenergo, Latvia's state energy power and heating industry, is going to be sold for 10 per cent of its real value. Experts have estimated the company's value to be US$ 2 billion, although the selling price has been set at US$19 million. According to Bojars, Latvenergo is so profitable that it could have financed the modernization of its power stations from its profits. The curious point is that one of the main buyers will be state-owned Svenska Vattenfall. Consequently, the Swedish state will own part of the Latvian state. Bojars cannot understand what sense it makes to have state-owned foreign companies, such as Neste and Statoil, in Latvian markets, when Latvia does not tolerate any state-owned Latvian enterprises. Oil business is another field which Latvians should control by themselves because it involves huge money flows. Bojars cites Argip in Italy as a good example for Latvia of how to collect the profits for the state. The same holds for the alcohol industry.[267]

Such giants as Latvenergo should remain state-owned and under public control. Privatization of small and medium-sized enterprises should be sponsored and promoted by cutting down private monopolies. Privatization should aim at the demonopolization of the national economy, because monopolies are incompatible with democracy. Currently anti-monopoly legislation is not supervised adequately in Latvia.[268]

The opening of the Latvian markets to foreign monopolies has led to the demise of domestic industries. Tilts Communications destroyed VEF, Latvia's biggest factory, which had an almost monopolistic position in the Soviet tele markets. VEF used to employ 25,000 workers and 3,000 researchers, and its R&D budget was bigger than that of the Academy of Sciences. The destruction of both urban and agricultural industries as a source of exports has resulted in the downfall of the economy. The production sector has been left underdeveloped, while attention has been focused on banking. Speculation instead of production, the cash economy (massive payment transactions outside banks), the permission to take foreign currencies freely out of the country and the neglect of export markets are further reasons for the bad economic situation.[269]

Monetary and exchange rate policies should contribute to export promotion. Economists should calculate a right value for the lats, which would balance the foreign trade account, and the lats should then be devalued to that level. The unbearable trade deficit results from the overvalued currency, which favours imports, while impeding exports. Buying of foreign currencies should also be restricted in order to balance foreign trade. The LSDP contrasts the selfish, corporate interests of the Bank of Latvia as well as commercial banks with those of industrial production, demanding priority setting in favour of the nation's survival. The Bank of Latvia is made responsible for the robbery of citizens' bank savings as a result of the ill-considered currency reform. According to Bojars, the alleged success in stabilization is mere propaganda.[270]

The budget should be balanced in principle, but if a deficit is needed to let people survive, it must be tolerated. It is a crime to pay pensions that fall short of the crisis minimum, when people have worked hard for 40 years or more. According to Bojars, the budget deficits have not been created by social expenses but by unnecessary credits that have been stolen from the state budget. Simultaneously the state is incapable of collecting taxes from private enterprises. This deficiency is in turn compensated by unreasonably high tax rates, although tax policies should make Latvia appealing to investors. The practical discrimination against Latvian entrepreneurs in comparison with foreign investors should be ended in taxation. A special tax policy should be applied to capital of speculative origin. Bojars advocates progressive taxation in order to reduce social inequality.[271]

The LSDP demands state stimulation of private investment in manufacturing. Transit, electronics, telecommunications, textiles, construction materials, paper, pulp and wood-processing are the most promising branches with a good export potential. Latvia should be turned from a supplier of raw materials into a high-tech country.[272]

Bojars regards agriculture as the backbone of the Latvian economy. Latvia cannot afford a depopulation of the countryside. A thriving countryside is also a precondition for green tourism, which may develop into a profitable business in the future. Bojars refers to the example of Switzerland. Latvia should protect its markets from subsidized imports in agriculture, because it has no money in the budget to subsidize its own agriculture. Moreover, Latvian products are cleaner than the products cultivated in the industrialized countries, where far more pesticides are being used. The opening of the borders to agricultural imports has helped to ruin Latvian agriculture. The fatal blow was given by the dissolution of collective farms, because the infrastructure was destroyed simultaneously. Collective farms should have been modernized to work in a cost-efficient manner. Private farmers were not given a real chance to start up due to the lack of affordable credits. Agriculture is closely related to the survival of a Latvian culture. European high culture flourishes in the cities, while ethnic culture is kept alive in rural areas. 'You are killing a nation, if you kill agriculture', argues Bojars.[273]

The LSDP does not believe in free trade. 'There is no such thing as free trade in the world', claims Bojars. 'Trade is restricted somehow everywhere as far as nationally important endangered branches or transitional periods are concerned. Both the GATT and EU principles provide instruments for that.' Latvia must develop balanced trade relations with the whole world – even the Far East countries – because it is dangerous to be dependent on one country. Russian markets should not be abandoned at any cost, since they are so very profitable. Latvians know how to do business with Russians, they have old connections there and many Latvian products are still competitive in the East. Latvia should join the EU with the speed Europe permits; in other words, as quickly as possible. The LSDP urges a closer integration of the Baltic and Nordic countries.[274]

As a professor of international law, Bojars derives his approach to the citizenship question from legal principles. The LSDP programme defines the task of the citizenship law to 'guarantee the existence of the state of the Latvian nation for the unlimited future'. Latvia is the nation state of Latvians and Livonians, whose justification rests on each nation's right to self-determination. International law and practice of nation states allow the so called positive discrimination, which determines imprescriptible priorities for nations living in their own historical territory. National policy in Latvia should aim at the satisfaction of the legitimate interests of Latvians and Livonians, the diminishing of the intercultural tension and reconciliation. The prevalence of imported pop culture and degradation of Latvian and Livonian culture should be fought against.[275]

Acceleration of the deoccupation must be supported. Latvia is not an immigration country: mass immigration of manpower is not permissible. Non-Latvians are given a full opportunity to gain their rights in accordance with international standards. Russian-speakers have a possibility to migrate to their own nation state, if the level of ethnic comfort in Latvia does not satisfy them. Latvians and Livonians do not have such a possibility. Latvia is the only place in the world where they can exercise the idea of a nation state, where they can develop their own language and culture at the state level. It is a tragedy that Latvians and Livonians are one of the most endangered ethnic groups in Europe, being a minority in seven of the biggest cities, including the capital. The state can have only one official language, otherwise there will be nothing that would keep the state together. A bilingual state would lead to a babel of tongues.[276]

All Latvians and Livonians have inalienable rights to return to their fatherland and receive Latvian citizenship. The LSDP is furious because deported Latvians who return from Siberia to Latvia after 50 years have not been accepted as Latvian citizens. A person to be naturalized should be loyal to Latvia, be fully integrated into Latvian society, know the Latvian language and support the Latvian nation state. The main distinction between citizens and non-citizens is that citizens have the right to determine state policies as well as to hold senior posts in state administration.[277]

The LSDP fights for social justice. According to the party programme, the whole development of the Latvian state should be centred on the improvement of people's living standards. The first priority is to ensure an appropriate human subsistence level for each and everyone – a worker, a woman, a child, a student, a disabled person. World market prices should not be introduced for consumer goods only but also for labour. The state should develop a strategy for raising wages to the level of the industrial countries, starting with manufacturing and creative sectors, including science, education and health care. Investments in health care, education, science, culture and social security should be increased. Construction of inexpensive state and cooperative apartments should be restarted. The legislation on restitution of residential buildings should protect tenants in the denationalized houses.[278]

8 The Political System and its Special Features

To be able to analyse the party programmes in a systematic fashion, it is necessary to introduce some contextual elements that make parties' positions on individual issues understandable. Respectively, it is essential to understand how separate issues are related to each other as well as to the underpinnings of a party ideology. Furthermore, if any generalizations are to be made, proper conceptual tools need to be put in place. The first step in sketching the context of economic policy is to outline the structure of party competition in Latvia. A dimensional analysis focusing on the configuration of political cleavages is helpful in this task.

The formation of party systems in East Central Europe has stimulated a proliferation of political science literature trying to conceptualize this process. Different authors have proposed divergent interpretations of the pattern of political alignment. A model that seems to fit with the political reality in Latvia has been introduced by Evans and Whitefield (1993). Evans and Whitefield's model matches the empirically constructed model by Nørgaard (1994) as well as the findings of the present study.

Evans and Whitefield extrapolate three cleavage dimensions, constituting the general categories of party competition: socioeconomic, ethnic and valence. The socioeconomic dimension centres around traditional left–right issues, including their area-specific applications. Such universal themes as the role of the state in the economy, regulation versus deregulation, social guarantees versus private initiative, political redistribution versus spontaneous market allocation, have found their expression also in the postcommunist countries. Topics related to a reform strategy are typical to the transitional economies exclusively but they still derive from the same left–right constellation. Gradualism versus shock therapy division lends itself to an example of the latter subcategory of the left–right issues. The ethnic dimension deals with such questions as citizenship rights, repatriation versus integration of immigrants, nationalism versus cosmopolitanism, traditional nation state versus multicultural bilingual state. The ethnic dimension overlaps the traditionalism–modernism dimension which has influenced, among others, the debate over the Constitution. The third dimension discerned by Evans and Whitehead is called the valence dimension. Evans and Whitehead reserve the valence category for such cases in which the socioeconomic or ethnic bases of competition are lacking. In the absence of substantial conflict dimensions, the principal issues around which parties compete are consensual. What will concern voters is the ability of parties to achieve agreed-upon goals.[279]

In the case of Latvia, the valence dimension is relevant to some extent, in spite of the existence of the socioeconomic and ethnic cleavages. This can be explained by the fact that the socioeconomic cleavage is neither so deep nor so firmly rooted as the appearance of the political conflict might suggest. To the extent that the socioeconomic cleavage fails to discriminate between parties it is partly replaced by the valence dimension. When policy programmes are relatively similar, results become decisive. Hence, Evans and Whitehead's reservation concerning the absolute exclusiveness of other cleavages can be relaxed. A modified version distinguishes between cleavage systems according to their degree of polarization and severity of conflict. If the prime cleavage is diluted or blurred, some issues inherent in it probably turn out to be consensual valence issues.

The content of the valence dimension depends on the content of a given political situation. Due to its conditional, volatile nature, it cannot be defined as precisely as the socioeconomic or ethnic dimension. In the case of Latvia, it takes its content primarily from the failures in economic policy. The valence dimension is obviously a secondary dimension the influence of which varies from time to time. For these reasons, the valence dimension does not need to be included in the basic demonstrations of Latvia's political cleavage structure but when analyzing electoral results, one must carefully scrutinize whether it is the valence dimension, rather than the socioeconomic dimension, that exerts influence.

The axes of party competition as well as individual parties' locations along these axes can be delineated in terms of a two-dimensional spatial model. Applying Evans and Whitefield's concepts to the political reality in Latvia, the axes can be specified as follows. The socioeconomic dimension consists of two intercorrelated subdimensions, namely a statism–liberalism and a gradualism–shock therapy dimension. The ethnic dimension is based on a nationalism–universalism division. The 'coordinates' of the parties in the spatial model are derived partly from the programme reviews displayed in the previous chapter (objective evaluation), partly from the self-location of parties[280] (subjective evaluation). It cannot be denied, though, that the location of parties in such a system of coordinates contains intuitive elements, too. One has to have an overall view of the political scene. In addition to analysing the programmes and the questionaires, I discussed the subject with several knowledgeable observers of Latvian politics. These informants included a specialist from Parliament's Press Centre, professors of the University of Latvia, diplomats of the Latvian Embassy in Helsinki and a counsellor of the Finnish Embassy in Riga. Moreover, I compared my own assessments with a similar spatial model delineated by Peters Strubergs, the party secretary of Latvia's Way, who also thoroughly explained the premises of his model to me. Relying on these various sources, I drew my own conclusions, and the final result is to be seen in Figure 8.1. The assessments of the party positions reflect the elites' appeals in the electoral campaign in September 1995.

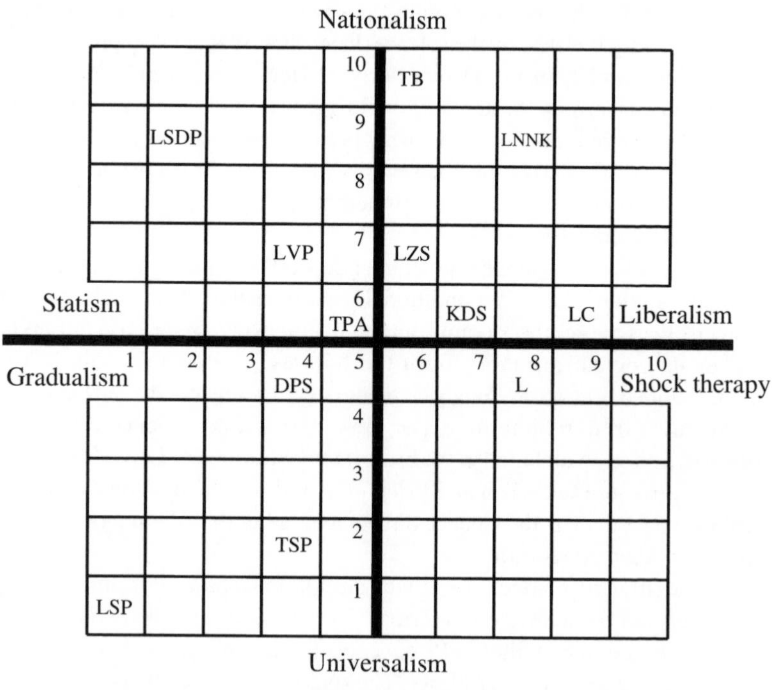

Figure 8.1   Political Cleavages and the Location of Parties in
the Competitive Space

SOCIOECONOMIC CLEAVAGE ON AN ISSUE BASIS

The main conflict in Latvian politics centres around the socioeconomic issues which can be defined in terms of left–right categories. In the pre-electoral campaign in 1995, parties set their sights on privatization, the banking crisis, the budget deficit, tax cuts, devaluation of the lats, the state monopoly on alcohol and pension reform. The same themes that dominated the electoral slogans constituted the core of the political programmes. Thus, the simplest way to analyse the content of the socioeconomic cleavage is to focus on the party programmes outlined in Chapter 7.

Many observers and researchers might be sceptical about such an approach, suggesting that party programmes cannot shed light on any issue. A persistent, widespread prejudice asserts that parties do not bother themselves with programmatic questions and their rhetoric consists merely of sporadic, populistic slogans. According to this view, parties have neither comprehensive programmes nor practical action plans. Parties are supposed to be incapable of thinking in terms of ideologies or other coherent belief systems.[281] My thesis is that the tendency to underrate the quality of party policies reflects a general ambivalence toward politics discussed at the end of this chapter. Although I do not dispute the alleged defects, my understanding of the state of politics is more positive.

In the first place, it must be clarified what is understood by a programme – a printed leaflet or fundamental principles guiding the party's policy formulation. To use an analogy, in common law countries, like Britain, the Constitution need not be written in full. It is true that the documented materials produced by parties are often unclear and incomplete. Many parties have in a written format only superficial short programmes the content of which would fit any political organization. Yet deficiencies in documents do not automatically imply that parties have no insight into the premises of their policy. Rather, this state of affairs reflects a lack of organizational resources. Young, inexperienced organizations with meagre financial means are not in a position to formulate their ideas on paper but, what is decisive, the ideas still exist in the heads of party leaders. Most parties are consistent in their approach in the sense that the various elements in their programmes are compatible with each other, which confirms the assumption that they rely on organized value systems. In the interviews, the representatives of parties appeared to be very well aware of their ideological underpinnings. The assertion that parties have no real programmes is based on a false method of collecting evidence; that is, one-sided reliance on published or other official documents. Discussions with parties give quite a different picture of the facilities of political actors from that obtained from the short programmes. What works in the advanced Western countries does not always work in the postcommunist countries.

Consensual Topics

Party programmes contain a substantial body of consensual themes that are shared by all parties. These consensual issues do not differentiate among parties and cannot thus constitute a source of political conflict. Therefore, such issues are irrelevant for our analysis which tries to extrapolate the divides within the political system. We shall first 'filter' the consensual topics from the programmes so that we can better concentrate on the controversial questions. The extent of general agreement also provides valuable information about the nature of political conflict.

Before going into the concrete cases, it should be mentioned once again – and for the last time – that the marketization of the economy is a self-evident starting point in all propositions, although this basic premise will not be repeated later on. The common ground implies that political conflict does not focus on the foundations of the economic system. Respectively, all parties understand that the rehabilitation of the economy is the cornerstone of future well-being as well as the prerequisite for the expansion of the social sector. Hence, all parties put their first priority on the development of the economy, because they realize it is impossible to proceed in a reverse order. Electoral slogans of some parties may have hinted at social populism but the attitude is more serious on the level of actual policy formulation.

All parties agree on the principles of taxation. The common demand is that tax rates should be cut, while at the same time an effective mechanism of tax collection should be put in place in order to combat widespread tax evasion. Tax incentives should be used as an instrument to foster private business and employment opportunities.

Modernization of Latvia's industry should be concentrated on competitive export branches which have a base in Latvia. These priority sectors should benefit from the country's natural resources, including the qualified work force, but they must be neither energy nor raw material intensive. Textiles, furniture, wood-processing, building materials, food processing and high-tech industries are mentioned as prospective branches of the future. Latvia's advantageous geographical location automatically allows a prominent role for transit to Russia. However, massive infrastructure investments in harbours and transport facilities are needed, if Latvia is going to win a position as a transit country. Foreign credits should be directed specifically into these kinds of infrastructure projects. Although nobody disputes the importance of transit trade, there are divergent opinions as to the question whether or not transit can constitute a mainstay of the economy. Left-leaning parties, which emphasize the primacy of a productive sector as the main employer in the economy, accuse Latvia's Way of an exclusive focus on transit and banking, the consequence of which was the complete destruction of Latvia's industry.

According to the prevailing public opinion, agriculture is an integral part of Latvia's economic structure and more resources should be devoted to its revitalization. The goal is to reach self-sufficiency in food production as well as to develop domestic food-processing industries. Parties admit that the agricultural question is not solely an economic one but there are deeper national and cultural values involved. The relation of Latvians to the countryside is very sensitive and emotional due to historical factors. Market principles cannot be introduced in agriculture too rapidly because the proportion of rural dwellers is so high that abrupt changes would cause a sharp rise in the unemployment rates. Except for the most liberal wing in Latvia's Way, all parties find it necessary to protect the domestic market from the dumping prices of subsidized farm imports. Thus, they are forced to accept both higher import tariffs and agricultural subsidies. The government is asked to fix guaranteed purchasing quotas for farm products for the state food reserve. Regional policies should stimulate the development of a provincial enterprise sector, which could gradually absorb the excess labour in agriculture. Despite the principal consensus on the protection of agriculture, it should be noted that there are differences in the intensity of commitment to the rural problems, depending on the main constituency of a given party. The National Bloc parties have agriculture very much at heart, since the major part of the Latvian nationals live in the countryside. The Russian parties are understandably oriented more toward industry, as the Russian workers populate the biggest cities. The Farmers' Union and the Unity Party are first and foremost devoted to the representation of rural interests.

A surprising unanimity was reached on the EU issue, as Latvia forwarded a formal EU application two weeks after the elections in October 1995. Following an invitation by the president, the faction leaders of all the political parties in the new parliament signed a declaration supporting Latvia's EU application. Contrary to expectations, the Socialist Party also endorsed the EU applications, abruptly breaking with its previous policy. The Socialist Party used to be the only party openly against Latvia's EU membership. 'This question cannot be solved to everyone's liking', commented co-chair Filip Stroganov after the party declaration signing. 'History moves forward and everyone has to work for Latvia to be an EU member.' The ratification of the agreement proved that an overwhelming majority of Latvia's political forces supports integration into the EU. Joining the EU has been a keystone of Latvia's foreign policy since the country regained independence. The sudden move was a symbolic reaction to the perplexing electoral result which raised doubts about the route Latvia wishes to follow. It made Latvia's resolve to join the EU unquestionable. The signing of the document was designed to keep Latvia on the road to EU membership, whoever takes power. In the same connection, the Cabinet agreed that Latvia must continue to reform its educational, legislative, agricultural and social security systems to meet EU standards.[282]

Conflictual Topics

Differences in individual issues and policies often derive from the fundamental differences in the underlying economic system that is aspired to. The economic models proposed by the Latvian parties vary from the Siegerist Party's Thatcherite ideal to the Socialist Party's China model and the Social Democratic Party's welfare state, to pick the extremes. The main bulk of the parties, however, stands for a socially responsible market economy, resembling the German *soziale Marktwirtschaft*. In spite of the common notion, there are slight differences in terms of exactly what is meant by a socially responsible market economy. The left-wing parties are more socially oriented, whereas the right-wing parties put more emphasis on the market elements. The essential point is that the mainstream is firmly committed to a market economy, although it rejects the boldest versions of the Anglo-American system pursued, for instance, by Mart Laar's conservative government in Estonia.

   Another basic division, which provides a framework for concrete policy choices, is based on the attitude toward economic liberalism. Parties can be grouped according to the influence of liberal ideas on their policies. Thus, we arrive at a basic classification of economic approaches with four clusters: (1) liberals (LC, LNNK, L), (2) qualified liberals (LZS, KDS, TB), (3) moderate interventionists (DPS, TPA, TSP, LVP), and (4) postsocialists (LSP, LSDP).

   Reflecting a worldwide trend, the neoliberal reform strategy triumphed in Latvia at the outset of the transition, but it was later challenged. Liberal principles are clearly evident in the profile of Latvia's Way and the liberal wing of the LNNK. The economic programmes of the Siegerist Party and the Christian Democratic Union also meet the standards of a liberal strategy. Fatherland and Freedom, the Farmers' Union and the conservative wing of the LNNK base their approach on liberalism but they reject what they call 'ultraliberalism', meaning that they are more cautious in their policy than, say, the LNNK liberals and Latvia's Way. Judging the recent policies, it seems that the liberal wing of the LNNK has strengthened its position within the party at the cost of the conservatives. Therefore, the LNNK is nowadays identified with the vigorous advocates of economic liberalism. A detail worth noting is that the Harmony Party has a very liberal businessman wing whose position corresponds to that of Latvia's Way and the LNNK. What attaches the businessmen to Harmony is probably the party's liberal citizenship policy, as a great part of Latvian business is in the hands of Russian-speakers.

   Economic liberalism is objected to by Saimnieks, Tautsaimnieks, Harmony and the Unity Party who equate the prevailing order with anarchy. These four parties share an approximately similar conception of economy which appeals for state support to industry. While centrist elements have become more and more conspicuous in post-election policies of Saimnieks, a truly leftist, anti-liberal alternative has emerged through the Social Democratic Party, which questions the foundations of the current reform strategy in a more fundamental way than the left-of-centre parties. In a category of its own is the Socialist Party with its adherence to the Chinese model for a gradual, state-led transition. The Socialist Party stands for a mixed economic system with considerable state influence on the economy.

The principal dissension on economic policy concerns the state's influence over the economy. Everybody agrees that state involvement must be drastically reduced in comparison with the previous system but the controversial question is exactly how much. The answer to this basic question has a bearing on choices in several related spheres, such as privatization and industrial policy. The positions taken by parties on this issue display the left–right divide within the party system very clearly. As a matter of fact, if that were not the case, the left–right dimension would not be relevant in the Latvian politics, since the question of the state's role in the economy is one of the most fundamental components defining the left–right dimension. The right-wing parties do not accept any state involvement in economic life, and they push for deregulation and promotion of competition. In their view, the sole task of the government is to provide the legislative framework for freely functioning markets. The Farmers' Union causes the only rift in the otherwise solid bloc configuration. Its view on the need for state control resembles that of the left-of-centre bloc. The left-wing parties leave room for economic regulation and state supervision, because they fear market anarchism. According to them, wild, unrestrained markets can lead to unpredictable consequences, as evidenced by the banking crisis.

A specific variation of the same theme concerns state ownership in industry. The LNNK, the Christian Democratic Union, Latvia's Way and the Siegerist Party take the most uncompromising stance on this issue, demanding that, with the exception of a few infrastructure objects, state ownership must be reduced to a minimum. State-owned industries will have no future in Latvia. Fatherland and Freedom as well as the Farmers' Union wish to retain some state influence in certain key sectors of industry, including the maintenance of state monopolies. Saimnieks, Tautsaimnieks, the Unity Party and the Harmony Party believe that the state must retain the ownership and management of strategic objects of national importance so that they can buttress capital accrual as well as the economic independence of the state. State-owned enterprises may exist alongside private enterprises at least in the short run, if they work efficiently under competitive conditions. The Social Democratic Party goes one step further, advocating explicitly a mixed economy, where a strong, dynamic state sector competes with the private sector. Replacement of state monopolies by private monopolies is not permitted by left-wing parties. Special attention is diverted to the creation of a state monopoly for the production, import and sale of alcohol after the traditional Nordic pattern. The Socialist Party shares the goals of the moderate left-wing parties, but its programme assigns the state-owned sector a considerably more pronounced role. Private entrepreneurship is to be favoured in services and small business, while big industries must be kept in the state's hands. While the National Conciliation Bloc parties view state-owned companies as exceptions to the rule, the Socialist Party builds its economic system on a predominant state sector. All the left-wing parties acknowledge the equal status of all property forms; the right-wing parties tend to prioritize private property.

A position taken on the question of the role of the state in the economy is logically reflected in the approach to privatization. An outline of a complete privatization strategy consists of a bundle of separate questions to be addressed when a privatization policy is being designed. All parties declare they want to accelerate the privatization process. This announcement, however, does not mean that parties would agree upon a unanimous privatization strategy. The real question is the way in which they want to speed up the privatization process: (a) by simplifying the procedure and making it more open or (b) by selling solely small enterprises and keeping the biggest ones under state control.[283] A fundamental disagreement centres on the essence or true meaning of privatization. The Siegerist Party and the Christian Democratic Union refer to the implicit assumptions behind various privatization concepts. The popular interpretation treats state property as people's property, aiming at redistribution of common wealth. The economist's view ties privatization with the promotion of investments and profit-making opportunities.

The conflict between the different objectives of privatization manifests itself in one's acceptance or rejection of accelerated privatization at any cost, that is, whether the speed per se is esteemed. The liberal parties are pushing for a fast, thorough programme which eliminates state ownership in the economy as quickly as possible. Latvia's Way, the Siegerist Party, the Christian Democratic Union and the business wing of Harmony believe that the purpose of privatization is to make the property work efficiently rather than to collect money for the budget. In their view, it is short-sighted to try to maximize the revenue from the sale of state enterprises, because it is much more important to create jobs and involve investments than to sell at a profit. Therefore, an entrepreneur with a sound business plan must be allowed to buy a privatization object at a nominal price so that he can start to work on the property as soon as possible. This line of argument implicitly values private property as superior to public property in that it assumes efficiency gains through a transfer of ownership to private hands.

The opposite view represented by Saimnieks, Tautsaimnieks and other non-liberal parties emphasizes the budget revenue obtained from selling state enterprises. These parties reject sales at a nominal price. An additional argument for not hurrying with privatization maintains that profitable state enterprises make a permanent contribution to the state budget. A Tautsaimnieks representative on the Supervisory Board of the Privatization Agency justified the idea with the metaphors 'the state should not kill the goose that lays golden eggs'.[284] The leftist forces rely on the ability of commercialized state enterprises to operate efficiently in a market environment.

The same above-mentioned Tautsaimnieks representative accused the Privatization Agency of selling only bad enterprises that would have required restructuring before sale. Restructuring by the state means price maximization at the cost of speed. Behind the demand for restructuring by the state is often a wish to postpone the sale of state enterprises and to keep them in the state's hands a little longer. Sometimes it can be used as an excuse to delay the liquidation of unprofitable enterprises, if the maintenance of working places takes precedence over other objectives. The liberals want to leave the responsibility for restructuring to the purchaser, because they do not consider it to be a task of the state. In addition, they remind their critics of the fact that the Latvian state does not possess the necessary means for a restructuring programme.[285]

Both sides argue in the name of employment but they choose the opposing means to achieve the same goal. The left-wing parties believe that jobs are better secured by postponing mass privatization, whereas the right-wing parties assume that private entrepreneurship can best enhance employment. The former view adheres to the preservation of the existing jobs in the short run, while the latter view puts its hope on the creation of new jobs in the long run. The concern about working places is reflected in the acceptance of liquidation as a means of privatization. The right-wing parties cannot accept that bankrupt state enterprises continue accumulating losses, which have to be covered by the state budget; that is, the money is ultimately taken from the pockets of tax-payers. The left-wing parties believe that a rescue plan is needed to save jobs. The variation in political views on liquidation has been presented in detail in Chapter 6 (p. 100–1). Generally taken, the leftist and nationalist parties show unfounded optimism about the market value of state enterprises, while the liberals see their condition more realistically. According to the leftist view, many state enterprises would be capable of surviving, if more efforts were made to restore the Eastern markets. The liberals doom the bankrupt enterprises as uncompetitive and non-viable.

Opinions diverge as to the procedure appropriate for conducting the sale of state assets. Latvia's Way and the other liberal parties urge the freeing of all operations and submitting them to market forces. The left-wing parties and Fatherland and Freedom want to bring the privatization process under stricter state control, claiming, among others, that the privatization of strategic enterprises should always be discussed in Parliament. The left-wing parties stress that the state must not lose sight of the social and economic consequences of enterprise privatization. Fatherland and Freedom is interested in preventing Latvian property from falling into the wrong hands. Fatherland and Freedom demanded that the background of prospective buyers should always be checked by the Privatization Agency to prevent an undesirable ownership structure. The Fatherland and Freedom faction organized a meeting in Parliament to discuss how many enterprises have been sold to former KGB agents, Communist Party members and Soviet citizens.[286]

The other aspect related to the appropriate sale method concerns the openness versus closedness of sales. The question has to do with competitiveness of the procedure. Latvia's Way and the LNNK advocate open actions without preferential treatment as to the type of buyers. Free competition among bidders implies that the selection of a buyer must be based on economic considerations solely – neither social nor political. The movement against free competition and open auctions consists of the forces inclined to the interests of domestic producers. State enterprise managers and representatives of former export industries are organized under the auspices of Saimnieks and Tautsaimnieks. They favour closed tenders with preference to insiders or specific groups of capital. The Social Democratic Party prioritizes employee ownership and workers' self-management.

Parties' approaches to privatization can be summarized by a triple classification. A liberal position is confronted from two different directions by nationalist and socially oriented forces. Latvia's Way pursues liberal policies; Fatherland and Freedom takes national concerns into account; the Social Democrats and the Socialists have a social emphasis, although the Socialists give way on socialist policies when the ethnic interest of Russian-speakers requires it. Saimnieks is hovering between a liberal and mildly socially oriented position. The populist Siegerist Party makes it a principle to always disagree, even though its programme is basically quite liberal. Correspondingly, the voting behaviour of the Socialist Party is sometimes motivated by the desire to oppose Latvian nationalists with the result that it may agree with more liberal solutions than Fatherland and Freedom. Voting behaviour of the smaller parties usually follows from their political reference group.

Latvia's Way and Fatherland and Freedom fully support high speed privatization and open methods in implementation. Saimnieks stands for privatization too, but it is tempted to manipulate the conditions in favour of specific investor groups and it would like to invite Eastern capital. It is not committed to procedural transparency to the same extent as Latvia's Way. It is not willing to expose all the information about prospective buyers it may hold, a feature which reflects Eastern business culture. One part of the Siegerists has reservations about the privatization of state monopolies, while the other part is very liberal right down the line. The Socialist Party prefers a liberal privatization strategy without qualifications, since exclusions are mostly directed against Russians. The Social Democrats declared themselves against privatization during the pre-electoral campaign of the second local elections, because in their opinion, privatization has been realized in an illegal fashion. These 'criminal' privatizations must be cancelled by rena-tionalizations. Social Democrats do not object to decent privatization, which takes into account social aspects, such as workers' rights and the protection of jobs. They accept neither liquidation of large state enterprises nor priva-tization of state monopolies. Their privatization policy is restrictive.

Two other issues that overlap with the privatization issue are foreign direct investment and foreign ownership of land. The largest investments in the near future are expected through privatization, but the prerequisite for a favourable development in investments is the establishment of a free land market.

The attitude toward FDI manifests a double-standard policy among one group of Latvian politicians. Superficially treated, FDI appears a consensual topic. All parties seem to welcome foreign investors to Latvia to provide the country with the badly needed capital, technology and know-how necessary for the diversification of the economic structure. Investors' contribution to jobs and exports is considered to be of vital importance to Latvia. Each party declares its dedication to create a favourable business environment, which will make Latvia an attractive business site. Parties claim to understand how hard the competition for Western investment is. However, when it comes to concrete cases, reservations begin to appear. The long-lasting political battle on Lattelekom's privatization with foreign capital is a shining example of resistance. Foreign monopolies in strategic sectors are rejected by the nationalist and left-leaning forces.

The basic fear is that foreign investors will buy the Latvian assets cheaply for well under their real value, enrich themselves at the cost of Latvians, repatriate the profits and crush the weak Latvian enterprises through competition. At the same time, Latvians will lose control over the national economy to foreigners who will be able to abuse their dictating position in the economy so that Latvia will be colonialized once again. The protectors of Latvian property tend to overestimate the standard and the capacity of Latvian industry, as if the old Soviet factories could be restarted with a little restructuring and as if the markets for their products had been given away voluntarily for political reasons. A typical error is to emphasize the uniqueness of Latvian resources or business opportunities and to put a lot of restrictions on their use in order to preclude their exploitation. Too many preconditions and provisos for the protection of various good things may create such an impenetrable jungle that a foreign investor loses his nerve when he is troubled by excessive regulations. Those who have a restrictive attitude toward FDI policies should remember that foreign investors do not exactly queue at the border waiting to rush into Latvia in masses. When a foreigner sets up a profitable business in Latvia, enviers claim that it would be better if Latvians handled the operation themselves to enjoy the profits themselves. Strangely they seem to forget that Latvians have neither the capital nor the managerial skills. Often it is not the public interest that worries the opponents of a specific investment but rather the vested interest of an economic lobby which does not tolerate foreign competition in its field. Of course, the resistance will be disguised in noble political rhetoric. Apart from these egoistic motivations, the desirability of free competition may not be understood adequately by all groups in Latvia.

Latvia's Way has the most consistent FDI strategy. It stands for foreign investment genuinely in practice too, trying to dismantle the remaining barriers. The Siegerist Party cannot afford to object to FDI, because German Siegerist has boasted of his actions to promote FDI from Germany. As business people, Saimnieks members are principally supportive of FDI, but they are more biased toward Eastern capital than the right-of-centre bloc. Fatherland and Freedom is cautious about the intrusion of foreign capital, as it would like to see Latvian capital dominating. While Fatherland and Freedom protects the interests of Latvian citizens, the Social Democrats defend the rights of labour but they also have a somewhat narrow interpretation of the national interest. Preconditions and restrictions cannot be avoided, even when FDI is not rejected as such. The Socialists have not been active in the FDI question.

Although each party officially welcomes foreign investors to Latvia, each party is not ready to grant foreigners the right to purchase land, especially in the rural regions. Hence, the question of land ownership reveals the true willingness to liberalize the investment climate. Land ownership is a very sensitive issue to Latvians because it has to do with the national mentality. Latvian peasants were liberated from serfdom as late as the beginning of the nineteenth century, 50 years before Russian peasants. Still, the Latvian peasants had to buy the land they had cultivated. Until the Second World War Latvia was primarily an agrarian country, implying that a great part of the native population has its roots in the countryside. Against this historical background, it is understandable that public opinion is against the sale of land to foreigners.[287] Decision-makers are beginning to realize that the economy cannot be developed without selling land without restrictions. The majority of political parties have yielded to this necessity, with the exception of parties attached to either rural interests or traditional values. The dividing line follows the rural–urban and the traditionalism–modernism cleavage rather than the left–right dimension.

The main force in Parliament against the establishment of a free land market was Fatherland and Freedom, whose stubborn resistance endangered the passing of Skele's bill. Fatherland and Freedom's claims are the primary reason why the privatization of land has not yet been started. The Farmers' Union, the Unity Party and the Social Democratic Party have also opposed a free land market. Tautsaimnieks requires that the state and the municipalities must control the purchases of land by foreigners. The sharpness of attitudes can vary within one party: radicals want to forbid the sale of land altogether while moderate opponents accept partial restrictions on certain areas or groups of people as well as other control measures.[288]

The opponents of a free land market want to prevent the 'sell-out of Latvia'. They have three kinds of argument. The emotional argument says that land is the only property the poor Latvians have left. The anti-Russian argument warns Latvians about increasing Russian influence in Latvia. Russians are supposed to control banks and oil transit already, but if they also buy all the land, what will happen to the Latvian state? Western investors are not much more popular. According to traditionalists, land is very valuable, although its price is temporarily very low. Hence, rich Westerners can buy the most fertile land for a song and line their pockets at Latvians' expense.[289]

Intercessors fear that the prohibition against selling land freely would limit foreign investment. The commonly used argument points out that one cannot build a factory without a plot of land under the building. The business parties Latvia's Way and Saimnieks are intrinsically interested in a free land market. The Siegerist Party and the Christian Democratic Union advocate the East German pattern in order to prevent eventual speculation with land. Land could be sold only to investors who commit themselves to definite projects which are bound with a certain number of employees. The land ownership question is further complicated by the citizenship issue. Harmony and the Socialist Party argue that it is totally unreasonable that non-citizens are deprived of the right to own land, if foreign investors are allowed to buy land in Latvia. Although the Socialist Party does not favour private ownership of land ide-ologically, the dismantling of restrictions serves the interest of

Russian-speakers. In addition, it provides an opportunity to be in opposition to Fatherland and Freedom, which it can never agree with.

Party positions on privatization, FDI and foreign ownership of land are summarized in Table 8.1.

Table 8.1   Attitudes Toward Privatization, Foreign Direct Investment and Foreign Ownership of Land by Parties Representing a Liberal, Nationalist and Socially Oriented Position*

Party	Privatization	FDI	Free land market
Latvia's Way	+ +	+ +	+ +
Fatherland & Freedom	+	¤	– –
Siegerists	+ / ¤	+ / ¤	+
Saimnieks	¤	+	+
Socialists	– / +	+	– / +
Social Democrats	–	–	– –

Key: + positive support without preconditions
        – reserved, restrictive attitude with many preconditions
        ¤ in-between position with minor exceptions, or an inconsistent, unclarified
        position
Note: * Sometimes the position taken in the programme differs from the actual practice realized in the voting behaviour. In those cases both the theoretical and practical definition have been presented in the table so that the former stands on the left side of the '/' division and the latter on its right side. Particularly pronounced, explicit formulations or activities either for or against have been denoted by a double plus or minus.

The use of a stable exchange rate as a means of macroeconomic stabilization was one of the most intensely debated topics in 1995. Almost all parties acknowledge the importance of macroeconomic stabilization so that they give their support to stringent monetary and financial policies as well as other measures needed to combat inflation and to curb the budget deficit. Only the Socialist Party argues that controlled inflation is a prerequisite for economic growth. While the government parties proudly present the excellent results of macroeconomic stabilization, the opposition parties call their bluff, claiming that the economy is not in balance.

The proper value of the lats is a more controversial question, which is also bound with the independent status of the central bank and the personality of the president of the Bank of Latvia. Latvia's Way, the LNNK, Fatherland and Freedom, the Siegerist Party and the Christian Democratic Union support unconditionally the policy of the strong lats as well as the current role of the Bank of Latvia in the economic policy-making. According to them, a devaluation would accelarate inflation with the result that everyone, exporters included, would be worse off afterwards. A stable currency and low inflation are defined as the cornerstones of the stabilization programme, which is the prerequisite for economic recovery. They are also marketed to foreign investors as the advantages Latvia is offering. Those parties that represent themselves as spokesmen for Latvian producers – Saimnieks, Tautsaimnieks, Harmony, the Socialist Party, the Unity Party, the Farmers' Union and the Social Democratic Party – attack the 'artificially high' rate of the national currency because it harms exports. The value of the lats should be determined so that it would balance the foreign trade account. The proponents for a devaluation consider the prevailing state of affairs tragicomical: Latvia has a totally ruined economy but a very stable currency, which is like a millstone. The critics claim that central bank policy must respond to the requirements of the economic situation.

During the pre-electoral campaign, there were voices demanding both the devaluation of the lats and Einars Repse's, the Governor of the Bank of Latvia, dismissal. After the elections, the tone became more moderate. Saimnieks leader Cevers announced his party's stance in October 1995 as follows:

> It is an abnormal situation, for example, herring caught by our fishermen cost three times more than those caught in Denmark. We are not saying that the lats should be devalued immediately. It has to find its real value to stimulate the country's export versus import ... World Bank experts say that the lats is propped up artificially. One person [Repse] had this idea to tie the lats 1:2 with the US dollar, disregarding the economy. He simply liked to play this computer game with his own big computer. Such childish games are too expensive ... Mr Repse is not critical to the Latvian state. We have to discuss how professionally he can lead the central bank.[290]

There are two slightly controversial points within the mostly consensual agricultural policy: the form of production and the form of protection. Land reform in combination with the prevailing restitution practice has created a class of small family farmers who live at the subsistence minimum and who cannot satisfy the domestic demand due to the demechanization of agriculture. Latvia used to export farm products during the Soviet era. The rightist bloc, which emphasizes restitution and denationalization on moral and ideological grounds, defines a family farm as the basic unit of Latvia's agriculture. Even if the dissolution of the collective farms initially leads to too small a farm size, the establishment of a real estate market will ensure a competitive farm size in the future. The leftist parties regard complete decollectivization as a mistake, although they recognize that it is now too late to restore collective farms, except in cases where they are still functioning. The left-wing parties campaign for the creation of voluntary producers' cooperatives to give an impetus for the development of marketing and processing facilities. They favour concentration of the agricultural production into bigger units than family farms. Latvia's Way and the LNNK are not enthusiastic about higher tariffs on agricultural imports but they have been forced to accept the idea. According to the LNNK, the state should rely on credits and subsidies rather than on customs tariffs in supporting agriculture. All other parties want to protect agriculture by all available means.

Latvia's international orientation and the direction of foreign trade – East or West – have induced a passionate dispute among the political parties. The parties are divided into two groups, the Europhiles and the Slavophiles, following the bloc division. The right-wing parties are eagerly piloting Latvia to Western Europe, calling to speed up the EU integration process. They are railing against any possible policy shift to a more eastward orientation, because they suspect the ultimate intentions of those parties that campaign for the need to build ties with Russia and the CIS. The rightist parties frighten voters by a future inclusion in the CIS, which would mark de facto the end of the independent Latvian state. The left-wing parties and the Siegerist Party rationalize their interest in the Eastern market on purely economic grounds, while accusing the rightist parties of unnecessarily politicizing the issue. They believe that the Eastern market is too valuable to be lost because the recovery of the industrial sector depends on the expansion of Latvian exports. They assure voters that the intensification of commercial relations with the CIS does not mean turning their back on the European integration. Neither Slavophiles nor Europhiles exclude economic contacts with either of the two spheres but they simply have reverse priorities. These differences in emphasis may have given the impression in the public debate as if one or the other side would totally neglect the development of trade relations with the less prioritized sphere. Creating such an image serves the political interests of the adversaries but it does not correspond to the truth.

A cross-cutting divide in trade policy revolves around the significance of the Baltic orientation. Hardly anyone disputes the desirability of intra-Baltic cooperation in principle but the sceptics do not believe in the possibility of its realization. Neither do they value it as highly as the active advocates of the Baltic economic space. Harmony, Latvia's Way, the Farmers' Union, the Christian Democratic Union and the Social Democratic Party actively advocate the intensification of cooperation among the Baltic states.

Summary

The main cleavages in Latvian politics, as far as economic policy is concerned, can be abstracted in terms of the six interrelated issue dimensions: state–market, regulation–deregulation, mixed ownership–private property, 'national' economy–open economy, protectionism–free trade and East–West. The conflict dimensions derive from the attitude toward economic liberalism. Although the 'shock versus gradualism' distinction is not an actively discussed issue in the public debate, parties are aware of its relevance and they are capable of taking a stand on it when explicitly asked. The variation in the reform strategies can be conceptualized in terms of four continuums: slow–fast, cautious–bold, conditional–unconditional and partial–complete.

To turn the perspective the other way around, the clustering can be organized around the classification of parties as well as around the issues. The different classifications created in the above text are not mutually exclusive but rather they are complementary, illuminating the various sides of the same position. Parties group in a similar fashion in relation to one another, irrespective of the specific criterion for the grouping. The consistency reflects the logical coherence among the elements of economic thinking. The separate issues form a chain in which all elements are interconnected with one another. For instance, the question of land ownership can be seen as a special case of the general readiness to grant freedoms to foreign investors as against the strict protection of national values. Equal opportunity brings about open, transparent privatization methods and emphasis on free competition. The chain could be followed indefinitely but the point is just to demonstrate how a liberal party takes a liberal stand on all problems right down the line and vice versa.

Parties divide into some four groups with distinctive profiles. Latvia's Way is the unswerving proponent of liberalism, being followed more or less consequently by the smaller right-of-centre parties. Conspicuous populism and a vague programme of the Siegerist Party make it difficult to determine its reference group, although the materials presented in this study would attach it to liberals. Fatherland and Freedom sticks to nationalism even in its economic policies, which the party itself defines as conservative. Its policies may not only occasionally contradict liberal principles but in the most far-reaching versions they paradoxically come close to the leftist strategy. Leftist parties divide into two groups according to the degree of ideologism. Saimnieks with its allies constitute the moderate left-of-centre bloc. The Social Democratic and the Socialist Party are truly leftist forces, although they are not allies. The relationship to the CP and national policies make the difference.

In sum, liberals, nationalists, left-leaning centrists and socialists make up the political spectrum in Latvia.

EVOLUTION OF THE PARTY SYSTEM

The present configuration of party competition displayed in Figure 8.1 can be fully comprehended only if the origins of the political alignment are known. Therefore, a short review of the evolution of the Latvian party system is necessary.

The first embryonic forms of political organization could be perceived in the spring of 1990 when the last legislative elections to the Supreme Soviet of the Latvian SSR were held. The political arena was dominated by two opposing forces – the Popular Front of Latvia (PFL), founded in 1988, and the Latvian Communist Party (LCP). The principal issue in the elections was Latvia's independence. The Popular Front functioned as a loose umbrella organization incorporating a wide spectrum of different political movements with various political persuasions. The only single cause which united these heterogeneous groupings was the idea of gaining Latvia's independence. After this immediate goal had been achieved and the legislature was faced with drafting laws on a range of disparate matters, the divergent views held by the Popular Front's members came to the fore. Inner tensions weakened its ability to act as a cohesive force. The Popular Front held an unrealistic desire to remain a unifying force for all people in Latvia but the rapid growth of non-aligned deputies in the legislature attributed to its dissolution. The unavoidable splintering of the Popular Front gave an impetus to the emergence of the Latvian party system. As a result of this political diversification, the Popular Front shrank to insignificance. It reconstituted itself as a political party in October 1994 but all prominent politicians had left the sinking ship long ago and gone over to other parties. The Popular Front ran for both the 5th and 6th Saeima elections but each time it failed to gain any seats in Parliament. In 1993, it won 2.6 per cent of the vote. In 1995, its defeat was even more crushing: 1.2 per cent of the vote.[291]

While the pro-independence organizations managed to keep their internal disagreements to themselves until the restoration of independence in August 1991, the weight of dissension was too heavy in the Latvian Communist Party to subdue the strife. Unable to maintain unity at its 25th congress in April 1990, the Communist Party lost the chance to retain its majority in the legislature where it had dominated throughout the decades of Soviet rule in Latvia. Unhappy with the party's reactionary leadership, liberal delegates (mostly Latvians) walked out of the convention. Most of the liberals joined forces with the Popular Front, voting for PFL candidates or even running as candidates endorsed by the front. With the walkout, the Communist Party became a bastion of communist conservatism. Its final demise came in August 1991, after the Supreme Council had ordered it to suspend its activities on the grounds that it had sought to overthrow the lawful government and legislature of Latvia. Consequently, the hard-core of standpatters (mostly Russians) transformed themselves into the Equal Rights movement which, in turn, was later re-formed into the Socialist Party.[292]

At the initial stage of the realignment process, like-minded deputies organized themselves as factions within the Popular Front. In anticipation of the forthcoming elections in June 1993, the political spectrum expanded with a leap as new organizations were founded and old ones splintered or redefined themselves. Most of the major actors on Latvia's political scene emerged during this first wave of realignment. Many of them were first established as public organizations or electoral associations; only later were they registered as political parties. (See Tables 8.2 and 8.3)

Twenty-three political organizations competed for Latvians' votes in the 5th Saeima elections held on 5–6 June 1993. Eight parties or electoral coalitions managed to exceed the 4 per cent barrier needed to obtain seats in Parliament: Latvia's Way, the LNNK, Harmony for Latvia – Rebirth of National Economy, the Farmers' Union, Equal Rights, Fatherland and Freedom, the Christian Democratic Union and Democratic Centre Party. The dominating issues in the pre-electoral campaign dealt with the citizenship law, withdrawal of the Russian troops, desovietization and denationalization of confiscated property. The nationality question was sharper and much more pronounced than in the next elections in 1995, while socioeconomic issues were overshadowed by the problems related to the survival of the nation. Reflecting a national consensus on the return to Europe, the Latvians gave their firm support to an economic reform course. Latvia's Way, a liberal reform party, came out a triumphant winner with 36 deputies, taking the lead in Latvian politics. The second largest party had less than half the number of seats gained by Latvia's Way. A notable feature in the election result was that left-wing parties were weakly represented in Parliament. Three left-wing parties totalled only one-fourth of the seats. The victory of the right was easy to explain as a reaction against communism. The Communist Party had discredited itself in the eyes of the population so completely that people distrusted all leftist forces.[293]

Table 8.2   Political Parties in Latvia: Ideological Profiles

Party	Ideology	Left–right position	Dominant cleavage	Party leader
For Fatherland and Freedom (TB)[NB]	National conservative	Right	Citizenship	Maris Grinblats
Latvian National Conservative Party (LNNK)[NB]	National conservative	Right	Socioeconomic	Anna Seile
Latvian Christian Democratic Union (KDS)[NB]	Christian democratic	Right-of-centre	Socioeconomic	Paulis Klavins
Latvian Farmers' Union (LZS)[NB]	Agrarian	Right-of-centre	Socioeconomic	Andris Rozentals
Latvia's Way (LC)	Liberal	Right-of-centre	Socioeconomic	Valdis Birkavs
People's Movement for Latvia/Siegerist Party (L)	Populistic	Right	Socioeconomic	Joachim Siegerist
Latvian Unity Party (LVP)	Agrarian populistic	Left-of-centre	Socioeconomic	Alberts Kauls
Democratic Party Saimnieks (DPS)	Pragmatic	Left-of-centre	Socioeconomic	Ziedonis Cevers
Political Union of Economists (Tautsaimnieks) (TPA)	Social liberal	Left-of-centre	Socioeconomic	Edvins Kide
National Harmony Party (TSP)	Left liberal	Left-of-centre	Citizenship	Janis Jurkans
Social Democratic Party of Latvia (LSDP)	Social democratic	Left	Socioeconomic	Juris Bojars
Latvian Socialist Party (LSP)	Pro-communist	Extreme left	Citizenship	Larisa Lavina and Filip Stroganov

Note: [NB] = National Bloc party

Table 8.3   Political Parties in Latvia: Distribution of Votes (%) and Seats in the
5th and 6th Saeima Elections, 1993 and 1995

Party	5th Saeima		6th Saeima		Trend
	Share of votes	Number of seats	Share of votes	Number of seats	
Fatherland and Freedom	5.4	6	11.9	14	+
LNNK	13.4	15	6.3	8	–
Christian Democrats	5.0	6	coal.	coal.	–
Farmers' Union	10.7	12	coal.	coal.	–
[LZS & KDS & LDP]	*	*	6.3	8	
Latvia's Way	32.4	36	14.6	17	–
Siegerist Party	*	*	14.9	16	+
Unity Party	< 4.0 (–)	0	7.1	8	+
Democratic Party	4.8	5			
→ Saimnieks			15.1	18	+
Tautsaimnieks	coal.	coal.	1.5 (–)	0	–
Harmony	coal.	coal.	5.5	6	–
[TSP & TPA]	12.0	13	*	*	
Socialist Party	5.8	7	5.5	5	–
TOTAL	89.5	100	87.2	100	

Key:
coal. = The party had joined an electoral coalition before the elections and did not
run separately.
* = The party or electoral association did not participate in the elections.
(–) = The party's share of the national vote is subtracted from the share of the parliamentary parties of the national vote (total), because the party gained no
seats in Parliament.

Sources: *Baltic Observer*, 5–11.10.1995; *Current Latvia*, 16–23.10.1995; Saeima
Information Department, 3 September 1995.

Personalities were decisive to the electoral result: many Latvians voted
for leaders without understanding the real content, not to mention the
consequences, of reform policies. Latvia's Way had succeeded in gathering
under its wing a lot of prominent, influential politicians, including Anatolijs
Gorbunovs, Latvia's first president. Anatolijs Gorbunovs had been the most
popular politician in Latvia since the late 1980s, and people followed him
in 1993, too. Gorbunovs is still a heavyweight politician who enjoys exceptionally high esteem among a large number of Latvians. He stands out
clearly from ordinary politicians. One might speak about statesmanship and
strong charisma in his case.[294]

Latvia's party system did not reach its final shape even after the first wave of party formation in 1993. The political landscape was continuously shifting. Again, new parties were founded and old organizations split up. The realignment of political forces peaked at the outset of the 6th Saeima elections held on 31 September–1 October 1995. Nineteen political parties or electoral coalitions submitted their candidate lists to the Central Election Committee in the hope of surpassing the 5 per cent threshold. Nine groupings gained seats in the 6th Saeima: the Democratic Party Masters (newcomer), the Siegerist Party (newcomer), Latvia's Way, Fatherland and Freedom, the Unity Party (newcomer), the LNNK, the coalition Farmers' Union, the Christian Democratic Union and Latgale's Democratic Party, the National Harmony Party and the Socialist Party. The election winners were primarily newly established parties that had not yet existed when the last elections took place. The previous winner Latvia's Way lost more than half of its support. Despite the crushing defeat, it ended up third in the polls and second in the seats because its votes were favourably distributed by region.[295]

The election result contributed to a splintered vote and, accordingly, a fragmented Parliament with no clear leader. There were four parties of almost equal strength which all represented incompatible political orientations. The most successful party was left-of-centre Saimnieks, followed by the right-wing populist Siegerist Party and right-of-centre Latvia's Way. The best performer of the National Conservative Bloc was national radical Fatherland and Freedom, surprisingly in fourth place. Compared to the elections of 1993, Latvia turned slightly to the left in 1995. Saimnieks's good performance was foreseen, but the triumph of the populists – Siegerist and Kauls – was a shock.

Local elections are observed less for their own sake but rather in anticipation of the next general election: local results are assumed to give hints of trends in national politics, although such indications are by no means watertight. The national conservative LNNK was the big winner in the first local elections in 1994, but the premature success did not ensure it a good showing in the 1995 general elections. Left-of-centre Saimnieks made a promising breakthrough in 1994 and also triumphed in the next Saeima elections. In the second local elections Saimnieks came out on the losing side, with only 6 of its 46 fielded lists landing candidates council seats. Bojars's Social Democratic Party came out as the big winner in March 1997, as it was able to collect the protest votes from the disgruntled masses of pensioners and factory workers (Table 8.4). The mainstream parties from the centre-right and centre-left were knocking on the wrong door. Technocratic pro-market themes were jettisoned in favour of socially oriented themes, as the disaster striking the newly founded conservative Reform Union proved. Reform's mobile phone-toting leaders relied on the young urban professional vote, but it was not enough in Latvia. Two of the main electoral themes were rent control and apartment heating. The Social Democrats took a decisive stand in favour of freezing rent controls and subsidizing housing. In Riga the government coalition Fatherland and Freedom, Latvia's Way and Saimnieks managed to maintain a governing majority by allying themselves against the Social Democrats.[296]

Table 8.4 Winners of the Second Local Elections and
Their Shares of the National Vote, 1997 (%)

Party	Share of Votes
Social Democratic Party	23.5
Saimnieks	11.5
Latvia's Way	10.5
Fatherland and Freedom	9.8
Farmers' Union	7.2

Source: *Baltic Times* 20–26.3.1997.

The electoral victory of the populist Siegerist Party in the 6th Saeima elections served as a catalyst to launch a two-phased realignment process, which had far-reaching implications for the political system. The attitude toward the Siegerists – a total rejection or a lukewarm, calculating acceptance – divided the political field into two parts, but of course the division reflected deeper political differences in substantial issues as well. In the first phase, left- and right-wing parties managed to close their ranks, which led to the formation of two equally strong blocs, the National Conciliation Bloc and the National Bloc complemented by Latvia's Way. The National Conciliation Bloc consisted of three left-leaning parties – Saimnieks, Harmony and Unity – which joined hands with the Siegerist Party. The Socialist Party, though not a member of the coalition, declared its support for the National Conciliation Bloc. The cohesiveness of both blocs in the first votings seemed to cement a left–right divide in Latvian party politics – but only for a while.[297]

Latvia's Way and the National Bloc parties were united by their firm objection to cooperation with the Siegerists. Particularly Fatherland and Freedom moderated its course with view to the coalition building, compromising many of its principles. Before the elections, Fatherland and Freedom had proclaimed that it would not cooperate with Latvia's Way but frightened by Siegerist and leftist dominance, both parties showed willingness to put aside their secondary disagreements. As long as the blocs kept their coherence, the left-leaning National Conciliation Bloc needed the support of the Siegerists in Parliament. Cevers commented on the coalition with

Siegerist pragmatically: 'This was not a wedding of love but rather a matter of following political purpose in a very uncertain time.' Harmony leader Jurkans maintained that agreeing with Siegerist was a matter of respecting the voters' will. 'All the talk about Siegerist's negative influence on Latvia's relations with the EU and Germany is greatly exaggerated', Jurkans said.[298]

The prolonged, difficult negotiations on the post-electoral government shuffled the cards anew. Siegerist was once again the initial source of problems. The leading principle that guided President Ulmanis's choices during the government formation was his resolution to exclude Siegerist from the government. Ulmanis dismissed the For Latvia Movement as an 'oppressive and hostile force'. Siegerist's nomination as an economic minister in the planned Saimnieks-led government cost Cevers a candidacy for premier in the first round. Instead of nominating election winner Cevers, Ulmanis invited Fatherland and Freedom leader Grinblats to form the new government. When Cevers's turn finally came he was no more successful than Grinblats. As two premier candidates had been rejected in the vote of confidence, it became obvious that the country could not be ruled effectively with a two-bloc system where one of the blocs held only a slim majority. Grinblats and Cevers's failed attempts to form a government on a bloc basis paved the way for more far-reaching mergers.[299]

In the second phase, the bloc boundaries crumbled as rightist and leftist parties joined forces. Cevers's change of tune made a broadly based 'rainbow government' possible after two months of negotiations. Earlier Cevers had refused to sacrifice his bloc's stability, but the political stalemate scrapped his bloc loyalty in favour of a stable majority government. The rainbow government was supported by six of nine parliamentary factions: Saimnieks, Latvia's Way, Fatherland and Freedom, the Unity Party, the LNNK and the Farmers' Union/Christian Democratic Union coalition. The new prime minister Andris Skele was a non-political compromise figure – he is a businessman – who was nominated as the competing blocs could not agree on a political person for reasons of prestige.[300] The rainbow government is undoubtedly the best solution to guarantee efficient governance when Parliament is divided, but this arrangement is not without its pitfalls either, because the existence of two wings within the coalition shifts the locus of political conflicts from the legislature to the government.

The rainbow solution left the Siegerist Party in opposition together with two fringe parties, Harmony and the Socialists. Despite its solid number of seats, the effective isolation of the Siegerist Party curtailed its influence on politics considerably. Ulmanis could be content, whereas furious Siegerist announced he would be in 'fierce opposition' to Skele's 'mafia cabinet'.[301] He has kept his word. The political strategy of the Siegerist Party is built on opposition for opposition's sake, even when the differences in economic thinking were not so sharp. Its aim is to undermine the stability of the government by all thinkable means, including the use of filibuster tactics. Still, its opportunities to shake the majority parliamentarism are quite limited. Today the Siegerists are even less of a menace to political stability than at the beginning of the legislative period, since the party was split into two parts in 1996. The splinter group called 'For People and Justice', which had supported Skele's first government systematically in all votings, was invited to participate in Skele's second government. In the second local elections the Siegerist Party fielded only a few candidate lists in a small number of municipalities, and the electoral success was likewise limited, as its voters had shifted to the Social Democrats. Siegerist seems to have realized that his story in Latvian politics has come to an end, since he has been spending increased time in Germany.[302]

The viability of the rainbow government was mistrusted beforehand, because it was composed of very heterogeneous political forces with a history of vigorous rivalry. Latvia's Way had the best match with Skele's policy vision. Saimnieks had political scuffles with Skele over privatization and budget policy. Fatherland and Freedom locked horns with other coalition parties especially on land reform and the citizenship question but it also held a different position on many points in economic legislation. Unity earned the reputation of being a coalition recalcitrant, which caused its exclusion from the next government.[303] Constant intra-coalition rows could not be avoided, but they did not block the work of the government, let alone tear apart the coalition. On the contrary, the implementation of a stiff-necked reformist platform was accelerated and many epoch-marking bills were pushed through Parliament. Skele's grim determination, talent for mediating between bickering ministers and ability to take drastic measures, if need be, together with the basic consensus on the ultimate goals saved the coalition from wreckage for a long time.

Saimnieks, in its exhalation of strength, had its share of differences with Skele and other ruling parties over 1996. Self-willed Cevers resigned as deputy premier in November 1996 as a consequence of long Skele–Cevers run-ins, blaming the premier for an authoritarian style of leadership. A month before Cevers had ousted his own Minister of Finance Aivars Kreituss from both the party and the ministry as a culmination of an intra-party spat. Kreituss had introduced a balanced budget in line with Skele's programme but against the deficit demands of Saimnieks. When Kreituss was dismissed from the party, his politician wife Ilga Kreituse, the Saeima Speaker and a former candidate for the presidency, also resigned from Saimnieks. The hunt for a new Minister of Finance was a long drawn-out process, and finally the dispute over the minister candidate toppled the whole government.

Saimnieks, who assumed the Ministry of Finance according to the government coalition contract, nominated businessman Vasilijs Melniks a candidate for the post on 13 January 1997. Prime Minister Skele approved the suggestion on the same day. Skele's approval raised heavy criticism because of Melniks's dubious business background. Melniks was suspected of having violated the anti-corruption law, since he was faced with charges ranging from tax evasion to selling contraband alcohol to having played a role in the collapse of Daugava Bank, a small commercial bank at which he was a shareholder and bank council member. A number of leading politicians, joined by President Guntis Ulmanis, started a campaign against Melniks before the parliamentary vote of confidence in his nomination, which resulted in Skele's defeat. What stuck in Skele's craw particularly was that a total of 13 coalition deputies from Latvia's Way, Fatherland and Freedom, LNNK and Unity voted against Melniks, and a number of others abstained from voting.[304]

In conjunction with the polemics over the nomination of Melniks, the 'moral spirits' in which Skele's coalition government was formed was questioned even by the President. Some coalition politicians complained that Skele had forced them to make unethical decisions in the name of reform. Skele took issue with the criticism flung at him and tendered his resignation on 20 January complaining about insufficient support: 'To my mind, these unprecedented accusations are too hard for me to swallow, as I am without real support [in the government coalition] to continue my work in this post.' Cevers blamed Ulmanis for having stirred up the anti-Melniks camp and declared that the government fell because of an intrigue and an artificially generated dispute. To those who remembered the events of the previous autumn, Saimnieks's sudden outburst of pro-Skele sentiment came as a surprise.[305]

A week-long series of interparty deliberations saw two forerunners for the post of prime minister emerge: Andris Skele (independent), the resigned Prime Minister, and Guntars Krasts (TB), the Minister of Economy. Saimnieks, the largest parliamentary faction, as well as the LNNK, the Farmers' Union, the Christian Democratic Union and For People and Justice, expressed support for Skele. Latvia's Way and Fatherland and Freedom, respectively the second and third largest factions, nominated Krasts for the post. The latter vigorously pushed the view that a member of a leading party would have more success in the government post than any outside candidate. According to them, Latvia needed a party-affiliated politician as prime minister. President Ulmanis picked up Skele and, following the renomination, Latvia's Way and Fatherland and Freedom came over to Skele's side. Skele returned to power with an almost identical government to the previous one. Only the Unity Party was replaced by For People and Justice and a couple of ministers were changed. The parliamentary factions backing Skele and coming together to form the government were Saimnieks, Latvia's Way, Fatherland and Freedom, the coalition Farmers' Union/Christian Democratic Union, the coalition LNNK/Green Party and For People and Justice. A majority of 70 deputies voted in favour of Skele's new government, 17 voted against and one abstained.[306]

After the government reshuffle many Latvians raised the legitimate question of what had changed. The same coalition headed by the same prime minister claimed the same ministerial posts. The coalition party leaders admitted that Skele had lacked a sufficient reason to resign from his post. Nor was Skele known as an oversensitive, soft-skinned weakling who is startled by criticism. Therefore, his offended reaction smacked of playacting. Skele was famous for his strong-arm style to pressure disagreeable coalition members into towing the government line, which caused accusations of non-democratic leadership. In the previous year he had threatened to resign more than once if coalition members did not come around to his way of thinking. Skele repeated demands for more coalition discipline after the formation of the new old government, warning that the rules would be stricter this time.[307] It seems likely that the government crisis was not genuine but a mere trick to tighten Skele's hand on the government and to get rid of an awkward ministerial candidate.

CENTRE-ORIENTATION DESPITE FRAGMENTATION

The alliance of leftist and rightist forces reveals something very essential about the political climate in Latvia. First of all, it effectively disproves the false notion which tries to equate the current situation with the prewar situation. In the 1920s, many European countries, including Latvia, suffered from illnesses of ultrademocratic constitutions: fragmented, polarized legislatures, constantly changing weak minority governments and sharp ideological conflicts with extremist tendencies. The deadlock of democracy paved the way for authoritarian movements which seized power in the early 1930s – and not entirely against the will of disillusioned citizens. Without going into the conditions that make the difference between the past and the present, it is evident that extremist fringe groups are not eroding the political middle in today's Latvia.

Splintering of the party system cannot be denied but, contrary to the prewar legislation, the 5 per cent barrier prevents the smallest splinter groups from gaining seats in the legislature. If the Anglo-American two-party system is used as a yardstick, the number of parties represented in Parliament still remains high. However, the Anglo-American system is not the sole viable model for democarcy, as some authors appear to believe. The Nordic countries have traditionally had multiparty systems – Denmark even an atomized one – though the tendency has been toward more coherent systems. Finland has at the moment ten political parties in the legislature where the two smallest factions consist of merely one deputy. In this light, Latvia's nine-party system does not look so alarming. It is easy to cast the blame for the fragmentation of the party system on the electoral system based on proportional representation. Yet single-member districts would not be a good solution to the problem because majority voting would not mirror the diversity of political opinions, which could cause the discontent to be channelled into extra-parliamentary movements. The social cleavage structure as well as the infantile stage of political development has to be taken into account when party systems are being compared.

Parties are not positioned along one dominant competitive dimension in Latvia but rather the space of party competition is composed of several cross-cutting cleavages: left–right (Latvia's Way, [the LNNK], Saimnieks, Tautsaimnieks, the Social Democratic Party), nationalism–universalism (Fatherland and Freedom, [the LNNK], Harmony, the Socialist Party) and rural–urban (the Farmers' Union, Unity). In addition, populists and Christians are competing for the votes of the Latvians. The traditionalism–modernism dimension exerts indirect influence, which cannot be measured easily in the number of seats. Fatherland and Freedom and the Social Democratic Party defend traditional values against Latvia's Way and Saimnieks's modernism. The two first-mentioned dimensions are the dominating cleavages in politics that have most impact on coalition building.

Another indication of the viability of the Latvian party system is that the parliamentary parties collect the major part of the given votes. Unlike in the last Duma elections in Russia, the share of redundant votes is low, in spite of the threshold. In 1993, eight parliamentary parties totalled 89.5 per cent of the national vote; in 1995, the respective figure was 87.2 per cent. The electoral support of political organizations not being elected varied from 0.1 per cent to 4.6 per cent (average 1.2 per cent) in 1995. That is to say, the drop-outs belonged to quite another size class than the elected parties. The extra-parliamentary parties are so tiny that they cannot shake the foundations of the political system. Moreover, nobody can claim that significant political forces are excluded from Parliament, since the votes are clearly concentrated on the main parties.

Political concentration will most probably reduce the number of political parties in the future as the socioeconomic cleavage is gradually superseding the pre-industrial cleavages. The first signs of a unification process within the party system are already in the air, in spite of the tendency that merger plans induce the splinter groups to form new parties but, at least thus far, the splits have been fatal to the dissolved parties (cf. Harmony and Tautsaimnieks, and For Latvia and For People and Justice). Unity and Harmony hover at the edge of a merger with Saimnieks. Unity has consented to merge with Saimnieks by the spring 1997. The party congress of Harmony ruled out a similar merger, but some propagators of the merger defected to Saimnieks anyway with the consequence that Harmony was deprived of its status as a parliamentary faction.[308] The LNNK united with the fellow national conservative party, Fatherland and Freedom. The LNNK dissidents who opposed the coalescence formed the Latvian National Reform Party.

Another counterweight to the political fragmentation is the strong centre-gravitation of the party system, which mitigates the negative effects of the former characteristic. The majority of the political parties are moderate right-of-centre or left-of-centre parties and there are no powerful extremist forces pushing for anti-system policies. Ideological distances between the political parties are relatively small at the programmatic level. Electors complain that the party platforms are so similar that they cannot discern any difference between political alternatives, which makes the choice in the elections difficult. Experts confirm this observation. Three days before the 6th Saeima elections, 30 per cent of the electorate had not yet decided which party they would vote for because of the vagueness of the party profiles. The pull toward the centre is growing stronger all the time. Saimnieks, which was not recognized by its right-leaning competitors to be a centrist party before the 6th Saeima elections, has now commonly admitted to being a left-of-centre force. The established parties show preparedness to close their ranks against radical challengers. They are conscious of the image required to become accepted as a 'serious' political alternative.

The main factor that pulls political parties toward the centre is the lurking threat of Russia. If Russia is considered to be the explanatory (independent) variable in the constellation, the EU can be defined as an intervening variable. Latvia's firm determination to join the EU is motivated by security considerations to a great extent, when the NATO option appears highly unlikely. The commitment to the EU, in turn, imposes strict restrictions on policy choices. Extremist solutions are automatically excluded, if Latvia wishes to meet with the approval of the EU countries. The other explanatory factor stems from the internal structure of the party system. Paradoxically, the fragmentation maintains a kind of 'balance of terror' by making coalition building inevitable. It was illustrative to observe how swiftly Fatherland and Freedom deradicalized its outlook after the 6th Saeima elections in order to qualify for the government. Centrist parties are always better positioned in coalition building, because they are acceptable to many political orientations.

The paradox of Latvian politics is that, in spite of minor differences in political programmes, parties are all too often incapable of arriving at an agreement. The hindrance to interparty cooperation is not a polarization of the party system in terms of sharp ideological contrasts but rather it reflects an immature political culture, entailing an inability to make compromises. Typically, the difference in opinions may be relatively small and, thus, seemingly reconcilable but still the political controversy may be long and spectacular. Even if all parties saw that it would be more advantageous for everyone to reach any decision than to leave the matter unresolved, they may be unwilling to conciliate. Politicians' stubbornness and unreasonable inflexibility often block urgent measures to the disadvantage of the public interest. Personal power struggles may give the impression that the political conflict would be sharper than it is in principle.[309]

An amusing example of politicians' childish ambition is the electoral coalition 'Labour and Justice' (*Darbs un Taisnigums*), which ran for the 6th Saeima elections with modest success, winning only 4.6 per cent of votes. This leftist coalition with trade union links was composed of four separate political parties and four public organizations. The point here is that although all the coalition partners were tiny in size and they shared approximately the same political aspirations with only slightly divergent shades, they could not agree on a unified party under one leader. One cannot avoid a feeling that everybody simply wanted to be a party leader. The phenomenon may well be generalizable to the whole political culture.

Latvian politics is highly personalized and the political elite is small with the result that personal animosities and sympathies play an essential role in bargaining. If the key persons of two parties, for instance, do not get along together, the coalition building may be hampered, even if there are excellent grounds for an alliance on a policy basis. A great proportion of political quarrels deal with nominations for various posts. The government crisis in January 1997, which led to the Prime Minister's resignation, was incited by a disagreement over the nomination of a new finance minister. The elitist drive of Latvian politics reflects the condition in which the social differentiation and the organization of civil society are underdeveloped. Political parties are not mass parties in the true sense of the word. Electoral shifts in political support ensue more from distrust in the ability or morals of the present rulers than from fundamental reconsiderations.

Attitudes toward sensitive political issues are often influenced by emotion rather than by reason. Latvian politicians have not yet learned to play the game with detachment. The grasp of sentimentality is especially apparent in relation to Russia. Nor have politicians been good at making a distinction between public and private affairs. In the formative years of the republic particularly, it was questionable whether they were pushing their own aims or Latvia's aims. The latter defect is closely related to a widespread corruption problem.

CORRUPTIVE SYMBIOSIS OF BUSINESS AND POLITICS

The origin of capital as well as the links between business and politics belong to the most closely guarded secrets in Latvia.[310] If one asked a Latvian to name the most prominent and influential figures in Latvian business, one would not get an answer, because nobody – except for a small circle of insiders – knows the rich. Faceless business hides behind the tinted black glasses of imported luxury cars. The name of the president of a company does not necessarily reveal anything about the true owners, since the president may act as a mere front without real decision-making power. A piece of Russian satire describes a man whose job was to get imprisoned. Many presidents serve a similar function in a figurative sense. With the exception of Parex, all Latvian banks have a Latvian president, even though it is commonly known that Russian-speaking capital is heavily involved in banking. For the same reason, it is difficult to draw a distinction between Latvian- and Russian-speaking business. Russian off-shore capital often enters Latvia under the guise of a Western investor. A 'Swedish' investor may turn out to be an off-shore company of a Russian firm.[311]

The veil of secrecy around Latvian business reflects the condition that the origin of capital is usually dubious. Typical sources of money are crime, the Communist Party, spontaneous privatization and Russia. Most business in Latvia is 'grey', as black money becomes whiter and whiter over the course of time. The lack of effective control mechanisms and established business traditions facilitate the features associated with the Wild East. The uninstitutionalized relationship between business and politics especially casts a long shadow of suspicion over the Latvian elite. The structure which relates political and economic forces to each other is carefully concealed. The link, though invisible, is nevertheless believed to be intimate. The yellow press regularly makes big headlines out of politicians' shady transactions, although black-and-white evidence is usually scarce. The third pillar in this triangular constellation is crime, which is amalgamated in both economic and political structures. Symbiotic relations are based on mutual interdependency: none of the three actors can survive without the others.[312]

All available information is based on guesses and rumours, but, of course, those outsiders who are engaged in big business in Latvia cannot avoid forming a rough picture of the situation around them. It is commonly believed that there might be half a dozen conglomerates that have divided the Latvian economy into exclusive spheres of control. These conglomerates are ramified holding companies which have extended their tenacles into various branches or they at least dominate the different stages of production process within one branch. Often they have achieved an oligopolistic position in their field, but there are a few examples of monopolies, too. The highly profitable transit of precious non-ferrous metals from Russia to the West, for instance, is monopolized by Russian-speaking companies. The conglomerates are not so much competitors in economy, since they are operating in distinctive fields. The rivalry comes to the fore in politics, because different business branches have different needs and priorities to be realized through economic legislation or policy-making. To cite a simplistic example, exporters need a weak currency, while importers want a strong currency. The diverging interests in economic policy prompt lobbying and political sponsoring, thus, explaining why the link with politics is of vital importance.[313]

It is not quite unambiguous to name the economic groupings, because they are not clearly defined nor well known, they are partly overlapping and they are in a constant state of ferment. Oil transit in general is believed to be the most powerful pressure group in Latvia. Skonto (multi), Mono (multi), Avelat (food) and Turibas (food) are names of the huge holding companies that are mentioned as the strong actors in Latvia's economy. Skonto's activities range from oil transit and wood-working (doors and windows) to restaurants/catering, banking and a radio station. The leader of the Skonto group is a former high-ranking KGB officer, and its managers are former Komsomol executives. Avelat keeps control over a great part of the food-processing industry, including bakeries, meat, fish, sweet and alcohol production. Prime Minister Skele is connected with the Avelat group in public, although his name cannot be found on the official documents.[314]

The common denominator for all conglomerates is that their founders were in a position to participate in the privatization at the very early stages of the process, when the privatization procedure was not yet institutionalized under one roof. Lease and employee privatization were the primary methods of transferring state property into private hands, implying that insiders had an advantage over others. Juris Bojars, an opposition politician, cites the privatization of the food-processing industry as a prime example of the abuse of authority in the creation of private wealth. Andris Skele was the Deputy Minister of Agriculture at the outset of the privatization process, being responsible for the privatization of the food-processing industry. No laws existed at that time so that nobody had the slightest idea of how to accomplish the task. It is perhaps unsurprising that Skele found himself as a major shareholder and a board member of the companies to be privatized. According to Bojars, Skele privatized a large number of monopoly factories for himself and his relatives.[315]

Political parties are lobbies of economic groupings. The hardest assessments deny the existence of genuine political parties in Latvia, claiming they are mere interest groups. Such claims are exaggerated, although they contain grains of truth and disclose something essential about the nature of the Latvian parties. The most clear-cut rivalry is embodied in the Latvia's Way–Saimnieks axis. Both parties are rooted in business rather than social groups. According to a simplistic interpretation, Latvia's Way represents the interests of Latvian-speaking, West-oriented capital, whereas Saimnieks is backed by Russian-speaking, East-oriented capital. Saimnieks supporters include the remains of the traditional export industries and domestic producers, whereas Latvia's Way supporters deal with imports. Skonto and Manntess are said to be the main sponsors of Latvia's Way. Saimnieks was founded by those who were dissatisfied with the rule of Latvia's Way. Challengers had not received from Latvia's Way those benefits they would have wished for either in economy or in politics.[316]

A third group is composed of those sponsors who identify themselves with no single party but distribute their financial aid between several political forces that are strong enough to have some say in politics. Parex Bank, which represents Jewish-Russian capital, finances all major parties simultaneously. In fact, all the strongest groupings, such as transit, give some money to everybody, even when they are primarily attached to one particular party. Therefore, the categorization above should not be taken too literally. Besides, divides are neither exclusive nor absolute. For instance, Latvia's Way has strong connections with Russian-speaking capital, while it would be a mistake to label Saimnieks as a Russian party. Apart from the fact that Latvia's Way and Saimnnieks are the 'number one' parties through which business exerts influence, they constitute no exceptions. The entire party system is exposed to lobbying.[317]

The pressure group activity is focused rather than universal. Private companies have neither the incentive nor the means to interfere with the formulation of the general direction of the country's economic policy at an abstract level. They become active on specific questions where their business interests are directly invloved. 'They just buy decisions they want to be adopted or they buy particular politicians or officials whom they want to act in their favour.' It is not quite exceptional for a company manager to go into politics in order to promote his business interests, although of course he would not proclaim it to the electors. Parties have to be responsive to businessmen's desires, because they depend on financing from the private enterprise sector. Parties make deals before the elections to have their campaigns financed, and after the elections the promises must be redeemed as reciprocal services. If one listens to the discussions in Parliament on legal acts related to commercial interests, it is easy to recognize who is whose lobby-fodder. Free ports, car insurance, trade and taxation of alcohol are randomly selected illustrative examples of the bills that have mobilized the lobbies. A concrete case from the oil business in Ventspils shows how Latvia's Way was promoting Lukoil's interests and Saimnieks Jukos's, but the Mayor of Ventspils wanted neither company because he was on friendly terms with a third supplier.[318]

Privatization is a target of intense pressure-group activity. Therefore it is necessary to agree on the nationally important large-scale projects at the political level among parties before submitting them to the Board of the Privatization Agency. A board membership in a significant corporatized state enterprise is a way of balancing interests and rewarding politicians. The composition of the board of Ventspils Nafta is a good barometer of the prevailing balance of power. Small and medium-sized enterprises are of interest to individual deputies and minor sponsors of political parties. A party may try to influence the privatization decision through the Supervisory Board of the Privatization Agency or by sending its representative – a member of the Supervisory Board or a deputy – to visit the General Director of the Privatization Agency. A further possibility is to negotiate with Latvia's Way, which is responsible for privatization.[319]

Lobbying occurs everywhere, and at first sight it might appear that the Latvian phenomenon differs little from the universal practice. Although that is true in principle, there are country-specific factors that give a peculiar nuance to the Latvian case. The most important distinctive features are that the politico-economic relations are not regulated by any legal or moral norms and the economic interests are not organized at all with the consequence that the forms of lobbyism are more primitive than in the West. The uninstitutionalized situation feeds the distrust of all sides and especially of the mass public. In the same way as it is difficult to detect where legal business ends and illegal business starts, it is difficult to make a distinction between bribery and normal lobbying in Latvia. The entanglement of crime and corruption with business and politics fouls the interaction. A noteworthy aspect, which explains the vitality of unofficial influencing, is that money speaks Russian in Latvia but Russian-speakers cannot use the official channels of influence due to their exclusion from politics.

The coalescence of political and economic power involves hazards caused by the concentration of power in the hands of a few. Plurality of competing power centres, a cornerstone of Western liberalism, is endangered by the politico-economic blocs. Extra-parliamentary Cabinet politics also weakens democratic control. If politics is made by special interest groups, the citizenry is not likely to belong to the beneficiaries. One implication may be the allocation of the funds in the budget in favour of the rich. Moreover, politicians who rely on the economic elite are not interested in educating citizens to become active participants who are conscious of their democratic rights. It is much more convenient for them to keep the masses passive, alienated and ignorant.

The secretive nature of the business–politics relation makes it prone to corruption. Corruption, contraband and tax evasion are the besetting sins of the Latvian society. An unofficial EU report classifies corruption and criminality as being equally severe problems in Latvia as they are in Russia.[320] To equate Latvia with Russia is considered an exaggeration by most observers, but the magnitude of the phenomenon cannot be understated and Latvia is undoubtedly one of the most corrupt countries in Europe. Because effective control mechanisms have not yet been put in place, the economy is in a chaotic, anarchistic state – firms appear and disappear overnight – which makes shady transactions possible. The state's losses in tax and customs revenues are considerable due to the illegal streams of goods. The alcohol sector is the best-known example of the rampant contraband. About half of the imported alcohol is estimated to have been smuggled to the country. A great many illegal activities are concentrated in the ports as well as other strategic transit points. Therefore, it is not insignificant who controls them. Most importantly, borders should be closed and border-guarding tightened up.

Economic criminality is not the monopoly of short-haired, broad-shouldered, leather-jacketed Russian-speaking men. In contrast, its spread and permanence hint at a wide network of beneficiaries at all layers of society. The phenomenon cannot be polarized by dividing people into 'sheep' and 'wolves', since the whole structure, including the so-called respectable elements, is penetrated by corruption. Because so many people live off it, its eradication is extremely difficult. The low salaries of civil servants expose them to bribery. The protection by customs authorities and border guards is a necessary precondition for the prevalence of contraband. This is realized by the man in the street, too. When the Estonian border guard detachment advertised a few vacant posts it received hundreds of applications, even though the salary offered was the lowest possible. Fringe benefits were assessed to be substantial.

Moreover, it is obvious that top politicians are involved in unlawfulnesses, although their involvement is often impossible to prove. The dilemma is that the offenders can be traced merely to an operational level which is then given the whole blame, while the real initiators are never caught. Nevertheless, the press concentrates on attacking the selected scapegoats, who are usually civil servants. Crime is integrated into the societal system due to the weakness of the state. Bandits are fulfilling those functions that the judiciary and the fiscal system are unable to carry out in Latvia.

An attempt to fight corruption involves the streamlining and simplifying of the tax and customs systems as well as other economic regulation to eliminate the space for rent-seeking. If the same rules are valid for each and everyone, then one will not benefit from offering a bribe, because the end result will be the same anyway. To cite an example, Latvia has adopted a unified tax rate of 25 per cent, which applies to all types of businesses. The anti-corruption law requires ministers, deputies and senior civil servants to report their income, real property and bank deposits. The law states that they shall not hold an economic post as president, council chairman or director in a private business. The implementation of the anti-corruption law contributed to the overthrow of Skele's second short-lived government in July 1997.

INTELLECTUALS' SCHIZOPHRENIC ATTITUDE TO DEMOCRACY

The features described above have nurtured suspicion of democracy among the Latvian intelligentsia, who used to be the leading political force, the vanguard, before the first democratic elections. Intellectuals are prone to emphasize the populistic and clientelistic aspects of politics, while denying the existence of real political programmes. Many intellectuals judge political parties as cadre-type groupings around power-seeking greedy leaders without any principles or engagement in societal problems. They consider political conflict disruptive, egoistic and degenerative and long for harmony in place of discordance. As Ambassador Anna Zigure puts it:

> Democracy has not been uplifting in a spiritual sense. On the contrary, it has been very disruptive so far. It has brought about progress in economy and legislation but not on the intellectual plane. If democracy is supposed to be something constructive, we have not democracy yet.[321]

The overly critical view of politics is steeped in the older tradition of democratic theory, which predominated in political philosophy from ancient Greece until the eighteenth century, with representative democracy. According to the classical view, factionalism and conflict are destructive. Citizens both could and should pursue the public good rather than their private ends.[322] Exactly the same point constitutes the core of the criticisms voiced by the cultural intelligentsia. They disapprove morally of the self-interested behaviour of politicians and interest groups because it is not addressed to serve the public good. The classical Greek vision of democracy presupposes a homogeneous *polis*, given the requirement for a harmony of interests. Citizens have to be homogeneous with respect to the characteristics that would otherwise tend to produce political conflict. No state could hope to be a good *polis* if its citizens adhered to, say, different ethnic groups.[323]

The monistic conception of democracy has points of convergence with the organic interpretations of the nation or the public good, which have entrenched traditions in Eastern Europe. The organismic view likens a political collectivity to a living organism as if it were a holistic entity like a person. If the nation is an organism, it is not a body that can breed divisions and conflicts. This kind of thinking easily leads to nationalism (though not inevitably). If the nation is an organism, it is not a body that can tolerate alien elements.[324] The unity of the Latvian nation was embodied in the Popular Front during the struggle for independence, when the common goal united heterogeneous social groupings under a single umbrella organization. There are still some people who are yearning for such unity, while they consider the emergence of a party system regrettable.

Hence, it can be seen how these two traditions – classical democratic theory and organistic ideologies – reinforce each other. A third element, which further reinforces the aversion to controversy, is the communist ideology. The Soviet system denied the existence of internal tensions, while trying to maintain an artificial façade of unanimity. In reality, conflicts of values and of interests are inherent in all societies. Democracy is needed precisely because people cannot agree. Conflicts are absent only in authoritarian systems.[325]

The search for consensus is often nothing more than a guise for a new authoritarian temptation, even when the authoritarian temptation might appear subconscious. Some Latvian intellectuals speculate on a new, unparalleled political system that would surpass the imperfect party democracy. They consider the much debated crisis of the party system and the traditional political ideologies in the West as a proof of the decay of party democracy. Time has passed it by. On the other hand, the idealists cannot define precisely what the futurist system should look like. Half jokingly, somebody once proposed a dictatorship of the poets as a way to the superior political order at a discussion about an ideal system. The analogy to Marxism is tangible, even though the given person himself did not realize it. This shows that democratic principles are not understood thoroughly even among the so-called intellectuals, while the idea of guardianship, one version of which is Marxism-Leninism, is very much alive in its various guises. In the above-cited naive case, the poets were supposed to be more qualified to rule than others, but the 'Philosopher Kings' can be replaced with economists, natural scientists or whatever. The elitistic assumption behind guardianship is always that only few people are competent to rule.[326] The group which believes itself to qualify as a guardian does not see itself as a party representing particular interests and particular views against representatives of other interests or projects. Such a distorted self-perception leads these people to strive for a monopoly in representing the 'national interest'.[327]

The persuasiveness of guardianship stems from a negative view of the moral and intellectual competence of ordinary people. This belief motivates the aspirations of the Latvian intellectuals, too. They do not trust ordinary people's ability to make decisions concerning their own life, including their political choices. They point out how intellectuals' removal from politics created a vacuum which was filled by Siegerist. They underscore emphatically the characterization that Siegerist's voters are poor, humble, simple-minded, uneducated people who cannot judge populistic slogans duly. To start a counter-attack, the intellectuals are preparing a comeback into politics because they feel they are needed as intermediaries between the people and the rulers. They have organized meetings to discuss whether the intelligentsia should form a political party to restore its position as 'a force that moves the society forwards'. The intelligentsia moans that they were pushed aside or that they could not tolerate the dirty world of politics.[328]

Körösenyi's (1994) keen analysis demonstrates how the motivations of the intelligentsia are as partial and self-interested as those of anyone else, despite pretences to the contrary. Furthermore, it converges on the conclusion that not all anti-authoritarian movements are pro-democratic. Körösenyi's thesis is that the democratic myth becomes the greatest danger to democracy. Intellectuals' political dissatisfaction is not manifested in the rejection of democracy itself; rather, it is just the opposite: disappointment begins precisely in the mythologizing of democracy. It stems from using some idealistic or utopian conditions as the measure, as a consequence of which the democracy that has formed is not considered the 'real' democracy. The intelligentsia is attracted to democracy as a concept, but it likes it less as a working political system.[329]

The psychological roots of frustration reflect jealousy and resentment, following from the loss of status. In the era of oppression, intellectuals represented the nation or society in opposition to power. They were able to preserve this honoured prophet role during the transition period so that it seemed they would form the political elite within the democratic regime. However, the intelligentsia soon found themselves on the losers' side, facing political marginalization. With the quick collapse of the anti-communist popular fronts and the emergence of party pluralism, the monopoly over representation of the nation or society was gone. After the channels of political articulation were opened, intellectuals turned from main players to one of many players. Disappointed intellectuals started to attack constitutional institutions and particularly the political elite that had received a mandate in the elections. Körösenyi concludes that the role perception of the intelligentsia is in contradiction with the logic of democracy.[330]

The term 'intelligentsia' has been used here, as it is a common practice, to refer exclusively to the representatives of culture, arts and humanistic sciences. The cultural-humanistic elite is often separated from or even contrasted with the economic-technical experts. In Latvia that kind of distinction is highly relevant. The culture (in a broad sense, including humanistic sciences) versus economy (in a similarly broad sense) split constitutes a significant social cleavage that divides the elite into two camps. The same phenomenon is observable among both the ethnic Latvians and the Russian-speakers, implying that the culture–economy divide cuts across the ethnic cleavage. There is no strong antagonism between the cultural and economic camps; the mutual contacts are simply scarce.[331] Neither is the cleavage highly politicized, as most politicians are reckoned to number among the 'economists', irrespective of their specific education. The content of the culture–economy cleavage can be depicted by the *Gemeinschaft–Gesellschaft* dichotomy, which is a close cousin of the traditionalism–modernism dimension.

9 Ideologization of Economic Policies

A great part of politics is easy to explain by interest conflicts. According to this account, voting is primarily an expression of social position and interests associated with it: parties develop in order to express these interests.[332] Some parties in Latvia represent the interests of the poor, others those of the farmers or specific business sectors and so on. To make a rough grouping, parties divide into economically and socially oriented parties, a division which follows from their approach to economic policy. Liberals who give precedence to economic results adhere to shock therapy, whereas socially oriented parties that are concerned with the costs of the transformation are influenced by gradualism. Why some parties promise to alleviate the burden on the population can be understood against the initial assumption. What is puzzling is the existence of parties whose programmes punish a majority of the population in the short term and whose political demands cannot be extrapolated from the demographic features of any constituency. A party's detachment from the social group interests raises the question of the coherence-maintaining force behind the party: what is the *primus motor* that prescribes its course of political and economic action? This is basically the question of what makes economic transformation possible in a democracy.

Latvia's Way does not appeal to any clearly defined structural location. People who vote for it must believe that a horse therapy is the most effective way to achieve the envisioned objectives of the transition. This confidence is to a large extent based on persuasion by ideas, because it cannot be attributed to personal experience or incontrovertible facts. Such attitudes have an exogenous character in the sense that they derive from such beliefs about politics or economics whose origins are not to be found in social cleavages. That suggests that ideas play an independent role in politics. Structural accounts can tell us a great deal about the constraints facing policy-makers, but policy-making is based on creation as well as constraint. It is the ideas about what is efficient, expedient or just that motivate the movement from one line of policy to another. Ideas prescribe a course of economic or political action. In this sense, ideology comprehends not only various political points of view, which specify what sorts of public activities are possible and desirable, but also economic theories, which specify what economic consequences will follow from the pursuit of particular policies. When the 'objective' situation is unclear, ideology can be seen as a cognitive map, a way of economizing in the face of excess or imperfect information.[333]

210

In line with the above reasoning it is stated that neoliberalism triumphed in Eastern Europe, not as an economic science, but as a political ideology.[334] The ideological nature of economic reform strategies can be derived from their underlying values. To demonstrate this thesis, the proof must be filtered through a wider context.

To begin with, let us consider the role of ideas in the policy process. Policy-makers customarily work within a framework of ideas that specifies not only the goals of policy and the kind of instruments that can be used to attain them, but also the very nature of the problems they are meant to address. Like a *Gestalt*, this framework is embedded in the very terminology through which policy-makers communicate about their work, and it is influential because so much is taken for granted. From the viewpoint of policy-makers, a framework of ideas becomes the prism through which they see the economy as well as their own role within it.[335]

The deceptive self-evidency of the interpretative framework easily obscures its partiality. Still, each policy paradigm, like scientific paradigm, contains a particular account of how the world operates, prioritizing some aspects of reality over others. Such restrictions on perspective are necessary to bring order and sense to the jumble of otherwise unmanageable information flow. It is, however, essential to acknowledge that setting priorities inevitably involves conscious choices that can be neither objective nor value-free. A choice of the perspective that lays the ground for any intellectual construction reflects implicit valuations. After the first step has been taken, the derivation of further higher-order axioms and the like may *appear* neutral, value-free and 'scientific', but one should not forget that the underlying approach is always based on some assumptions that are taken for granted in the later phases. If scholars or policy-makers are unable to identify the subjectivity of their decisions to rely on one paradigm rather than another, they will suffer from a self-myopia which will make them prisoners of their own convictions. Fascinated and blinded by the complexity of their mathematical models or expert jargon, they will fail to recognize the value-laden premises of their sophisticated models.

Real-life experience shows unambiguously how different theories are related to different political ideologies and how they serve conflicting political aims. The affinity between economic theories and political ideologies is demonstrated in the relations between Keynesianism and social democracy, on the one hand, and between monetarism, public choice theory and the Austrian school and the so-called new right (including Thatcherism and Reaganism), on the other hand. In the case of economics of transformation, the presence of ideological elements is exceptionally pronounced because the positions in the transition debate are mainly grounded on beliefs rather than on rigorous analyses or empirical verification, because the theoretical basis of 'transfonomics' is weakly developed and applicable previous experience is missing. The lack of indisputable, objective expert knowledge means that there are merely competing interpretations for the requirements of the situation, which deprives the justification of the claim for absolute scientific neutrality. Instead, the judgement always entails political, ideological or other exogenous factors affecting the power of one set of actors to impose its vision over others. The first conclusion is thus that economic reform strategies should be conceived of as being derivatives of ideological belief systems rather than eternal theoretical rationalizations.

A common-value basis is hypothesized to be the link which makes certain economic theories persuasive to specific political orientations. In fact, political ideologies and economic theories appear as different sides of the same coin which stem from the same origin. The derivation of the transition strategies from their underlying values converges with the value approach to the study of political ideology first introduced by Milton Rokeach (1973). Rokeach's famous two-value model of political ideology reduces society's main ideological-cum-political conflict dimension to a two-value continuum. Rokeach formulates his thesis as follows:

> It may be hypothesized that all major varieties of political orientation will have to take an explicitly favourable, a silent, or an explicitly unfavourable position with respect to two values in particular – *freedom* and *equality* – not only ideologically to advance one's own perceived self-interest but also to oppose perceived competing interests. Thus, the major variations in political ideology are hypothesized to be fundamentally reducible, when stripped to their barest essence, to opposing value orientations concerning the political desirability or undesirability of freedom and equality in all their ramifications.[336]

The assumption of a single continuum does not imply unidimensionality. On the contrary, the basic opposition between freedom and equality germinates different variations that reflect time- and place-specific social conditions. The most pressing problems at hand give a concrete expression to these fundamental values. In the context of the postcommunist transitions, the confrontation materializes in the form of gain maximization for shock therapists and pain minimization for socially oriented parties. The different approaches to transition are instruments to attain the terminal values, freedom and equality. In the theoretical discussion the collision of priorities was expressed in the paradoxical relationship between liberalism and democracy. Which is more important, the freedom of self-regulating markets or the introduction of mechanisms for popular control and inclusive participation?

The fundamental differences in the basic premises of the alternative reform models make it often impossible for the advocates of different strategies to agree on a common body of data against which a technical judgement in favour of one strategy might be made.[337] The lack of a common standard of measurement resembles a classroom problem from the introductory courses on price theory: how should one compare bread with meat? Analogously, how should one compare the growth of gross national product with the consolidation of democracy?

Rokeach's two-value model of political ideology is in fact a definition of the left–right continuum along which the major ideological orientations and political parties are traditionally arranged. A high ranking for equality indicates a leftist orientation, while emphasis on freedom reflects a rightist orientation. Latvia's Way's emphasis on competition, deregulation, market mechanism, openness and free trade clearly mirrors a liberal value system which ranks economic freedoms high. Fast marketization of the economy has an overwhelming priority over all other objectives to the extent that the social costs of transition are tolerated as an unavoidable evil. Attachment to equality can be conceived in the heightened attention to social questions in the Social Democratic platform. Redistribution through wage increases, workers' self-management and better social guarantees as well as public control of the strategic sectors seek to equalize economic power.

To summarize, the distinguishing feature of the analytical scheme developed here is that the sphere of ideologies is not confined to politics alone. The very definition of ideology presented at the beginning of this discussion also touched on other realms, including the realm of economics. Even the economic theories underlying the proposed reform strategies can be analysed like ideologies. Economists as well as other technocrats often tend to raise themselves above all partiality and subjectivity, although the preceding analysis demonstrates that their prescriptions are no less value-laden than those of anyone else. Economic policy is a product of valuations as much as any other field of policy. Economists' objectives represent just one particular kind of set of objectives among different sets of objectives that are always bound with terminal values. As all human thinking is penetrated by intrinsic value biases, there exists no black-and-white distinction between irrational, chaotic politics and universally rational economics.

The question remains why one set of ideas acquires influence over policy-making in some times and places but not others. Why did the Popular Front embrace a liberal transition strategy in Latvia? The super-ideology which dominated over all other objectives at the launch stage of reforms was Westernization. Latvians wanted to shake off the Soviet yoke and facilitate the 'return to Europe' as fast as possible. Western Europe was seen as a proven model which had delivered prosperity, but the desire of becoming European had not only a material underpinning but also a sociopsychological one. Latvians stress their historical and cultural ties with Central and Northern Europe, because they identify themselves with 'Europeans' rather than with Slavs. In Latvia a consensus prevails on what to escape and where to head in the future.

A complete rejection of the former system was easier in the Baltic states than in other parts of the Soviet Union, since it was always perceived as alien and as imposed from the outside. The big difference compared with the other Soviet republics is that the Baltic states have a tradition of national independence (1918–40). Because of their late involuntary annexation, the Baltics were never so fully Sovietized as most other Soviet republics. Consequently, the strong antipathy toward all things Soviet fuelled the drive to dismantle the main pillars of the Soviet system, such as communism, central planning and the rouble.[338] An essential factor was also that the postcommunist elite abandoned the Communist Party (CP) and went over to newly established political organizations. The Latvian CP was not reformed from inside, as happened in Lithuania where the leadership of the CP consisted of nationally minded Lithuanians. In Latvia the CP degenerated into a bastion of Russian standpatters so that the CP could not develop into a social democratic party like its Lithuanian sister party. Ideas do not acquire political force independently of the constellation of institutions already presented there.[339]

While politicians have only a limited understanding of reform programmes, what they decide depends on their confidence in their economic advisors. In the FSU countries the knowledge of market economy and Western economics was virtually nil at the outset of transition. The international community launched a number of initiatives to assist East European countries in their attempts to restructure their economies according to market principles. The spirit of the era, imprinted by the hegemony of neoliberal economics, favoured a particular kind of solutions which were eagerly adopted by the trend-conscious elites who wanted to create the right image for the country. What was in conformity with the supreme goal of Westernizing Latvia was accepted automatically as a part of the 'deal'. The economic strategy was a component of a transitional package, ranging from the democratization of polity to the marketization of economy. Complete belief systems were transferred to a fertile, receptive soil which found itself in a virginal state after the demise of communism.

The persistence of democracy can be explained in a similar fashion as the commitment to economic reform. Latvians view the relationship between capitalism and democracy in the light of the West European example, although that connection is a product of a peculiar historical conjuncture. Due to this optical delusion, the historical affinity between democracy and capitalism has become the dominant model in the eyes of both political leaders and citizens. Moreover, the postcommunist countries are strongly encouraged in their way toward liberal democracy, by, for example, conditioning their entry into the Western cooperation organizations by the degree of democratization. The commitment to democracy is reinforced especially by the plausible prospect of eventual admittance to the European Union, a prospect that also provides detailed standards for many aspects of reform.

With the collapse of communism, democracy has become 'the only legitimate and viable alternative to an authoritarian regime of any kind'. When democracy is valued intrinsically for its own sake, authoritarian solutions lose their appeal. Democratic leadership in the current wave is more powerful than ever before because of the confluence of two sets of newly emerging forces: domestically, a surge of public demand for democratic reforms; internationally, sharp increases in material, moral and strategic assistance and pressure from governmental and non-governmental organizations. The electronic media and other sophisticated communication linkages continually feed a global democratic *Zeitgeist* of unprecedented scope and intensity.[340]

10 The Nationality Question

THE FALLACY OF RESEARCHERS

Most foreign researchers used to emphasize permanent dominance of the nationality conflict in Latvian politics. Evans and Whitefield, among others, predicted that 'party competition in Estonia and Latvia will be structured on non-pluralist, ethnic and nationalist lines with valence issues forming the axis of political disputes within each community'. They argued that 'the emergence of a class-basis support for parties is unlikely because of the similarity in size of the two communities. In these conditions intra-ethnic cohesion is likely to pay a premium.' So they concluded that 'the importance of ethnic divisions, heightened by the insecurity of break-away status, should focus party competition on ethnic or nationalistic issues. Therefore, the most influential bases of interests are likely to be precommunist identities relating nationality and ethnicity.'[341] The prognosis is erroneous insofar as the perspective exceeds the initial stage of democratization. Contrary to expectations, the significance of the nationality/citizenship cleavage is gradually diminishing.

The discrepancy between the outsiders' expectations and the actual situation can be explained by an anomaly in the Latvian case. Drawing on the bitter history of national conflicts in Eastern Europe, many scholars have tried to force Latvia in the same mould by turning the nationality question into a self-fulfilling prophecy. Yet one cannot draw conclusions for Latvia based on the evidence from the former Yugoslavia or Northern Ireland. Concentration on demographic statistics to the exclusion of everything else leads to a twisted logic which appears convincing on the desk of an armchair researcher but which does not correspond to the empirical reality. The general weakness of cross-national 'large-N' comparative studies is that they are insensitive to the social, cultural and institutional variations evident among different countries. Comparativists of this type are generalists who cannot be familiar with the specific local conditions characterizing each case. Conclusions are drawn from a limited number of statistical variables on the basis of logical inference.

Too many Western scholars have also been susceptible to Russian propaganda, as if these professional researchers had never heard of criticism of sources. The Russian diplomatic corps is very effective in selling its psychological problem to the West. Russia until quite recently, persisted in accusing the Baltic states of human rights violations, although numerous international organizations, including the OSCE and the EU, have confirmed repeatedly that there are no human rights violations. Furthermore, the results of survey studies and in-depth interviews do not fit with the image of national animosity (see below). The majority of Latvian residents – both Latvian- and Russian-speakers – believe in national conciliation and peaceful development of the ethnic relations.

The problem is whether the word of a 'commoner' carries any weight against the word of a learned academic, if he or she has already drawn the conclusions in advance. Only the future will show who was right. I have no intention of speculating on any theoretical options so as to predict the unforeseen future. Nor am I looking for verification for any hypothesis. I shall simply report the prevailing moods of Latvia's residents according to the principle 'let the facts speak for themselves'.

A HETEROGENEOUS MINORITY AND ITS DIVISIONS

The background of the minority problem stems from the Russification policy practised by the Soviet Union which artificially changed the proportions of the national groups in Latvia (Table 10.1). After the occupation, the Soviet Union started an unprecedented genocide policy against Latvians. The genocide expressed itself in deportations of civilian population to Siberia, forced emigration, confiscation of Latvian property and Sovietization of everyday life. Throughout the years of Soviet rule, Latvia experienced a substantial inflow of immigrants, mainly from Russia, Belarus and the Ukraine. The increase in population during the postwar years was dominated by an increase on account of immigration. Due to this migration, Latvia had the highest growth of population in the whole of Europe. Yet the natural population was on a continual decrease owing to low birth rates. In 1935, the share of Latvian nationals was 75.5 per cent. In 1989, the proportion of Latvian nationals had diminished to 52.0 per cent. Latvians were about to become a minority in their own country.[342]

The terminology referring to the non-Latvian minority is not just a result of a random lingual formulation but it contains political nuances, which reflect the ambitions of each side. Latvians insist on calling the Slavic population 'Russian-speakers', a term which has been adopted for official use in the international arena, too. Latvians stress emphatically that the minority does not consist merely of ethnic Russians, but also of Belarusians and Ukrainians as well as many other nationalities. They sometimes tend to overemphasize the proportion of other nationalities at the cost of Russians. Russia, by contrast, is not so accurate in its use of terms. It prefers homogenizing the minority and referring to it as 'Russians' in order to legitimize its interference

218 Empirical Case Study

in the internal affairs of Latvia. The Latvian concept is of course correct, even though it must be admitted that Russians are overwhelmingly the biggest nationality group after Latvians with their share of 30.3 per cent as against Belarusians' share of 4.3 per cent and Ukrainians' share of 2.7 per cent. The latter nationalities constitute the second and third largest national minorities in Latvia. The proportion of Russians has decreased slightly after independence. In 1989 Russians constituted 34.0 per cent of the population.

Table 10.1   Ethnic Composition of the Population, 1996 (%)

Nationality	%
Latvian	56.6
Russian	30.3
Belarusian	4.3
Ukrainian	2.7
Polish	2.6
Lithuanian	1.4
Others (< 1.0 % each)	2.1

Source: *Riga in Your Pocket*, February–April 1997, p. 9.

Another noteworthy point is that the categories 'non-Latvians' and 'non-citizens' are not converging (Table 10.2). Not all non-Latvians are non-citizens. The proportion of non-citizens (29 per cent) is much smaller than that of non-Latvians (some 43 per cent). The proportion of citizens will slowly grow by virtue of naturalization.

Table 10.2   Proportion of Permanent Residents Classified as Citizens or Non-Citizens, 1996 (*percentage and absolute figures*)

Permanent Residents	%	Number
Citizens	71	1,769,300
Non-citizens	29	721,260
Whole population	100	2,490,560

Source: *Riga in Your Pocket*, February–April 1997, p. 9.

Not even Latvia's Russians are a homogeneous body in the sense that one could speak of a genuine Russian community. First of all, there is a split between citizens by descendancy, citizens by naturalization and non-citizens. The former group consists of the members or descendants of the Russian minority having lived in Latvia in the interwar period. The proportion of Russians was 10.6 per cent in 1935. An alternative possibility is to divide

Latvia's Russians into four categories according to the point of time and the way in which they arrived in Latvia.

The citizens are primarily people who came to Latvia before the First World War. A great part of them are Old Believers who were persecuted in Russia in the seventeenth and eighteenth centuries. Old Believers escaped to the peripheries of the Russian empire with the result that some of them migrated to the outlying county of Latgale. All those Russians who have lived in independent Latvia before the Second World War are now well-integrated into society. There is no question of their loyalty to the Republic of Latvia. They are Russian-speaking Latvians in the true sense of the word, and they usually speak Latvian as well. One could compare them to Finnish Swedes. Relations between the traditional Russian minority and the Russian immigrants are not always friendly. Because of the immigrants, Russians are labelled an undesirable mass. The 'old' Russians are annoyed at being lumped together with the late-comers.[343]

The largest group of Russians are workers who were transported to Latvia to satisfy the huge demand for labour prompted by forced, rapid industrialization. Latvia was a victim of a purposeful Russification campaign to a greater extent than the other Baltic republics. Russian workers were pawns in the unscrupulous game the Soviet leaders were playing. The most unfortunate ones are those unskilled workers from the nearby regions of Russia who were invited to work in Latvia 10–15 years ago. They were recruited for simple unskilled manual work in state factories; because of their limited education and lack of knowledge of the Latvian language, they are now in difficult straits.[344]

A substantial number of the Russians voted for independence at the referendum, since they expected to live in a Western-oriented economically prosperous country. Disappointment came when they were denied citizenship. Despite this drawback, most of them want to stay in Latvia instead of returning to Russia. It is not only the economic calculation but also the sense of homeland that ties them to Latvia. They have strong positive feelings for Latvia, although the economic distress (which is common to all) and the lack of political rights frustrates them. The majority of Russian-speakers understand the changed realities – the Soviet Union has ceased to exist – and, accordingly, acknowledge the necessity to adjust to it. If Latvians play their cards right, there will be a great potential to win the sympathies of the majority of Russians.[345]

Russian hard-liners consist of the communists who were sent to Latvia as the representatives of Moscow and of the retired army officers who regarded themselves as liberators. They show no willingness to adjust to the new circumstances. The attitudes of these people cannot much be influenced.[346]

The bulk of the communists' supporters consists of the poor old-age pensioners who are yearning for 'the good old days'. They would like to restore the Soviet Union as well as the Soviet system in economy and politics. Many of them really believe in communism deep in their heart. Now they are following the progress of the communists in Russia watchfully.[347]

Old communists do not usually hold a hostile attitude toward Latvian nationals as such. However, there is a tiny group of aggressive Russian chauvinists who do not recognize Latvians as a separate nation. 'Even if they were standing two metres away from a Latvian, they would not see him.' Aggressive chauvinists are primarily people with a limited education from all age groups.[348]

The thin layer of the new rich is interested only in profit opportunities. Many new rich businessmen are former members of the communist *nomenklatura* who have done a complete U-turn in their ideology.[349]

Generation plays an important role, too. Irrespective of background, the younger generation is more positive and more adaptable. Many young Russians understand that adaptation to Latvian culture together with a command of the Latvian language is the shortest way to realize economic and human capacities. This tendency can be observed in the field of business education. Many Russian-speaking parents send their children to Latvian schools for the same reason.[350]

Since Russian-speakers are by no means a uniform group, there cannot be a single outlook which reflects their attitude at a universal level. Any categorization does not do full justice to the infinite spectrum of attitudes, if variation in the intensity of opinions is taken into consideration. Various subjective and personal factors affect the viewpoints, not merely the general sociopolitical situation. The case of two taxi drivers is illustrative in this respect.

Objectively taken, both taxi drivers were in the same position. Still, one was quite happy and satisfied with his life, whereas the other was very bitter and negative. The contented taxi driver, an elderly man, is an ethnic Russian but he proudly explained that he speaks Latvian fluently. He defined Latvia as his fatherland, even though he was not a citizen. The unsatisfied taxi driver, a handsome man in his forties, was a mix of Lithuanian, German, Swedish and Polish origin, although he belonged to the Russian-speakers. He was highly critical of Latvia's language policies, as he did not speak Latvian well; instead, he spoke Lithuanian. The latter taxi driver had been a naval officer in the Soviet army, but after losing his job he was compelled to drive a taxi. The elder taxi driver had probably driven a taxi all his life. The former officer's discontent reflects the loss of social position and secure income in an understandable way, although the dissatisfaction is disguised in sharp criticism of Latvia's national policies. Personal ambitions are being ideologized and scapegoats are being sought. A man who has faced such a hard lot would be bitter – for good reason – in any country. The same phenomenon can be generalized to explain the radical attitudes of the Russian-speaking hard-liners. The vanguard of the conservatives consists mainly of the former *nomenklatura* who used to enjoy a privileged position in the Soviet system but who have not succeeded in going over to business. They treat the loss of their previous privileges as a violation of human rights. Russians used to have 19 listed privileges over Latvians – in addition to real power – during the Soviet period.[351] Thus, socioeconomic interests are wrapped up in nationality or human rights rhetoric. Those who lost most are likely to have the most uncompromising attitudes. Those whose position has remained roughly the same are indifferent to political changes. To sum up, the ethnic conflict is entangled with an interest-based struggle over societal influence.

Typically, the aggressive section of the Russian-speakers tends to be the most vocal group. Though a minority, the radicals are eager to monopolize the representation of the Russian-speakers. The hard-liners have better organizational resources thanks to their past activities, while the silent majority remains unarticulate. It is very telling that the prime party that champions the rights of the Russian-speakers is the follow-up party of the Moscow-minded Latvian Communist Party which supported the August coup. The biggest Russian newspapers in Latvia, *SM* and *SM Cevodnja*, take positions close to *Lidztiesiba*'s line. Their writing style is confrontational on many issues. Although they constantly make a noise about the necessity to integrate the Russian-speakers into Latvian society, their articles undermine their own demands. When they frighten people with stories of terrible naturalization tests and merciless officials, or when they stick to alleged injustices in an unconstructive way, they foment antagonism and prejudice between the ethnic communities rather than encourage naturalization and national conciliation. Russian business newspapers, like *Bizness & Baltija*, provide neutral, matter-of-fact information.[352] Western observers should keep in mind that the opinions they are likely to be faced with first do not necessarily tell the whole truth.

A representative survey study is the most reliable way to examine the general trends in public opinion. Interviewing a representative cross-section of the population is especially appropriate, when nationalists as well as other *Besserwissers* talk as if everyone in the ethnic group thinks alike. As part of its programme monitoring mass response to transformation in postcommunist societies, the Centre for the Study of Public Policy (SPP) at the University of Strathclyde in Glasgow has created the New Baltic Barometer, a six-nationality survey covering Estonia, Latvia and Lithuania, with separate questionnaires and samples for Russian-speakers as well as the titular nationalities. The New Baltic Barometer is designed to measure to what extent people with the same nationality think and act uniformly.[353]

The SPP paper 284 reports the results of the third New Baltic Barometer survey, undertaken in November 1996. Fieldwork was conducted in Latvia by Baltic Data House (formerly Lasopec). The universe was defined as permanent residents of Latvia between the ages of 15 and 74. The sample was selected through a multistage random sampling procedure, with stratification by region, district and urbanization. In the event, 1,006 interviews were undertaken in 103 sampling points. Of the respondents, 551 were Latvians and 455 Russian-speakers. The sample was checked for appropriate weights for age and gender to match the national census figures for the distribution of the population.[354]

The statistical results of the New Baltic Barometer will be complemented and commented on by means of qualitative in-depth interviews conducted by the author of this book. The interviews were undertaken in Riga and Liepaja in April–May 1997. They addressed such issues as the relations between the ethnic communities, the conditions on which citizenship should be granted, Russian-speakers' identity and loyalty to the independent Latvian state. The interviews were directed especially toward Russian-speaking business. Two core questions for businessmen were whether Russian-speaking companies feel themselves to be discriminated against and whether they have enough channels of influence available.

The only reason why the emphasis was placed on the business community was not the bias of the study at hand: it discusses economy-related topics in the first place. More importantly, Russian-speaking business holds a key position in the debates on internal security. Businessmen possess quite different financial, intellectual and network resources than, say, poor pensioners. Latvian nationalists consider a strong presence of Russian-speaking capital a threat to the country's independence. They see Russian-speaking businessmen as potential lobbyists of Moscow who want to sabotage Latvian economy. Their orientation toward the Eastern markets is regarded with suspicion, because nationalists are afraid that increasing Russian influence will lead to unpredictable political consequences. The line of argument is as follows: 'If the Latvian economy falls into the hands of Russians, the next day the whole country will be in the hands of Russia.'

A considerable part of Latvian capital is of Russian origin and Russian-speakers are more active in business life than Latvians. Because the highest positions were manned by Russians in Soviet-Latvia, Russians were able to convert their former political privileges into economic advantages. Currently most Russians have no choice but to do business, since non-citizens cannot hold a public office with the consequence that administration and politics are excluded from them. Psychologically it is likely that the active part of the population is proportionally overrepresented among the immigrants. Those people who leave their native place in search of a better life are characteristically more able and ambitious than those who stay.[355]

PEACEFUL COEXISTENCE BUT LATENT TENSIONS

Both Latvians and Russian-speakers agree unanimously that the relations between the ethnic groups are based on peaceful coexistence. 'Our relations are not exacerbated in the sense that Latvians and Russians could not talk and keep company, live and work together.'[356] In shops one automatically receives friendly service in both languages, irrespective of the native tongue of the clerk. In mixed work places Latvian and Russian-speaking colleagues get along quite normally without forming cliques according to the nationality. This is confirmed by foreign investors whose staff consists of both Latvians and Russian-speakers. A trade union boss describes the relations between Latvian and Russian-speaking workers with an anecdote. In Soviet times, workers of the same factory used to go to a forest restaurant after the working day and share a bottle of vodka. Today nothing has changed. It is not exceptional to have personal friends of different nationalities. A 40-year-old Moscow-born Russian lady says: 'I have Latvian friends. My daughter has Latvian friends. She has been dancing in a Latvian dancing school for eight years.' The daughter speaks Latvian perfectly but the mother has difficulties with the language.[357]

When the New Baltic Barometer asked people how they would describe the relations between nationalities and ethnic groups in Latvia, around three-quarters of both Latvians and Russian-speakers defined them as unproblematic (Table 10.3). The average respondent was convinced that they can handle whatever problems arise. Only 2–3 per cent regarded the relations as bad.

Table 10.3   Assessment of Ethnic Relations (%)

	Latvians	Russian-speakers
No problems	2	4
All right	72	72
Not so good, difficulties	22	21
Bad	3	2

Source: Rose 1997, 48.

Politicians are often more uncompromising in their demands than the public. A commonly held view among all nationalities is that the fomentation of the national conflict serves only the interests of certain politicians. The man in the street is reluctant to turn the ethnic question into a political one.[358] 'Questions related to nationalism or pressure on Russians are questions of high political spheres. Simple Latvians and Russians understand this situation.'[359] 'There are many nations living here. If we fight with each other, it won't be better. Some politicians need such a war, but normal people don't like a war between nations.'[360]

Life is so very hard for most Latvian inhabitants that they have no energy to think about ethnic politics. 'The main question is the question of survival for each man and for each business company ... A lot of Russians are indifferent to the actual government in Latvia. They think about their family, business and so on but they don't think about political issues.'[361] Economic hardships are shared by the whole population, irrespective of nationality or citizenship. The prevalence of socioeconomic problems undermines the ethnic basis of politics.

In Latvia a majority does not believe that ethnic relations could ever become aggravated to the level of open conflict. When the New Baltic Barometer asked whether ethnic conflict between Latvians and Russian-speakers is a threat to peace and security, 76 per cent of Russian-speakers and 58 per cent of Latvians disagreed with the statement (Table 10.4). Latvians saw the ethnic conflict as more threatening than did the Russian-speaking minority. Hard-line nationalist politicians of both sides (especially those of the opposite side) were considered to disturb social peace. In the prevailing climate of opinion such a view can be interpreted as a condemnation of national radicalism, when this particular question is related to the attitudes expressed in other connections.

Table 10.4   Threats to Internal Peace and Security
(*% agreeing with the statement*)

	Ethnic conflict *	*Hard-line nationalists in Russia*	*Hard-line nationalists in Latvia*
Russian-speakers	23	45	55
Latvians	41	73	48
Difference	−18	−28	7

Note: * Between Latvians and Russian residents in Latvia.
Source: Rose 1997, 34–5.

The in-depth interviews confirmed the survey results. People want to believe in the levelling-out of the remaining differences. The willingness to live in peace is pronounced. The interviewees disputed the contention according to which a serious crisis either in economy or in relations to Russia could inflame the situation. 'I don't believe in that, because we had a crisis situation in 1991–92. Before the probability was higher than now.' 'A few years ago there was pressure on Russians in Latvia but now the situation is more tolerant. After some years we can adjust the relations between the Russian community and the Latvian community.'[362] The Russians who were interviewed suggested that the significance of issues related to nationality divisions will continue to lose significance in politics and society. 'In the future, problems of nationality will not play a big role. The situation will develop in a positive direction, a direction of increasing tolerance in Latvian society. It will be a more human society.'[363]

Optimism is the prevailing mood as far as the future is concerned.

Come to Latvia after two years. There will be another country, a much better country. All good things: social policy, the economic status of people, differences in language ... Everything will be normal step by step. Now is the time for political games but there will be a time for economy. Economy is higher than all the current problems. This is not optimism but a consequence of the normal laws of society's development. We live close to Europe. We cannot make laws that reverse the world-wide laws.[364]

It is easy to see that Latvia is not Tsetchynia, which Latvians, by the way, are proud of. Latvia has never witnessed ethnically based violence. Ethnic strikes or demonstrations have not taken place since 1990.[365] However, to claim that ethnicity plays no role at all or that absolutely no problems exist would be an exaggeration. Tensions are latent and delicate. One does not notice them at first glance but they still smoulder under the apparently calm surface. Sometimes it is difficult to conceptualize them; they deal with fine sentiments and insinuations rather than plain words and deeds. It is telling that the interviewees normally started the conversation by stressing the friendly relations between Latvians and Russian-speakers. When the discussion proceeded further, negative points started to emerge. This kind of behaviour proves that Latvian residents have firmly decided to move on toward a better society. By understating problems and sweeping them under the carpet, people want to avoid conflicts. The same conciliatory, constructive spirit was expressed explicitly in words, too.

Russian-speakers do not blame Latvians for open hostility or intentional discrimination. What makes the integration difficult is the closed, inward-looking nature of the Latvian community. Latvians admit themselves that they are reserved people who regard too much openness as intrusive. As the Latvian community is small, the interpersonal links often stem from early childhood so that there are strong bonds between Latvians. It is not easy for outsiders to enter a cohesive society where everybody knows everybody. In large state factories where the proportions of Latvian- and Russian-speaking workers are roughly the same, communication does not cause any problems. To be the only Russian-speaking employee in a Latvian company is much harder. Latvians require that one must speak Latvian perfectly, otherwise they do not recognize one as belonging to their community. Latvians do not say it directly, but the end result is that the Russian-speaker will feel isolated.[366]

People's ethnic thinking is composed of two distinct layers. One of them operates on an abstract context, the other on a concrete person-to-person level. Feelings are more negative and reserved when the other ethnic group is conceived as an abstract entity in terms of a 'them and us' constellation. Then different stereotypes are being attached to the other nationality. For instance, Latvians regard Russians as too open, noisy and aggressive in business. 'Russians drink vodka together with their neighbours. Latvians don't do that.' A Latvian compares the mentality difference between Russians and Latvians with the corresponding difference between Americans and Europeans, by referring to the Americans' superpower mentality.[367] Both groups recognize the mentality difference strongly. Eastern and Western cultures are experienced as antagonistic.[368]

Neither side is free from bias. The main stereotypic generalization is to treat Russians as occupants. Consequently, Russian-speakers feel themselves unwanted second-class residents. The source of the pyschological problems is historical in the case of the Latvians. The heritage of a 50-year occupation does not disappear from people's minds all of a sudden. Russian-speakers, in turn, feel offended when they hear occupant accusations. 'I cannot recognize myself as a civil occupant. My father was deported by force to Latvia. I was born here. I could not make a choice where to be born. Such points of view are insulting.' The prejudices of Russian-speakers result from limited, one-sided information, because many of them do not speak Latvian.[369]

When people engage in face-to-face contact, they normally have no problems in communication. Nobody is thinking of nationality problematics in the midst of daily life. As Russian Irina puts it: 'Life shows that beliefs and practice are two different things.' In her previous work place Irina used to share a room with a colleague who was an active rank-and-file member of a nationalist political party. Her basic attitude toward Russians corresponded with her political beliefs. As Irina and the nationalist continued to share the same room, they got to know each other and – surprise, surprise – became good friends. Friendship has been maintained, even though Irina has since changed jobs.[370] What is most encouraging is the understanding both ethnic groups show for each other's positions, despite some differences in opinion. The recognition of the opponent's problems lays a promising foundation for the formation of an integrated society in the future. Russian-speakers would prefer a bilingual state, but they can understand Latvians' fear of the Latvian language being assimilated. They rationalize that national values are much more sensitive for a small nation whose survival is at stake. Similarly, moderate Russian-speakers see the reasons for Latvians' insistence on restricting citizenship. The demographic situation threatens to turn Latvians into a minority in their own country. One interviewee reasons that Latvians first want to accumulate capital to themselves as well as consolidate their hold on government before opening citizenship to wider circles.[371]

The historical roots of the ethnic question are discerned by empathic Russian-speakers. They treat Latvia as a small nation which used to be under the pressure of a great power. Finally the small nation reacted to that pressure. Perhaps all these counter-reactions are not solely positive – but they are understandable. Unavoidably, Soviet power is being identified with Russians. Russian-speakers try to accentuate the difference between a policy of the totalitarian state and ordinary people. Former Soviet citizens cannot be rendered guilty of what happened. The last point is usually acknowledged by Latvians – at least in principle. In their defence, Russian-speakers maintain that they did not know about the occupation until Latvia's national reawakening in the late 1980s. They considered the Baltic states a well-developed part of Russia.[372]

There are Russian-speakers who are even open to self-criticism. According to them, Russian-speakers were lulled into a comfortable feeling of being citizens of a multinational superpower with the implication that they did not take into consideration the national feelings of Latvians. It was not necessary to learn the native language, because Russian was the lingua franca of the Soviet Union. A small minority of Russian-speakers had an uneasy, guilty feeling because of the neglect of the national language, but the majority did not pay attention to it.[373] To sum up, if there are so many consensual elements and so much readiness to meet the other side half-way in even a part of the population, the future looks promising.

Despite some uneasy feelings as a collective group, Russian-speakers do not complain of unfair treatment in concrete situations any more than Latvians. When the New Baltic Barometer asked people whether they expect fair treatment from a variety of public and private institutions with which they are likely to have contact in their community, no systematic bias, which would have indicated discrimination, could be observed in the answers (Table 10.5). The good news is that Russian-speakers and Latvians agree about the likelihood of being treated fairly. The bad news is that this is sometimes due to large numbers of Latvians as well as Russian-speakers expecting unfair treatment. Equitable treatment is not the same as fair treatment.[374]

Table 10.5   Expectations of Fair Treatment (% *expecting fair treatment*)

	Post Office	Bank	GP, hospital	Shop	Work	Social security	Municipal housing	Police
Russians	85	79	79	78	58	57	56	41
Latvians	81	81	77	74	58	60	60	41
Difference	+ 4	− 2	+ 2	+ 4	0	− 3	− 4	0

Source: Rose 1996.

The average Russian-speaker does not claim that Russian-speakers would be under pressure from Latvian nationalism. The preference most Russian-speakers show for life in Latvia as against living in Russia or a Greater Russia incorporating their present homeland also indicates that they are not a deprived minority. The interviewed persons trust in the respect of the rights of the ethnic minority by the Latvian government. They recognize that a lot of efforts have been made to create a democratic society. Latvian politicians and authorities do not offend Russian-speakers in their public speeches. The occasional insulting comments in the mass media are made by reporters, artists, academics or other private entities.[375]

CITIZENSHIP AND POLITICAL ATTITUDES

De jure Latvian residents are divided into citizens and non-citizens but de facto one could speak about two different categories of citizenship, because non-citizens are treated in the same way as citizens in most respects. Their position differs favourably from that of aliens. Non-citizens have almost equal socioeconomic rights as citizens; they are guaranteed state protection; they are issued a travel document, a non-citizen's passport. The main difference in citizens and non-citizens' rights concerns political rights. Non-citizens can neither vote nor run for elections nor hold public office. Nevertheless, the rights of a non-citizen are broader than the rights of a Soviet citizen. This is an essential factor explaining why non-citizens have not demanded political rights more vocally on a mass scale. People who have got used to living in a dictatorship do not understand the value of democratic rights.[376]

The neglect of political rights can be seen in survey studies, as well. From the point of view of ordinary Russian-speakers, conventional political rights of a citizen do not appear to be a high priority. Social and economic rights come first. The same attitude holds for Latvians. Virtually everyone, irrespective of nationality, agrees that those who live in Latvia have rights to welfare benefits.[377]

The evidence from the New Baltic Barometer challenges the claims of the hard-line politicians of both sides when it shows that there is no uniformity of opinion about who should be a citizen. Each nationality divides into absolutists and moderates. Nationalities differ only in the way in which they divide (Table 10.6). Among Latvians the biggest split is between those who think that the criterion for citizenship should be the position as of 1940 and those prepared to grant citizenship to an increasing number of Russian-speakers on the basis of birth or even of long-term residence. Among Russian-speakers the dividing line is between those who want citizenship now and those accepting restriction to people born in the country or resident for a substantial number of years. The median response among Russian-speakers states that citizenship should be restricted to residents of more than ten years' standing. The proportions of the absolutists versus moderates are 42:58 among Latvians and 47:52 among Russian-speakers.[378] The result supports the view that a great part of the Latvian residents finds the current citizenship law as a reasonable compromise which has successfully stabilized the situation in the country.

Table 10.6   Who Should Be Citizens? (%)

	Latvians	Russian-speakers
Pre-1940 family	42	4
Born in Latvia	33	24
Resident over 10 years	17	24
Resident at independence or now	8	47

Source: Rose 1997, 18.

The command of the Latvian language is a close concomitant of the citizenship issue, not least because a language exam is an essential part of the naturalization test. While it is hardly surprising that Latvians are virtually unanimous that everyone who lives there should learn the national language, it is striking that 91 per cent of Russian-speakers agree (Table 10.7). The language exam as a condition for citizenship is not quite as uncontroversial. Nevertheless, almost two-thirds of Russian-speakers accept it. The most significant difference between Latvians and Russian-speakers does not lie in the recognition of the duties of a resident or a citizen but in the strength of the obligation. A more detailed statistical analysis reveals that Russian-speakers are more likely to say that people 'usually' owe the country a duty, such as learning of the national language, whereas Latvians are more inclined to say that everyone definitely has an obligation.[379] Latvians tend to believe that Russian-speakers are reluctant to learn Latvian on principle, but these results disprove such a claim.

Table 10.7   Command of the National Language as a Resident's Duty and as a Condition for Citizenship (% *agreeing with the statement*)

	Every resident should learn Latvian	*Every citizen should pass a language exam*
Russian-speakers	91	61
Latvians	99	93
Difference	− 8	− 32

Source: Rose 1997, 38, 41.

What undermines, in the eyes of Latvians, Russia and the Socialist Party's demand for immediate, all-inclusive citizenship is the extremely low rate of naturalization. Only a small fraction of the non-citizens entitled to apply for Latvian citizenship try to pass the naturalization test. Naturalization statistics from 1996, during which non-citizens between the ages of 16 and 20 were eligible to apply for naturalization, paint a bleak picture: of the 33,000 eligible non-citizens, only 525 submitted applications.[380] When the New Baltic Barometer asked non-citizens whether they planned to apply for citizenship, 43 per cent of the respondents spoke about such plans; 23 per cent was unsure and one-third said no.[381] Many Latvians interpret the passiveness of non-citizens as a sign of disinterest:

> Russians say they have lived here and want to become citizens. At the same time there are very few persons who take the naturalization exam. The test is not a problem if you just go and try it. People are very passive ... The main problem is not the citizenship law but the people who don't apply for naturalization, even if they were entitled to it. They have been shown the way.[382]

The reasons for the low naturalization rates are manifold. First, as indicated above, the significance of citizenship is not understood, just as the significance of democracy is not understood. Moreover, it is not perceived that citizenship brings tangible benefits, as well. To cite an example, a non-citizen who is entitled to apply for citizenship but who has not yet done so argues: 'I have all possibilities to work here and to travel abroad. Everything depends on the person himself, his education and personal abilities.' There are also prevailing misunderstandings concerning the nature of citizenship: citizenship is believed to restrict a person's freedom to move to another country. Such misconceptions sound strange to a Westerner but they reflect experience from the Soviet reality. Soviet citizenship was indeed restrictive. Some Russians point out rightly that travelling to Russia will become more complicated, if a Russian takes Latvian citizenship. A Latvian citizen needs a visa to enter Russia, whereas holders of the FSU passports can travel to Russia freely. A visa-free regime is important to those Russians who have relatives in Russia.[383]

Second, preparation for the naturalization test takes time and effort. 'I have neither time nor energy to occupy myself with this matter. I prefer living without citizenship now. I don't know about the future.' There seems always to be something more urgent or important to do than to read Latvian history and constitutional law. The price of the naturalization test, LVL 30, is quite expensive by Latvian standards. Therefore people do not take the exam simply to see if they can pass it. For the poorest strata the price of LVL 30 can act as a barrier. Pensioners and invalids are allowed a discount but students are not.[384]

Third, non-citizens are afraid of both the exam and the Latvian authorities. A rumour has spread that the multiple-choice test in history and law is terribly difficult. On the one hand, it presumes very detailed rote learning of, for instance, exact dates; on the other hand, it contains taxing questions which require university-level inference, not just general knowledge. Nobody could expect such kinds of questions beforehand. The test is also long. Irina tells: 'My daughter is a graduate. She has tried to pass the exam twice but each time she has missed a few points in history. She had revised for the exam. My daughter says she will never pass it.' Irina is convinced that the exam has been made difficult deliberately, because Latvians do not want to have Russian-speaking citizens. A representative of the OSCE does not believe this is so – university professors, who have created the test, have simply failed to set the right degree of difficulty. The language test is easy enough.[385]

Certain Latvian institutions have a bad reputation among Russian-speakers. The Citizenship and Immigration Department as well as the board of examiners for professional language exams earlier behaved unreasonably and high-handedly. They made the process extremely distressing for some people. Consequently, Russian-speakers fear being humiliated again. In reality the fear is unfounded, since candidates are treated well at the Naturalization Office.

The Naturalization Office shows a friendly, positive face, trying to do its job as well as possible in a matter-of-fact way. The Citizenship and Immigration Department and the language board have also improved their practices.[386]

Fourth, young men have a disincentive to apply for citizenship, because male citizens must enter military service. When the first cohort entitled to naturalization was approved, the twelve-person group was composed of eleven females and one male who limped badly.[387]

Fifth, pride may prevent some from going to the naturalization test. Abstention demonstrates a conscious protest then. Some Russian-speakers cannot understand why they have to apply for citizenship, if they were born in Latvia and possibly speak Latvian, while a person who comes from America or Australia gets citizenship automatically.[388]

Sixth, family hierarchy restricts the freedom of choice of the young generation. Typically adult children live at home with their parents, as both generations are economically dependent on one another. It is not psychologically easy for a young person to take citizenship, if the family will be divided along this sensitive line. As a result, children will have rights that parents have not, which contradicts the hierarchial structure of a Russian family, where senior family members are respected.[389]

As distinct from the main trend, well-educated business people are very much aware of the significance of political rights. They mention the lack of citizenship rights and political power as the chief grievance in Latvia. They refer to the fact that there are no political forces defending their economic and political interests. The Lithuanian variant is raised as a model for an exemplary approach to citizenship policy. The defenders of a lenient citizenship law argue that granting citizenship to everybody would increase the loyalty of Russian-speakers to the Latvian state. The wish to reverse the current citizenship law is pronounced. Some of the interviewees show optimism in this respect as far as the future is concerned. They assume that the law may become more lenient in the course of time when economic and social conditions start to improve. 'The state will think about it.' The initiative by President Ulmanis is seen as an encouraging sign of a softening stance. President Ulmanis invited public discussion about the citizenship issue in society and among political parties. He called for legal amendments easing naturalization requirements. Better information, easier exams, appropriation of money for courses and textbooks are ways of accelerating naturalization without changing the current law.[390]

In spite of the dissatisfaction with nationality policies, most non-citizens are not prepared to take action in an effort to influence the situation. The New Baltic Barometer reports that only about one-third would take part in a protest demonstration about citizenship (Table 10.8). Former Soviet citizens are not familiar with political participation and they have little idea of the possibilities open to them. Instead, they stress their being unpolitical persons. Shortage of time owing to the necessity to work long days is mentioned as another constraint. 'Foreign subsidiaries excluded, our company [FIS] employs over a hundred people in Riga. I work in the office from 8 am till 11 pm each day. I have no time for anything else.' Latvia's Russian-speaking minority is totally unorganized at the level of civil society perhaps because the Russian-speaking world has no organizational tradition.[391]

Table 10.8   Interest in Politics and Readiness to Take Political Action
(% answering positively)

	Interested in politics	Ready to take part in demonstrations about citizenship
Russian-speakers	49	34
Latvians	57	15
Difference	– 8	19

Source: Rose 1997, 17, 35.

A low interest in politics supports the interpretation that political rights are not valued much (Table 10.8). The difference in political interest between Latvians and Russian-speakers to the disadvantage of Russian-speakers can be explained by the latter's exclusion from politics. Why would they be interested in something which they cannot influence? Rather, it might be painful to watch Latvian politics as an outsider. Furthermore, Russian-speakers are unfamiliar with the basic categories of politics: about half of them cannot place themselves on the left–right scale (Table 10.9). Of both Latvians and Russian-speakers, 68 per cent do not feel close to any party or movement.[392] Symptoms of political alienation are recognizable. Russian-speakers do not trust in the contemporary political alternatives. In their view, party politicians are interested only in money and power. 'Politics is dirty everywhere. Only before elections do politicians speak nicely: "We are together. We will be strong."'[393] According to the New Baltic Barometer, 85 per cent of both Latvians and Russian-speakers distrust political parties.[394]

The interviewees maintained that no political party represents the interests of Russian-speakers. Accordingly, they did not spontaneously mention any party by name. When the Socialist Party, Harmony and Saimnieks were mentioned, which are usually classified more or less as Russian-speakers' parties, the interviewees expressed their disappointment with these parties: 'The leaders of these parties are working for their own personal political interests, not for those of electors.'[395] Entrepreneurs did not conceive of the Socialist Party as being their party at all: 'It has other targets. Its main objective is to resolve political and humanitarian problems and to level differences between citizens and non-citizens. It does not take care of business questions.'[396]

Table 10.9   Self-placement on a 'Left–Right' 10-point Scale, Ranging from 1 (Furthest Left) to 10 (Furthest Right) (%)

	Latvians	Russian-speakers
Extreme left (1, 2)	2	6
Left (3, 4)	8	10
Centre (5, 6)	34	30
Right (7, 8)	13	4
Extreme right (9, 10)	3	0
Don't know/no answer	38	49

Source: Rose 1997, 17.

Many Latvians do not want the Russian-speakers to be enfranchised, because they are convinced that the new voters would vote for the Socialists or politicians like Belarusian Lukashenko. A uniform voting pattern looks highly unlikely in the light of the diversified structure of the ethnic minority. As indicated earlier, Russian-speakers are by no means a homogeneous group. Survey results of the Russian-speakers' party affiliations confirm the hypothesis of the dispersion of votes between different parties (Table 10.10). The most popular parties are left-of-centre Saimnieks (35 per cent) and left liberal Harmony (21 per cent). The left radical Socialist Party ranks only third with considerably lower support (13 per cent). Right-of-centre Latvia's Way (11 per cent) and coalition Farmers' Union and Christian Democratic Union (10 per cent) are not far behind the Socialists in popularity. The national conservative parties have, understandably, hardly any support among Russian-speakers. Correspondingly, the Socialist Party and Harmony are shunned by Latvians.

It can be concluded that parties which put strong emphasis on the nationality question lean on a constituency composed of a single ethnic group. The National Bloc parties will be the biggest losers when the number of Russian-speaking voters starts to grow. The leading centre parties which are oriented toward socioeconomic issues attract electors across ethnic divisions. At the moment it appears that socioeconomic questions have the highest priority in people's thinking, overriding the ethnic question. Hence, it is not self-evident

that Russian-speaking voters would polarize the Latvian party system along
ethnic lines, as Western scholars typically forecast. A new Russian party will
most probably emerge, but it will not achieve a monopoly over the votes of
Russian-speakers.

Table 10.10   Party Preferences (%)

Party	Latvians	Russian-speakers
Saimnieks	10	35
Harmony	3	21
Socialist Party	1	13
Latvia's Way	15	11
Farmers' Union & KDS coalition	10	10
Siegerist Party	3	5
Fatherland and Freedom	27	2
Unity Party	2	1
Social Democratic Party	12	1
LNNK	16	–
Others	2	–

Source: Rose 1997, 42–3.

Thus far the attempts to organize so-called Russian parties have been
unsuccessful. They have often been unserious local groupings without a
genuine political platform. The Russian Citizens' Party (*Krievu pilsonu
partija*), which ran for the 6th Saeima elections, has since vanished from the
political scene. The party was founded by the Abreve community, which
demanded compensations from Russia for their losses by virtue of Abreve's
annexation to Russia in 1944. The Russian Citizens' Party was labelled a
puppet party of the LNNK, whose main function was to divide Russian-
speakers' votes in order to weaken Harmony and the Socialist Party. It had
no distinguished leaders. In the local elections held in March 1997, another
Russian party (*Krievu partija*) gained two seats in the Riga City Council.
The party was supported by Old Believers. The success of a totally unknown
political force was explained by the voters' disappointment with established
parties and a low electoral turnout (less than 50 per cent). There being no
barrier, the composition of the city councils became extremely fragmented.[397]

People's self-placement on the left–right divide is in conformity with their
party preferences (Table 10.9). A moderate left-of-centre position is the most
frequent choice among both Latvians (26 per cent) and Russian-speakers (25
per cent). Russian-speakers are more left-leaning than Latvians but the

proportion of an extreme left identification is still relatively small. The attitudes of Latvia's residents are far from radical.

NON-CITIZENS' LEAGUE

The Non-Citizens' League (NCL) was a failed attempt to organize a non-political body which would represent the interests of non-citizens with respect to the government. It was founded in late 1993 by a group of persons from various political parties and NGOs. The stimulus for the establishment of the NCL came from the perception of a severe sociopolitical problem in Latvia: almost one-third of the population has no practical mechanism to participate in political decision-making. Consequently, that part of the population is excluded from decision-making in certain other areas, as well. The founders of the League considered this state of affairs as a problem not only for non-citizens but also for the state, because, in their view, no country can claim to be really democratic if a large section of the population is denied full democratic rights; that is, the right to participate in political life. The situation was seen as unjustified, regardless of historical or legal reasons why these people were not recognized as Latvian citizens. 'That is altogether a different story', the NCL stressed.[398]

The NCL called into question the very foundations of the adopted citizenship law, calling them 'dubious'. It declared itself an heir of the Popular Front. 'It is not fashionable to talk about this today but let's not forget that the so-called "zero option" was clearly envisaged by the Popular Front's pre-electoral programme in 1990. That is why many Russian-speakers voted for the Popular Front then.' Now Russian-speakers feel themselves betrayed. Yet non-citizens cannot change existing laws. The NCL was invented as a way to address what they define as the most fundamental problem of the Latvian society. It wanted to start a dialogue with the government.[399]

The NCL organized a poll to elect authorized representatives to conduct a dialogue with the government on behalf of non-citizens. In essence, the poll was a quasi-election, but the NCL deliberately wanted to avoid calling it an election so as not to arouse suspicion. About 45,000 non-citizens – less than 10 per cent – took part in the action. The participation remained low partly due to the lack of an effective mechanism for organizing the poll, and partly due to difficulties with the police. The poll was preceded by a media campaign and an appeal to different political parties and NGOs to nominate their candidates for the poll. The NCL prepared a bulletin which contained a list of the candidates. On the reverse side of the bulletin, the goals of the

NCL were defined. The 'zero option' was not amongst them. Three principal demands were as follows:

1. to eliminate all restrictions in non-citizens' rights in the field of social and economic rights;
2. to provide non-citizens with the right to vote in municipal elections;
3. to redress the malpractices in the registration of citizens, conducted by the Citizenship and Immigration Department.[400]

One of the primary activities of the NCL was the identification of the differences in citizens' and non-citizens' rights beyond political rights. Officially the only difference should concern political rights, but the NCL found over 60 distinctions in social, economic and property rights as well as in political freedoms (which is not the same thing as political rights). To make the violations known both in Latvia and abroad, the NCL compiled for publishing a list of the differences[401] and urged human rights experts to evaluate them. The State Human Rights Committee gave its report three years later, at the end of 1996. The latter organization found ten cases in which the Latvian legislation contradicted the country's international obligations. According to Tsilevich, the main grievances deal with employment rights, social security and travel documents.[402]

The law prohibits non-citizens from working in certain professions. Tsilevich understands that particular offices, such as judge, public prosecutor or diplomat, are reserved for Latvian citizens only, but some restrictions appear ridiculous to him. He mentions the positions of head of a pharmacy, crew of commercial airlines and barrister as examples of incomprehensible restrictions. Second, in the case of non-citizens, years worked outside Latvia are not taken into account in the calculation of an old-age pension. For citizens it does not matter where they have worked. Considering the low level of pensions, each santimi may be crucial for survival. Third, bilateral agreements with certain countries allow only citizens to enter these countries without a visa. One such country is Britain. After the visa-free regime was taken into effect, Britain closed its consular section in Riga. Now non-citizens have to go to Moscow, Stockholm or Helsinki to obtain a British visa. In Moscow queues are enormous and Russian citizens have a priority. To get to Stockholm or Helsinki, a non-citizen needs a Swedish or Finnish visa.[403]

It was not only the differentiation in legal rights but also the implementation of the laws – the manner in which the laws are put into practice – that caused complaints from the NCL. The NCL criticized the Citizenship and Immigration Department heavily. Tsilevich is convinced that malpractices there were not merely arbitrariness of isolated officials but a state policy. Arbitrariness was more large-scale and systematic than otherwise would have been possible. Radical nationalistic officials considered it their holy task to protect the purity of Latvian citizentry. Moreover, even if a non-citizen won a trial against the Citizenship and Immigration Department, he was not compensated for the extra costs.[404]

When the NCL applied for an official registration as envisaged in law, the Minister of Justice refused the registration. The main accusation against the NCL was that its activities were in essence of a political nature. Non-citizens are not permitted to establish political organizations in Latvia. The NCL was required to remove the idea of the representation of non-citizens and organize itself as a cultural association. The NCL denied being a political organization by referring to the law which defines what political activities are about. The NCL agreed to eliminate some items on its statute, but it did not help. When the registration was refused for the second time, the NCL appealed to the court in June 1995. Since then the NCL is waiting for its case to be taken to a hearing in the court. It has not tried to speed up the process because its leaders have concluded that 'the rain has gone'. If the government does not want a dialogue, the NCL can do nothing alone. The NCL is no longer active.[405]

The chairman of the NCL does not regard ethnic relations as problematic at the interpersonal level. According to him, the relations are normal. He refers to the frequency of interethnic marriages: every fifth Latvian marries a Russian. Instead, the problem must be formulated in terms of the relations between the state and the non-titular population. Tsilevich blames the deep segregation of society on state policies. Russian-speakers are squeezed out of administration, science and culture. They are concentrating on businessmen and blue-collar workers, while Latvians are becoming a nation of bureaucrats and peasants. The 'division of labour' resembles the situation that prevailed in prewar Latvia in the 1920s and 1930s. In Tsilevich's opinion, it is harmful for Latvians themselves, because it facilitates a permanent 'brain drain' and hinders healthy competition in the labour market. After the restoration of independence thousands of new jobs were created in state offices, which were all occupied by Latvians.[406]

Russians in the Baltics are finding themselves in a similar position to the Jews. A survey conducted in 1996 reveals that the same stereotypes that have traditionally been attached to Jews are now attached to Russians in the Baltics. The division into Latvian politics and Russian business also creates stereotypes. Some people believe that Russian businessmen have bought all Latvian politicians. Other people believe that Latvian politicians blackmail Russian businessmen. Neither contention is true, since politics and business are closely interdependent.[407]

IDENTITY AND LOYALTY

Latvia's Russian-speakers have developed an identity distinct from their original nationality. Russians living in Latvia are not the same Russians as those living in Russia. They are more Western. The other important point is that Russian-speakers' ethnic consciousness is weak. They do not actively think of their national identity. Russian-speakers believe that national values are more important for small nations which are struggling for the survival of their culture and language. Latvian nationalists level the accusation that Soviet workers were turned into a cosmopolitan mass which does not feel its national roots.[408] The contention contains a grain of truth. A quite separate question is the valuation of cosmopolitanism: is it negative or not?

The interviewees defined themselves as cosmopolitan in the first place. After that they added that deep in their heart they are Russian. Yet the Russian identity was dormant. Many interviewees introduced the category of a 'Latvian Russian', underscoring their ties to Latvia. As one person put it: 'I am Russian. My culture is Russian. Yet I could not live in Russia, because I am integrated into this society. I consider myself Western, cosmopolitan.' Despite the lack of citizenship, the Russian-speaking interviewees regarded Latvia as their homeland. 'I am a patriot of the Latvian state. Many Russians feel the same way.' Respectively, they confirmed their loyalty to Latvia and their standing for an independent Latvian state. Entrepreneurs defined their companies as internationally oriented Latvian enterprises, pointing out that business does not know borders.[409]

In contrast with Russian-speakers, Latvians are very conscious of their national identity, even when a person is not a nationalist. Nationality has a top priority in Latvians' self-definition. The Latvian language is given an intrinsic value. A 25-year-old Latvian woman said that she could never live abroad permanently, because she could not use her native tongue. (She speaks English, German and Russian fluently.) Young Latvians are often actively engaged in cherishing folklore traditions.[410]

Rose has constructed an indicator for the Baltic nationals' identities (Table 10.11). The New Baltic Barometer asked people to describe how they usually think of themselves, allowing two choices. By combining these two choices, five pairs of identities were formed: local, Baltic, Balteast, Soviet and European. Over two-thirds of Russian-speakers had a pair of identities: as residents of a city or region within Latvia and as Russians (Balteast). A majority put local identity before nationality. Local identity was more widespread than Soviet identity. As Latvians also tend to choose the combination of a local and national identification, the identities overlap at the local level, notwithstanding major divisions at the national level. Very few Russian-speakers identify themselves even secondarily with Latvians. Virtually no Latvians identify with the Soviet Union. Non-national identities are more frequent among Russian-speakers than among Latvians, which is consistent with the observations made above.

Table 10.11   Combined Identities (%)

	Latvians	*Russian-speakers*
Local	6	13
Baltic	88	3
Balteast	1	68
Soviet	0	8
European	4	8

Note:
Local   = 2 * city/locality/region.
Baltic   = 1* Baltic nationality + 1 * city/locality/region or vice versa.
Balteast   = 1 * Baltic nationality or city/locality/region + 1 * Slavic nationality or
                   Soviet or vice versa.
                   (Rose calls this type 'Baltic and Soviet'.)
Soviet   = 1 * Soviet + 1 * Slavic nationality or vice versa or 2 * Soviet or 2 *
                   Slavic nationality.
European = 2 * European.
[1* = one choice of two possible self-identities; 2 * = both choices of two possible self-identities]

Source: Rose 1997, 47.

Even though Russian-speakers identify themselves as Russians or as other Slavic nationals, they do not want to go back to former times. When the New Baltic Barometer asked people whether they would like a return to government as part of the Soviet Union, 57 per cent rejected this alternative. In 1995 the figure was 74 per cent. Even less is there a desire to return to communist rule: only 9 per cent of Russian-speakers endorsed this alternative. A major reason why Russian-speakers do not want to be integrated into a Moscow-led state is that over half of them believe that conditions for people like themselves are worse in Russia than in Latvia (Table 10.12). Over two-thirds are so detached from their ancestral home that they would have no place to live in Russia. Having lived all their lives in Latvia, they have no real ties to their native country. Russian-speakers have an interest in the future of the land in which they live. A clear majority is optimistic about the future of Latvia, especially in comparison with the prospects for Russia.[411]

What is important for Russian-speakers is the maintenance of cultural ties with Mother Russia. They would also like to ensure the opportunity to hear and use their native tongue along with Latvian. A usual complaint concerns the lack of a Russian-speaking television channel. Russian television can be seen only through a cable network, but poor pensioners, for instance, cannot afford to pay for cable television. These groups are least likely to understand Latvian.[412]

Table 10.12   Latvia's Russians not Longing for Russia (%[*])

	Russian-speakers
Conditions worse in Russia	55
Latvia has better prospects for future	62
No place to live in Russia	68

[*] percentage agreeing with the statement.

Source: Rose 1997, 50.

RUSSIAN-SPEAKING BUSINESS

Business is often defined as the most tolerant sphere of human acitivity where pursuit of profit overrides ethnic divisions. Many Russian-speaking businessmen put their hope on a 'spillover' effect, wishing that a similarly pragmatic attitude would gain ground in other sectors of society, too. 'Business is the main thing that gives hope for the future.' Businessmen unanimously assert that connections between Latvian- and Russian-speaking companies do not cause difficulties, because both sides clearly understand that business is business and the best option should always be chosen. 'If a business contact is useful, nobody will think about the language.' 'Our company [Terrabalt] has no problems with Latvian partners. In each situation we find a common language. It is the language of business.' The same holds for recruitment: the best applicant will be appointed. 'There is only one type of divide in information technology: this is a smart guy; this is a stupid guy. It is the best kind of division, because the language in information technology is English.'[413]

In spite of the working contacts between Latvian- and Russian-speaking companies, the business community is divided along ethnic lines. 'Ethnically pure' companies are more usual than mixed ones. Businessmen refer to practical and human reasons rather than to purposeful selection or animosity when explaining the existence of such a division. It simply appears natural for Russian-speakers to seek Russian-speaking employers and vice versa. The language and mentality difference makes it easier to work with people of the same nationality. Economic history explains in some cases why certain sectors or companies employ almost exclusively Russian-speaking workers. One entrepreneur admits that he feels uncomfortable when a Latvian employee is near, because he does not completely trust in a Latvian employee's loyalty. A Latvian may be loyal to the company at work, but at home his family may press him by complaining: 'Why do you have to work for that Russian? Couldn't you find a job anywhere else?'[414]

Latvian- and Russian-speaking business have their strongholds in different branches of economy. Transit and banking are normally classified as being the sphere of Russian-speaking capital. Latvian-speaking capital has concentrated on food and alcohol production as well as on wood-working. However, certain reservations should be kept in mind: the divide is not absolute, the trend points to the blurring of boundaries and the origin of the capital is often obscure. It is a false generalization to label all Russian-speaking business as illegal. Honest businessmen clearly want to break away from their dubious colleagues. Russian-speaking enterprises look for business opportunities in the East more actively, whereas Latvians are more oriented toward the West.

Russian-speaking business regrets the neglect of Eastern markets because of political reasons. Russian-speaking businessmen accuse 'political ambitions' of bringing about a too blinkered orientation toward Western Europe, where Latvian products are not competitive. They want to depoliticize economic questions and submit them only to considerations of rational calculation. In their view, Latvia should develop commercial relations in all directions, not solely to the West or the East. They draw attention to Latvia's unique geographical location as a gateway between the East and the West, stressing the necessity of taking full advantage of this position. The development of a strategic hub status requires the development of economic relations with Russia. 'Russia is a large market with vast resources, Latvia is a transit point.' They admit, though, that Latvian foreign trade policies have recently developed in the right direction.[415]

Russian-speaking businessmen argue for East trade in terms of welfare gains for the nation. The collapse of industrial production and the resulting poverty is seen as a consequence of breaking off relations abruptly. 'A black man cannot become a white man overnight – it is impossible. We tried to do such a thing. Now more than 60 per cent of the population lives below a subsistence minimum. It is one result of the abnormal strategy in economic development.' Practical men demand acknowledgement of realities: Latvia was a part of the Soviet Union for a long time. How it became a part of the Soviet Union is quite another issue, but the historical fact cannot be denied. During the Soviet period, strong business relations were established with different regions of the FSU. 'To break all these relationships once and for all is not smart.' Instead, these old contacts should be reactivated to 'make money for our people'. Business culture as well as many other forms of societal organization have more similarities with the FSU traditions than with Western Europe, although politicians want to introduce the Western model, which is suitable for a highly developed society but not for a sick economy.[416]

From the business point of view, there is hardly any difference in the operation of Latvian- and Russian-speaking companies. Both share the same rights and obligations in principle so that the conditions for business should not differ. In practice Russian-speaking companies feel slightly disadvantaged in comparison with Latvian-speaking companies, although contrasts are not glaring. Once again Russian-speakers do not blame Latvians for blatant cases of discrimination but point out fine mechanisms that indirectly work to the advantage of Latvians. The difference derives from missing political rights. Latvian entrepreneurs have better lobbying possibilities and better interpersonal contacts with the government with the result that they can get political support for their projects. Russian-speaking companies cannot count on any aid from above.[417]

The growth of Latvian influence in the Russian dominated banking sector is mentioned as an example of how mergers and buy-outs organized by the state-owned Latvian banks have paved the way for the expansion of the Latvian-speaking capital. Another example comes from Liepaja where the free port zone was set up recently. No single Russian-speaking representative was elected to the administrative body of the free port zone. The administration was elected by Liepaja's municipal council, composed of Latvians, which, in turn, was elected by the primarily Latvian electorate owing to the restrictions on franchise.[418]

When the Democratic Party Saimnieks came into being, Russian-speaking businessmen hoped that it would become their political arm. They financed Saimnieks's pre-electoral campaigns. What appealed to Russian-speaking business in the party programme was its openness to Eastern markets, liberal attitude in the free land market controversy and disregard of the language divide. Despite the electoral victory in the 6th Saeima elections, Saimnieks did not reach a leadership position in the party system, as it had expected as the biggest parliamentary faction. It floundered in its own self-complacency as well as in personal scandals. The scandals discredited the party's image in the eyes of its supporters, including businessmen. As it did not win a position in which it could dictate political decisions and make policies of its own, Saimnieks could not provide an effective channel of influence for its financers. The lack of results led to disappointment. Today Russian-speaking businessmen do not believe in politics. One interviewee stated openly what

Latvian nationalists are afraid of: the most realistic way for Russian-speaking business to increase influence is to increase economic relations with Russia.[419]

ETHNIC CLEAVAGE IN PARTY POLITICS

The most important manifestation of the ethnic cleavage is the political controversy over the citizenship law. The National Bloc parties, especially Fatherland and Freedom and the LNNK, pushed for a restrictive citizenship law whereas the Russian parties – Harmony and the Socialist Party – pleaded for a lenient version. Latvia's Way held an in-between position. As mentioned before, the citizenship issue was one of the main themes of the pre-electoral campaign in 1993.

The dispute culminated in the summer of 1994 when the highly controversial draft law was forwarded to Parliament's readings. Despite strong pressure on the part of Russia, the CSCE, the Council of Europe and the European Union, the Latvian Parliament passed a tough citizenship law on 21 June 1994. The distribution of the vote was 66 to 11 with 3 abstentions. The adopted law allowed the naturalization of non-citizens born in Latvia from 1 January 1995 until the year 2000. At the turn of the century there would still have been 500,000 remaining non-citizens. A quota system would have applied to these non-citizens not born in Latvia. The latter's naturalization was estimated to proceed at the rate of 2,000 per year. The Council of Europe and CSCE officials raised objections to the quantitative principle as well as the lack of a solid time schedule for naturalization. The basis for objections was the fact that the status of a large number of inhabitants was not defined in the citizenship law.[420]

President Guntis Ulmanis responded to a government appeal to reject the law and returned it to Parliament for reconsideration. Ulmanis feared the consequences of signing the law. The strict formulation of the law threatened to block Latvia's entry to the Council of Europe and the European Union. In the end, Parliament yielded to international pressure with the result that the amended law was accepted on 22 July 1994. The quota principle was replaced with a four-wave naturalization process, characterized as a window system.[421]

Naturalization started in 1995 with special groups: spouses of Latvian citizens, ethnic Estonians and Lithuanians as well as former citizens of Estonia and Lithuania. In 1996, the window was opened to 16–20-year old non-citizens who were born in Latvia. In 1997 the upper limit was raised to 25 years, in 1998 to 30 years and in 1999 to 40 years. In 2000 all Latvian-born non-citizens will be entitled to apply for citizenship. In 2001 all those who have come to Latvia as minors will be encompassed by the naturalization process. Those who were under 30 years of age when they came to Latvia will be entitled to naturalization in 2002. All the rest will have this right in 2003. Hence, by the year 2004 all residents will have the opportunity to apply for citizenship. The window never closes. The only restrictions are placed on criminals and former Soviet military personnel.[422]

After passing the citizenship law, the issue lost its relevance for a majority of the electorate. The adopted law was conceived of as being a satisfactory and at the same time the only politically possible compromise. The overriding wish to ensure social stability in the face of burning economic problems calmed feelings down, too. Most parties dropped the citizenship issue from their active agendas and settled for working within the existing legislation. Even the LNNK and Harmony, originally opponents of the law, agreed to work within it. They stressed that any changes to be made should be done through Parliament. The only parties that stubbornly kept on addressing the citizenship issue were Fatherland and Freedom and the Socialist Party.

Fatherland and Freedom insisted on abrogating the adopted citizenship law, which it considered disadvantageous to Latvians. It put forward an alternative bill to be endorsed by a referendum. The Fatherland and Freedom proposed law suggested a narrower definition of groups who can apply for citizenship and more restrictive annual numbers for people who can become citizens through the naturalization process. In the late summer of 1994, Fatherland and Freedom began a massive signature collection campaign to move its bill into a referendum. However, it did not manage to collect enough signatures required by law to start proceedings on a new law. Thus, the attempt miscarried. Having realized it cannot influence the status quo, Fatherland and Freedom concentrated its efforts on precluding further relaxation of the current law. When Fatherland and Freedom joined Skele's first government, it demanded a stipulation to be included in the government programme that nothing will be changed in the citizenship law. Otherwise it will break the coalition and leave the government. The mood of the electorate as well as of most other parties is in accord with the clause. At the moment it seems politically impossible to introduce any changes in the citizenship law.[423]

The opposite parties in the citizenship controversy base their arguments on different historical and legal facts. Neither side can dispute the tenability of the other's evidence, but rather the point hinges on which factors should be considered to be the most relevant ones under contemporary circumstances. As the opponents perceive the situation from different angles, there is a danger their paths of thinking will never cross, so that the debate will lead to no conclusive result. First of all, the treatment of the citizenship question reflects the degree of acceptance of the prevailing demographic situation. The different approaches to the citizenship law diverge in terms of their temporal points of comparison: proponents of a restrictive version take the prewar situation as a point of departure, whereas proponents of a lenient variant stress the necessity to accept the actually existing situation. The other fundamental source of division derives from one's perception of the potential threat posed by Russians to the Latvian nation and how best to deal with that threat. The approaches of Fatherland and Freedom, on the one hand, and the National Harmony Party, on the other, embody these distinctions.

The legal approach advocated by Fatherland and Freedom looks back to the demographic situation that prevailed before the Soviet occupation in 1940. It emphasizes the legal continuity of the Latvian state, and accordingly the descendancy of citizenship. Repatriation of 'illegal occupants' is seen as a logical implication of the Geneva Convention on the status of occupied states. The consequences of the colonialization should be eliminated as quickly as possible, instead of legalizing the residence of intruders.[424] The argument is founded on the production of evidence that the occupation violated international law and was morally unjustified, which, indeed, is an indisputable fact. The weakness of the approach is that it relies solely on normative thinking without taking into account political realities. The illusion of a euphoric prewar Latvia is an unrealizable dream.

The National Harmony Party disputes neither the content of legal reasoning nor the occurrence of injustices but it considers past events irrelevant to the current problems. It makes a distinction between causes (Sovietization policy) and consequences (changed proportions between Latvians and non-Latvians). The burning problem is now how to manage a country in which almost one-third of the population is without citizenship. These people have lost their political rights. The question is exacerbated by differences in social, economic and property rights which, according to the Harmony Party, are totally unfounded. As Latvia cannot escape the existing situation it must adapt to it and try to make the best of it.[425] In contrast to the principled position of Fatherland and Freedom, the Harmony Party stands for pragmatism and political realism.

Many Latvians continue to feel threatened by Russians. The starting point of their thinking is the idea that the Soviet policy drove the Latvian nation to the verge of extinction. Simultaneously Latvians were de facto deprived of the right to use their own native tongue in all situations of everyday life, because immigrants were not obliged to learn Latvian. A telling example is a Russian children's doctor who did not know a word of Latvian. Latvians are afraid of the assimilation of their language, culture and national traditions. A large number of Russians living in Latvia do not speak Latvian, while most

Latvians speak Russian. If all Russian-speakers were automatically granted citizenship, they might never learn the state language.[426]

An additional aspect is that the loyalty of the Russian minority is under suspicion. The political effects of increasing Russian influence on politics are regarded as unpredictable. Proponents of a tougher citizenship law fear that those who are naturalized will be ethnic Russians who will derail Latvia's political orientation toward a market economy and inclusion in the EU. Instead, they will shift the country toward protectionism, Russia and possibly future inclusion in the CIS. Comparing Latvia to Belarus, Aigars Kimenis, the acting chair of the Fatherland and Freedom Coordination Centre, says: 'If pro-Russian politicians get a majority in Parliament, then, when Parliament keeps changing to the left and again to the left, it will be the end of the Latvian state.' In order to keep control over the Latvian state, it is necessary to restrict naturalization of non-citizens.[427]

The spokesmen for the integration of Russians try to convince their opponents that Russians do not constitute a threat to Latvia's independence. Russians living in Latvia have a different mentality and orientation from Russians in Russia. According to the inclusionists, the key issue for Latvia's Russians is not the ethnic question but the socioeconomic one. The difference between Latvian and Russian mentalities became apparent from the very beginning of the national awakening. Ethnic consciousness was much lower among Russians than among Latvians. Hence, the attitudes of the Russian-speakers depend mainly on their social and economic conditions. From this perspective, active participation of Russians in business is desirable rather than alarming. If Russian businessmen develop a vested interest in the existence of an independent Latvian state, they will have no reason to act against Latvia – on the contrary, they will serve to stabilize the situation. Furthermore, business is international. If Russian business is legal, pays taxes and provides jobs it is as welcome as any other business. National economy is about internal economic structures, not about ethnic economic structures. In other words, it is the economy of Latvia, not the economy of Latvians. At the present stage of economic reform the state needs the commitment of all people to economic rebuilding. If Latvia refuses to accept part of its residents as citizens, the excluded people are not likely to be motivated to work for the country. Finally, the normalization of relations with Russia requires that the conditions in which the Russian minority lives in Latvia do not give cause for complaints.[428]

Thus far the nationalism–universalism dimension has been reduced solely to the citizenship issue. There are also other manifestations of this cleavage, although they do not carry as much weight as the dispute over the distribution of political rights. The question of desovietization is one such manifestation.

Nationalists demand radical desovietization, squaring up with the past and opening of KGB archives. Several Parliament deputies have undergone highly publicized, inconclusive trials for alleged KGB collaboration. Foreign Minister Georgs Andrejevs (LC), one of the then most popular politicians in Latvia, resigned after admitting he had worked as a KGB agent. The most spectacular trials have been held in the cases of Alfreds Rubiks, the former First Secretary of the Latvian Communist Party, and Alfons Noviks, the former KGB head in the Stalin era. Noviks was prosecuted for the deportation of tens of thousands of people in the 1940s and 1950s. The leftist forces want to avoid confrontation with the former representatives of Soviet rule. They plead for a general amnesty. Respectively, they oppose general restrictions on present activity of former CP and KGB members due to the unreliability of evidence.

Cases in which the ethnic and socioeconomic cleavages reinforce each other are exceptions to the rule. Yet those rare manifestations which connect citizenship rights with social, economic, labour and property rights are highly politicized. Restitution, restrictions on ownership of land, differentiated social benefits and ethnicity as a criterion for the selection of administrative personnel are examples of the intertwinement of the two dimensions. The Riga City Council's decision to pay social allowances only to the citizens of Latvia sparked an uproar in the country's political life in January 1995. According to the resolution, indigent non-citizens could receive municipal allowances for heating and apartment rent only in special cases. The restriction was motivated by shortages in Riga's social budget: the city budget was not sufficient to pay social allowances to all indigent residents. The governing party in the City Council was the LNNK. Latvia's national parties supported the decision and asked all other municipalities to act equally. The majority of parliamentary factions opposed the differentiation between poor people, calling the decision discriminatory. Leftist parties argued that taxes are paid by all residents regardless of citizenship. Therefore the law on social allowances is equal for all. The local government's decision was struck down as illegal by the then Minister of State Reform (LC).[429]

Paralleling the diminishing visibility of ethnic issues in politics, it is becoming more and more difficult to uphold a distinctive political profile for parties that are not firmly anchored in other issue dimensions. Because both the socioeconomic and ethnic dimension offer a limited range of variation, the clearly discernible positions on them can be occupied only by a finite number of parties. After the 'quota' is full, the valence category becomes operative. Parties that are substitutes for each other compete in terms of their ability to achieve consensual goals. If one party falls short of its promises, voters will try the competing alternative. Competition along the valence dimension is likely to ruin the weaker parties in time. The simple rules of combinatorics apply to the explanation for decreasing party fragmentation. The number of possible combinations increases with the number of independent, mutually exclusive variables and vice versa. If one conflict dimension fades, the number of political parties can be expected to diminish.

The concentration process in the Latvian party system has started with the parties that have held an in-between position between parties with a more categorical outlook. The same phenomenon can be observed both in the National Conservative Bloc and in the cluster of Russian-speaker-friendly parties. The LNNK and Harmony have been in sharp decline since the 6th Saeima elections, while Fatherland and Freedom, and likewise Saimnieks, have grown in size at the former's expense. Part of the leadership in both parties drew conclusions from the drop in electoral support and suggested a merger with the programmatically close competitor. Harmony's party congress took a vote on a merger with Saimnieks in July 1996. The party congress rejected the proposed merger in a voting, which resulted in a fatal split within Harmony. Over seventy Harmony members, including two deputies, defected to Saimnieks. As a consequence of the defection, the number of Harmony's seats was reduced to four. Harmony was deprived of its status as a parliamentary faction, since by law a minimum of five deputies is required to form a faction. The party congress of the LNNK consented to merge with Fatherland and Freedom in April 1997.[430]

If we analyse the spatial locations of the LNNK and Harmony according to the model delineated before, we can see that the parties hold a symmetric position in the competitive space. The LNNK is an intermediary between Latvia's Way and Fatherland and Freedom, Harmony between Saimnieks and the Socialist Party. The LNNK and Latvia's Way agree on economic policy, but disagreement on citizenship policy separates them. The LNNK and Fatherland and Freedom share a similar approach to national policies, but their economic policies differ. Identically, Harmony's economic programme is very similar to that of Saimnieks, while the citizenship question connects it with the Socialist Party. Latvia's Way and Fatherland and Freedom, on the one hand, and Saimnieks and the Socialist Party, on the other, have mutually exclusive political orientations in each respect. It is easy to infer logically why a decline in the ethnic cleavage will first touch the LNNK and Harmony, not Fatherland and Freedom or the Socialist Party.

It is not only the abstract logic that explains the reconfiguration of the Latvian party system but also real-life setbacks, failures and scandals have a definite impact on the misfortune of certain parties. In the case of Harmony, two such factors contributed to its electoral defeat in the 6th Saeima elections: a split with Tautsaimnieks and a scandal about the party chairman's love affairs.

The bad publicity in the latter aspect alienated voters especially in the Catholic Latgale county, which has traditionally been a stronghold of Harmony's support.[431] Being a small party in opposition, Harmony has attained only a low visibility in the mass media during the ongoing legislative period. Big parties with diversified social and economic programmes and greater political influence attract more and more moderate voters across the ethnic boundaries. Single-issue parties are not viable, as the short history of the Unity Party proves.

The LNNK was whittled away by Fatherland and Freedom. The more moderate LNNK used to be the more popular of the two parties in the early 1990s. In the first local elections in May 1994, the LNNK came out a winner. It was also one of the favourites in the 6th Saeima elections. On the evidence of poll results, it was commonly believed that the LNNK would lead the next government. The surprising electoral defeat came as a shock to the LNNK leadership. The fallacy of the LNNK was that it was identified with the ruling parties, even though it had been in opposition at the national level. The first reason for such an image was the Pyrrhic victory in the local elections. The LNNK governed many city councils but it had no success in putting its policies in practice. During its electoral campaign in 1994 it had made unrealistic promises of a rapid change for the better which it could not keep. As the promised miracle did not happen, disappointed voters lost their trust in the party. The second reason for the electoral defeat in 1995 was that the LNNK was a supportive rather than a fighting opposition in Parliament. Its economic policy resembled very closely that of Latvia's Way. Fatherland and Freedom, by contrast, was always in bitter opposition to the government, agreeing on hardly any issue with Latvia's Way. It was able to exploit this tactical advantage so that people thought it would know the solutions to economic problems.[432]

Even in the government, Fatherland and Freedom has been able to maintain an image as an upright party which is less corrupt and more principled than other political forces. It appears as a creditable alternative, because it has always pursued consequent policies to attain its principal goal, a Latvian Latvia. Bojars's evaluation of Fatherland and Freedom can be presumed to be shared by many voters: 'It is less responsible for the prevailing economic chaos than the other governing parties, especially Latvia's Way.' After moderating its demands, Fatherland and Freedom has become capable of participating in political coalitions. Fatherland and Freedom follows a double strategy: the pragmatists of the party work in the government, while the orthodox nationalists make speeches in Parliament to uphold the right image. Fatherland and Freedom has won heavy posts in Skele's second government, including Minister of Finance, Minister of Economy and Minister of Justice.

The work of the Fatherland and Freedom ministers has been judged with general satisfaction.[433]

The increasing popularity of Fatherland and Freedom cannot be explained by an upsurge in nationalism; rather, the reasons are manifold, as the discussion above shows. Several factors together have contributed to the growth of the party. Notably, none of these factors is directly related to the citizenship question or other manifestations of the ethnic cleavage. The briefest explanation, comprising all the partial explanations, is that Fatherland and Freedom has won because the LNNK has lost. The valence dimension comes into the picture here. Both parties lean on a solid constituency which adheres to national conservative values. This part of the electorate treats the LNNK and Fatherland and Freedom as national conservative alternatives in general. Within the involatile national conservative community, the parties compete for the same votes.[434] Their combined share of the vote hardly changed from election to election. In 1993, the support of the LNNK and Fatherland and Freedom totalled 18.8 per cent. In 1995, the respective figure was 18.2 per cent.

The same phenomenon can be recognized with the Socialist Party. Its electoral results have also remained stable: it gained 5.8 per cent of the national vote in 1993 and 5.5 per cent in 1995. A party with such an extremist ideological outlook does not attract mobile voters but relies on steady supporters. For the same reason it is easy to conceive why left-of-centre Harmony did not plan to join forces with the Socialist Party.

The LNNK had a choice: would it stress national conservative values or liberal economic values? A majority put emphasis on the former values which connected the party with Fatherland and Freedom. The liberal wing of the LNNK, including Aleksandrs Kirsteins and Andrejs Krastins, opposed the coalescense. They announced they would never join Fatherland and Freedom. The Reform Party, which emerged shortly before the local elections in March 1997, was an unsuccessful attempt (at least in those elections) to provide a reform-minded conservative alternative in the place of the LNNK. Some Fatherland and Freedom members fear that the homogeneity of their party will suffer from the merger with the LNNK, if Fatherland and Freedom were to split into a liberal and conservative wing over economic questions.[435]

THE DECLINE OF THE ETHNIC CLEAVAGE

There is no coherent Russian-speaking community which could act as a united force in society. Given the multiple divisions, there cannot be a unity of interests or opinions either. Political rhetoric is prone to describe all people of a given nationality as thinking alike, although that is not the case in any community. Universal generalizations over the orientation of a nation are nothing but stereotypes. To treat all Russians as communists is as mistaken as it is to treat all Germans as Nazis. A democratically minded Russian is annoyed and embarrassed when he must stand next to pensioners who carry portraits of Stalin on Victory Day. Latvians should make a distinction between proponents of the Soviet Union and Western-oriented Russian-speakers who are willing to find a place in Latvian society. The latter group should be appealed to strongly and their integration should be encouraged in order to create a positive spillover effect. State policies can affect which ideas the majority of Russian-speakers become receptive to. If they see conditions improving, they are motivated to work for the future. In contrast, if they feel abandoned as outcasts, the propaganda of the hard-liners becomes verified by empirical reality.

Those people who are mostly concerned with the nationality question are incapable of conceiving the difference in the thinking of businessmen and ordinary people as opposed to their own approach. Practical people do not put much emphasis on ethnicity or language; their worldview is compiled of quite different values and concerns. A nationalist who fears Russian businessmen makes inferences from his own way of thinking and internal logic without realizing that it is different factors that count for businessmen. Nationalists emphasize the nation state and the language as a bond that keeps the state together. They require from citizens loyalty through a commitment to national values. Protection of ethnicity and national culture has the highest esteem for them. It is not only the Russian influence but also the Anglo-American pop culture that is seen as a threat. Interestingly, Latvia's EU membership receives more support from Russian-speakers (66 per cent in favour) than from Latvians (52 per cent in favour).[436] The cosmopolitan attitude rests on the old Latin *'ubi bene, ibi patria'* ('where man lives well, there is his fatherland') thinking. Loyalty can stem from interest calculation as well as from national sentiments or blood ties. In the future Latvia is faced with the task of creating a political nation in the place of an ethnic nation.

The best way to dispel prejudices is to increase interpersonal contacts between the ethnic communities. The segregation of society into two exclusive communities should be fought against by all possible means. Removal of unnecessary restrictions on non-citizens' rights could be the first step in the desirable direction. Strengthening the awareness of socioeconomic interests serves the same goal. Such a tendency is already recognizable. 'People have started to realize that the language is not the main reason for all the problems they have to cope with.'[437] The nationality question was overshadowed by economic concerns in the 6th Saeima elections as well as in the second local elections. When parties were asked which conflict dimension in their view exerts dominant influence in Latvian politics, ten out of twelve parties named the socioeconomic dimension as the most important cleavage in Latvia. The emergence of 'mixed' political parties that attract voters across the ethnic divide is encouraging. Populistic parties in Latvia have not tried to appeal to national sentiments by looking for scapegoats among the Russian-speakers.

Three principal orientations can be discerned among the Latvian parties to be used as a source of classification: nationalist, mainstream and universalist. Fatherland and Freedom pursues distinctly nationalist policies and the fellow party LNNK accompanies it closely. The latest initiative they have been jointly pushing for is a shift to an all-Latvian-language education system, advocating the gradual phasing out of Russian-language schools.[438] The Social Democratic programme contains views that resemble the nationalist line, but the party is not talking about the ethnic question actively. Traditionalism of a different variety governs Bojars's values, which emphasize the protection of native Latvian culture from foreign influences. The other National Bloc parties approach the centrist compromise position represented by Latvia's Way. The left-of-centre parties, with the exception of Harmony, share an approximately similar approach, belonging to the mainstreamers, as well, although they may be rather more liberal than some of the right-of-centre parties. The mainstream line can be characterized as a conciliatory pro-Latvian policy. Harmony and the Socialist Party/Equal Rights faction fight for the political rights of Russian-speaking non-citizens.

Latvia's wish to join the EU will force the political leaders to reconsider the citizenship law, because naturalization of non-citizens is progressing too slowly. The current silence around the citizenship question is largely due to people's inexperience of democracy and the conspicuousness of economic problems. The situation is favourable when a country comes from a dictatorship: people are not accustomed to demand democratic rights. The change in status from a Soviet citizen to a non-citizen meant an enlargement of rights and freedoms. To use an economic metaphor, it meant a Pareto improvement, although the Pareto optimum was not reached. A time may come when non-citizens do not compare their rights in terms of a longitudinal development in their personal history but cross-sectionally with their fellow countrymen. Ivan may start to ask why Ivars in the neighbourhood may vote but he may not, even when he pays the same taxes.[439] A rise in the awareness of political rights can make the prevailing structure unbearable. This is exactly the scenario which Western scholars and observers are anticipating.

Maintaining the status quo is always an option, but in the Baltic context it does not provide long-term security for people of either nationality. It leaves Baltic peoples fearful of the government of the Russian Federation, or even Russians in their own country. It leaves some Russians fearful of conflicts with a dominant Baltic majority, and some fearful of conflicts whipped up by hard-line Russians in Moscow.[440]

Latvians do not recognize the potential menace, thus, seeing no urgent need to cope with the problem. The current situation is stable and a mechanism for naturalization has been created. Some political parties may be reluctant to witness a substantial increase in the number of Russian-speaking voters for egoistic reasons of survival. If they calculate they are on the losers' side after shifts in the political landscape, they will oppose the extension of citizenship. More importantly, the wounds of the Soviet occupation are still too fresh to allow introduction of drastic moves, but the development so far indicates that tolerance will gain ground in the course of time. When attitudes mature, people will be able to distinguish between political guilt and individual guilt. Now the average Latvian is ready to accept a Russian-speaker as a neighbour but not as a co-citizen.[441] Thus, the political behaviour of Latvians is more nationalistic than their social behaviour. A step-by-step erosion of the distinction between citizens and non-citizens could parallel the evolution of the attitudinal climate. In order to avoid a repoliticization of the citizenship issue, incentives aimed at the acceleration of naturalization could start with technical changes in the naturalization tests as well as other measures that do not presuppose changes in the citizenship law.

To acknowledge that the citizenship issue must be dealt with in a more efficient way in the future is not to say that ethnic or nationalistic themes would dominate party competition. Latvia is not polarized into two camps with mutually exclusive outlooks.[442] There are a lot of consensual elements as well as common interests based on a similar socioeconomic position. Economic divisions undermine ethnic divisions, instead of reinforcing them. Politicians should respect the will of the people and not artificially inflame ethnic tensions. Virtually everyone agrees that Latvians and Russian-speakers can get along normally in everyday life. A human rights activist of the Harmony Party also acknowledges this fact in the discussion, but at the same time the title of the publication of which the activist is co-author is 'Ethnic Conflict in the Baltic States: The Case of Latvia.' The man-in-the-street is well aware of the destructiveness of a nationality conflict. Latvian residents are firmly committed to not allowing the events of Yugoslavia or Tsetchynia to be repeated in their country.

Part V

Politics versus Markets?

11 Political Constraints on Economic Reform

AVAILABILITY OF POLITICAL SUPPORT

For the take-off of reform, determination among the political elites was decisive. Latvia's leadership was unanimous in its decision to take a new course in the economy. The next challenge was to rally initial support behind the idea of transition to a market economy. Under the prevailing pro-independence enthusiasm, the mobilization of people was not difficult at all. First, people were prepared to make sacrifices for the sake of a better future, as long as the nation was seen as a unified monolith and intra-societal conflicts had not yet come to the fore. Second, people did not know what the market economy was about, not to mention the social consequences of a market-oriented reform. Nobody thought to analyse the effects of market-ization on society. It appeared self-evident that independence, democracy, a return to Europe and a market economy belong together automatically, although no logical connection exists between these components. The results of the Eurobarometer public opinion survey conducted in the autumn of 1991 show that a clear majority (60 per cent) felt Latvia was generally going in the right direction (wrong 18 per cent). The ratio supporting the idea that the creation of a free market economy was right for the country's future was more than two to one (57:25). Nearly half (49 per cent) of the population wanted to speed up economic reforms, one-fifth (21 per cent) was satisfied with the speed and only around one-tenth (12 per cent) said reforms were going too fast.[1]

In 1991–92, the undisturbed introduction of a reform package was secured by the hegemony of the reform-minded Popular Front in the legislature. In the 5th Saeima elections in June 1993, Latvia's Way triumphed as a successor of the Popular Front, gaining almost a third of the vote. No anti-reform protest party gained a firm foothold in Parliament. The ex-communists, who might have been suspected to cause a potential hazard for reform, although they did not openly oppose economic transformation, won less than 6 per cent of the vote. People were still willing to follow the popular leaders from the era of the struggle for independence, although the postcommunist recession had shaken people's faith in the glamour of capitalism. Increased pessimism was measured in a conspicuous downward trend in attitudes toward the direction the country was taking. In November 1992, less than a third (31 per cent) felt Latvia was generally going in the right direction, while almost a half (48 per cent) said the country was going in the wrong direction. A similar change was to be observed in attitudes toward the market economy. Of all Phare countries, the fall in support was greatest in Latvia, reversing previous majority support: 36 per cent for and 48 per cent against the market economy. Despite widespread dissatisfaction with the economic situation, people did not turn their backs on economic reform. Negative changes in attitude to economic reform were of minor significance (too slow: 44 per cent; right speed: 13 per cent; too fast: 16 per cent). The percentage of those saying economic reform was proceeding too slowly was greater than the percentages of those saying it was too fast and those saying it was the right speed together.[2]

When the survey results are compared to the electoral results of the following summer, it becomes apparent that, despite some sort of disillusionment, a majority of people wanted economic reforms to proceed at full speed. This willingness was crucial for the political sustainability of economic reform, because it implied that people saw reforms as the only way out of the bad situation. Reform leaders were not rendered guilty of the misery but, on the contrary, reforms were conceived of being a rescue from the crisis. Russia's economic blockade against Latvia, resulting in a severe fuel crisis, made it easy to find scapegoats outside the system. The expression of dissatisfaction with the economic state was not necessarily a revolt against the marketization of the economy. It is thinkable that the survey questions concerning the direction of the country as well as satisfaction with the market economy conveyed an immediate response to the prevailing situation rather than an anti-reform mood. If everything seems to be falling apart, it would be odd to show great optimism and contentment. Yet the recognition of facts need not lead to more far-reaching conclusions in the short run, especially when there are intervening factors that help to explain the course of events. This line of reasoning seems to be affirmed by the observation that in the next year improved confidence in the country's direction was matched with an increasing commitment to a market economy, while the prospects for economic reform remained relatively stable in comparison with previous years (Tables 11.1, 11.2 and 11.3).

Table 11.1   Direction of Country – Right or Wrong? (%)

	1991	1992	1993
Right	60	31	41
Wrong	18	48	34

Table 11.2   Market Economy – Right or Wrong? (%)

	1991	1992	1993
Right	57	36	41
Wrong	25	48	39

Table 11.3   Economic Reform – Too Fast or Too Slow? (%)

	1991	1992	1993
Too slow	49	44	44
About right	21	13	17
Too fast	12	16	11
No reforms	?	10	11

Sources: *Central and Eastern Eurobarometer* 2/1992, 3/1993 and 4/1994.

Availability of political support for the transition to a market economy can also be measured in a more subtle, indirect way, which may shed light on the real receptiveness to capitalism even better than direct formulations. The question is then whether the mental climate is ripe for a market economy and whether commonly held values are consistent with those of the market. Deep-rooted, partly unconscious prejudices can block the implementation of a marketization process even when people convey support of a market economy but do not actually understand the essence of capitalism. These attitudinal aspects also can be examined by survey methods.

'Profit is theft' was the message of the communist indoctrination. Private entrepreneurship and affluence are still regarded as suspect in the eyes of the mass public. It is not a merit to be a successful businessman, especially when one's business is based on trade and not on production.[3] Strong involvement of organized crime in business, *nomenklatura* transforming their political privileges into economic power, spontaneous privatizations, tax evasion, money laundering and contraband are not helpful in dispelling old suspicions. These phenomena only serve to affirm that a great deal of Latvian business is indisputably 'dirty' by any standards. When interviewees were asked to characterize people who have been able to earn a lot of money with liberalization of the economy, the phrases given in the questionnaire were agreed with either definitely or somewhat – that is, given characteristics were attached to the new rich – to the following extent: 'enterprising' 86/81 per cent, 'use job connections' 83/77 per cent, 'exploit other people' 66/63 per cent, 'dishonesty' 53/46 per cent, 'have foreign connections' 50/38 per cent, 'work hard' 31/31 per cent, 'help make our economy grow' 28/34 per cent.[4]

An overwhelming majority (85 per cent) held the view that individual achievement should determine how much people are paid; only a tenth (11 per cent) considered that incomes should be made more equal.[5] The reserved attitude toward businessmen seemed to stem from the conviction that businessmen's wealth is acquired by virtue of connections and dishonesty rather than of hard work, that is, individual achievement. Thus, the spirit of capitalism was accepted but the realization of this spirit was distrusted. More than two-thirds (69 per cent) of Latvians and over a half (53 per cent) of Russians considered capitalism very or somewhat important, while only 7/14 per cent adhered to socialism.

Latvian soil is receptive to marketization in principle, if recurrent perceptions of malpractices or undesirable side effects of reforms do not reverse the positive basic mood. For instance, the majority of people are in favour of privatization in principle, but simultaneously they are well aware of its pitfalls. According to Rose and Maley's survey, 75 per cent of Latvians and 59 per cent of Russians believe that an enterprise is best run by private owners; 10 per cent and 15 per cent, respectively, hold the view that state ownership is the best way to run an enterprise; 57/41 per cent think privatization will make the economy more productive, and 71/67 per cent say it will put more goods in the shops. These positive effects are unfortunately overshadowed by worries about the consequences of privatization for unemployment (76/70 per cent) and concentration of wealth in few hands (80/73 per cent).[6] Entrepreneurs have definitely adopted the capitalist spirit.

POLITICAL FEEDBACK

Disappointment with economic development remained latent for a while but as the pressure mounted predictable outcries were voiced. The first major manifestation of distributional conflicts of political significance was the teachers' strike in December 1994. The strike brought to the fore the explosive potential smouldering in the impoverished public sector. Public poverty, caused by insufficient tax revenues, has pushed the salaries of public sector employees so low that teachers, doctors and civil servants can hardly survive without extra hours or jobs. Young, talented teachers are leaving schools for better paid jobs in the private sector. At the beginning of the strike, a teacher's salary was LVL 51 (US$ 102) per month. Teachers demanded a rise in salary of 16 per cent. The strike lasted for over a week and culminated in one of the largest demonstrations since independence. Approximately 14,000 teachers and their supporters marched through Riga to the government building, where the demonstrators sang folk songs. The Prime Minister said 'the government supports teachers' demands and considers them fair, but the state budget lacks money for the immediate implementation of the demand'. The end of the conflict marked a significant victory for the trade unions in all of the Baltic states. Neither governments nor workers themselves had taken the unions seriously because of their dubious role during the Soviet period.[7]

A minor modification in the government's reform strategy was introduced in response to political pressure in connection with the government reshuffle in 1994. Birkavs was known as more market-oriented and rightist than Gailis, who was classified as slightly more socially oriented and less liberal. The Gailis government increased the share of social expenditure in the state budget and tried to appeal to citizens' emotions by putting more weight on political rhetoric. Optical changes included the stepping aside of the key persons of the Birkavs government, Minister of Economy Uldis Osis and Minister of Finance Ojars Kehris, who had earned a bad reputation during their period in office. Osis and Kehris were the fathers of Latvia's market economy as well as the *éminence grise* of the Latvia 2000 and Latvia 2010 programmes. Liberalism, which had meanwhile become a swearword, was identified with these persons – with good reason, in fact. Because of their immense unpopularity, Osis and Kehris were not put up as candidates for the 6th Saeima elections. Latvia's Way attempted to soften its image in the eyes of the voters.[8]

The real test of political feedback came in the 6th Saeima election in the autumn of 1995, when the social and economic consequences of the transition were already being tangibly felt. The acute economic crisis and the budget deficit diverted the attention to economic and social problems in the pre-electoral campaign. The second round of free elections had returned the old communists to power in Lithuania, Poland and Hungary; in Estonia the conservative government had been replaced with a centrist one. Observers waited with excitement to see what the Latvian postelectoral government would look like and whether the new power constellation would endanger the continuation of vigorous reforms. The worst fears appeared to have come true: leftist, populistic and nationalistic forces with an extremist flavour defeated West-oriented reformers. As expected, Latvia's Way, which had energetically pursued liberal reform policies in the government, suffered a crushing defeat, although it maintained its position as the second largest party in Parliament. Latvia was at first doomed to political chaos and economic disaster, although the gloomy predictions soon proved premature. The main reason for such a misapprehension was insufficient familiarity with Latvian parties.

Saimnieks emerged as the backbone of the left-leaning camp. The crucial point is that Saimnieks is not a pro-communist anti-system party but a centre-left party which prefers to cooperate with centre-right parties to strongly leftist parties. It does not pursue radical policies that would ruin Latvia's marketization course. It is a matter of taste whether one approves or disapproves of Saimnieks's methods on specific questions, just as it is a matter of political preference what stand one takes on a political controversy in any country. Unity was a populistic trouble-maker but its protest did not stem from ideological extremism. It was a left-of-centre party like Saimnieks. Its role in politics was reduced to zero by the middle of the legislative period. The Siegerist Party shared Unity's fate. At first sight, the Siegerist Party appeared to match perfectly the textbook stereotype of anti-reform, anti-democratic populism. It played on social discontent, promising higher pensions, free medical care and all possible improvements in social security. Yet the crucial difference was that its programme was not directed against fast-moving reforms; on the contrary, it spoke in favour of shock therapy, open economy and accelerated transformation. It announced the rehabilitation of the national economy to be a necessary precondition for the solution of social problems. It also rejected aggressive nationalism. Fatherland and Freedom could agree with the guidelines of reform policies with the liberal parties, although it had reservations concerning some points.

Latvia was lucky in that the predictable dissatisfaction was channelled through relatively moderate, market-friendly alternatives. The emergence of a counterpole to Latvia's Way and its allies was a natural, inevitable phenomenon which corresponds to the normal dynamics of democratic politics. The impressive results of Skele's rainbow government affirm that the electoral result did not bring the reform process into a stalemate. The beginning looked troubled but Skele's strong-arm tactics pressured quarrelsome coalition members into toeing the government line. The government crisis in January 1997 was not a reaction to social pressures originating from a popular protest. Nor did it bring about any changes to the government policies. To conclude, Latvia came away from its first ordeal with a fright.

The second local elections were proclaimed a poll of the government support, in anticipation of the result of the next Saeima elections. As the rebels of the previous Saeima elections had either disbanded or become tamed into joining the establishment, new political challengers were needed to channel the protest votes. Bojars's Social Democratic Party took over the role of crusader against the entrenched leadership this time. The difference was, as compared to the previous elections, that Bojars advanced with a radical leftist programme which contained elements inconsistent with thoroughgoing marketization and economic liberalism. The practised policies were questioned with quite a new level of sharpness. The leftist economic platform was combined with national traditionalism and moral conservatism. Is Bojars the long-anticipated spectre who embodies the East European symptom?

It is too early to say, because demands put before elections are typically harder than those put after shouldering the government responsibility, but even if he were a real threat to reform the electoral result would never allow him to reign alone. Although the Bojars Party emerged as the single biggest party in the local elections, the share of the ruling coalition far exceeded Bojars's support. The press concentrated on Bojars's advance but the distribution of votes in the local elections can be looked at from another viewpoint, as well. The ruling parties continued to have a steady backing, which confirms the poll results suggesting that Skele's reform course is viewed with confidence by part of the population. Young professional middle-class people especially are firmly committed to the maintenance of the marketization strategy despite economic distress because they are ideologically convinced of the felicity of liberalism. The most hard-hit groups are naturally looking for an escape from the nightmare, and they are the target of politicians who want to exploit disillusionment for partisan advantage. The questions are simply: How extensive is the opposition? What kinds of goals does it set forth? Are the pro-reform parties capable of joining forces against the populists?

There are also various external factors that constrain the latitude of any party in power. First, the international financial institutions (the IMF, the European Bank for Reconstruction and Development (EBRD), the World Bank, etc.) have their say in the formulation of national economic policy because they control the credit flows on which Latvia is heavily dependent. Second, integration into the EU requires that Latvia's legal acts and regulations are approximated to EU standards in order to ensure a conformity with European legislation. For instance, protectionist measures and monopoly arrangements contradict EU provisions. As all the political parties have signed the declaration addressed to the EU Council containing Latvia's application for full membership in the EU, they are committed to the rules of the game. Third, the budget constraint is so hard that it does not leave many options available. Finally, the balance of power among the political forces permits only a heterogeneous multiparty coalition, if a majority government is striven for. A homogeneous government, in turn, would confront a strong opposition composed of parties with a strength almost equal to that of the leading government party.

SOLID GROUND BUT MINOR DRAWBACKS

The fundamental question to be answered in this study is connected with the impact of political constraints: has politics hampered the progress of economic reforms in Latvia? The preceding analysis of political constraints, structured in accordance with Majone's classification, provides a relatively optimistic outlook. The reform leaders were able to mobilize initial support for reform with ease; disillusionment with economic development did not take radical forms of expression; the profilereration of parties was compensated by their approaching the political middle. Hence, the basic preconditions seem to be secured – no dramatic upheavals are conceived on the horizon.

An exclusive focus on the very general trend paints too rosy a picture of the effect of political constraints. It would be exaggeration to claim that politics has not constrained the implementation of reform at all. Political constraints intervene in the process on the level of concrete measures or projects. Typically, social concerns or particularistic interests conflict with economic optimality. Interests need not be merely material ones, they also include nationalist motivations which can place restrictions on the range of acceptable methods. The nationalist opposition has obstructed the passage of many bills when it has considered given proposals disadvantageous to the so-called 'national interest', as the prolonged readings of the bill on the free land market exemplify. Obstructionism is not always intentional in the sense that it would directly serve certain rational calculation. Sometimes resistance stems from nothing but ignorance and stupidity. The borderline between deliberate intentionalism and simple-mindedness is obscure in many cases.[9]

According to a stereotypic horror picture, quarrelsome politicians persist in disputing reform measures in Parliament week after week, without bringing matters to a conclusion until it is too late. Admittedly, unnecessarily long discussions postpone decisions in a harmful way from time to time or the focus shifts to secondary quarrels when urgent matters are waiting for a decision. Parliament may also be so fractured on the issue under consideration that it is difficult to find a sufficient majority in the decisive voting. However, such cases are not the general rule. Excessively long speeches are interrupted quickly by the Speaker. Executors of the reform regard Parliament's working as satisfactory.

From the perspective of an entrepreneur, the impediments to private sector development are in the first place bureaucratic rather than political. Two bureaucratic traditions come together in Latvia with unfortunate results: the native Latvian and the communist. One can, of course, argue that political will determines the setting of bureaucratic regulation in the end but simultaneously one should take into account the mitigating background factors that may explain the shortcomings. First, the Soviet heritage will not disappear overnight. Organizational culture and operational models are passed on from the administrative economy because people have no experience of a market environment. Second, the legislature is under tremendous pressure to develop the legislative framework, when the country is making a profound transition with little existing legislation in place. The process of drafting and enacting laws must occur with speed and it does not leave room for consultation with the interested parties. The sheer quantity of the undertaking makes coordination difficult, leading to contradictions and chaos. The same item may have been stated differently in different laws. Frequent changes in regulations combined with insufficient training of finance inspectors and customs officials cause situations in which one gets different answers to the same question from different people in different posts.

Overly detailed bureaucratic regulation causes a great deal of unnecessary extra work for the companies operating in Latvia. The reason for an excessive bureaucratic control is the attempt to combat illegal transactions, smuggling and tax evasion. What irritates businessmen mostly is the arbitrary dispersal of authority among various agencies. Repeated visits are required to several authorities where the same questions must be answered each time. Businessmen demand one-stop shopping in a coordinating office where they could have access to all necessary information. An example from the oil industry illuminates the scale of red tape bureacracy in Latvia. Dozens of different licences, permits and stamps are required before an oil company can build a service station. When the building is finished, 37 permits are again required to set up a business and start sales.[10]

Foreign investors sometimes have a feeling that everything is made as difficult as it can possibly be. Occasionally they cannot avoid the impression that the inertia in bureaucracy is intentional, if the reasons for the complaints appear artificial. To cite an example, a foreign company had simultaneously submitted six identical projects for approval. The authorities granting the licences had complaints about the realization of each project but the reproaches concerned different details in each case. One of the most publicized projects that met with stubborn underground resistance was Neste and Statoil's oil terminal, the building of which was seriously delayed due to alleged sabotage. The Ministry of Economy was in favour of the oil terminal but the local competitors bribed bureaucrats to impede construction work. Local entrepreneurs often act against the public interest and against the official policy in order to protect themselves from increasing competition. Furthermore, foreign investors fear unfair competition if foreign firms, which are known to have money and know-how, are expected to meet the required standards fully, while local competitors are allowed exceptions to the rules.[11]

Foreign investors highlight the excess of red tape bureaucracy, slow privatization, confusing financial laws and problems with getting appropriate visas as their main problems. Corruption, racketeering and organized crime also create a nuisance.[12] The government's resolve to improve the business environment is nevertheless trusted. Investors are convinced that Latvians are determined to facilitate the transition to a market economy and to incorporate the country into Europe. They are not afraid of about-turns in economic policies even in cases of government reshuffles. With regard to the country risk, Latvia is considered to offer sufficient political and economic stability, no major turbulences being in sight. The basic prerequisities for starting up a business safely are in place and society is moving in the right direction creditably with observable progress in the development of economic, political and legal systems. The state is found to be reasonably responsive to investors' concerns regarding what makes a country attractive to a foreign investor. Considerable improvements in taxation are cited as an example of such responsiveness.[13]

Administrative inefficiency can be seen as one expression of the persistence of Soviet man. The once-and-for-all transfusion of an exogenous belief system has only scratched the thin surface of people's thinking but not yet penetrated their natural way of reacting to incentives. Their understanding of things is rooted in the institutional setting of the administrative economy, which used to dominate their previous life experience. For instance, they may give different meanings to concepts borrowed from the Western terminology with the result that apparently unanimous communication with Westerners can lead to distinct interpretations of the situation. Another consequence of the deficient internalization of a market-confirming logic is the frequent collision of the official ideology with the means of implementation; that is, the speeches of the ruling political elite collide with the measures of the executive level. The contradiction is not brought about by a deliberate sabotage. Even if one swore by the market economy and honestly believed to act according to one's best judgement, it is not certain that the proposed action will match the requirements of the market economy. The mental transition to a market economy takes much more time than the economic and institutional change.

12 Reflection on the Theoretical Discussion

The honeymoon has ended but Latvia has been able to build a positive consensus on the basic direction in which society should be moving. The irreversibility of the transition to a market economy is commonly understood among the political forces in Latvia. Almost all Latvian parties are assuring people that their path will lead to (some version of) capitalism. As a return to communism can be discounted with good reason, the real question centres on the government's ability to maintain the coherence of the reform programme.

According to the pro-authoritarian thesis, democratic leaders, constrained by the local version of the political business cycle, find it difficult to stand firm when they face demands to expand government expenditure. The Latvian experience effectively disproves the central contention of the 'conventional wisdom', asserting that democratic regimes are distinctly disadvantaged in undertaking macroeconomic stabilization. Ironically, the success in macroeconomic stabilization is one of the chief achievements of Latvia's economic policies. Skele's government continued a harsh austerity programme aimed at the elimination of macroeconomic imbalances, particularly the cutting of inflation rates. Inflation has been brought down swiftly from over 1,000 per cent in 1992 to under 10 per cent in 1997 – five short years. The budget is balanced, the currency is freely convertible and stable, privatization is about to be finished and the trend in legislation points to the further liberalization of economic activities. These randomly selected achievements demonstrate that the Latvian governments have not yielded to economic populism. Latvian politicians, irrespective of their party membership, are extremely critical of the country's economic state and insist on concentrated efforts to get Latvia on the right track. Foreign observers often see the situation more positively than Latvians themselves who tend to disregard the remarkable achievements of the economy when struggling in the midst of daily problems. The attitude of Latvians is quite the opposite to the mentality ascribed to South America where self-satisfied politicians are always convinced that things are going just fine, even if the state is near to bankruptcy.

The political opposition is currently weak in comparison with the seats occupied by the government parties in the Saeima, but the fallacy of majority parliamentarianism resting on a heterogeneous coalition is the cabinet's internal incoherency. The composition of the rainbow government exposes it to pressures from domestic producers interested in state subsidies, higher import tariffs, closed tenders, restrictions on competition as well as other protectionist measures to a greater extent than the previous Latvia's Way governments. The positive side of the arrangement is that the distributional conflict is firmly institutionalized, which reduces the space for populism. All the significant political forces share the governmental responsibility.

Each slight modification in the economic strategy should not be judged automatically as opportunism because such corrections, instead of being harmful deviations, can present improvements to an imperfect design, because the human factor is inherent in every programme. Diversity of impulses can also broaden the perspective of policy-making, check malpractices and introduce sound criticality, say, in the use of funds. To cite an example, Saimnieks stressed the need for economizing the use of public funds when it was in opposition and criticized Latvia's Way for spending money on unprofitable investments, such as the decoration of buildings, in the face of a huge budget deficit. When a Saimnieks man took the office of Finance Minister, financing for the second stage of National Opera reconstruction – that is, the enlargement of the opera house – was totally curtailed. The state budget had provided 1.3 million lati (US$ 2.6 million) to be paid in 1996 for the opera house's reconstruction.[14] In this case, the democratic process brought about an economically reasonable correction in the wake of the cabinet reshuffle. The shortcoming of an authoritarian system is that it runs the risk of suppressing both constructive and detrimental opposition with the consequence that it loses valuable inputs.

The technocrats responsible for the implementation of reform measures have respect for the fact that they are operating in a democratic polity. They do not feel excessively constrained by democratic politics, although they admit the existence of political constraints. Talis Linkaits, Head of the Administrative Department in the Privatization Agency, formulates the democratic understanding as follows: 'Privatization is also a political process. We [in the Privatization Agency] have to make such decisions that are acceptable at least to the majority of the parties. Of course, we are sometimes forced to take such decisions we would not like to.'[15] Prime Minister Skele expresses the same idea by using a metaphor that neatly captures the relationship of economic reform to democratic polity:

> The state is not one big rock, the democratic state is built by many small bricks. All these little bricks that don't fit in right now need to be carefully reattached to the wall. This is a very difficult and time-consuming job. If Latvia weren't a democratic state, then we would operate with big blocks and then maybe we would much more quickly have the type of building we want, but Latvia is a democratic state. Therefore, we have to deal with

each individual brick which has its own facets, its own characteristics. And this is very time-consuming.[16]

The weakest link in democratic transitions is believed to be citizens. Citizens have less reason to believe in optimistic forecasts than technocrats or politicians. Citizens look at economic reforms from a very simple perspective: they want to eat. They cannot be persuaded by technocratic blueprints or political rhetoric in the long run. The development of public opinion in Latvia corresponds roughly to Przeworski's theoretical model of the political dynamics of economic reform.

According to Przeworski, radical strategy may enjoy popular support, if voters have a high degree of confidence that they will benefit in the future from the transitional sacrifice. People are willing to suffer in the short term if they believe that their future after reforms will be sufficiently superior to the status quo to compensate for temporary deterioration. Hence, radical reforms, though they engender high social costs, are not necessarily always imposed on the population by technocrats and politicians.[17]

This was the case in Latvia, too, where the initial strategy was adopted with a convincing consensus. A critical observer might claim in this connection that the man in the street could not understand the extent of the coming sacrifice and the consequences of market-oriented reform on society. The salesmen of reform marketed their 'product' to ignorant people who lacked the cognitive capacities to assess the byproducts of transition but who were at the same time very receptive to any anti-Soviet ideas owing to strong currents of national enthusiasm. The initial choice in favour of reform was based on unrealistic beliefs, hopes and fantasies, having hardly anything to do with the factual knowledge needed to make an informed decision. This condition raises serious questions regarding the intrinsic value of democratic voting. The problem is neither new nor specific to Latvia or other transitional societies: political science pondered the dilemma intensively already in the 1930s, when pessimism about the functioning of democracy was widespread even among the democratically-minded political scientists. Recently, the same question has come up in the public debate centring around the viability of the referendum as a method of direct democracy. Because this is not the right place to go deeply into the normative discussion about democratic theory, the prevailing commitment to democracy is taken as given.

Even if the initial strategy were adopted with a wide consensus, it is unlikely that the path of reform will be smooth and it remains uncertain that the valley will be traversed. The support for reform tends to erode as its social costs are experienced. The erosion of support can be explained in terms of declining confidence in the success of reforms. Once consumption falls below the status quo, people will be tempted to return to it. Public expectations count more heavily than the actual economic results. If politicians promise immediate improvements but consumption in fact declines, the competence of the government is put in question. The LNNK made this classic mistake in the first local elections, whereas Skele has been wise enough not to make any great promises. Paradoxically, continuation of reforms is also threatened when the economy shows the first signs of recovery, since people read the current situation symptomatically.[18]

Latvian people have shown amazing tolerance in the face of a declining living standard. People have not flocked to the streets with red flags; pauperization has not given rise to extremist movements. Political centre-orientation among the main part of the population, registered in surveys, is interpreted by many Latvians as a counterpart to a moderate national character, sometimes approaching phlegmatism and indecisiveness. Latvians liken their calm, peaceful mentality to that of the Nordic peoples, as opposed to the fiery, quick-tempered southerners. A Latvian never acts without thinking first: either a Latvian thinks first and acts only then or he thinks first and even after that fails to act.[19] Another anecdote tells about a Latvian who comes to a fork in the road. The Latvian hesitates and ponders for a long time which way to go. Finally he decides to go in both directions. National character is, of course, also a metaphysical concept to be used as an explanatory variable in a scientific analysis but, though not measurable, it undoubtedly gives intuitive hints about a country's political culture. The national character may help outsiders to understand why the economic hardships have not caused a political explosion in Latvia. The Latvian nation is a very patient nation that has become used to suffering.

Another aspect is that the daily struggle for survival absorbs so much energy that nothing is left for public participation. The masses are passive, alienated, unmobilized and indifferent to ideologies. The destruction of a civil society and the ban on free political association during the communist regime eradicated the tradition of organizational activity and inhibited the formation of a social identity from which political interests might develop. Consequently, people are incapable of perceiving their interests clearly and their ability to organize themselves is very low. This state of affairs will not last forever. Latvia has already evidenced a reorganization of the temporarily disarrayed elite groups; mobilization of the masses will follow in the next stage, although it will not happen in a short time. To the rescue of reform, the rising level of political activism is paralleled by increasing pragmatism and conciliatory spirit among the politicians. Political views have approached each other on many questions, and the development of attitudes has moved in a liberal direction.

Until the present day, it has been easy to legitimize giving priority to the rebuilding of the economy over and above the expansion of the social sector, in spite of widespread poverty. If the economic development continues encouragingly, the confrontation with the distributional problem can no longer be avoided. There are already signs hinting at the strong appearance of the social question in the pre-electoral campaign of 1998. It is not only Bojars or Siegerist-type populistic politicians that now raise the issue, but also Latvia's Way will slightly reverse its course before the 7th Saeima elections in order to put more emphasis on the social aspects of the market economy. However, the attitudes of the new middle class are not receptive to welfarism. The better-off have often adopted the hard Social Darwinistic ethic of 'survival of the fittest', and according to which egoism is a virtue. They understand capitalism as *laissez-faire* capitalism where materialistic and individualistic values prevail. They concentrate on private consumption, reject collective action and imitate the Western life style. The poor are rendered guilty of their misfortune by explaining that they are lazy drunkards who do not seize the available opportunities. The outcome of 'egalitarian' communism has been an atomized, unsolidary society where people have not gained a mature sense of responsibility.

In line with logical expectations, the liberal reform party Latvia's Way, identified with shock therapy, has been in decline but nevertheless it has maintained its position as one of the key parties. It is no longer a unifying force among Latvians but it has cemented its own constituency. Liberal values appeal to committed, pro-Western voters who are looking for a right-of-centre alternative. These people shun leftist parties, and Fatherland and Freedom is also considered to pursue too 'leftist' economic policies in their eyes. In addition, many of them reject national conservatism. Even if a new untainted liberal party were to replace Latvia's Way, which has had its share of corruption scandals just like the other parties, there would continue to be a social need for a right-of-centre force. In the distant future it might be possible that a reformed Fatherland would develop into a catch-all party capable of incorporating Latvia's Way or its follow-up party, but that is already a shaky speculation without factual grounds. Currently Fatherland and Freedom is experiencing a strong upward surge in support, because it is trusted by people. The opposite holds for Saimnieks, which disappointed its voters by earning the notorious reputation of the most corrupt party in Latvia. Some journalists have doomed Saimnieks to perish but one should not forget its strategically favourable location in the party system. The rapidly strengthening Social Democratic Party will be the locus of attention in the near future and thus the other parties will have to decide how to get along with it. Bojars will take the place of Siegerist but his influence on politics may be more long-lasting than Siegerist's since he is advancing with a coherent programme and a disciplined team. What is common to the two climbers, the rightist Fatherland and Freedom and the leftist Social Democrats, is nationally flavoured traditionalism (not chauvinism) and moral conservatism, as opposed to the losers', Latvia's Way and Saimnieks, cosmopolitan modernism.

In addition to the four above-mentioned major parties, the Farmers' Union and the Socialist Party are likely to maintain a steady support, although they will never grow large. A miscellaneous group of fringe parties will also form part of the picture. Newcomers can still bring surprises in the future. Rumour has it that three popular persons – President Guntis Ulmanis, composer Raimonds Pauls and poet Ambassador Janis Petersons – might found a presumably centrist party when the President's term expires. It is also speculated that Skele will found or join a party, although he has repeatedly asserted that he will remain independent. Many people now regard him as a one-man party.

The political participation and thus the open influence of Russian-speakers have been modest at best so far. Their parties have primarily concentrated on human and political rights, while businessmen have relied on Cabinet politics. Russian-speakers have no distinct ethnic interests in the economy that could not be derived from their structural location. Equally positioned Latvians and Russian-speakers have similar socioeconomic interests. A poor Russian pensioner shares the same hard lot as a poor Latvian pensioner; a Russian entrepreneur is no more sympathetic to communism than a Latvian one. The only major difference is that Russian-speaking business is more oriented toward Eastern CIS markets than Latvian-speaking business or official Latvia, and this affects their preferences for FDI and foreign trade policies. However, the general detachment of interests from ethnicity is an important condition in anticipating the evolution of the party system when the proportion of Russian-speaking voters increases. The heterogeneity of the Russian-speaking minority weakens the likelihood that party competition would focus on ethnic or nationalistic issues exclusively. The pluralist basis of the political contest (in terms of the content of political disputes) has already been created in Latvia. The determining of economic policies has so far been independent of the existence of the ethnic minority. The silent majority of this minority is excluded from politics so that there has been no need to take its opinion into consideration. Ad hoc lobbyism does not target the foundations of the economic regime.

Latvia has succeeded in stabilizing the situation, even though the prevailing circumstances could have turned events into a fiasco as well. The achievement indicates that structural accounts or abstract theorizing alone do not warrant conclusions about economic and political success. Respectively, policy outcomes cannot be extrapolated directly from popular demands without taking into account the independent role of government actors, organizational relations and external pressures. When the popular support for reforms starts to crumble, the political will of the leaders comes under stress. Willingness is shaped not only by pragmatic calculation but also by ideological motives. The strongest form of political resolve is ideological dedication. History proves how mighty the power of ideological dogmatism can be and how it can lead to disastrous consequences in the worst case. The Russian October Revolution, followed by the forced collectivization of the national economy, is a sad example of the power potential of ideologies. On the other hand, a reasonable sense of mission in a democratic context can stimulate a positive drive that elicits a determination to resist populistic temptation or self-serving pressure group activity. The driving force behind economic liberalization both in the West and the East has been ideological as much as economic. The creation of capitalism in Eastern Europe can be seen as an ideological project similar to the creation of communism.

Determinism was rejected in this study when the alleged dependence of the transition strategy on a regime type was examined. Both democracy and authoritarianism are compatible with various economic strategies. The decision to employ a specific strategy is a political choice within the range of options open to decision-makers. The contemporary historical and geographical setting has excluded the authoritarian option from Latvia's political leaders. The authority of the democratic process has become an inviolable artefact all over the world after the third wave of democratization. Although the attachment to democracy ultimately rests on a subjective valuation, the consequences of this valuation are converted to an objective reality with concrete results.

Notes

Part I: The Research Question and its Foundations

1. Haggard & Kaufman 1992, 4; Hall 1986, 4; Nelson 1990, 6.
2. Haggard & Kaufman 1992, 3, 319–20; Hall 1986, 4.
3. Hall 1986, 4–5.
4. Comisso 1991b, 162; Schmitter 1994, 67.
5. Prosi 28.4.1995.
6. ECE 1992, 43; Nelson 1993, 448–9.
7. Rodrik 1993, 356.
8. Comisso 1991a, 22–3; Herrmann-Pillath 1991, 177; Pickel 1993, 145; Rodrik 1993, 360.
9. Comisso 1991b, 180; O'Donnell 1995, 24–6; Rose & Haerpfer 1994, 3.
10. O'Donnell 1995, 25.
11. Przeworski 1991, 136.
12. Bruszt 1992, 71; Stark 1992, 49.
13. Huntington 1992, 210; Pickel 1993, 156.

Part II: Theoretical Underpinnings

1. Ekiert 1991, 310–11; Frederiksen et al. 1993, 32; Nørgaard 1992, 41; Rose 1994, 13.
2. Rose 1994, 22–3.
3. Bruszt 1992, 55; Dewatripont & Roland 1992, 291; Przeworski 1991, 138; Rose 1994, 24.
4. Comisso 1991b, 184; Przeworski 1991, 138; Rose 1994, 24.
5. Bruszt 1992, 56; Comisso 1991b, 180–4.
6. Fukuyama 1992, 108; Schmitter 1994, 66–7.
7. Bealey 1993, 221–2; Fukuyama 1992, 108; Schmitter 1994, 66.
8. Dryzek & Torgerson 1993, 128, 130; Pierson 1992, 83.
9. Bellamy 1994, 419.
10. Bellamy 1994, 419–20.
11. Bellamy 1994, 421–3.
12. Bellamy 1994, 423–5.
13. Hayek 1982, 86.
14. Pierson 1992, 84–5.
15. Buchanan 1992, 93; Pierson 1992, 83–4; Williamson 1994, 14.
16. Beetham 1993, 201–2.
17. Beetham 1993, 193.
18. Beetham 1993, 195.
19. Beetham 1993, 197–8.
20. Beetham 1993, 199–200.
21. Dryzek & Torgerson 1993, 127, 130–1; Kornai 1990, 139; Sachs 1992a, 41.
22. See Williamson 1994.
23. Comisso 1991b, 162–3.

24. Beetham 1993, 187; Lipset 1993, 43–6, 50.
25. Bellamy 1993, 118; Lipset 1993, 43, 49.
26. *Journal of Democracy* 5(4): 3.
27. Geddes 1994, 104; Haggard & Kaufman 1994, 5.
28. Armijo et al. 1994, 165–7; Geddes 1994, 106.
29. Maravall 1994, 17–18.
30. Armijo et al. 1994, 162–3; Nelson 1994, 55.
31. Armijo et al. 1994, 164–5.
32. Pickel 1993, 141.
33. Kornai 1992b, 3.
34. Lipton & Sachs 1990a, 100, 132. Lipton and Sachs's argument is analogous to Hayek's criticisms of contemporary democratic practice. Hayek criticizes a pluralist conception of democracy on the grounds that it leads to 'a deadlock between these organized interests, producing a wholly rigid economic structure which no agreement between the established interests ... could break' (Hayek 1979, 93).
35. Kaltefleiter 1988, 71.
36. Kaltefleiter 1991; Pickel 1993, 141; Lipton & Sachs 1990a, 88.
37. Kornai 1992b, 4.
38. Lipton & Sachs 1990a, 87–8.
39. Pickel 1993, 142–3; Przeworski 1991, 138.
40. Pickel 1993, 143–4.
41. Nelson 1993, 459–60; Przeworski 1991, 86, 183.
42. Przeworski 1991, 86, 179.
43. Pickel 1993, 142; Przeworski 1991, 180.
44. Pickel 1993, 143.
45. Poznanski 1993a, 53.
46. Haggard & Kaufman 1994, 8.
47. Pickel 1993, 144, 147.
48. Pickel 1993, 144.
49. Pickel 1993, 144.
50. Haggard & Kaufman 1994, 8; Pickel 1993, 145–6; cf. Comisso 1991a, 18–22.
51. Pickel 1993, 146–8.
52. Pickel 1993, 153.
53. Pickel 1993, 153.
54. Huntington 1992, 258–9.
55. Maravall 1994, 18.
56. Maravall 1994, 19.
57. Bresser Pereira et al. 1993, 4, 10, 166; Pickel 1993, 153–4.
58. Geddes 1994, 111–12.
59. Nelson 1993, 459.
60. Bresser Pereira et al. 1993, 9, 133.
61. Bresser Pereira et al. 1993, 9–10, 133–4; Maravall 1994, 24.
62. Bresser Pereira et al. 1993, 10.
63. Di Palma 1991, 80.
64. Poznanski 1993a, 52.
65. Geddes 1994, 105–7; Maravall 1994, 20.
66. Maravall 1994, 20.
67. Maravall 1994, 20–1; Åslund 1994, 63.

276   *Latvia's Transition to a Market Economy*

68. Geddes 1994, 107; Maravall 1994, 21; Åslund 1994, 63–4.
69. Geddes 1994, 107–8; Maravall 1994, 19.
70. Geddes 1994, 109.
71. Armijo et al. 1994, 174; Geddes 1994, 113.
72. Haggard & Kaufman 1994, 13; Maravall 1994, 19; Pickel 1993, 160.
73. Maravall 1994, 19, 22.
74. Maravall 1994, 19.
75. Haggard & Kaufman 1994, 13.
76. Armijo et al. 1994, 167–8; Bresser Pereira et al. 1993, 5; Maravall 1994, 23; Pickel 1993, 157.
77. Pickel 1993, 160.
78. *Journal of Democracy* 5(4): 4; Nelson 1994, 49.
79. Balcerowicz 1994, 82; *Journal of Democracy* 5(4): 4.
80. *Journal of Democracy* 5(4): 4; Nelson 1993, 438.
81. Haggard & Kaufman 1994, 12; Nelson 1993, 438; Nelson 1994, 51.
82. Nelson 1993, 436, 438; Nelson 1994, 51.
83. Haggard & Kaufman 1994, 15; Nelson 1993, 437; Nelson 1994, 51, 52, 55.
84. Balcerowicz 1994, 84–6.
85. Haggard & Kaufman 1994, 12, 15; *Journal of Democracy* 5(4): 4; Nelson 1993, 440; Nelson 1994, 55.
86. Haggard & Kaufman 1994, 15; Nelson 1994, 54.
87. Nelson 1993, 439; Nelson 1994, 54–5.
88. Ofer 1992, 83; Poznanski 1992a, 1; Slay 1994, 31.
89. Haggard & Kaufman 1992, 6.
90. Sachs 1992c, 7; Åslund 1992, 33; Åslund 1994, 69.
91. Armijo et al. 1994, 169–70; Poznanski 1992b, 56; Poznanski 1992c, 654; Slay 1994, 31–2; Åslund 1992, 33; Åslund 1994, 69.
92. Armijo et al. 1994, 168–9; Åslund 1992, 32; Åslund 1994, 69.
93. Balcerowicz 1994, 86–7; ECE 1992, 45; Slay 1994, 32.
94. Armijo et al. 1994, 34; ECE 1992, 45; Ofer 1992, 84; Åslund 1992, 34; Åslund 1994, 69–70.
95. Murrell 1992b, 80; Åslund 1992, 35.
96. Slay 1994, 32–3.
97. Armijo et al. 1994, 170; ECE 1992, 45; Poznanski 1993a, 44; Stark 1992, 18; Åslund 1994, 65.
98. Slay 1994, 31, 33.
99. Burke, Edmund (1790), *Reflections on the Revolution in France*; Nelson, Richard & Winter, Sidney (1982), *An Evolutionary Theory of Economic Change*, Cambridge, Mass.: Harvard University Press; Oakeshott, Michael (1962), *Rationalism in Politics and Other Essays*, New York: Basic Books; Popper, Karl (1971), *The Open Society and Its Enemies*, Princeton: Princeton University Press; Schumpeter, Joseph A. (1942), *Capitalism, Socialism and Democracy*, London: Allen and Unwin.
100. WIDER 1992, 6.
101. ECE 1992, 232; Murrell 1992b, 92; Lipton & Sachs 1990b, 297.
102. Berliner 1992, 217; Murrell 1992a, 11; Murrell 1992b, 91.
103. Dallago 1991, 139; Poznanski 1993b, 420; Sachs 1992b, 44.
104. OECD 1992, 79.
105. Dallago 1991, 143, 145; Poznanski 1992b, 57.

106. Bornstein 1992, 292–4; Dhanji & Milanovic 1991, 17; Murrell 1992b, 90; OECD 1992, 18.
107. Dhanji & Milanovic 1991, 26–7; Stark 1992, 25–6.
108. Dhanji & Milanovic 1991, 19; Poznanski 1992c, 649.
109. Murrell 1992a, 14; Murrell 1992b, 87.

Part III: Setting the Research Task

1. Gomulka 1994a, 89; Majone 1975, 259–61.
2. Nørgaard 1992, 45, 46, 49.
3. Hall 1986, 271.
4. Yin 1993, 3; Yin 1994, 13.
5. Comisso 1991a, 16; Poznanski 1992c, 641, 646.
6. Gourevitch 1989, 100; Hall 1986, 13–14; Hall 1989, 13, 389.
7. Gourevitch 1989, 89; Przeworski 1991, 166.
8. Gourevitch 1989, 199.

Part IV: Empirical Case Study

1. Vacic 1992, 2–4.
2. Przeworski 1991, 158; WIDER 1992, 1.
3. Ahrens 1994, 23; ECE 1992, 43; Milenkovitch 1991, 155.
4. *Baltic Observer* 4–10.1.1996.
5. ME 1996, 8.
6. Ahrens 1994, 22–3; Apolte 1992, 157; Camdessus 1992, 3; EBRD 1993, 54–5; Schrader 1994, 262, 264.
7. Lainela & Sutela 1994a, 179; Starrels 1993, 13; World Bank 1993, 4.
8. IMF 1994, 10; Lainela & Sutela 1994a, 180.
9. EBRD 1994, 29; IMF 1994, 93–4.
10. Bungs 1993a, 33; EBRD 1994, 111; IMF 1994, 39; Lainela & Sutela 1993, 21.
11. Lainela 1994b, 182.
12. *Baltic Observer* 3–9.11.1994; IMF 1994, 37; Lainela 1994a, 36; MER 1994, 28.
13. IMF 1994, 96–7; Lainela 1995, 27; Paeglis 1994, 45–6.
14. Lainela & Sutela 1994a, 129; FIAS 1993, 21.
15. Elerts 1997a.
16. LDA 1996b, 27.
17. Elerts 1997a; Karklins 1993, 28; Law on Foreign Investment, Paragraphs 8 and 11.
18. Kushners 19.2.1997.
19. Vitolins 1993, 24–5.
20. LDA 1996a.
21. Ahrens 1994, 22–3; Blanchard et al. 1991, 5; Bresser Pereira et al. 1993, 2; Camdessus 1992, 3; Charap & Dyba 1991, 40; Gomulka 1994b, 4; Milenkovitch 1991, 153; Starrels 1993, 10; WIDER 1992, 6.
22. Lainela & Sutela 1994a, 70; Polkowski 1993, 26.
23. Elerts 1997b; LDA 1996b; ME 1996.
24. PlanEcon 1994, 86, 93.
25. Lainela & Sutela 1994a, 54–5; Paeglis 1994, 45–6.

26. Paeglis 1994, 47.
27. IMF 1994, 93; Latvijas Banka 1994, 3, 6; Polkowski 1993, 29; Starrels 1993, 12.
28. Lainela 1995, 28; LDA 1994, 63; Latvia 1992, 14; Paeglis 1994, 41; Schrader & Laaser 1994, 97.
29. Lainela & Sutela 1994a, 73–6; Polkowski 1993, 33.
30. LDA 1996b.
31. LDA 1997.
32. Ahrens 1994, 23; van Brabant 1992, 128; Charap & Dyba 1991, 42; Schrader 1994, 260; Van Arkadie & Karlsson 1992, 215; Williamson 1994, 26.
33. Bolz & Polkowski 1994a, 13–14; FIAS 1993, 5–6.
34. Bolz & Polkowski 1994a, 13–14.
35. IMF 1994, 91; Wäre 24.1.1997.
36. Vaivars 6.10.1995; various issues of the *Baltic Independent* from 19.5–3.8.1995 and of the *Baltic Observer* from 4.5–26.7.1995.
37. *Baltic Times* 16–22.1.1997; Repse 1996; Salonen 27.9.1995.
38. BfAI 1995, 1; Blanchard et al. 1991, 64–6; Bolz & Polkowski 1994a, 90; Hansson 1992, 12.
39. Shteinbuka 1993a, 96; Shteinbuka 1993b, 36; World Bank 1993, 101–2.
40. Polkowski 1993, 35–9.
41. Bolz & Polkowski 1994b, 152–3; Shteinbuka 1993a, 111; various unpublished materials from the LDA.
42. ME 1996, 9.
43. Bolz & Polkowski 1994a, 29–30; FAZ 1992, 15; Lainela 1994b, 182; Latvia 1992, 2; MER 1993, 5.
44. LDA 1997.
45. LDA 1997.
46. Linkaits 22.9.1995.
47. van Brabant 1992, 9–12.
48. Bornstein 1992, 314; ECE 1992, 214; Dhanji & Milanovic 1991, 14–15.
49. van Brabant 1992, 12; EBRD 1993, 32, 118.
50. van Brabant 1992, 12; Coopers & Lybrand 1994, 16; EBRD 1993, 32, 118.
51. Bungs 1992, 73; Shen 1994, 133.
52. EBRD 1993, 32.
53. *Baltic Observer* 2–8.3.1995; LPA 1996, 6, 27; LPA 1997, 1.
54. LPA 1996, 6–7; LPA 1997, 1.
55. Independence refers here to the declaration of the sovereignty of Latvian over Soviet law in May 1990. The declaration asserted that the independent Republic of Latvia, as recognized internationally in the interwar period, legally still existed, although the break with the USSR was not made complete until the declaration of full independence in August 1991.
56. Frydman et al. 1993, 217; LPA 1995a; MER 1994, 13.
57. Blukins un Elksne 1993, 13; Bolz & Polkowski 1994b, 154; EIU 1993, 26; Frydman et al. 1993, 218–20; Linkaits 22.9.1995; Zvejs 20.9.1994.
58. IMF 1994, 27; *Latvian Business Guide* 1994, 59–61; LPA 1997, 1.
59. LPA 1995a; LPA 1996, 9; MER 1993, 10; MER 1994, 14–15.
60. *Latvian Business Guide* 1994, 60–1; Law on the Privatization of State and Municipal Property, Article 3; LPA 1996, 26.
61. LPA 1996, 19.

62. LPA 1996, 22.
63. *Latvian Business Guide* 1994, 60–1; LPA 1997, 2; MER 1994, 15.
64. LPA 1996, 26–7.
65. *Baltic Observer* 7–13.12.1995; Bornstein 1992, 294; Dhanji & Milanovic 1991, 29.
66. *Baltic Independent* 23.2–1.3.1995; Linkaits 22.9.1995; Zvejs 20.9.1995.
67. IMF 1994, 25.
68. Blukins un Elksne 1993, 14; Draft Law on Certificates; Frydman et al. 1993, 226–7; LPA 1995b, 8; LPA 1997, 2; MER 1992, 10–11; MER 1994, 16–17; Shen 1994, 137; Van Arkadie & Karlsson 1992, 208; Zvejs 20.9.1995.
69. LPA 1996, 18.
70. Linkaits 26.3.1997.
71. Frydman et al. 1993, 223.
72. See Stark 1992 and Pedersen 1993.
73. LPA 1997, 4.
74. ECE 1992, 214–15; Poznanski 1992c, 641.
75. Linkaits 22.9.1995; Rozenfelds 1992, 356.
76. Lainela 1994b, 178; Linkaits 22.9.1995; World Bank 1993, 36.
77. Bungs 1992, 78.
78. Linkaits 22.9.1995; Apinis 1993, 112.
79. Apinis 1993, 117; Bungs 1992, 78; Draft Law on Certificates; Rozenfelds 1992, 119,
80. *Baltic Independent* 30.6–6.7.1995.
81. *Baltic Times* 29.5–4.6.1997 and 5–11.6.1997.
82. Linkaits 26.3.1997.
83. Linkaits 26.3.1997.
84. Linkaits 26.3.1997; LPA 1996, 14.
85. Linkaits 26.3.1997; LPA 1996, 14.
86. *Current Latvia* 19–27.12.1994.
87. *Current Latvia* 19–27.12.1994.
88. *Baltic Observer* 8–14.6.1995 and 8–14.2.1996; Linkaits 22.9.1995.
89. Apinis 18.9.1995; Boman 26.9.1995; Tsilevich 7.5.1997; Vaivars 6.10.1995.
90. *Baltic Observer* 2–8.2.1995, 8–14.6.1995 and 22–28.6.1995; Vaivars 6.10.1995.
91. *Baltic Observer* 8–14.6.1995; Boman 26.9.1995; Linkaits 22.9.1995; Vaivars 6.10.1995.
92. *Baltic Observer* 22–28.9.1994, 24–30.11.1994, 27.7–9.8.1995, 28.9–4.10.1995.
93. *Baltic Observer* 24–30.8.1995, 7–13.9.1995, 21–27.9.1995 and 28.9–4.10.1995; Silins 19.9.1995.
94. Vaivars 6.10.1995.
95. Linkaits 22.9.1995; cf. Apinis 1993, 115.
96. Apinis 18.9.1995; Linkaits 26.3.1997; Pavlovskis 20.9.1995; Zdanok 25.9.1995.
97. Linkaits 26.3.1997.
98. Linkaits 26.3.1997.
99. *Baltic Observer* 23.2–1.3.1995; Bolz & Polkowski 1994a, 21–2.
100. Linkaits 26.3.1997.
101. Linkaits 26.3.1997; Zalans 14.4.1997.
102. Linkaits 26.3.1997.
103. See Chapter 8, pp. 201–6.
104. Linkaits 26.3.1997.

105. Linkaits 26.3.1997.
106. Apinis 1993, 112; Linkaits 22.9.1995 and 26.3.1997.
107. Zalans 14.4.1997.
108. Grinbergs 4.4.1997.
109. Bornstein 1992, 285; Van Arkadie & Karlsson 1992, 206.
110. MER 1992, 5; Frydman et al. 1993, 227; Schrader & Laaser 1994, 47–8; World Bank 1993, 35.
111. Rozenfelds 1992, 357; Vaarmann 12.10.1993; Zalans 14.4.1997.
112. Blukins un Elksne 1993, 13; Law on the Privatization of State and Municipal Property, Article 17; Linkaits 22.9.1995.
113. Kirsis 27.1.1997.
114. Zalans 14.4.1997.
115. MER 1992, 5–6; Denton Hall 1992, 2, 4; Lainela 1994b, 177.
116. Hansson 1992, 11; Linkaits 22.9.1995.
117. Rozenvalds 21.9.1995.
118. Brence 19.9.1995; Bungs 1993c, 32; Indans 1995, 17.
119. TB 1995a; TB 1995c.
120. Brence 19.9.1995; TB 1995a.
121. *Baltic Independent* 24–30.11.1995; Brence 19.9.1995; TB 1995a; Vaivars 16.10.1995.
122. Brence 19.9.1995.
123. Brence 19.9.1995.
124. Brence 19.9.1995; TB 1995a; TB 1995c.
125. Zdanok 25.9.1995.
126. Brence 19.9.1995; Rasnačs 26.9.1996; TB 1995c.
127. Brence 19.9.1995.
128. Grinblats 1995, 6; Indans 1995, 17. Linkaits 22.9.1995; Putnaergle 6.9.1995; Rasnačs 26.9.1995; Zalans 22.9.1995.
129. Indans 1995, 17; Linkaits 22.9.1995; Rasnačs 26.9.1995; TB 1995c.
130. Grinblats 1995; Rasnačs 26.9.1995; TB 1995c.
131. Grinblats 1995; Rasnačs 26.9.1995; TB 1995c.
132. Rasnačs 26.9.1995; TB 1995b.
133. Rasnačs 26.9.1995; TB 1995c.
134. Grinblats 1995; Rasnačs 26.9.1995; TB 1995c.
135. Bungs 1993c, 31; Indans 1995, 21; Lambergs 25.9.1995.
136. Runcis 27.9.1995; Vaivars 16.10.1995.
137. Lambergs 25.9.1995.
138. Brence 19.9.1995; Lambergs 25.9.1995; Zalans 22.9.1995.
139. Lambergs 25.9.1995.
140. Vaivars 16.10.1995; Zalans 22.9.1995.
141. Lambergs 25.9.1995; Seile 1995.
142. Lambergs 25.9.1995; Seile 1995.
143. Lambergs 25.9.1995; Seile 1995.
144. Lambergs 25.9.1995.
145. Lambergs 25.9.1995; Seile 1995.
146. Indans 1995, 21; Lambergs 25.9.1995.
147. Indans 1995, 21; Seile 1995.
148. Klavins 22.9.1995; Rozentals 1995.
149. Klavins 22.9.1995.

150. The adherence of the KDS to religious principles in its party programme resembles the Finnish Christian League rather than the German CDU, which is a secular catch-all party fulfilling the function of a moderate conservative party.
151. KDS 1994; Klavins 22.9.1995.
152. KDS 1994; Klavins 22.9.1995.
153. KDS 1994; Klavins 22.9.1995.
154. Klavins 22.9.1995.
155. Klavins 22.9.1995.
156. Klavins 22.9.1995.
157. KDS 1994; Klavins 22.9.1995.
158. KDS 1994; Klavins 22.9.1995.
159. Klavins 22.9.1995.
160. Klavins 22.9.1995.
161. KDS 1994; Klavins 22.9.1995.
162. KDS 1994; Klavins 22.9.1995.
163. *Baltic Observer* 21–27.7.1994; Bungs 1994a, 8; *Helsingin Sanomat* 23.12.1994; Indans 1995, 5.
164. Lukins 18.9.1995.
165. Bungs 1994a, 9; Lukins 18.9.1995.
166. Bungs 1994a, 9; Lukins 18.9.1995.
167. Indans 1995, 5; Lukins 18.9.1995.
168. Lukins 18.9.1995; Rozentals 1995.
169. Lukins 18.9.1995; Rozentals 1995.
170. Lukins 18.9.1995.
171. Indans 1995, 5; Rozentals 1995.
172. Bungs 1991, 19; Bungs 1993b, 17; Bungs 1993c, 33; LC 1995a.
173. *Baltic Observer* 21–27.7.1994; Birkavs 1995; Bungs 1994a, 8–9; LC 1995a.
174. *Baltic Observer* 15–21.8.1994 and 1–7.9.1994; *Current Latvia* 15–22.8. and 22–29.8.1994; Zalans 22.9.1995.
175. LC 1995a; LC 1995b, 3–5; LC 1995c.
176. *Baltic Independent* 8–14.12.1995; Birkavs 1995; Strubergs 25.9.1995.
177. Strubergs 25.9.1995.
178. Birkavs 1995; LC 1995b, 7, 11; Pavlovskis 20.9.1995.
179. Birkavs 1995; LC 1995b, 10; Pavlovskis 20.9.1995.
180. LC 1995b, 10–11; Pavlovskis 20.9.1995.
181. LC 1995a; LC 1995b, 9.
182. Birkavs 1995; LC 1995b, 8–9.
183. LC 1995b, 12; Pavlovskis 20.9.1995.
184. Bungs 1994a, 9; LC 1995b, 17–19; Pavlovskis 20.9.1995.
185. LC 1995b, 18–19.
186. Birkavs 1995; LC 1995b, 7, 16; Pavlovskis 20.9.1995.
187. LC 1995a; Zalans 22.9.1995.
188. *Baltic Independent* 13–19.10.1995; Indans 1995, 16; *Helsingin Sanomat* 3.10.1995.
189. Saulitis 25.9.1995.
190. *Baltic Independent* 6–12.10.1995 and 13–19.10.1995; *Baltic Observer* 31.8–6.9.1995; *Financial Times* 3.10.1995; *Helsingin Sanomat* 3.10.1995.

191. *Baltic Independent* 13–19.10.1995 and 27.10–2.11.1995; *Baltic Observer* 12–18.10.1995; *Frankfurter Allgemeine Zeitung* 6.10.1995.
192. *Financial Times* 3.10.1995; *Helsingin Sanomat* 3.10.1995; Zigure 6.10.1995.
193. *Baltic Independent* 13–19.10.1995; *Baltic Observer* 5–11.10.1995 and 30.11–6.12.1995; Zalans 22.9.1995.
194. *Baltic Independent* 13–19.10.1995; *Baltic Observer* 12–18.10.1995; *Helsingin Sanomat* 3.10.1995.
195. *Baltic Independent* 27.10–2.11.1995.
196. *Helsingin Sanomat* 3.10.1995.
197. *Baltic Independent* 13–19.10.1995 and 27.10–2.11.1995; *Baltic Observer* 12–18.10.1995; Saulitis 25.9.1995; Ziedins 27.9.1995.
198. Saulitis 25.9.1995; Ziedins 27.9.1995.
199. Saulitis 25.9.1995; Ziedins 27.9.1995.
200. Saulitis 25.9.1995; Ziedins 27.9.1995.
201. *Baltic Independent* 3–9.11.1995; Saulitis 25.9.1995; Ziedins 27.9.1995.
202. Saulitis 25.9.1995; Ziedins 27.9.1995.
203. Indans 1995, 16; Saulitis 25.9.1995.
204. Indans 1995, 16; Ziedins 27.9.1995.
205. Indans 1995, 17; Ziedins 27.9.1995.
206. Saulitis 25.9.1995; Ziedins 27.9.1995.
207. Indans 1995, 7; Zalans 22.9.1995 and 14.4.1997.
208. *Baltic Independent* 29.9–5.10.1995 and 6–12.10.1995; *Baltic Observer* 28.9–4.10.1995; The Saeima Election Law; Zalans 22.9.1995; Zigure 5.9.1995.
209. *Baltic Independent* 29.9–5.10.1995; Vaivars 16.10.1995.
210. Valdmanis 27.2.1996.
211. Putnaergle 6.9.1995; Vaivars 16.10.1995; Valdmanis 27.2.1996; Zigure 5.9.1995.
212. *Baltic Observer* 28.9–4.10.1995; Indans 1995, 7; Valdmanis 27.2.1996.
213. *Baltic Observer* 5–11.10.1995 and 7–13.12.1995; Bungs 1994b, 2–3; Cevers 1995; Nørgaard 1994, 85.
214. Apinis 18.9.1995; *Baltic Independent* 6–12.10.1995.
215. Apinis 18.9.1995 and 11.2.1997; *Baltic Independent* 6–12.10.1995; Kreituss 21.9.1995.
216. Apinis 18.9.1995 and 11.2.1997.
217. Apinis 18.9.1995; *Baltic Independent* 6–12.10.1995; Cevers 1995; Kreituss 21.9.1995.
218. Apinis 18.9.1995.
219. Kreituss 21.9.1995; Saimnieks 1995.
220. Kreituss 21.9.1995; Saimnieks 1995.
221. Apinis 18.9.1995; Kreituss 21.9.1995; Saimnieks 1995.
222. Apinis 18.9.1995; Saimnieks 1995.
223. Apinis 18.9.1995; Saimnieks 1995.
224. Freivalds 18.9.1995; Kide 1995; Skudra 18.9.1995.
225. Skudra 18.9.1995.
226. Skudra 18.9.1995; Tautsaimnieks 1995, 2.
227. Freivalds 18.9.1995; Skudra 18.9.1995; Tautsaimnieks 1995, 3.
228. Freivalds 18.9.1995; Skudra 18.9.1995; Tautsaimnieks 1995, 3.
229. Kide 1995; Tautsaimnieks 1995, 2–3.
230. Skudra 18.9.1995.

231. Skudra 18.9.1995.
232. Indans 1995, 9; Rozenvalds 21.9.1995; Zalans 22.9.1995.
233. Rozenvalds 21.9.1995.
234. Rozenvalds 21.9.1995.
235. *Baltic Independent* 6–12.10.1995; Rozenvalds 21.9.1995; Saskana 1995.
236. Aboltins 22.9.1995.
237. Aboltins 22.9.1995; Rozenvalds 21.9.1995; Saskana 1995.
238. Rozenvalds 21.9.1995; Saskana 1995.
239. Aboltins 22.9.1995; Rozenvalds 21.9.1995.
240. Rozenvalds 21.9.1995; Saskana 1995.
241. Indans 1995, 13; Tsilevich 7.5.1997.
242. Bungs 1993c, 29–30.
243. *Baltic Observer* 13–19.7.1995, 27.7–9.8.1995 and 17–23.8.1995; Bungs 1993c, 30.
244. Zdanok 25.9.1995.
245. Putnaergle 6.9.1995; Zdanok 25.9.1995.
246. The interviewee comes inadvertently to a very fundamental conclusion of general significance. Zdanok's conclusion derives, of course, from a specific context – her presentation of 'conditional expectations' – but, despite this condition, it is generalizable. In this particular case, the statement is thrilling as the line of argumentation leads to a logical result that contradicts the ideological position of the interviewee. More importantly, it seriously questions the alleged superiority or even the justification of social systems that restrict liberal freedoms. Is it not the system providing the greatest amount of opportunities and equal chances to every man that is superior to all other systems? If so, why does one advocate something else? Obviously not for the common good. The communist system is the most anti-liberal system of all systems. Does Zdanok indirectly admit that it does not give people as much possibility to realize themselves as liberalism?
247. Boman 26.9.1995; Zdanok 25.9.1995.
248. Zdanok 25.9.1995.
249. Zdanok 25.9.1995.
250. *Opponent* 9/1995; Zdanok 25.9.1995.
251. *Opponent* 9/1995; Zdanok 25.9.1995.
252. *Opponent* 9/1995; Stroganov 1995; Zdanok 25.9.1995.
253. Indans 1995, 13; Zdanok 25.9.1995.
254. Zdanok 25.9.1995.
255. Zdanok 25.9.1995.
256. Bojars 3.4.1997.
257. *Baltic Times* 20–26.3.1997.
258. *Baltic Times* 13–19.3.1997 and 20–26.3.1997.
259. Bojars 3.4.1997.
260. *Baltic Times* 13–19.3.1997; Bojars 3.4.1997.
261. *Baltic Times* 8–14.5.1997.
262. *Baltic Times* 13–19.3.1997; LSDP 1997, 3–5.
263. *Baltic Times* 13–19.3.1997; Bojars 3.4.1997; LSDP 1997, 5, 19.
264. Bojars 3.4.1997.
265. Bojars 1997; LSDP 1997, 27.
266. Bojars 3.4.1997.

267. Bojars 3.4.1997.
268. Bojars 3.4.1997.
269. Bojars 3.4.1997; LSDP 1997, 5.
270. Bojars 3.4.1997; LSDP 1997, 28.
271. Bojars 3.4.1997; Bojars 1997.
272. Bojars 3.4.1997; Bojars 1997.
273. Bojars 3.4.1997.
274. Bojars 3.4.1997.
275. Bojars 1997.
276. Bojars 3.4.1997; Bojars 1997.
277. Bojars 1997.
278. Bojars 1997.
279. Evans & Whitefield 1993; Nørgaard 1993; Nørgaard 1994; cf. Kitschelt 1992, Márkus 1993.
280. The interviewees were asked to place their parties on various issue dimensions (on a scale of 1–10) indicating both the ethnic and socioeconomic dimension. The methodological problem with such self-placements is that they are not mutually comparable due to subjective perceptions of the scale. What represents a moderate position to one can be an extreme position to another. Also normative standards can affect the self-placement. To be a socially acceptable political force, each party wants to avoid the imprint of an extremist party. Consequently, parties tend to place themselves toward the middle of the scale, while shunning the extreme poles, irrespective of their objective position. Hence, self-locations can be treated only as suggestive of a general direction. They undoubtedly reveal whether the party is leftist or rightist but the inaccuracy of the classification permits only very rough conclusions.
281. Runcis 27.9.1995.
282. *Baltic Independent* 20–26.10.1995; *Baltic Observer* 19–25.10.1995; *Current Latvia* 9–16.10.1995.
283. Linkaits 22.9.1995.
284. Linkaits 22.9.1995.
285. Linkaits 22.9.1995.
286. Linkaits 22.9.1995.
287. Rozenvalds 21.9.1995.
288. Linkaits 26.3.1997; Zalans 12.1.1997.
289. Zalans 12.1.1997.
290. *Baltic Observer* 5–11.10.1995.
291. *Baltic Observer* 5–11.10.1995; Bungs 1991, 17; Bungs 1993c, 30; Bungs 1994b, 1.
292. Bungs 1993c, 31.
293. Nørgaard 1994, 78; Runcis 27.9.1995.
294. Nørgaard 1994, 78; Runcis 27.9.1995.
295. *Baltic Independent* 6–12.10.1995; *Baltic Observer* 5–11.10.1995.
296. *Baltic Times* 6–12.3.1997 and 13–19.3.1997.
297. *Baltic Independent* 13–19.10.1995; *Baltic Observer* 9–15.11.1995.
298. *Baltic Independent* 13–19.10.1995; *Baltic Observer* 9–15.11.1995.
299. *Baltic Independent* 13–19.10.1995; *Baltic Observer* 9–15.11.1995.
300. *Baltic Observer* 14–21.12.1995, 21–27.12.1995 and 4–10.1.1996.
301. *Baltic Observer* 14–21.12.1995, 21–27.12.1995 and 4–10.1.1996.

302. Zalans 14.4.1997.
303. *Baltic Times* 30.1–5.2.1997 and 13.2–19.2.1997.
304. *Baltic Times* 16–22.1.1997 and 23–29.1.1997.
305. *Baltic Times* 23–29.1.1997 and 30.1–5.2.1997.
306. *Baltic Times* 30.1–5.2.1997, 6–12.2.1997, 13–19.2.1997 and 20–26.2.1997.
307. *Baltic Times* 6–12.2.1997.
308. *Baltic Business Weekly* 8–14.7.1996.
309. Boman 26.9.1995; Zigure 5.9.1995.
310. The issue is so sensitive that some interviewees wish to remain anonymous when discussing these themes. One person I contacted refused to give an interview at all.
311. Grinbergs 4.4.1997; Tsilevich 7.5.1997.
312. Grinbergs 4.4.1997; N.N.; Tsilevich 7.5.1997.
313. Flick 11.2.1997; Grinbergs 4.4.1997; N.N.
314. Flick 11.2.1997; Liela 1997; Tsilevich 7.5.1997.
315. Bojars 3.4.1997; Flick 11.2.1997.
316. Flick 11.2.1997; Tapiola 24.1.1997; Tsilevich 7.5.1997.
317. N.N.; Tsilevich 7.5.1997.
318. Apinis 11.2.1997; Flick 11.2.1997; Linkaits 26.3.1997; Tsilevich 7.5.1997.
319. Flick 11.2.1997; Linkaits 26.3.1997.
320. *Helsingin Sanomat* 21.1.1997.
321. Zigure 6.10.1995.
322. See Dahl 1989, 18–30.
323. Dahl 1989, 18.
324. Dahl 1989, 72; Przeworski 1991, 92.
325. Przeworski 1991, 95.
326. Dahl 1989, 65.
327. Cf. Przeworski 1991, 92.
328. Trapenciere 26.9.1995.
329. Körösenyi 1994.
330. Körösenyi 1994.
331. Zalans 12.1.1997.
332. Evans & Whitefield 1993, 523.
333. Gourevitch 1989, 100; Hall 1989, 13, 361.
334. John Toye questions the scientific status of the Washington consensus: 'Is the Washington consensus a statement of what economists actually believe about economic policy (i.e. the outcome of an opinion survey)? Is it instead a statement of what economists ought to believe, at least if they are "serious" economists (i.e. a synthesis of normative economics)? Or is it a statement of "wisdom" ... which liberal economists must believe (i.e. a core vision, a professional creed or a neoliberal ideology)?' (Toye 1994, 39)
335. Hall 1993, 279.
336. Rokeach 1973, 169.
337. Hall 1993, 280.
338. EIU 1993, 1; Hansson 1992, 2; Lainela & Sutela 1994a, 10.
339. Hall 1989, 390.
340. Huntington 1992, 58; Shin 1994, 168–9.
341. Evans & Whitefield 1993, 543, 547.
342. Supreme Council 1990; LNNK 1990.

343. Avotins 29.1.1997; Boman 26.9.1995; Tapiola 24.1.1997.
344. Avotins 29.1.1997; Loginov 23.4.1997.
345. Avotins 29.1.1997; Loginov 23.4.1997; Tapiola 24.1.1997.
346. Avotins 29.1.1997.
347. Loginov 23.4.1997.
348. Loginov 23.4.1997.
349. Loginov 23.4.1997.
350. Avotins 29.1.1997; Bahn 10.4.1997; Loginov 23.4.1997.
351. *Helsingin Sanomat* 13.7.1997.
352. Zalans 14.4.1997.
353. Rose 1996, 2; Rose 1997, iii–iv.
354. Rose 1997, 63.
355. Grinbergs 22.4.1997.
356. Rižanskij 11.4.1997.
357. Horoših 8.4.1997; Luhtanen 19.3.1997; Šilins 19.9.1995.
358. Zigure 5.9.1995.
359. Bahn 10.4.1997.
360. Horoših 8.4.1997.
361. Bahn 10.4.1997.
362. Bahn 10.4.1997; Korolenko 8.4.1997.
363. Korolenko 8.4.1997.
364. Kadish 4.4.1997.
365. Zigure 5.9.1995.
366. N.N. 1997.
367. Grinbergs 4.4.1997.
368. Bahn 10.4.1997.
369. N.N.; Zalans 14.4.1997.
370. Horoših 8.4.1997.
371. Horoših 8.4.1997; Rižanskij 11.4.1997; Tšernousov 11.4.1997.
372. Bahn 10.4.1997; Rižanskij 11.4.1997.
373. Bahn 10.4.1997; Loginov 23.4.1997.
374. Rose 1996, 5.
375. Loginov 23.4.1997; Rose 1996, 8.
376. Tapiola 24.1.1997.
377. Rose 1996, 3, 6.
378. Rose 1996, 9–10.
379. Rose 1996, 4.
380. *Baltic Times* 29.5–4.6.1997.
381. Rose 1997, 59.
382. Zalans 14.4.1997.
383. Horoših 8.4.1997; N.N.; Tapiola 24.1.1997.
384. N.N.; Tapiola 24.1.1997.
385. Horoših 8.4.1997; Tapiola 24.1.1997.
386. Tapiola 24.1.1997.
387. Tapiola 24.1.1997.
388. Tapiola 24.1.1997.
389. Tapiola 24.1.1997.
390. Bahn 10.4.1997; Horoših 8.4.1997; Kadish 4.4.1997; Korolenko 8.4.1997; Rižanskij 11.4.1997; Tšernousov 11.4.1997.

391. Kadish 4.4.1997; Tapiola 24.1.1997.
392. Rose 1997, 41.
393. Korolenko 8.4.1997.
394. Rose 1997, 30.
395. Bahn 10.4.1997.
396. Kadish 4.4.1997.
397. Tsilevich 7.5.1997.
398. Tsilevich 7.5.1995.
399. Tsilevich 7.5.1995.
400. Tsilevich 7.5.1995.
401. See Opalski, Magdalena, Tsilevich, Boris & Dutkiewicz, Piotr (1994). *Appendix to Ethnic Conflict in the Baltic States: The Case of Latvia.* Kingston, Ontario: Canada Communications Group.
402. Tsilevich 7.5.1995.
403. Tsilevich 7.5.1997.
404. Tsilevich 7.5.1997.
405. Tsilevich 7.5.1997.
406. Tsilevich 7.5.1997.
407. Tsilevich 7.5.1997.
408. For Latvians thinking like this, Russians living in Russia are more acceptable than the immigrants who have left their fatherland. Russia's Russians have a sense of nationality.
409. Bahn 10.4.1997; Horoših 8.4.1997; Kadish 4.4.1997; Korolenko 8.4.1997; Loginov 23.4.1997; Rižanskij 11.4.1997; Tšernousov 11.4.1997.
410. Zalans 14.4.1997.
411. Rose 1996, 6; Rose 1997, 28–9.
412. Bahn 10.4.1997; Horoših 8.4.1997.
413. Bahn 10.4.1997; Kadish 4.4.1997; Korolenko 8.4.1997; Loginov 23.4.1997; Rižanskij 11.4.1997; Tšernousov 11.4.1997.
414. Bahn 10.4.1997; Kadish 4.4.1997; Korolenko 8.4.1997.
415. Kadish 4.4.1997; Korolenko 8.4.1997; Rižanskij 11.4.1997; Tšernousov 11.4.1997.
416. Bahn 10.4.1997; Kadish 4.4.1997.
417. Bahn 10.4.1997; Kadish 4.4.1997; Korolenko 8.4.1997.
418. Bahn 10.4.1997; Korolenko 8.4.1997.
419. Bahn 10.4.1997; Kadish 4.4.1997; Korolenko 8.4.1997.
420. *Baltic Independent* 24–30.6.1994 and 1–7.7.1994; *Baltic Observer* 18–24.1.1996; *Current Latvia* 20–27.6.1994, 27.6–4.7.1994 and 18–25.7.1994.
421. *Baltic Independent* 24–30.6.1994 and 1–7.7.1994; *Baltic Observer* 18–24.1.1996; *Current Latvia* 20–27.6.1994, 27.6–4.7.1994 and 18–25.7.1994.
422. Tapiola 24.1.1997.
423. *Current Latvia* 31.7–7.8.1995; Zalans 14.4.1997.
424. Brence 19.9.1995.
425. Rozenvalds 21.9.1995.
426. Zalans 22.9.1995.
427. *Baltic Observer* 18–24.1.1996; Brence 19.9.1995.
428. Rozenvalds 21.9.1995; Zdanok 25.9.1995.
429. *Baltic Observer* 19–25.1.1995.
430. *Baltic Business Weekly* 8–14.7.1996.

431. Zigure 6.10.1995.
432. *Baltic Independent* 22–28.9.1995; Vaivars 6.10.1995; Zalans 22.9.1995.
433. Tapiola 24.1.1997; Zalans 14.4.1997.
434. Zalans 3.10.1995.
435. Zalans 14.4.1997.
436. Rose 1997, 44.
437. Kadish 4.4.1997.
438. *Baltic Times* 6–12.3.1997.
439. Tapiola 24.1.1997.
440. Rose 1996, 10.
441. Tsilevich 7.5.1997.
442. Rose 1996, 11.

Part V: Politics versus Markets?

1. *Central and Eastern Eurobarometer* 2/1992.
2. *Central and Eastern Eurobarometer* 3/1993.
3. Putnaergle 6.9.1995.
4. The first percentage refers to the Latvian sample, the second to the Russian one. Owing to the unusually stark ethnic and linguistic divisions, the Baltic states were treated as being composed of two 'publics' defined by nationality. Rose is surprised at the extent of similarity among the Baltic and Russian nationalities in their replies to many questions. Differences within ethnic communities are often greater than differences between ethnic communities. (Rose & Maley 1994, iii–iv.)
5. Rose & Maley1994.
6. Rose & Maley 1994.
7. *Baltic Independent* 16–22.12.1994; *Baltic Observer* 8–14.12.1994.
8. Strubergs 20.9.1995; Zalans 22.9.1995.
9. Zigure 5.9.1995.
10. Salonen 27.9.1995.
11. N.N.; Salonen 27.9.1995.
12. *Baltic Observer* 7–13.12.1995.
13. Results of the survey among foreign investors in Latvia conducted by the LDA in October 1996.
14. *Baltic Observer* 11–17.1.1996.
15. Linkaits 22.9.1995.
16. *Baltic Times* 21–27.3.1996.
17. Przeworski 1991, 164–73.
18. Przeworski 1991, 164–73.
19. Vaivars 16.10.1995.

Bibliography

Ahrens, Joachim (1994). 'The Transition to a Market Economy: Are There Useful Lessons from History?' In Schipke, Alfred & Taylor, Alan M. (eds) *The Economic Transformation – Theory and Practice in the New Market Economies*. Heidelberg: Springer-Verlag.

Apinis, Paulis (1993). 'Privatisierung von Betrieben in Lettland.' In Meissner, Boris & Loeber, Dietrich A. & Levits, Egils (Hrsg.) *Die Wirtschaft der baltischen Staaten im Umbruch*. Köln: Verlag Wissenschaft und Politik.

Apolte, Thomas (1992). *Politische Ökonomie der Systemtransformation: Gruppeninteressen und Interessenkonflikte im Transformationsprozeß*, Duisburger Volkswirtschaftliche Schriften Band 15. Hamburg: S + W Steuer- und Wirtschaftsverlag.

Armijo, Leslie & Biersteker, Thomas & Lowenthal, Abraham (1994). 'The Problems of Simultaneous Transitions.' *Journal of Democracy* 5(4): 161–75.

Åslund, Anders (1992). *Post-Communist Economic Revolutions: How Big a Bang?*, Creating Post-Communist Order 14(9). Washington, DC: The Center for Strategic and International Studies.

Åslund, Anders (1994). 'The Case for Radical Reform.' *Journal of Democracy* 5(4): 63–74.

Balcerowicz, Leszek (1994). 'Understanding Postcommunist Transitions.' *Journal of Democracy* 5(4): 75–89.

Bealey, Frank (1993). 'Capitalism and Democracy.' *European Journal of Political Research* 23(2): 203–23.

Beetham, David (1993). 'Four Theorems About the Market and Democracy.' *European Journal of Political Research* 23(2): 187–201.

Bellamy, Richard (1993). 'Introduction: Joseph A. Schumpeter and His Contemporaries.' *European Journal of Political Research* 23(2): 117–20.

Bellamy, Richard (1994). 'Dethroning Politics: Liberalism, Constitutionalism and Democracy in the Thought of F. A. Hayek.' *British Journal of Political Science* 24(4): 419–41.

Berliner, Joseph S. (1992). 'Strategies for Privatization in the USSR.' In Keren, Michael & Ofer, Gur (eds) *Trials of Transition: Economic Reform in the Former Communist Bloc*. Boulder, CO: Westview Press.

BfAI (Bundesstelle für Außenhandelsinformation) (1995). *Lettland: Wirtschaftstrends zum Jahreswechsel 1994/95*. Länderreport.

Blanchard, Olivier, Dornbusch, Rudiger, Krugman, Paul, Layard, Richard & Summers, Lawrence (1991). *Reform in Eastern Europe*. Cambridge, MA: The MIT Press.

Blukins un Elksne (1993). 'Privatization – Step by Step.' *Muuttuva Itä-Eurooppa – Uudistuvat Markkinat* 37: 13–18.

Bolz, Klaus & Polkowski, Andreas (1994a). *Lettland: Die Entwicklung der Wirtschafts- und Sozialpolitik*, HWWA-Report 144. Hamburg: HWWA-Institut für Wirtschaftsforschung.

Bolz, Klaus & Polkowski, Andreas (1994b). 'Trends, Economic Policies and Systemic Changes in the Three Baltic States.' *Intereconomics* 29(3): 147–56.

Bornstein, Morris (1992). 'Privatisation in Eastern Europe.' *Communist Economies and Economic Transformation* 4(3): 283–320.

Bresser Pereira, Luiz Carlos, Maravall, José María & Przeworski, Adam (1993). *Economic Reforms in New Democracies: A Social-Democratic Approach.* Cambridge: Cambridge University Press.

Bruszt, László (1992). 'Transformative Politics: Social Costs and Social Peace in East Central Europe.' *East European Politics and Societies* 6(1): 55–72.

Buchanan, James (1992). 'Public Choice After the Revolutions: 1989–91.' *Journal of Public Finance and Public Choice* 2(3): 93–101.

Buchanan, James & Tullock, Gordon (1962). *The Calculus of Consent: Logical Foundations of Constitutional Democracy.* Ann Arbor: University of Michigan Press.

Bungs, Dzintra (1991). 'Political Realignments in Latvia after the Congress of the People's Front.' *Report on the USSR* (20 December 1991): 17–20.

Bungs, Dzintra (1992). 'Latvia: New Legislation Opens Door to Reform.' *RFE/RL Report* 1(17): 73–9.

Bungs, Dzintra (1993a). 'The Lats Returns to Latvia.' *RFE/RL Report* 2(16): 33–8.

Bungs, Dzintra (1993b). 'The New Latvian Government.' *RFE/RL Report* 2(33): 14–17.

Bungs, Dzintra (1993c). 'The Shifting Political Landscape in Latvia.' *RFE/RL Report* 2(12): 28–34.

Bungs, Dzintra (1994a). 'Latvian Government Resigns.' *RFE/RL Report* 3(28): 8–10.

Bungs, Dzintra (1994b). 'Local Elections in Latvia: The Opposition Wins.' *RFE/RL Report* 3(28): 1–5.

Camdessus, Michel (1992). *Economic Transformation in the Fifteen Republics of the Former U.S.S.R.: A Challenge or an Opportunity for the World?* Washington, DC: IMF.

Central and Eastern Eurobarometer (1992). No. 2. Brussels: European Commission.

Central and Eastern Eurobarometer (1993). No. 3. Brussels: European Commission.

Central and Eastern Eurobarometer (1994). No. 4. Brussels: European Commission.

Charap, Joshua & Dyba, Karel (1991). 'Economic Transformation in Czechoslovakia.' *Osteuropa-Wirtschaft* 36(1): 35–47.

Comisso, Ellen (1991a). 'Political Coalitions, Economic Choices.' *Journal of International Affairs* 45(1): 1–30.

Comisso, Ellen (1991b). 'Property Rights, Liberalism, and the Transition from "Actually Existing" Socialism.' *East European Politics and Societies* 5(1): 162–188.

Coopers & Lybrand (1994). *Latvia: A Business and Investment Guide.* Riga: Coopers & Lybrand Europe.

Dahl, Robert A. (1989). *Democracy and Its Critics.* New Haven: Yale University Press.

Dallago, Bruno (1991). 'Hungary and Poland: The Non-Socialized Sector and Privatization.' *Osteuropa-Wirtschaft* 36(2): 130–53.

Denton Hall (1992). 'Privatisation in Latvia: Review of Legislation.' London. Unpublished report.

Dewatripont, M. & Roland, G. (1992). 'The Virtues of Gradualism and Legitimacy in the Transition to a Market Economy.' *Economic Journal* 102(411): 291–300.

Dhanji, Farid & Milanovic, Branko (1991). 'Privatisation.' In OECD (Organization for Economic Cooperation and Development) *The Transition to a Market Economy*. Paris: OECD.

Di Palma, Giuseppe (1991). 'Legitimation from Top to Civil Society: Politico-Cultural Change in Eastern Europe.' *World Politics* 44(1): 49–80.

Downs, Anthony (1957). *An Economic Theory of Democracy*. New York: HarperCollins Publishers.

Dryzek, John S. & Torgerson, Douglas (1993). 'Democracy and the Policy Sciences: A Progress Report.' *Policy Sciences* 26(2): 127–137.

EBRD (European Bank for Reconstruction and Development) (1993). *EBRD Economic Review: Current Economic Issues and Annual Economic Outlook*.

EBRD (European Bank for Reconstruction and Development) (1994). *Transition Report: Economic Transition in Eastern Europe and the Former Soviet Union*.

ECE (Economic Commission for Europe) (1992). *Economic Survey of Europe in 1991–1992*. New York: ECE secretariat.

EIU (The Economist Intelligence Unit) (1993). *Baltic Republics: Estonia, Latvia, Lithuania*, EIU Country Report 2nd quarter 1993. London: EIU.

Ekiert, Grzegorz (1991). 'Democratization Processes in East Central Europe: A Theoretical Reconsideration.' *British Journal of Political Science* 21(3): 285–313.

Elerts, Maris (1997a). 'Doing Business With Latvia.' Speech given by the Director General of the Latvian Development Agency at an investment seminar and exhibition in Copenhagen, January 1997.

Elerts, Maris (1997b). 'Investment Incentives and Opportunities in Latvia.' Speech given by the Director General of the Latvian Development Agency at an investment seminar and exhibition in Hannover, April 1997.

Evans, Geoffrey & Whitefield, Stephen (1993). 'Identifying the Bases of Party Competition in Eastern Europe.' *British Journal of Political Science* 23(4): 521–48.

FAZ (Frankfurter Allgemeine Zeitung) (1992). *Länderanalyse der Frankfurter Allgemeine Zeitung GmbH Informationsdienste: Baltikum*. Frankfurt: FAZ.

FIAS (Foreign Investment Advisory Service) (1993). 'Diagnostic Study of the Foreign Direct Investment Environment in Latvia.' Unpublished report.

Frederiksen, Bernhard Trier, Johannsen, Lars & Pedersen, Anette (1993). 'De baltiske demokratiens konsolidering.' *Politica* 25(4): 381–98.

Frydman, Roman, Rapaczynski, Andrzej & Earle, John S. (1993). *The Privatization Process in Russia, Ukraine and the Baltic States*, CEU Privatization Reports Volume 2. London: Central European University Press.

Fukuyama, Francis (1992). 'Capitalism & Democracy: The Missing Link.' *Journal of Democracy* 3(3): 100–10.

Geddes, Barbara (1994). 'Challenging the Conventional Wisdom.' *Journal of Democracy* 5(4): 104–18.

Gomulka, Stanislav (1994a). 'Economic and Political Constraints During the Transition.' *Europe-Asia Studies* 46(1): 89–106.

Gomulka, Stanislav (1994b). *Lessons from Economic Transformation and the Road Forward*, Occasional Paper No. 5. Norway: Centre for Economic Performance.

Gourevitch, Peter A. (1989). 'Keynesian Politics: The Political Sources of Economic Policy Choices.' In Hall, Peter A. (ed.) *The Political Power of Economic Ideas: Keynesianism across Nations*. Princeton, NJ: Princeton University Press.

Haggard, Stephan & Kaufman, Robert R. (eds) (1992). *The Politics of Economic Adjustment: International Constraints, Distributive Conflicts, and the State.* Princeton, NJ: Princeton University Press.

Haggard, Stephan & Kaufman, Robert R. (1994). 'The Challenges of Consolidation.' *Journal of Democracy* 5(4): 5–16.

Hall, Peter A. (1986). *Governing the Economy: The Politics of State Intervention in Britain and France.* Cambridge: Polity Press.

Hall, Peter A. (ed.) (1989). *The Political Power of Economic Ideas: Keynesianism across Nations.* Princeton: Princeton University Press.

Hall, Peter A. (1993). 'Policy Paradigms, Social Learning, and the State: The Case of Economic Policymaking in Britain.' *Comparative Politics* 25(3): 275–96.

Hansson, Ardo (1992). *Transforming an Economy while Building a Nation: The Case of Estonia*, Working Paper No. 62. Stockholm: Institute of East European Economies.

Hayek, Friedrich A. (1979). *The Political Order of a Free People.* London: Routledge.

Hayek, Friedrich A. (1982). *Law, Legislation and Liberty.* London: Routledge and Kegan Paul.

Herrmann-Pillath, Carsten (1991). 'Systemtransformation als ökonomisches Problem.' *Aussenpolitik* 42(2): 171–81.

Huntington, Samuel P. (1992). *The Third Wave: Democratization in the Late Twentieth Century.* Norman: University of Oklahoma Press.

IMF (International Monetary Fund) (1994). *Latvia.* Washington, DC: IMF.

Indans, Ivars (1995). *Political Forces of Latvia and Their Platforms Before the Elections of the 6th Saeima.* Riga: Information Department of the Chancellery of the Republic of Latvia.

Kaltefleiter, Werner (1988). 'Bedingungen für die Durchsetzung ordnungspolitischer Grundentscheidungen nach dem Zweiten Weltkrieg.' In Fischer, Wolfram (Hrsg.) *Währungsreform und soziale Marktwirtschaft: Erfahrungen und Probleme nach 40 Jahren*, Schriften des Vereins für Sozialpolitik Band 190. Berlin: Duncker & Humblot.

Kaltefleiter, Werner (1991). 'Wer wählt freiwillig Schmerzen?' *Rheinischer Merkur* 40, 4 October 1991.

Karklins, Janis (1993). 'Latvia and Finland: Practical Aspects of Cooperation and Business Opportunities.' *Muuttuva Itä-Eurooppa – Uudistuvat Markkinat* 37: 28–34.

Kitschelt, Herbert (1992). 'The Formation of Party Systems in East Central Europe.' *Politics & Society* 20(1): 7–50.

Kornai, Janos (1990). 'Comments and Discussion [of the Lipton & Sachs Paper].' *Brookings Papers on Economic Activity* 1: 134–45.

Kornai, Janos (1992a). 'The Affinity Between Ownership Forms and Coordination Mechanisms: The Common Experience of Reform in Socialist Countries.' In Poznanski, Kazimierz Z. (ed.) *Constructing Capitalism: The Reemergence of Civil Society and Liberal Economy in the Post-Communist World.* Boulder, CO: Westview Press.

Kornai, Janos (1992b). 'The Postsocialist Transition and the State: Reflections in Light of Hungarian Fiscal Problems.' *The American Economic Review* 82(2): 1–21.

Körösenyi, Andras (1994). 'Intellectuals and Democracy in Eastern Europe.' *Political Quarterly* 65(4): 415–24.

Lainela, Seija (1994a). 'Baltian maat vuonna 1993.' *Review of Economies in Transition* 4/94: 21–40. Helsinki: Bank of Finland.

Lainela, Seija (1994b). 'Private Sector Development and Liberalisation in the Baltic Countries.' *Communist Economies and Economic Transformation* 6(2): 175–86.

Lainela, Seija (1995). 'Baltian maat vuonna 1994.' *Review of Economies in Transition* 1/95: 25–46. Helsinki: Bank of Finland.

Lainela, Seija & Sutela, Pekka (1993). 'Introducing New Currencies in the Baltic Countries.' *Review of Economies in Transition* 8/93: 5–32. Helsinki: Bank of Finland.

Lainela, Seija & Sutela, Pekka (1994a). *The Baltic Economies in Transition*. Helsinki: Bank of Finland.

Lainela, Seija & Sutela, Pekka (1994b). 'The Comparative Efficiency of Baltic Monetary Reforms'. *Review of Economies in Transition* 10/94: 5–26. Helsinki: Bank of Finland.

Latvia (1992). 'Memorandum of Economic Policies.' Unpublished administrative document.

Latvijas Banka (1994). *Bulletin*. Riga.

LDA (Latvian Development Agency) (1994). *Latvian Business Guide 1994*. Riga: LDA.

LDA (Latvian Development Agency) (1996a). 'Business Attitude in the Latvian Latitude.' Unpublished draft for marketing material.

LDA (Latvian Development Agency) (1996b). *Information on Latvia for Investment Partners*. Riga: LDA.

LDA (Latvian Development Agency) (1997). *Latvian Business Guide 1997*. Riga: LDA.

Liela, Elita (1997). 'Information from Newspapers About Ave Lat and Ave Lux.' Unpublished report, Latvian Development Agency.

Lipset, Seymour Martin (1993). 'Reflections on Capitalism, Socialism and Democracy.' *Journal of Democracy* 4(2): 43–55.

Lipton, David & Sachs, Jeffrey (1990a). 'Creating a Market Economy in Eastern Europe: The Case of Poland.' *Brookings Papers on Economic Activity* 1: 75–133.

Lipton, David & Sachs, Jeffrey (1990b). 'Privatization in Eastern Europe: The Case of Poland.' *Brookings Papers on Economic Activity* 2: 293–341.

LNNK (Latvia's National Independence Movement) (1990). *The Genocide of Latvians*. LNNK.

LPA (Latvian Privatization Agency) (1995a). *Latvian Privatization Agency*. Riga: LPA.

LPA (Latvian Privatization Agency) (1995b). *Privatization Programme, Its Execution and Subsequent Tasks*. Riga: LPA.

LPA (Latvian Privatization Agency) (1996). *Annual Report 1995*. Riga: LPA.

LPA (Latvian Privatization Agency) (1997). *Latvian Shipping Company*. Internet: http://www.lpa.bkc.lv/InfoLatvianShippingCompanyGB.htm.

Majone, Giandomenico (1975). 'On the Notion of Political Feasibility.' *European Journal of Political Research* 3(3): 259–74.

Maravall, José María (1994). 'The Myth of the Authoritarian Advantage.' *Journal of Democracy* 5(4): 17–31.

Márkus, György G. (1993). 'Politische Konfliktlinien und Legitimation in Ostmitteleuropa: Der Fall Ungarn.' *Osteuropa* 42(12): 1167–80.

ME (Ministry of Economy of the Republic of Latvia) (1996). *Economic Development of Latvia*. Riga: Publishing House in Ogre.

MER (Ministry of Economic Reforms of the Republic of Latvia) (1992). 'Country Privatization Report.' Unpublished administrative document.

MER (Ministry of Economic Reforms of the Republic of Latvia) (1993). 'Programme of Macroeconomic Stabilization.' Unpublished administrative document.

MER (Ministry of Economic Reforms of the Republic of Latvia) (1994). 'Independence, Stabilization and Reform.' Unpublished administrative document.

Milenkovitch, Deborah (1991). 'The Politics of Economic Transformation.' *Journal of International Affairs* 45(1): 151–64.

Murrell, Peter (1992a). 'Conservative Political Philosophy and the Strategy of Economic Transition.' *East European Politics and Societies* 6(1): 3–16.

Murrell, Peter (1992b). 'Evolutionary and Radical Approaches to Economic Reform.' *Economics of Planning* 25(1): 79–96.

Nelson, Joan (ed.) (1990). *Economic Crisis and Policy Choice: The Politics of Adjustment in the Third World*. Princeton, NJ: Princeton University Press.

Nelson, Joan (1993). 'The Politics of Economic Transformation: Is Third World Experience Relevant in Eastern Europe?' *World Politics* 45(3): 433–63.

Nelson, Joan (1994). 'Linkages Between Politics and Economics.' *Journal of Democracy* 5(4): 49–62.

Nørgaard, Ole (1992). 'The Political Economy of Transition in the Post-Socialist Systems: The Case of the Baltic States.' *Scandinavian Political Studies* 15(1): 41–60.

Nørgaard, Ole (1993). 'Politik og økonomi i Baltikum: Inledning.' *Politica* 25(4): 374–80.

Nørgaard, Ole (red.) (1994). *De baltiske lande efter uafhængigheden: Hvor så forskellige?* Århus: Forlaget Politica.

O'Donnell, Guillermo (1995). 'Do Economists Know Best?' *Journal of Democracy* 6(1): 23–8.

OECD (Organization for Economic Cooperation and Development) (1992). *Methods of Privatising Large Enterprises*. Paris: Centre for Cooperation with the European Economies in Transition.

Ofer, Gur (1992). 'Stabilizing and Restructuring the Former Soviet Economy: Big Bang or Gradual Sequencing?' In Keren, Michael & Ofer, Gur (eds) *Trials of Transition: Economic Reform in the Former Communist Bloc*. Boulder, CO: Westview Press.

Paeglis, Imants (1994). 'The Financial Sector and Monetary Reform in Latvia.' *RFE/RL Research Report* 3(22): 40–7.

Pedersen, Ove K. (1993). 'Selling the State or Building a Society: Private Property Reforms in West and East.' Paper presented at a ECPR-Conference in Leiden, April 1993.

Pickel, Andreas (1993). 'Authoritarianism or Democracy? Marketization as a Political Problem.' *Policy Sciences* 26(2): 139–63.

Pierson, Christopher (1992). 'Democracy, Markets and Capital: Are There Necessary Economic Limits to Democracy?' *Political Studies* 40 (Special Issue): 83–98.

PlanEcon (1994). *Review and Outlook for the Former Soviet Republics*. PlanEcon.

Polkowski, Andreas (1993). *Lettland: Wirtschaftspotential und Wirtschaftsordnung*, HWWA Report 112. Hamburg: HWWA-Institut für Wirtschaftsforschung.

Poznanski, Kazimierz Z. (1992a). 'Radical Transition Versus Self-Grown Transformation in Eastern Europe and the Former Soviet Union: Introduction.' *Economics of Planning* 25(1): 1–3.

Poznanski, Kazimierz Z. (1992b). 'Market Alternative to State Activism in Restoring the Capitalist Economy.' *Economics of Planning* 25(1): 55–77.

Poznanski, Kazimierz Z. (1992c). 'Privatization of the Polish Economy: Problems of Transition.' *Soviet Studies* 44(4): 641–64.

Poznanski, Kazimierz Z. (1993a). 'Property Rights and Civil Liberties: Evolutionary Perspective on Transition in Eastern Europe and the Soviet Union.' In Schönfeld, Roland (Hrsg.) *Transformation der Wirtschaftssysteme in Ostmitteleuropa*, Südosteuropa-Studien 51. München: Südosteuropa- Gesellschaft.

Poznanski, Kazimierz Z. (1993b). 'Restructuring Property Rights in Poland: A Study in Evolutionary Economics.' *East European Politics and Societies* 7(3): 395–421.

Przeworski, Adam (1991). *Democracy and the Market: Political and Economic Reforms in Eastern Europe and Latin America.* New York: Cambridge University Press.

Repse, Einars (1996). *The Latvian Banking System – Moving Forward.* A speech given by the Governor of the Bank of Latvia at the 'Second Annual International Conference on Banking and Finance in the Baltics' in Riga, October 1996.

Rodrik, Dani (1993). 'The Positive Economics of Policy Reform.' *The American Economic Review* 83(2): 356–61.

Rokeach, Milton (1973). *The Nature of Human Values.* New York: Free Press.

Rose, Richard (1994). 'Postcommunism and the Problem of Trust.' *Journal of Democracy* 5(3): 18–30.

Rose, Richard (1996). *Rights and Obligations of Individuals in the Baltic States.* Draft for an article. Glasgow: Centre for the Study of Public Policy at the University of Strathclyde.

Rose, Richard (1997). *New Baltic Barometer III: A Survey Study*, Studies in Public Policy Number 284. Glasgow: Centre for the Study of Public Policy at the University of Strathclyde.

Rose, Richard & Haerpfer, Christian (1994). 'Mass Response to Transformation in Post-Communist Societies.' *Europe-Asia Studies* 46(1): 3–28.

Rose, Richard & Maley, William (1994). *Nationalities in the Baltic States: A Survey Study,* Studies in Public Policy Number 222. Glasgow: Centre for the Study of Public Policy at the University of Strathclyde.

Rozenfelds, Janis (1992). 'Problems of Legislation on Privatization in Latvia.' In Seiffert, Wolfgang (Red.) *Wirtschafts-und Gesellschaftsrecht Osteuropas im Zeichen des Übergangs zur Markwirtschaft.* München: C. H. Beck'sche Verlagsbuchhandlung.

Sachs, Jeffrey (1992a). 'Accelerating Privatization in Eastern Europe: The Case of Poland.' *Proceedings of the World Bank Annual Conference on Development Economics* 1991: 15–30. 'Floor Discussion of the Sachs Paper', 39–42.

Sachs, Jeffrey (1992b). 'Privatization in Russia: Some Lessions from Eastern Europe.' *The American Economic Review* 82(2): 43–8.

Sachs, Jeffrey (1992c). 'The Economic Transformation of Eastern Europe: The Case of Poland.' *Economics of Planning* 25(1): 5–19.

Schmitter, Philippe C. (1994). 'Dangers and Dilemmas of Democracy.' *Journal of Democracy* 5(2): 57–74.

Schrader, Klaus (1994). 'In Search of the Market: A Comparison of Post-Soviet Reform Policies.' In Csaba, László (ed.) *Privatization, Liberalization and Destruction: Recreating the Market in Central and Eastern Europe.* Aldershot: Dartmouth.

Schrader, Klaus & Laaser, Claus-Friedrich (1994). *Die baltischen Staaten auf dem Weg nach Europa: Lehren aus der Süderweiterung der EG*, Kieler Studien 264. Tübingen: J.C.B. Mohr (Paul Siebeck).

Shen, Raphael (1994). *Restructuring the Baltic Economies: Disengaging Years of Integration with the USSR*. Westport, CT: Praeger.

Shin, Doh Chull (1994). 'On the Third Wave of Democratization: A Synthesis and Evaluation of Recent Theory and Research.' *World Politics* 47(1): 135–70.

Shteinbuka, Inna (1993a). 'Latvia in Transition: First Challenges and First Results.' *Review of Economies in Transition* 8/93: 61–94. Helsinki: Bank of Finland.

Shteinbuka, Inna (1993b). 'The Baltics' Ways: Intentions, Scenarios, Prospects.' *Review of Economies in Transition* 8/93: 33–60. Helsinki: Bank of Finland.

Slay, Ben (1994). 'Rapid versus Gradual Economic Transition.' *RFE/RL Research Report* 3(31): 31–42.

Stark, David (1992). 'Path Dependence and Privatization Strategies in East Central Europe.' *East European Politics and Societies* 6(1): 17–54.

Starrels, John M. (1993). *The Baltic States in Transition*. Washington, DC: International Monetary Fund, Publication Service.

Supreme Council (1990). *About the Republic of Latvia*. Riga: Supreme Council.

Toye, John (1994). 'Comment.' In Williamson, John (ed.) *The Political Economy of Policy Reform*. Washington, DC: Institute for International Economics.

Vacic, Alexander M. (1992). 'Systemic Transformation in Central and Eastern Europe: General Framework, Specific Features and Prospects.' *Osteuropa-Wirtschaft* 37(1): 1–18.

Van Arkadie, Brian & Karlsson, Mats (1992). *Economic Survey of the Baltic States: The Reform Process in Estonia, Latvia and Lithuania*. London: Pinter Publishers.

van Brabant, Jozef M. (1992). *Privatizing Eastern Europe: The Role of Markets and Ownership in the Transition*. Dordrecht: Kluwer Academic Publishers.

Vitolins, Uldis (1993). 'Latvian Development Agency – Why You Need It and Where to Find It.' *Muuttuva Itä-Eurooppa – Uudistuvat Markkinat* 37: 24–5.

WIDER (World Institute for Development Economics Research of the United Nations University) (1992). *Report on the Conference 'Transformation from a System of Central Planning to a Market Economy'*. Helsinki: WIDER Institute.

Williamson, John (ed.) (1994). *The Political Economy of Policy Reform*. Washington, DC: Institute for International Economics.

World Bank (1993). *Latvia: The Transition to a Market Economy*. Washington, DC: World Bank.

Yin, Robert K. (1993). *Applications of Case Study Research*, Applied Research Methods Series Volume 34. Newbury Park, CA: Sage Publications.

Yin, Robert K. (1994). *Case Study Research: Design and Methods*, Applied Research Methods Series Volume 5. Newbury Park, CA: Sage Publications.

NEWSPAPERS, JOURNALS AND PAMPHLETS

Baltic Business Weekly, 8–14 July 1996.
Baltic Independent, various issues from 1994–96.
Baltic Observer, various issues from 1994–96.
Baltic Times, various issues from 1996–97.
Current Latvia, various issues from 1994–95.
Financial Times, 3 October 1995.

Frankfurter Allgemeine Zeitung, 6 October 1995.
Helsingin Sanomat, 3 October 1995, 21 January 1997 and 13 July 1997.
Journal of Democracy 5(4).
Riga in Your Pocket: February–April 1997. A periodical travel guide.

LAWS

Draft Law on Certificates.
Law on Foreign Investment, 5 November 1991 (last amendment 9 April 1996).
Law on the Privatization of State and Municipal Property, 3 March 1994.
The Saeima Election Law, 6 June 1995.

PARTY PLATFORMS

Bojars, Juris (1997). 'Programmatic Principles of the Social Democratic Party of Latvia.'
    Unpublished draft programme.
LSDP (*Latvijas Socialdemokratiska partija*) (1997). *Vadlinijas un programma*.
    Unofficial translation by Ilona Grave.
KDS (*Kristigo Demokratu savieniba*) (1994). *Latvian Christian Democratic Union:
    Principal Programme*.
LC (*Latvijas Cels*) (1995a). *A 4000 Character Programme for the 6th Saeima*.
LC (*Latvijas Cels*) (1995b). *Programme of the Union Latvia's Way*.
LC (*Latvijas Cels*) (1995c). *Savieniba Latvijas Cels*.
Opponent 9/1995. [Party organ of the Latvian Socialist Party] Unofficial translation
    by Ieva Raubisko.
Saimnieks (1995). *Apvienošanas kongresa dokumenti*. Unofficial translation by Ieva
    Raubisko.
Saskana (1995). *The National Harmony Party: Theses for the Election Campaign
    to the 6th Saeima*.
Tautsaimnieks (1995). *Political Union of Economists: Pre-election Programme*.
TB (*Tevzemei un Brivibai*) (1995a). *The National Conservative Association 'Tevzemei
    un Brivibai'*.
TB (*Tevzemei un Brivibai*) (1995b). *Taxation Policy*.
TB (*Tevzemei un Brivibai*) (1995c). *Union For Fatherland and Freedom*.

INTERVIEWS WITH THE LATVIAN PARTY LEADERS BY *DIENA* IN AUGUST 1995
(Unofficial translation by Anja Boman and Ellen Riekstina, Finnish Embassy, Riga.)

Birkavs, Valdis (LC)
Cevers, Ziedonis (DPS)
Grinblats, Maris (TB)
Kide, Edvins (TPA)
Rozentals, Andris (LZS)
Seile, Anna (LNNK)
Stroganov, Filip (LSP)

List of Interviewees

Interviews were taken in two separate sequences.* The first wave of interviews was conducted in Riga, 13–27 September 1995, and in Helsinki, 5–6 September 1995 and 6–16 October 1995. The second phase of interviews was carried out in Riga and in Liepaja between 24 January 1997 and 7 May 1997. The positions following the names of interviewees were those held at the time of the interviews. The abbreviations in parentheses refer to the nationality of interviewees.**

Aboltins, Janis	Adviser, Harmony; president, Rigas Komercbanka (Lat)
Apinis, Baldurs	Adviser to party leader, chief coordinator of the party's electoral campaign, editor of the party programme, Saimnieks (Lat)
Bahn, Arcady	Marketing manager, Terrabalt Ltd, Liepaja (Rus)
Bojars, Juris	Party leader, Social Democratic Party of Latvia; professor, head of the Institute of Foreign Affairs, University of Latvia (Lat)
Boman, Anja	Counsellor, Finnish Embassy, Riga (Fin)
Brence, Anita	Adviser to deputy, specialist in international affairs, Fatherland and Freedom (Lat)
Flick, Bert	Adviser, Latvian Privatization Agency (Ger)
Freivalds, Talivaldis	Adviser to deputy, Political Union of Economists (Lat)
Grinbergs, Maris	Investment consultant, self-employed, Riga (Lat)
Horoših, Irina	Economist, Lido Ltd, Riga (Rus)
Kadish, Boris	President, Frame Inform Systems Ltd, Riga (Rus)
Klavins, Paulis	Party chairman, Christian Democratic Union (Lat)
Korolenko, Victor	Director, West East Industries Ltd, Riga (Rus)
Kreituss, Aivars	Deputy chairman, next Minister of Finance, Saimnieks (Lat)
Lambergs, Aristids	Deputy chairman, LNNK (Lat)
Linkaits, Talis	Head of Administrative Department, Latvian Privatization Agency (Lat)
Lukins, Girts	Board member, former Minister of Environmental Protection and Regional Development, Farmers' Union (Lat)
Loginov, Sergei	Export consultant, self-employed, Riga (Rus)
Pavlovskis, Olgerts	Deputy, State Minister of Foreign Affairs, Latvia's Way (Lat)
Putnaergle, Dita	Consul, Latvian Embassy, Helsinki (Lat)
Rasnačs, Dzintars	Advisor to deputy, economic specialist, next Minister of Justice, Fatherland and Freedom (Lat)
Rižanskij, Vladimir	Technical director, Tosmare Ltd, Liepaja (Rus)
Rozenvalds, Juris	Board member, Harmony; professor, Department of Philosophy, University of Latvia (Lat)

---

*   With two exceptions: Vaarmann and Valdmanis
** Key: Est = Estonian, Fin = Finnish, Ger = German, Lat = Latvian, Rus = Russian who is a permanent resident of the Republic of Latvia

Runcis, Andris	Head of the Department of Political Science, University of Latvia (Lat)
Salonen, Matti	Managing director, Shell Latvia (Fin)
Saulitis, Andris	Deputy, People's Movement for Latvia (Lat)
Šilins, Andris	President of the Confederation of Trade Unions (Lat)
Skudra, Ojars	Advisor, Political Union of Economists; lecturer, Department of Communication and Journalism, University of Latvia (Lat)
Strubergs, Peters	Organizational secretary of party, Latvia's Way (Lat)
Tapiola, Pirkka	Deputy Head of Mission, Organization for Security and Cooperation in Europe (Fin)
Trapenciere, Ilze	Researcher, Institute of Philosophy and Sociology, Latvian Academy of Sciences (Lat)
Tšernousov, Dimitrij	Head of technological unit, Tosmare Ltd, Liepaja (Rus)
Tsilevich, Boris	Deputy of Riga City Council, adviser to party chairman, Harmony; chairman of the Non-Citizens' League; researcher (Rus)
Vaivars, Peteris	First Secretary, Latvian Embassy, Helsinki (Lat)
Valdmanis, Guntars	Financial expert of party, leading candidate in party list, Unity Party (Lat)
Wäre, Olli	Managing director, Jaunalko Ltd, Riga (Fin)
Zalans, Juris	Specialist of the Press Service, Saeima (Lat)
Zdanok, Tatjana	Former deputy, Socialist Party; professor, Department of Mathematics, University of Latvia (Rus)
Ziedins, Egils	Aide to party leader, People's Movement for Latvia (Lat)
Zigure, Anna	Ambassador, Latvian Embassy, Helsinki (Lat)
Zvejs, Visvaldis	Director of the Privatization Department, Ministry of Economy (Lat)
N.N.	Anonymous Russian

Occasional Discussions

Avotins, Valdis	Marketing director, Latvian Development Agency (Lat)
Kirsis, Janis	President, Lindeks Ltd, Riga (Lat)
Kushners, Eduards	Lawyer, Latvian Development Agency (Lat)
Luhtanen, Pentti	Director, Cecilia Ltd, Riga (Fin)
Prosi, Gerhard	Professor of Political Economy, University of Kiel (Ger)
Vaarmann, Mati	Economic counsellor, Estonian Embassy, Helsinki (Est)

Occasional discussions were also held with representatives of foreign companies operating in Latvia, who wish to remain anonymous.

Index

Index compiled by Auriol Griffith-Jones